Canadian **Content**

SEVENTH EDITION

NELL WALDMAN
SARAH NORTON

NELSON

NELSON

Canadian Content, Seventh Edition
by Nell Waldman and Sarah Norton

Vice President, Editorial Director:
Evelyn Veitch

Editor-in-Chief,
Higher Education:
Anne Williams

Executive Editor:
Laura Macleod

Senior Marketing Manager:
Amanda Henry

Developmental Editor:
Theresa Fitzgerald

Permissions Coordinator:
Natalie Russell

Content Production Manager:
Claire Horsnell

Copy Editor:
Kelli Howey

Proofreader:
June Trusty

Researcher:
David Oswald

Senior Production Coordinator:
Ferial Suleman

Design Director:
Ken Phipps

Managing Designer:
Franca Amore

Interior Design:
Sonya V. Thursby, Opus House
Incorporated

Cover Design:
Martyn Schmoll

Cover Image:
Susan Point

Compositor:
KnowledgeWorks Global Ltd.

Library and Archives Canada
Cataloguing in Publication Data

Canadian content / [edited by]
Sarah Norton, Nell Waldman. —
7th ed.

Includes bibliographical references
and index.
ISBN 978-0-17-650362-8

    1. College readers. 2. English
language—Rhetoric—Textbooks.

I. Norton, Sarah
II. Waldman, Nell

PE1417.C25 2011   808'.0427
C2010-906093-8

ISBN 13: 978-0-17-650362-8
ISBN 10: 0-17-650362-5

CONTENTS

By Unit

UNIT 1: TWO BASIC STRATEGIES: NARRATION AND DESCRIPTION

> "I would learn . . . that 'definitely attending' on *Facebook* means 'maybe' and 'maybe attending' means 'likely not.' So I probably shouldn't have taken it personally. But the combination of alcohol and solitude turned my thoughts to self-pity. Was I really that big a loser?"

> "If stunning aesthetics are the skin that covers Newfoundland and Labrador, then its people are the sinew. Sometimes they even look the part, strung together with twine and leather, their faces the image of being the next best thing to indestructible."

> "My friend Pujee is a hockey player from Ulaan Baator, Mongolia. . . . I was there making a movie for the CBC about my hockey travels abroad."

UNIT 2: EXAMPLE

UNIT 3: PROCESS ANALYSIS

UNIT 4: CLASSIFICATION AND DIVISION

UNIT 5: COMPARISON AND CONTRAST

"Cree, my mother tongue, . . . lives in the human body not
above the neck, as English does, not between the neck and the
waist, as French does, but one step lower . . . in the sex organs . . .
in the most fun-loving, the most pleasurable—not to mention the
funniest-looking—part of the human corpus."

"At first glance, science and poetry appear to have little in
common."

UNIT 6: CAUSAL ANALYSIS

"Addictions always originate in unhappiness, even if hidden.
They are emotional anesthetics; they numb pain. The first
question always is not 'Why the addiction?' but 'Why the pain?'"

"It is hard to avoid feeling vulnerable to this invisible enemy
who does not play by known or explicit rules. Of course, that is
precisely the anxiety that terrorists seek to produce."

"In time, I learned to smother the rage I felt at so often being
taken for a criminal."

"What if we come to decide jet travel has become too polluting
to risk our children's future? Or just far too expensive to
continue flying the kids to Disneyland? And if a million such
decisions were to cause the jet age to end, how would we come
back to earth?"

"Why this difference between men and women? When natural
selection shaped male–female differences, it didn't stop at muscles
and naughty bits. It also shaped differences in our psychologies."

"And the telephone, as it turned out was bad news. With its
coming, the face of the village began to change."

UNIT 7: DEFINITION

UNIT 8: ARGUMENT AND PERSUASION

"What if the modern, postindustrial economy is simply more congenial to women than to men?"

"To promise, as some politicians [do], that they are going to cut taxes in order 'to allow Canadians to keep more of their hard-earned dollars' is simply a way of saying, 'forget about pursuing your most noble aspirations collectively and do not worry about securing the blessings of real freedom.'"

"Perfectly good words are taken from our vocabulary, limiting the expression of a thought or an opinion. I recently read about high schoolers who are not allowed to use the word 'vagina.' And what should they say instead?"

"Of course, B.C. is a beautiful place. Many places are. But the best place on earth? Not likely. No place is. At the same time, it is our place, a unique place, and it is our responsibility not to wreck it."

"Real hope, real change, doesn't come from outside and never will."

"I am flesh, a flesh eater, whether the food is carrot or cow. Harvesting and killing are the same activity, the interrupting of one life cycle for the sake of another."

"The disturbing possibility is that Canada is not an asylum from hatred but an incubator of hatred."

UNIT 9: FICTION

"Everyone else I loved never went anywhere. And France was such a far away place, farther even than Vancouver, too far away to phone, too far away to hope you would ever come back."

"I have no longing for the meals themselves, but I miss the way we sat down together, our bodies leaning hungrily forward while my father, the magician, unveiled plate after plate. We laughed and ate, white steam fogging my mother's glasses until she had to take them off and lay them on the table. Eyes closed, she would eat, crunchy vegetables gripped in her chopsticks, the most vivid green."

"When the time came, Carson just stood and made for the doorway, the same slow bee-line stride he'd taken to the bar. Beside me, the bartender cleared our glasses and talked low into his beard. 'Think twice little girl, the Northern bushman's a different breed.'

But then Carson looked back at me over his shoulder, and just like a rockslide, I felt myself slip off the barstool and follow."

"If you run to the end of the shelterbelt and just keep going, across the quarter section that was the first one your dad had to sell, your legs get tired at first and it's hard to breathe, but before long you start feeling strong, like you could run forever, catch up to that big old setting sun and live in a land where all the houses are huge and airy like the fields, with walls the same gold colour as the sky, where the people are tall and beautiful, and wise and kind."

"Goldfinch was flapping clotheslines, a tenement delirious with striving. 6030 Bathurst: insomniac, scheming Odessa. Cedarcroft: reeking borscht in the hallways. My parents, Soviet refugees but Baltic aristocrats, took an apartment at 715 Finch, fronting a ravine and across from an elementary school—one respectable block away from the Russian swarm."

"We were just rounding the western point of the island, but he was really beginning to suffer. His steady strokes had broken into short, choppy grabs at the water. He was hardly swimming at all. He moved the way his life did, no movement forward, just treading water.

'I don't think I can make it, Don,' he said. 'I'm about beat.' . . .

I banged the paddle blade flat on the water. It sounded like a shot and sent a sheet of water into his face. 'Who'd care if I let you drown?'"

"I knew that soldiers were dying in battle overseas, that bombs were destroying the great cities of Europe. But now it seemed that death had leaped the vast ocean like a stream and settled into the street where we lived."

"Of all the girls that Kevin had been involved with, Anita had
the most substance. The least she could do for the girl is give her
a beautiful wedding."

"He would wake at night screaming that he had seen the *cù
mòr glas a' bhàis*, the big grey dog of death, and his screams filled
the house and the ears and minds of the listeners, bringing home
again and again the consequences of their loss."

APPENDIX

CONTENTS

By Subject

ANIMALS AND US

COMMUNICATION/WRITING

CULTURAL DIVERSITY

ETHICS AND MORALITY

MEDIA AND THE ARTS

MODERN LIFE

MOSTLY CANADIAN

NATURE AND THE ENVIRONMENT

RELATIONSHIPS, FAMILY, AND GENDER

RURAL LIFE/URBAN LIFE

TECHNOLOGY AND SCIENCE

WAR AND PEACE

WORK, SPORTS, AND LEISURE

YOUTH AND AGE

PREFACE

To the Instructor

Canadian Content is a reader designed for Canadian students who are studying English composition at the postsecondary level. Thirty-four of the forty essays new to this seventh edition are by some of Canada's best-known writers: Ian Brown, June Callwood, Lorna Crozier, Tomson Highway, Lawrence Hill, and Margaret Wente, to name just a few.

Our title, *Canadian Content*, is a play on the mandate of the Canadian Radio-television and Telecommunications Commission (CRTC), the federal broadcasting regulatory agency whose guidelines require that broadcasters provide a minimum of two-thirds Canadian content in their programming. Although print materials are not governed by the CRTC, we thought that the CRTC's content requirement was a worthy target for a postsecondary text. In this edition, 80 percent of our readings are by Canadian writers, some of them new to our country; the balance are well-written, thought-provoking essays by writers from around the world, addressing issues that concern us all.

This edition features some significant changes. First, an analysis of the curricula of first-year writing courses across Canada convinced us to separate narration and description (Unit 1) from example (Unit 2), so previous adopters of the text will find that the units have been renumbered. Second, we are delighted to introduce a unit devoted to contemporary Canadian fiction. Short stories can contribute in many ways (in addition to pure enjoyment) to the composition classroom. See the Instructor Resources section of our website (www.cancon7e.nelson.com) for ideas on how to incorporate fiction into your composition curriculum. And third, we have included more light-hearted, humorous selections, such as the satiric "How to Perform a Tracheotomy" in Unit 3 and "D'oh! An Analysis of the Medical Care Provided to the Family of Homer J. Simpson" in Unit 5.

In the Introduction, we have revised "How to Read with Understanding" and "How to Write to Be Understood" to provide a shorter, less technical overview of the complex tasks of reading and writing. "How to Write a Documented Essay" has been updated and includes a new example of a documented paper. A comprehensive treatment of researching, writing, revising, and documenting essays, in both MLA and APA styles, is available on our new website, along with a review of grammar basics and ESL tips.

The introduction to each unit offers a brief explanation of an organizational pattern, liberally supported by illustrations from the readings in that unit. In Unit 1, we introduce, explain, and illustrate narration and description—two strategies that are basic to all writing. Units 2 through 7 focus on traditional expository patterns: example, process analysis, classification and division, comparison and contrast, causal analysis, and definition. Unit 8 is devoted to argument and persuasion. We acknowledge that these rhetorical patterns are most often blended in "real-life" writing (most exposition has a persuasive element, for example). Nevertheless, we believe that students will be stronger, more confident writers if they learn the organizational possibilities individually, one at a time, before they attempt to combine them.

The selections within the units are arranged from simple to complex. This ordering allows for two different approaches to curriculum: instructors can fulfill their course requirements by assigning level-appropriate readings in a number of rhetorical patterns, or a class can be led through progressively challenging readings based on one or more rhetorical patterns. We have also included a table of contents by subject for those instructors who prefer to organize their courses around topics or themes rather than structural patterns.

The introductions to Units 1 through 8 conclude with a short model essay illustrating the structural pattern that is the focus of the unit. Together, these model essays demonstrate how a single topic—communication—can be approached from different points of view and developed in different ways. The model essays also exemplify the introductory and concluding strategies explained in the Glossary at the back of the book. Terms that appear in small capital letters throughout the text (AUDIENCE, DICTION, METAPHOR, and THESIS, for example) are defined in the Glossary.

Each essay is preceded by a short biographical note and followed by a "Words and Meanings" section that provides contextual definitions of words and phrases with which students may not be familiar. Next we provide two sets of discussion questions. Those under the heading "Structure and Strategy" lead students to identify and consider the techniques the author used to achieve his or her goal; those headed "Content and Purpose" guide students to a deeper understanding of the essay's meaning. Finally, we offer some suggestions for writing after each reading. Each unit concludes with "Additional Suggestions for Writing," a list of topics that lend themselves to the structure and development strategies explained in the unit.

ADDITIONAL RESOURCES

The following table outlines the contents of our website (www. cancon7e.nelson.com):

Instructor Resources

- How to Use *Canadian Content*
- Preventing Plagiarism: Why? What? How?
- Suggested Answers to Questions in the Text
- Alternative Set of Model Essays
- Suggestions for Writing Documented Essays Based on *Canadian Content*

Student Resources

- How to Research Your Topic
- Summarizing, Paraphrasing, and Quoting
- Format and Documentation
  - MLA
  - APA
- How to Revise Your Paper
- Grammar Basics:
  - Sentences: Kinds and Parts
  - Parts of Speech
  - ESL Tips
- Writing Essay Exams
- Writing Critical Evaluations

ACKNOWLEDGMENTS

We thank Kamal Al-Solaylee, Aileen Burford-Mason, Claudia Casper, Richard Lederer, Charles Montgomery, Ryan Van Meter, Alan R. Wilson, and Charles Weijer, who helped us secure permissions and, in some cases, supplied us with biographical information. We owe special thanks to David Oswald, who was a major contributor to this edition. David discovered, read, and critiqued numerous essays from both mainstream and off-beat sources for our consideration; he also contributed to many of the biographical notes that precede the selections. David's enthusiasm for contemporary fiction motivated us to realize a long-held dream: to include short fiction in

Canadian Content. We thank our executive editor, Laura Macleod, for her support in making this change.

We hope you enjoy using this new edition of *Canadian Content* as much as we enjoyed creating it.

Nell Waldman
Sarah Norton

INTRODUCTION

How to Read with Understanding

Every college and university student knows how to read—sort of. The trouble is that many of us don't read very efficiently. We don't know how to adapt our reading style to our reading purpose. Most people aren't even aware that there are different ways to read.

Basically, there are two kinds of reading: **surface reading**, which is casual reading for pleasure or for easy-to-find facts. This is the type of reading we do when we enjoy a novel or read a newspaper, whether in print, onscreen, or on a smartphone. The second kind of reading is **deep reading**. This is the kind required in postsecondary courses and on the job: reading to acquire the facts and ideas we need in order to understand a topic. Deep (or analytical) reading has practical rather than recreational purposes. Both kinds of reading can be satisfying, but analytical reading takes more time and also brings greater rewards. Good readers (and writers) tend to do well not only in college and university but also in their careers.

Students new to college or university often claim that they can read perfectly well while listening to music, watching television, or talking on the phone. These students are partly right: they can read under those circumstances, but they can't read for understanding. Unlike watching *YouTube* videos or TV, which uses less mental energy than eating, reading for understanding is an *active* process. It requires your full concentration and participation. You need to set aside a period of time each day to read without being interrupted.

Here's what you need before you begin to read:

- A quiet place
- A good reading light
- A pencil
- A current, comprehensive dictionary[1]

THE ANALYTICAL READING PROCESS APPLIED TO *CANADIAN CONTENT*

There are three steps to reading and understanding the selections in this text. These steps will help you read and understand any piece of academic or professional prose.

1. Preview before you read.
2. Read the selection all the way through.
   Look up the meaning of words you don't understand.
   Read the questions that follow the selection.
3. Read the selection a second time—slowly and carefully.
   Answer the questions following the selection.

STEP 1: PREVIEW BEFORE YOU READ

You cannot learn facts, ideas, or even words in isolation. Learning requires CONTEXT,[2] a sense of the whole into which each new piece of information fits. The more familiar you are with the context and content of an item before you begin it, the better you will understand what you read.

Begin by looking through the essay to get a sense of the following:

- *How long is the piece?* You'll want to estimate how much time you'll need to complete it.
- *What is the title?* The title often points to something significant about the content.
- *Who wrote the essay?* Knowing something about the author may help you predict the kind of essay you're dealing with. Is

---

[1] The *Collins Gage Canadian Paperback Dictionary* is convenient, portable, and inexpensive. For your desk, we recommend either Nelson's *Canadian Dictionary of the English Language* (1997) or the *Canadian Oxford Dictionary* (2004). ESL students will find the *Oxford Advanced Learner's Dictionary of Current English* (2010) a useful reference.

[2] Definitions of all words that appear in SMALL CAPITAL LETTERS are in the Glossary section at the back of this book.

the author dead or alive? A humorist or a social critic? A journalist or an academic? A student or a specialist? What is his or her nationality?

- *What about* the BODY *of the piece?* Are there subheadings or other visual cues that indicate the division of the topic into KEY IDEAS?

In this textbook, first read each unit's introduction for essential information on essay organization and development. The unit introductions are illustrated by examples taken from essays in the text.

STEP 2: READ THE SELECTION ALL THE WAY THROUGH

This is the tough one. Most inexperienced readers have a fairly short attention span, and they need to train themselves to increase it. You need to read a piece all the way through in order to get a sense of the whole; otherwise, you cannot fully understand either the essay or its parts. Here's how to approach your first reading of an essay or article:

- *Withhold judgment.* If you decide in advance that the topic is boring ("Who cares about toothpaste?") or the style is too demanding ("I couldn't possibly understand anything entitled 'How to Perform a Tracheotomy' "), you cheat yourself out of a potentially rewarding experience. Give the writer a chance. Part of an author's responsibility is to make the writing interesting and accessible to the reader.
- *Use your pencil.* Make notes, underline, and jot questions in the margin. Try to identify the THESIS of the essay as you read. When you come across a sentence or passage you don't understand, put a question mark in the margin.
- *Note the words that are marked with the symbol* °. This symbol indicates that the meaning of the word or phrase is given in the "Words and Meanings" section following the essay. If you're unfamiliar with the term, check the definition we've provided and keep reading. Mark any other words whose meaning you can't figure out from the context. You can look them up later.

Good writers set up their material for you: they usually identify their topic early and indicate the scope of their essay. Your first reading of an essay or article should be a read-through: your goal is to get a good idea of what the piece is about, its informational content. You need to read the piece a second or even a third time before you can analyze its structure and the strategies the author has used to convey the content effectively.

If you can't figure out the meaning of a word from its context, and if you need to know the meaning to understand a sentence or paragraph, it's time to turn to your dictionary. For every word you look up, your dictionary will provide you with more information than you need. Only one meaning will be appropriate in the context you are reading. When you're satisfied that you've located the appropriate definition, write it in the margin.

After you've finished reading an essay, go through the questions that follow it. These questions are divided into two parts. The "Structure and Strategy" questions will help you understand the **form** and STYLE of the essay—the techniques the writer has used to communicate his or her ideas. The "Content and Purpose" questions will help you understand the **meaning** of the essay—what the writer wanted to communicate and why. Together, these two sets of questions will guide you to a thorough understanding of the selection.

You won't be able to answer all the questions we've provided, but don't panic. The purpose of going through these questions now is to prepare yourself for a second, closer reading of the essay. All you need to know at this stage is the kind of questions you should be able to answer after your second reading.

STEP 3: READ THE SELECTION A SECOND TIME— SLOWLY AND CAREFULLY

Got your pencil ready? The physical act of writing as you read helps keep your attention focused on the essay and serves to deepen your understanding of its content and structure. Here are some guidelines to follow as you read the essay a second time:

1. Analyze the INTRODUCTION of the essay. What strategy has the writer used to establish the topic, the limits of the topic, and the TONE? Who is the writer's target AUDIENCE? Are you included in this group? If not, remember that your reactions and interpretations may differ from those of the writer's intended readers.

2. Underline the author's THESIS (if you haven't already done so during your first reading). Identify the writer's main PURPOSE. Is it to explain, to persuade, to entertain? Some combination of these?

3. Make notes in the margins. Use the margins to jot down, in point form, an outline of the piece, to add supplementary (or contradictory) EVIDENCE, or to call attention to especially significant or eloquently expressed ideas. Notice how the writer develops the KEY IDEAS. Be sure you can distinguish between main ideas and supporting details—the examples, definitions, ANALOGIES, and so on—that the writer has used to make key points clear to the reader. Circle key TRANSITIONS

(linking words and phrases). Transitions signal to the reader that the writer has concluded one idea and is moving on to another.

4. What is the TONE of the piece? Is it humorous or serious, impassioned or objective, formal or informal? Good writers choose their tone carefully, since it affects the reader's response more than any other technical aspect of writing.

5. Consider the CONCLUSION. Does it restate the thesis or expand on it in some way? Are you left with a sense of the essay's completeness, a feeling that all questions raised in the piece have been satisfactorily answered? Or do you feel that you've been left dangling, that some of the loose ends have yet to be tied up?

Now it's time to turn to the questions following the selection. Consider the questions carefully, one by one, and think about possible answers. Refer to the selection often to keep yourself on the right track. Most of the questions do not have simple or single answers. Some of them ask for your opinion. Write the answers out in full if that is your assignment. Otherwise, jot down your answers in point form or in short phrases in the margins of the text.

The purpose of the questions is to engage you as deeply as possible in the structure and meaning of each piece. As you analyze *what* the writer has said (the content and purpose) and *how* he or she has said it (the structure and strategies), you will come as close as you can to full understanding. At this point, you are ready to test your understanding in classroom discussion or through writing a paper of your own.

How to Write to Be Understood

Learning to read for understanding will help you to write clear, well-organized prose. As you practise the techniques readers use to make sense of a piece of writing, you will become increasingly skilled at meeting your own readers' needs when you write. For years, you've probably been told to keep your AUDIENCE in mind as you write. By itself, this is not a particularly helpful piece of advice. You need to know not only *who your audience is,* including how much they know and how they feel about your topic, but also *how readers read.* These two pieces of information are the keys to understandable writing. (We are assuming here that you have a firm grasp of your topic. You can't write clearly or convincingly about something you don't understand.)

Once you have decided who your audience is, there are five steps to ensuring that your readers will understand what you say. Writing a paper is like going on a journey: it makes sense—and it's certainly more efficient—to choose your destination and plan your route before you begin. Your THESIS is your destination. Your KEY IDEAS are signposts on the route to your destination. Together, your thesis and key ideas determine the kind of paper you are going to write.

We begin this book by discussing two basic writing strategies— narration and description—that are useful in every kind of writing. Then we explain and illustrate seven different ways to approach a topic. Please note: *there is no one right way to explain any topic.* Like a geographical destination, a topic can be approached via several routes.

Take a broad, general topic like communication skills, for example. If you flip through the introductions to Units 1 through 8, you will see that each contains a model essay illustrating the kind(s) of writing explained in that unit. The model essays all discuss communication skills, but they are all different. Read these model essays carefully to discover how the organizational pattern discussed in each unit gives COHERENCE and UNITY to the topic.

As you have already discovered, people who are reading analytically don't like surprises: they don't want to encounter sudden shifts in direction or dead ends. They need a smooth, well-marked path through the writer's prose. Your responsibility to your readers is to identify the destination, set them on the path to that destination, and guide them through to the end. If you can keep them interested on their journey, so much the better. As you read through the selections in this book, you will encounter a variety of stylistic devices that you can use to add interest and impact to your own writing.

Rhetoric is the art of using language effectively. The RHETORICAL MODES[3] are four classic kinds of non-fiction writing: NARRATION, DESCRIPTION, EXPOSITION, and ARGUMENT/PERSUASION. Good writers choose whichever mode is best suited to their topic and purpose.

RHETORICAL MODE	PURPOSE	UNIT
Narration	Tell a story	1
Description	Create a sensory picture	1
Exposition	Explain or inform	2–7
Argument/Persuasion	Convince	8

Most non-fiction writing falls into the category of exposition, which includes the organizational patterns of *example, process analysis, classification/division, comparison/contrast, causal analysis,* and *definition*. Units 2 through 7 explain and illustrate these patterns. Practising each mode in isolation is helpful when you are learning to identify and use basic writing techniques, but you should be aware that most writing is a blend of modes and purposes.

Here are the five steps to clear, well-organized writing:

1. Clarify your topic.
2. Discover your thesis.
3. Develop a thesis statement, including a preview of your key ideas.
4. Write your first draft.
5. Revise your paper (as many times as necessary), edit, and proofread.

The first three steps are the *preparation* stage of the writing process. Be warned: these steps may take you as long as—if not longer than—Steps 4 and 5, which involve the actual *writing*. In academic and professional writing, the more time you spend on preparation, the less time the actual writing will take—and the better your paper will be.

---

[3] Classifying writing into categories is useful for those who are learning how to arrange and develop their ideas effectively, in the same way that practising scales, tempo, and modulation is helpful to people who want to learn how to play a musical instrument. It is necessary to master the basics before attempting to create an original composition.

STEP 1: CLARIFY YOUR TOPIC

If you have been assigned a topic for your paper or report, don't grumble—be grateful! A large part of the work has already been done for you. You have been handed a limited topic along with a hint as to how to approach it. **Direction words** are reliable clues to the kind of paper/report your instructor/supervisor is looking for. If your assigned topic begins with one of the words in the first column below, it should lead to a paper based on the writing pattern in the second column.

DIRECTION WORD	WHAT IT MEANS
Compare/Contrast	Show similarities/differences (see Unit 5)
Define	Give the meaning of a term, with examples (see Unit 7)
Describe	Give specific details of what the topic looks like (see Unit 1)
Evaluate	Give the positive and negative points of the topic (see Unit 8)
Illustrate	Explain by giving detailed examples (see Unit 2)
Justify	Give reasons, supported by evidence (see Unit 8)

What should you do if you are asked to come up with a topic of your own? Choosing a satisfactory topic is critical to producing a paper your readers will understand. Inexperienced writers often choose a topic that is far larger than either their knowledge or the assignment can accommodate.

A satisfactory topic is one that is *significant, specific,* and *supportable.*

- A *significant* topic is one that is worth the time and attention you expect your readers to give to your work. You must have something original and interesting to say if you hope to capture and keep a reader's attention. There's a world of difference, for example, between the essay "Toothpaste" by David Bodanis (page 185) and a paper on "How I Brush My Teeth" by an inexperienced writer.
- A detailed discussion of a *specific* topic is always more satisfying to read than a superficial treatment of a broad one. This is why, in "The End of the Wild" (page 112), Wade Davis chooses to discuss three particular examples rather than generalize about ecological disasters.

You can narrow a broad topic to a specific one by applying one or more limiting factors to it. Think of your topic in terms of a particular *kind*, or *time*, or *place*, or *number*, or *person* associated with it. Davis, for example, limits his topic in terms of *kinds* (passenger pigeon, buffalo, and rainforest) and *place* (North American continent).

- A topic is *supportable* if you can develop it with examples, facts, quotations, descriptions, ANECDOTES, comparisons, definitions, and other supporting details. These supporting details are called EVIDENCE. Evidence, combined with good organization, is what makes your explanation of a topic clear and convincing.

STEP 2: DISCOVER YOUR THESIS

Once you've chosen a suitable topic, you need to decide what you want to say about it. A THESIS is *an idea about a limited topic*; it is a viewpoint that needs to be explained or proved. There are three ways to go about discovering a thesis. The first two are **freewriting** and **brainstorming**, techniques with which most postsecondary students are already familiar.

Another way to approach an assigned topic (especially if you are stuck for ideas) is to ask specific **questions** about it. If you apply one of the questions in the first column below, you'll probably answer your question about writing strategy (see second column) — and come up with useful key points as a bonus. Not all questions will apply to your topic. Try different ones until the right question clicks. Then read the introduction to the unit for tips about writing the kind of paper that you are aiming for. (The symbol X in the chart below stands for your topic.) The third column points you to model essays, all on the topic of communication, that illustrate the structural patterns identified in the middle column.

If this is the question that best fits your topic (X)	You will be writing this kind of paper[4]	Model essay
How did X happen? What does X look like?	Narration (Unit 1) Description (Unit 1)	"A Cultural Exchange" (page 37), a descriptive narrative of *mis*communication
What are some good examples of X?	Example (Unit 2)	"A Manner of Speaking" (page 81), examples of body language

Continued

---

[4] See the introduction to each unit for definitions, explanations, and examples.

If this is the question that best fits your topic (X)	You will be writing this kind of paper	Model essay
How is X made or done? How does X work?	Process Analysis (Unit 3)	"Metamorphosis" (page 134), how a baby learns to talk
What are the parts or characteristics of X?	Division (Unit 4)	"Listen Up" (page 177), three components of good listening
What are the kinds or categories of X?	Classification (Unit 4)	
What are the similarities and/or differences between X and Y?	Comparison/ Contrast (Unit 5)	"She Said, He Said" (page 207), the differences between men's and women's conversation
What are the causes and/or effects of X?	Causal Analysis (Unit 6)	"The Trouble with Readers" (page 252), causes of written miscommunication
What does X mean?	Definition (Unit 7)	"Talking Pidgin" (page 295), a definition of pidgin languages
What are the reasons for—or against—X?	Argument/ Persuasion (Unit 8)	"Why Good Writing Makes You Sexy" (page 326), an argument designed to convince readers that good written communication improves your sex appeal

When you discover the question that produces answers that are closest to what you want or need to write about, then you will know what kind of paper is required—that is, what kind of organizational pattern to follow. The answers to the best question are likely to become the key points of your paper, points you may choose to include in your thesis statement. We have provided marginal notes with the model essays to help you identify their structure and development.

STEP 3: DEVELOP YOUR THESIS STATEMENT

A thesis statement is the most efficient way to organize a short paper. It plans your paper for you and it tells your reader what he or she is going to read about. To continue the analogy between reading an essay and taking a trip, the thesis statement is a kind of map: it identifies your destination and the route you are going to take. Like a map, it keeps your reader (and you) on the right track. To be specific, a thesis statement does two things. It states the THESIS of your paper and previews the KEY IDEAS of your paper.

A. STATING YOUR THESIS

As concisely as possible, identify the topic of your paper and what you intend to **explain** or **prove** about that topic (your THESIS). Here are two examples:

- Men and women talk differently. (Thesis of "She Said, He Said," page 207)
- Three passions, simple but overwhelmingly strong, have governed my life. (Thesis of "What I Have Lived For," page 199)

Be sure to state an *idea* or *opinion* about your topic; don't just announce it and leave the reader to wonder how you intend to approach it. *Do not write,* for example, "I'm going to discuss how men and women talk" or "This paper is about my life." These are bald (and boring) topic statements, not thesis statements.

Once you've stated your thesis, look at it carefully. Is it appropriate for the length of your assignment and the amount of time you've been given to write it? Beware of a thesis that is too broad ("Men and women are different in many ways") or too narrow ("My life is enhanced by a hearty breakfast").

B. PREVIEWING YOUR KEY IDEAS

The second part of a thesis statement identifies the KEY IDEAS you will discuss in your paper and the ORDER in which you will discuss them. Go back to your prewriting activity (brainstorming, freewriting, or questioning) and find the two to four best points you came up with. These points are your key ideas.

Next, consider how to arrange your points. Should they be in *chronological, climactic,* or *logical* ORDER? Choose the arrangement that is most likely to achieve your PURPOSE, then write out your points in grammatically parallel form (see PARALLELISM in the Glossary section).

Now you are ready to combine your THESIS and your key ideas into an *expanded thesis statement.* Compare the following examples with the *simple thesis statements* we provided under "Stating Your Thesis," above. To highlight the difference, we've underlined the key ideas in each statement:

- When men and women engage in that intrinsically human activity called "talking," there is much that is different in <u>why</u>

they talk, the way they talk, and what they talk about. ("She Said, He Said," page 207)

- Three passions, simple but overwhelmingly strong, have governed my life: the longing for love, the search for knowledge, and unbearable pity for the suffering of mankind. ("What I Have Lived For," page 199)

Not all essays contain full thesis statements. In most of the selections in this book, for example, you will find a statement of thesis but not a preview of the key ideas. Why? Because professional writers don't need the organizational apparatus that non-professionals do. Through experience, they have learned less visible techniques to help their readers follow them through their writing. We recommend, however, that you include a full thesis statement in the papers you write. (The best place to put it is at the end of your introduction.) There is probably no writing strategy you can use that is more helpful to your readers' understanding of the content of your paper.

STEP 4: WRITE A FIRST DRAFT: PARAGRAPH DEVELOPMENT, TRANSITIONS, AND TONE

Before any paper is ready for submission, writers draft and revise, draft and revise—sometimes sequentially, sometimes simultaneously. The purpose of writing a first draft is to get something down on paper that you can work with until you have created a well-organized paper with solid PARAGRAPHS, effective TRANSITIONS, and an appropriate TONE.

A. DEVELOPING YOUR PARAGRAPHS

Every KEY IDEA should be developed in one or more paragraphs, each of which contains a TOPIC SENTENCE that states its main point. The topic sentence often starts the paragraph, so that the reader knows at the outset what to expect. All sentences that follow the topic sentence should support and develop it. Your paragraph will be unified (see UNITY in the Glossary section) if every supporting sentence relates directly to the topic sentence. An adequately developed paragraph includes enough EVIDENCE to make its main idea clear to your readers.

How do you decide the best way to develop a particular paragraph? How much evidence should you include? What kind of support should it be? To make these decisions, put yourself in your reader's place. What does he or she need to know in order to understand your point? Below is a list of ways that you can develop individual paragraphs. Note that many of the paragraph strategies correspond to the essay patterns identified in the chart on page 9–10.

- Narrating a story or a personal ANECDOTE
- Specific descriptive details, facts, or statistics
- Well-chosen examples or illustrations
- Relating a series of steps or stages
- A comparison or contrast
- A definition
- A quotation or paraphrase (using expert opinion), which of course, must be properly documented (see How to Write a Documented Essay on page 16)

You can, of course, use more than one kind of evidence to develop a paragraph. A definition is often complemented by one or more examples; sometimes an anecdote can be combined with a quotation or PARAPHRASE. There is no fixed rule that governs the kind or number of development strategies you can use. Your responsibility is to provide your readers with everything they need to know to understand your THESIS.

Once you have drafted your key ideas, you have two more paragraphs to write: the INTRODUCTION and the CONCLUSION. All too often, these parts of a paper are dull, clumsy, or repetitive. But they don't have to be. Carefully constructed, these paragraphs can catch your reader's attention and clinch your discussion. The Glossary section contains a number of ideas you can choose from when crafting a beginning and ending for your paper.

B. SUPPLYING TRANSITIONS

As you write and revise, keep in mind that you want to make it as easy as possible for your reader to follow you through your paper. TRANSITIONS are words or phrases that show the logical relationship between one point and the next, causing a paragraph or a paper to hang together and read smoothly. Like the turn signals on a car, transitions such as *first, next, therefore, however,* and *finally* tell the person following you where you're going. The Glossary section will give you suggestions for appropriate transitional phrases, depending on the kind of relationship between ideas that you want to signal.

C. ESTABLISHING AND MAINTAINING AN APPROPRIATE TONE

TONE is the term used to describe a writer's attitude toward a topic as it is revealed through his or her language. A writer may feel angry, amused, nostalgic, or passionate, and this attitude is reflected in the words, examples, quotations, and other supporting details with which he or she develops the thesis. Good writing is usually modulated in tone; the writer addresses the reader with respect, in a calm, reasonable way. Highly emotional writing is often not convincing to readers—what gets communicated is the strength of the writer's feelings rather than depth of knowledge or validity of opinion.

Tone is a complex idea to understand, and control of it is a difficult skill to master. As you read the selections in this book, observe how skilled writers convey a range of emotions. For example, "D'oh! An Analysis of the Medical Care Provided to the Family of Homer J. Simpson" is a comic contrast of two cartoon doctors. But the medical DICTION and dry wit of the essay make a subtle point about the quality of medical care we receive. David Bodanis's "Toothpaste" appears at first to be a straightforward analysis of the ingredients of a product we use every day. The essay could have been as dry and humourless as a chapter from a chemistry text, but Bodanis manages to make it both bizarre and funny.[5]

STEP 5: REVISE, EDIT, AND PROOFREAD YOUR PAPERS[6]

At last you've reached the final stage of the writing process. Even though you are probably sick of your assignment by now and eager to be done with it, *do not* skip this step. You need to revise your paper before you send it out into the world. Ideally, you should revise several days after writing your paper.

A. REVISING

A thorough revision requires at least two reviews of your paper. The first time you go over it, read it aloud, slowly, from beginning to end, keeping your AUDIENCE in mind as you read. Is your THESIS clear? Are the KEY IDEAS arranged in an appropriate ORDER? Are all points adequately explained? Has anything been left out? Are the PARAGRAPHS unified and coherent? Are there any awkward sentences that should be rephrased?

---

[5] Marking the text as you read can help you understand how writers manipulate tone. In "Toothpaste," for example, when you come to a descriptive phrase that makes you respond "Yecchh," mark it. Similarly, underline or note in the margin any phrases you find funny. When you've finished reading, you can go back and figure out how the author caught your attention: through a change in DICTION, perhaps? Unusual SYNTAX? A surprising example?

[6] For a detailed guide to revising, editing, and proofreading, see "The Three Steps to Revision" on our website: www.cancon7e.nelson.com.

B. EDITING

Begin editing by running your essay through the grammar- and spell-check functions of your computer. Don't just go through the document replacing your words with the computer's suggestions, however. Computers are programmed to question, not to decide, the appropriateness of a writer's choices. You must decide for yourself if the questions are useful and if any of the suggestions are suitable.

The second time you read through your paper, read it with the Editing Checklist (on the inside of the front cover) in front of you for easy reference. Pay special attention to the points that tend to give you trouble: for example, sentence fragments, verb errors, misplaced apostrophes, or dangling modifiers. Most writers know their weaknesses; unfortunately, it's human nature to ignore these and to focus on strengths. That is why editing your work can be a painful process. Nevertheless, it is an absolutely essential task. You owe it to yourself and your reader to find and correct any errors in your writing.

C. PROOFREADING

If your spelling, punctuation, or keyboarding skills are not strong, you will need to read your paper a third time. Grammar- and spell-check it again. Then read it through from the end to the beginning to check every sentence. When reading from back to front, you're forced to look at each sentence individually rather than in CONTEXT, and thus you are more likely to spot your mistakes. It's also a good idea to ask someone else to go over your paper and identify any errors you've missed.

A final word of advice: whether you are writing for a teacher or an employer, **always keep a copy of your paper for your files**.

If you follow these five steps carefully, your reader will arrive at your destination without any accident, mishap, or wrong turns. And if, as we have suggested, you keep your audience in focus throughout the process, you can make the journey informative and enjoyable. No reader can ask for more.

How to Write a Documented Essay

This section provides a quick overview of the process of writing research papers. For a detailed explanation of how to write and document a research paper, go to our website (www.cancon7e.nelson.com) and consult "Researching Your Topic," "Summarizing, Paraphrasing, and Quoting," and "Formatting and Documenting a Research Paper."

For some essays or research assignments, you will be required to find and integrate other people's ideas or expert opinion into your paper. You will use the written (or, occasionally, spoken) words of external sources to develop your KEY IDEAS and prove your THESIS. As any good lawyer knows, proving your point depends on the effective presentation of quality EVIDENCE. The evidence you assemble and the way you incorporate it into your own writing will determine the success or failure of your documented essay.

Keep in mind that the reason most instructors assign research papers is to give you an opportunity to demonstrate how well you can find, analyze, and evaluate source material, synthesize it, and use it to support your own conclusions about a topic. Very few research assignments require you simply to report other people's findings on a topic. Normally, you are expected to use source material as evidence to support your thesis. Writing a documented essay requires the use of high-order thinking skills: interpreting, summarizing, analyzing, and evaluating. That is why a research paper or term paper so often serves as the culminating test of learning in university and college courses. Such papers are good practice for the world of work, too. The critical thinking skills that a documented essay requires are the same skills that professionals must demonstrate on the job.

STEP 1: GATHERING THE EVIDENCE

Your first task is to find, evaluate, and make notes on source material that supports your thesis. Usually, you do this work using computer-based research tools, books, periodicals, and academic or professional journals as your sources. A research librarian can help you find current, relevant, and credible information.

After you have found a number of promising-looking sources, your next task is to evaluate the material to see if it is appropriate for your paper. Inexperienced writers often get bogged down at this point, spending days or even weeks reading potential sources in detail. A more efficient approach is to scan each work quickly and ignore anything that is not up to date or reliable.[7] Once you have identified a number of potentially useful sources, read them carefully, using the reading and note-taking suggestions provided in "How to Read with Understanding" (pages 1–5). Whenever you make notes from a source, be careful to record its publishing information; whether you are summarizing, paraphrasing, or quoting, you must always identify your source. This process is called **documentation**. Following are the basic guidelines for documenting electronic and print sources:

- **For electronic sources:** Name(s) of author(s) or editor(s) (if given); document title; title of the database or site; date of publication or last revision; name of the institution or organization sponsoring the site (if given); date you accessed the source; URL or DOI.
- **For print sources:** Name(s) of author(s) or editor(s); title; place of publication, publisher's name, and date of publication; page number(s) on which you found the information you are using.

Keeping detailed and accurate bibliographical records as you read your sources will save you hours of time and frustration when you come to provide documentation for your paper and can't remember where you found a crucial piece of information. Accurate bibliographical records will also help to keep you from falling into the trap of unintended plagiarism (more on this later).

STEP 2: PRESENTING THE EVIDENCE

Once your research notes are complete and you have begun your first draft, you need to know how to integrate the information you have found into your own writing. There are three methods you can choose from: summary, paraphrase, or direct quotation. A SUMMARY is a highly condensed version of another person's ideas or observations. A PARAPHRASE is a longer summary. It could include, for example, the KEY IDEA and several supporting details, whereas a summary would present only the key idea. Whether you are summarizing or paraphrasing, *you must put the source information into your own words.* If you use the actual words or phrases of the original, you are *quoting,* and you must signal that fact to the reader by using quotation marks or—for a quotation that runs more than four typed lines in your paper—by indenting the quoted passage 2.5 cm from the left margin and identifying the source. (See "Formatting and Documenting a Research Paper" on our website.)

---

[7] Be wary of Internet sources, especially if the source's URL does not end with a recognized domain such as ".gov" (government) or ".edu" (educational institution). You often can check the credibility of an author, company, organization, or institution by using an online search engine such as Google.

A word about **academic integrity**: Most students know that **plagiarism** is using someone else's ideas and presenting them as your own. Submitting someone else's term paper or collecting material from various articles and passing it off as yours are clear examples of academic dishonesty. Not everyone realizes, however, that neglecting to identify your sources, even if the omission is unintentional, is also plagiarism. Whenever you use another writer's ideas in an essay, you need to let your reader know whose ideas they are and where you found them. Careful documentation will not only ensure that you avoid plagiarism, it will also ensure that you are given credit for the reading and research you have done.

To document the online sources, books, articles, and other information you have used in your paper, you need to follow an approved system of documentation. Two basic styles are used in most colleges and universities: the Modern Language Association (MLA) format, usually required in humanities courses; and the American Psychological Association (APA) format, commonly used in the social sciences. Both formats have abandoned the old-fashioned and cumbersome footnote system in favour of in-text parenthetical referencing, which means indicating the source in parentheses immediately following the summary, paraphrase, or quotation. (You'll find detailed instructions and examples of in-text citations on this book's website: www.cancon7e.nelson.com).

The natural and physical sciences use a wide variety of documentation formats, and many colleges and universities publish their own style manuals. If your instructor requires a specific format, use the appropriate handbook to guide you through the task of acknowledging source material. Most systems of documentation require, in addition to parenthetical citations, that you list your sources for the paper in a separate section at the end, called either "Works Cited" (MLA) or "References" (APA). The format of this list—including spacing, order of information, capitalization, and punctuation—must be followed *exactly,* down to the last comma, for your paper and your list of references.[8] If your instructor leaves the choice of format up to you, choose one of the following style guides:

- Gibaldi, Joseph. *MLA Handbook for Writers of Research Papers.* 7th ed. New York: MLA, 2009. www.mla.org)

---

[8] We know this requirement sounds incredibly picky, and it is. However, the format of a documentation entry tells a professional reader just as much as the content of the entry (author's name, title, etc.) does. A documentation entry is like a line of computer code: those who know the language of the symbols can read the message. Your instructors know the code and expect to find it in your "Works Cited" or "References" list.

- American Psychological Association. *Publication Manual of the American Psychological Association.* 6th ed. Washington, DC: APA, 2009. (www.apa.org)

Detailed information about the MLA and APA styles is available on our website: www.cancon7e.nelson.com.

The essay that follows is documented and formatted in APA style. It shows you

- how to incorporate summaries, paraphrases, and short and long quotations into your writing
- how to indicate that you have altered a quotation, either by leaving something out (use ellipses) or by adding or changing a word or phrase (use square brackets)
- how to use parenthetical citations for different kinds of sources

We have added notes in the margin of the essay to identify the author's sources and the kinds of parenthetical citations they require. The References list is annotated to identify the different kinds of sources the writer relied on to illustrate and support her thesis.

SAMPLE ESSAY PRESENTED IN APA STYLE

APA-formatted essays are to be prepared on letter-size paper, with 2.5-cm margins at the top, bottom and sides. You should use a 10- or 12-point Times New Roman font or a similar font. (This same essay, formatted in MLA style, is in the Appendix, page 445.)

*Running head
to appear on
all pages*

WHAT MAKES YOU HAPPY?   1

*Essay title
and author's
name and
institutional
affiliation,
centred in the
upper half of
the page*

What Makes You Happy?

Jessica Marlowe

Canadian College

WHAT MAKES YOU HAPPY?   2

What Makes You Happy?

What makes you happy: A great new outfit? A baby's smile? A hefty bonus cheque? Human happiness is a complicated question, one that is attracting increased attention from psychologists, sociologists, and policy makers. There is even a new academic discipline, Happiness Studies, that focuses on what "happiness" means and how people try--and often fail--to achieve it. "Happiness" in this context does not mean joy, or merriment, or cheerfulness, or any other synonym you may find in your thesaurus. It means a high level of satisfaction with one's life. For most people, good health, meaningful work, and positive personal relationships are basic requirements for happiness. Those are the givens. The variables most often cited are material wealth, personal residence, and family ties.

Thesis statement

What we own is, of course, a function of how much disposable income we have. We often assume that the more money we have, the happier we will be because we can buy more "stuff": a high-end auto, designer clothes, state-of-the-art electronics, fabulous footwear, dazzling jewellery, a yacht--the list is endless. But beyond a certain level of comfort, research suggests

WHAT MAKES YOU HAPPY?   3

that owning more "stuff" does not translate into more

happiness. In "But Will It Make You Happy?" Stephanie

Rosenbloom (2010) recounts the experience of a young

couple with well-paying jobs, a spacious apartment, two

cars, and piles of household goods who felt, despite it

all, dissatisfied with their lives. They gave away most

Summary

of their possessions and downsized to a small studio

apartment, while he went back to school and she started a

business from home. Their income dropped dramatically,

but so did their spending. Now debt-free, they travel, do

volunteer work, and say that they are happier than they

have ever been.

Another example is software engineer Kelly Sutton,

who pared down his life to a laptop, iPad, Kindle, two hard

drives, a few items of clothing, and towels and bed linens,

and documented the purge on his blog, TheCultofLess.

com. Sutton sums up his experience this way:

Long quotation with words omitted (ellipses) and words changed (in square brackets)

> While I don't consider myself to be some sort of
> ascetic or societal recluse, I've found that more
> stuff equates to more stress. Each thing I own[ed]
> came with [an] expectation of responsibility. . . .
> I glance[d] into my desk drawers and [saw] my
> neglect. (Bielski, 2010, p. L4)

Full parenthetical source citation; see second item in References

WHAT MAKES YOU HAPPY?   4

These examples bear witness to the old adage that
money can't buy happiness, and the latest academic
research confirms that traditional wisdom. A recent study
finds that having money actually "impairs people's ability
to savor everyday positive emotions and experiences"
(Quoidbach, Dunn, Petrides, & Mikolajczak, 2010, p. 759).

Short quotation within the text; full parenthetical source citation; see item 7 in References

On the other hand, money can buy something
that does contribute to happiness: positive experience.
The experience could be a memorable vacation, a
backyard pool for the whole family to enjoy, a biking
excursion with friends, season's tickets to the theatre
or a sports event, a weekend camping expedition, or
even a relaxing day at the spa. While a new car provides
a pop of pleasure when we first drive it home, we
quickly get used to it, and the thrill is gone. Or, worse,
our neighbour comes home with a better one, and
we succumb to envy for his shinier, more expensive
vehicle.

The craving for material possessions is insatiable;
acquiring the new clothes or smartphone we long
for leads, sadly, to higher expectations but not increased
satisfaction. But the pleasure of a satisfying experience
can be savoured over time. British philosophy professor

WHAT MAKES YOU HAPPY?   5

*Quotation
from online
source;
author's name
given in text;
see item 3 in
References*

A. C. Grayling maintains, "A man who has a thousand pounds and spends it on a wonderful trip to the Galapagos Islands is a rich man indeed: the experiences, the things learnt, the differences wrought in him by both, are true wealth" (2008).

Related to conspicuous consumption is another happiness variable: our homes. Where we live influences our happiness, both on the macro (the country) and micro (the home) levels. The Scandinavian countries consistently score highest in happiness surveys. For example, in the 2010 *Gallup World Poll* survey, Denmark, Finland, and Norway topped the list of 155 countries surveyed. Denmark ranked first, with 82 percent of respondents reporting themselves as "thriving." Sweden tied with the Netherlands for fourth place. Canada placed eighth. Francesca Levy describes the survey methodology that Gallup used in this poll:

*Long quota-
tion (indented
2.5 cm on the
left-hand side)*

First, they asked subjects to reflect on their overall satisfaction with their lives, and ranked their answers using a "life evaluation" score between 1 and 10. Then they asked questions about how each subject had felt the previous day. Those answers allowed researchers to score their "daily experiences"--things like whether they felt well rested, respected, free

WHAT MAKES YOU HAPPY?   6

of pain and intellectually engaged. Subjects that reported high scores were considered "thriving." The percentage of thriving individuals in each country determined our rankings. (2010)

As one would expect, a certain level of affluence is reflected in these findings, but it is surprising to those of us living in the Frozen North to find that a warm climate is not a factor that contributes significantly to happiness. The five least happy countries (Sierra Leone, Cambodia, Comoros, Burundi, Togo) are all impoverished-and-hot countries. The United States, by most measures the richest country in the world, falls below Canada at number 14, with 57 percent of respondents reporting themselves as thriving. These rankings suggest that the happiness of a country depends on the degree to which its economic and social welfare--the social safety net--is assured.

Our immediate surroundings--the space we live in-- influence our happiness, too. People work hard to achieve a comfortable home with enough space for their family. Yet there is increasing evidence that bigger, fancier homes do not necessarily translate into happier occupants. For one thing, in Canada's major cities, affordable large homes with big lots exist only in the suburbs, a fact that means a long,

WHAT MAKES YOU HAPPY?   7

stressful daily commute for the family's breadwinners.

Apart from the huge carbon footprint of the jumbo house

and the two gas-guzzling cars, the personal costs to the

family can be very high. Charles Montgomery emphasizes

this point in "Me Want More Square Footage":

> [P]eople who live in low-density sprawl are more
>
> likely to die violently than their inner-city
>
> cousins--thanks mostly to car accidents. . . .
>
> [S]uburban kids are far more likely to get hooked
>
> on drugs and booze. Why? Not enough chill-out
>
> time with their parents, for one thing. And
>
> where are suburban parents in those crucial
>
> after-school hours? Drumming their dashboards
>
> on marathon commutes home from distant
>
> offices. (2011, p. 59–60)

Modified long quotation from article in an anthology; abbreviated source citation; see item 6 in References

Thinking about where we live, of course, leads

us to the third factor in the happiness equation: the

people with whom we live. While an adult may choose

to live alone or with a group of like-minded friends,

most of us live in families. Russian writer Leo Tolstoy

famously began his classic novel *Anna Karenina* with

the words: "All happy families are alike; each unhappy

family is unhappy in its own way" (1878/2000, p. 1).

WHAT MAKES YOU HAPPY?   8

Whether or not Tolstoy is right, there is no question that
a person's family--both the birth family and the family
one chooses or creates--significantly influences his or
her happiness. Coming from a troubled family is a strong
predictor of unhappiness. Those who have been born
into a dysfunctional family must work long and hard to
overcome the emotional damage of their background;
if they do not, they are likely to repeat the damaging
behaviour in the family they create as adults (Maté, 2011,
p. 254).

*Paraphrase
of article in
anthology;
see References
item 5*

On the other hand, healthy marriages and families
correlate to higher levels of happiness and well-being
in life. Studies tell us that married people tend to be
happier than single people. Adding children to the mix,
however, complicates the association between family and
happiness. Once an infant joins the family, caregiving
takes over one's life. The work is endless with small
children. Older parents especially, who have become
accustomed to independence, may find that a baby's
incessant demands lower their day-to-day satisfaction
with life. This dissatisfaction usually diminishes as the
child grows and becomes more independent, although
the adolescent years often present a whole new set

WHAT MAKES YOU HAPPY?   9

Paraphrase of article in online journal; see first item in References

of challenges. A 2009 study cited in the *Journal of Happiness Studies* reviews the positives and the negatives of having children and concludes that children greatly increase people's satisfaction with life if they have the time, the financial resources, and the right partner to share them with (Angeles, 2009).

Possessions, property, and parenthood: All are mixed blessings. Perhaps the key to happiness must remain a mystery. Some people maintain a happy equilibrium even in challenging circumstances; other people struggle to be happy with a life that most would envy. Mark Holder, a professor at UBC Okanagan, provides a helpful overview of advice from happiness researchers to put us on track (cited in Shore, 2010): Nurture social relationships, seek well-being rather than wealth, choose good friends, don't compare yourself to celebrities, cultivate gratitude, be active, complete tasks, help others, develop a hobby, appreciate the good moments, and don't bear grudges. Forgive people. Perhaps these deceptively simple maxims--not fame, fortune, or fabulous wealth--hold the key to lasting happiness.

WHAT MAKES YOU HAPPY?   10

References

Angeles, L. (2009). Children and life satisfaction. *Journal*

of Happiness Studies. doi: 10.1007/s10902-009-9168-z

Bielski, Z. (2010, August 28). Keeping down with the

Joneses. *The Globe and Mail,* p. L4.

Grayling, A. C. (2008, April 10). Happiness is the

measure of true wealth. *Telegraph.* Retrieved from

http://www.telegraph.co.uk/comment/3557112/

Happiness-is-the-measure-of-true-wealth.html

Levy, F. (2010, July 14). The world's happiest countries.

Forbes. Retrieved from http://www.forbes.

com/2010/07/14/world-happiest-countries-lifestyle-

realestate-gallup.html

Maté, G. (2011). Embraced by the needle. In N. Waldman

& S. Norton (Eds.), *Canadian Content* (7th ed.,

pp. 254–257). Toronto: Nelson.

Montgomery, C. (2011). Me want more square footage.

In N. Waldman & S. Norton (Eds.), *Canadian*

Content (7th ed., pp. 57–62). Toronto: Nelson.

Quoidback, J., Dunn, E. W., Petrides, K. V., &

Mikolajczak, M. (2010). Money giveth, money taketh

away: The dual effect of wealth on happiness.

Psychological Science, 21(6), pp. 759–763.

WHAT MAKES YOU HAPPY?   11

Rosenbloom, S. (2010, August 8). But will it make you
    happy? *The New York Times,* pp. B1, B4.

Shore, R. (2010, August 4). A scientific approach to
    happiness. *The Vancouver Sun.* Retrieved from
    http://communities.canada.com/vancouversun/blogs/
    greenman/archive/2010/08/04/a-scientific-approach-
    to-happiness.aspx

Tolstoy, L. (2000). *Anna Karenina* (R. Pevear & L.
    Volokhonsky, Trans.). New York: Penguin Books.
    (Original work published 1878.)

UNIT 1

Two Basic Strategies: Narration and Description

Narration and description are basic to all writing. Indeed, it would be difficult to write any essay or report without using one or both of these strategies. In this introduction, we use examples from essays in this unit to illustrate what narration and description are, why we use them, and how to write them.

NARRATION

WHAT IS NARRATION?

Narrative writing tells a story; it relates a sequence of events. Novels and short fiction are also narratives, but they are based on imagined events. In this book, we are primarily concerned with non-fiction—writing that is based on fact. When an essay includes a story (often called an ANECDOTE) to illustrate a KEY IDEA, the reader trusts that the story actually happened. For instance, Hal Niedzviecki's essay "*Facebook* in a Crowd" (page 39) tells the story of his *Facebook* party:

> One day this past summer, I logged on to *Facebook* and realized that I was very close to having 700 online "friends." Not bad, I thought to myself, absurdly proud of how many cyberpals, connections, acquaintances and

even strangers I'd managed to sign up. . . . So I decided to have a *Facebook* party.

Narrative essays tell readers what happened, often in chronological order, and readers assume that the events in the story actually occurred. The narrative is a way for the writer to make a point—assert a thesis—in a compelling way.

A new genre of narrative writing has gained prominence in recent years: *creative* (or *literary*) *non-fiction,* which is a hybrid of fiction and non-fiction. For a piece of writing to be creative non-fiction, it must be factually accurate but also demonstrate attributes of style and technique most often found in literature, specifically the short story. In other words, the experience recounted in the narrative must be based in fact but told in a way that approximates good fiction writing: setting a scene, creating a plot, developing character, and achieving a climactic moment when the narrator recognizes something that changes him or her in a fundamental way.

Ryan Van Meter's "First" is a fine example of creative non-fiction; he writes about a formative event from his own childhood in a way that achieves the crystalline clarity of the best short fiction. Lorna Crozier's "What Stays in the Family" and Michael Ignatieff's moving "Deficits" also share elements of this hybrid genre. Niedzviecki's *"Facebook* in a Crowd," Dave Bidini's "Mongolian Invasions," and Tommy Akulukjuk's "My Father and the Baby Seal" are examples of more traditional narrative essays.

WHY DO WE USE NARRATION?

Providing a narrative is often a good way to develop a key idea. For example, in the passage below from "My Father and the Baby Seal" (page 50), Tommy Akulukjuk narrates an episode from a hunting excursion with his father:

> . . . on our way back home, we decided to take a risk and travel on the sea-ice that my father had earlier deemed unsafe. Inuit hunters are always careful, checking what they think is dangerous. Along the way we tested the thickness of the ice with a harpoon. At one point, when my father got off the snowmobile to do this, he said to me, "Don't follow. Stay here." I felt apprehension in his voice, an uncertainty that I'd never heard before.

This anecdote illustrates the anxiety of a child who recognizes for the first time that his father can experience fear.

A writer may use narration as the sole organizing principle of an essay: What happened first? And then what happened? And then . . . ? "My Father and the Baby Seal" is an example of this kind of narrative essay. Another is "First," which tells the story of the moment the author learned his feelings were forbidden.

More often, however, writers use narration to develop a key idea in an essay that is structured as a classification, comparison, causal analysis, or some other rhetorical pattern. For example, the following anecdote from Brent Staples's causal analysis essay, "Just Walk On By" (page 263), supports a key idea about the racist assumptions he encountered as a young journalist in Chicago:

> . . . I was on assignment for a local paper and killing time before an interview. I entered a jewelry store on the city's affluent Near North Side. The proprietor excused herself and returned with an enormous red Doberman pinscher straining at the end of a leash. She stood, the dog extended toward me, silent to my questions, her eyes bulging nearly out of her head. I took a cursory look around, nodded, and bade her good night.

HOW DO WE WRITE NARRATION?

Narration is based on the principles of storytelling. A good story tells a sequence of events in a way that captures the reader's interest and imagination. Good narration re-creates an experience so that readers can see and hear and feel it as if it had happened to them.

Here are five guidelines for writing effective narration:

1. Decide on your THESIS. Every narrative you use should contribute to your thesis by developing one of your key ideas

2. Select details that are clearly and directly related to your thesis. What you leave out is as important as what you put in. Put yourself in the reader's position and tell enough of the story to make it both clear and vivid, but do not include so many details that your narrative wanders away from its PURPOSE: supporting a key idea.

3. Arrange the events in the most effective time order. Usually, a story moves in CHRONOLOGICAL (time) ORDER: first this happened, then this, and finally that. But sometimes a narrative is more effective if the writer begins at the end and then goes back to tell how the story began (this technique is called a **flashback**). It's even possible to begin in the middle of the chronological sequence, introduce a flashback to fill in details that occurred before the point at which the story began, and then proceed to the end. Michael Ignatieff uses this complex sequence in

"Deficits" (page 71), an essay about the devastating effects of Alzheimer's disease on his mother. Whatever time order you use, it is important to adhere to the next guideline.

4. Use TRANSITIONS to help your reader follow you as you proceed through the narrative. Provide time-markers (not in every sentence, of course) to indicate the sequence of events: *after, suddenly, next, as soon as,* and *finally* are the kinds of useful transition signals that keep your readers on track.

5. Maintain a consistent POINT OF VIEW. Point of view means the angle of narration: Who is telling the story? If you begin your anecdote with yourself as first-person narrator ("I"), continue telling the story yourself. Don't shift to a different narrator, such as a "you" or a "he" or "she." Readers need to experience a story from a single, consistent narrative perspective.

DESCRIPTION

WHAT IS DESCRIPTION?

Descriptive writing creates a picture in words. It tells readers what a person, a place, or a thing looks like. Effective description appeals not only to the reader's visual sense but also to other senses: hearing, taste, smell, and touch. For example, in "Clinging to The Rock" (page 42), Russell Wangersky creates a vivid sense of Newfoundland's tiny outport villages:

> There's life yet in gritty, tightly knit outport communities. In Reefs Harbour on Newfoundland's Northern Peninsula, a handful of fishing sheds, their sides weathered to a uniform silver-grey, stand like forgotten teeth on a half-buried lower jaw. Lobster markers hang from coils of yellow rope inside their dusty windows. A single boat curves in towards the harbour, its engine the only sound in the still air, a solitary fisherman at the stern. Every few seconds, a small wave breaks over the shoals in the harbour, loud enough to drown out the vessel's approach.

This passage re-creates the look, the feel, and the sounds of the isolated communities on Newfoundland's coast, and it supports Wangersky's topic sentence about their essential *life*.

WHY DO WE USE DESCRIPTION?

Description creates a sensory image of a topic. Concrete descriptive details help clarify abstract ideas; they also appeal to the reader on many levels, including the emotional. Description is an excellent way to make a point in a powerful way. Take, for example, Michael Ignatieff's poignant descriptions of his mother when she was young and as she is now:

> She always loved to swim. When she dived into the water, she never made a splash. I remember her lifting herself out of the pool, as sleek as a seal in a black swimsuit, the water pearling off her back. Now she says the water is too cold. . . .
>
> I bathe her when she wakes. Her body is white, soft, and withered. I remember how, in the changing-huts, she would bend over as she slipped out of her bathing suit. Her body was young. Now I see her skeleton through her skin. When I wash her hair, I feel her skull. I help her from the bath, dry her legs, swathe her in towels, sit her on the edge of the bath and cut her nails: they are horny and yellow. Her feet are gnarled. She has walked a long way.
>
> ("Deficits," 67)

People and places are often the focus of descriptive writing, but things—inanimate objects—can also be described in convincing detail. Consider the following passage and see if you can figure out what common substance David Bodanis is describing:

> To keep the glop from drying out, a mixture including glycerine glycol—related to the most common car anti-freeze ingredient—is whipped in with the chalk and water, and to give *that* concoction a bit of substance . . . a large helping is added of gummy molecules from the seaweed *Chrondus crispus*. This seaweed ooze spreads in among the chalk, paint, and anti-freeze, then stretches itself in all directions to hold the whole mass together. A bit of par-affin oil (the fuel that flickers in camping lamps) is pumped in with it to help the moss ooze keep the whole substance smooth.

Did you guess that this disgusting-sounding substance is tooth-paste? (See Bodanis's essay on page 185.)

Some pieces of writing are entirely descriptive. However, description is most often used to support KEY IDEAS within another organizational pattern. "Toothpaste" is a division essay and "Deficits" is primarily a narrative, yet both are enhanced by strong description. Short passages of description—a sentence or two, or even just a phrase—can help you ensure that your ideas are clear to the reader. Consider, for example, Jeffrey Moussaieff Masson's description of a penguin's egg in "Dear Dad," a process analysis essay (page 146): "Weighing almost a pound, and measuring up to 131 millimetres long and 86 millimetres wide, this is one of the largest eggs of any bird."

HOW DO WE WRITE DESCRIPTION?

To paraphrase Stephen King, good description begins in the mind of the writer and ends in the mind of the reader. Description provides details of what your reader needs to visualize in order to understand your point. Good description communicates the writer's attitude toward a topic as well as the objective details. Your goal should to be to convey, through the details you choose, a dominant impression that reflects your feelings about the person, place, or thing you are describing. Take another look at the descriptive examples above: Ignatieff's description of his mother, Wangersky's description of Newfoundland's outports, and Bodanis's description of toothpaste ingredients. These passages all clearly convey the writers' attitudes toward their topics.

Here are four guidelines for writing good description:

1. Determine your PURPOSE. Are you writing a purely descriptive essay? Or are you using description to develop a KEY IDEA in an expository or persuasive essay? Decide whether you want to present a factual, objective picture (Masson's penguin egg, for example) or if you need to create a dominant impression that reflects your feelings, as Ignatieff does in "Deficits."

2. Use sensory words in your description. What does the topic look, sound, feel, smell, and taste like? Choose words that contribute to the dominant impression you want to convey.

3. Select the most important physical details. You cannot describe every detail about a topic without losing your focus (and your reader).

4. Arrange your selected details so that your picture emerges coherently. Usually, you will choose a spatial order (from top to bottom, left to right), but sometimes a psychological order (e.g., from external features to internal character) is appropriate. Choose the arrangement that is most likely to accomplish your purpose.

Mastering narration and description is well worth your time and effort. Because they answer the fundamental questions readers ask—What happened? What did it look like?—narration and description are two of the most useful tools a writer can use to communicate meaning.

The following essay illustrates how narration and description can be used together to help convey a thesis.

A Cultural Exchange

Introduction (provides descriptive details)

The French bar-café is an institution, a unique national treasure. Its patrons are an eclectic mix of blue-clad workmen in cloth caps or berets; lawyers and stockbrokers in business suits; scruffy individuals who could be students, artists, anarchists, or all three; elderly retired gentlemen in tweeds and moustaches; and farmers in rubber boots. The haze of blue smoke that gives the interior such a warm aura is the most distinctive characteristic of a French bar: the unique smell of French tobacco. The harsh Gauloise produces a tangy, dark aroma that is unforgettable.

Narrative begins by describing the situation: a birthday celebration

I had entered this tiny bar on the ground floor of a country hotel in a small village in central France on a mission. My wife and I were staying in the hotel overnight, celebrating her fortieth birthday and recovering from lunch. Valerie's celebratory meal had taken place in nearby Roanne at Restaurant Troisgros, one of the gastronomic wonders of the world. "Lunch" had begun at noon and ended nearly four hours

More descriptive details

later when we staggered out to our car, stuffed with *foie gras,* lobster *breton poché, noisettes* of lamb, a profusion of French cheeses, and a mind-boggling array of rich desserts. Now, some hours later and a few kilometres away, we were ready to cap the big day with a bottle of champagne on the balcony of our room. Unwilling to guzzle the expensive nectar from bathroom tumblers, I had tottered down three flights of stairs to the bar to borrow a pair of proper champagne glasses.

General statement about communication; description of writer's weak grasp of French

We take communication for granted — so much so that only when it goes awry do we stop to think about what a complex process it is. My French is adequate, I'm told, so far as accent is concerned, but pathetically weak in grammar and vocabulary. Even the simplest conversation requires extensive rehearsal, so it was with some trepidation that I entered the crowded, smoky bar, muttering to myself the request I was about to make.

Narrative resumes here

"Oui, monsieur?" The bartender was a friendly sort, but possessed of one of those voices that, when pitched just right, can be heard in the next province.

*Narrative
(developed by
descriptive
details and
dialogue)*

Conversation gradually died as everyone turned to watch me struggle through my request.

I must have done well enough in my broken French accompanied by expressive hand gestures—shaping the glasses in the air and sipping imaginary bubbly—because the bartender grinned, reached under the bar, and produced two large flutes, polishing them elaborately with his apron.

"Et pour quelle grande célébration désirez-vous deux verres de champagne, monsieur?" he boomed as he set the glasses in front of me, winking theatrically. By now the entire bar was concentrating on our conversation, eager to hear what great celebration it was that required champagne glasses.

Confident that I was up to the task, I grinned and told the entire company, *"C'est aujourd'hui le quatorzième anniversaire de ma femme!"*

*Climactic
incident: the
"punch line"
(developed by
descriptive
details)*

The bar erupted in cries of congratulation and admiration. Blue-clad, Gauloise-smoking workmen toasted me, hoisting their glasses overhead and shouting their approval. Others, apparently helpless with laughter, sagged against the bar. Several tried to shake my hand, though I was encumbered by the champagne glasses, and more than one slapped my back resoundingly. One older gentleman, nattily dressed in a blue beret and sporting magnificent waxed moustaches, wept with laughter as he tried to pour some of his *pastis* into my precious glasses. The hilarity seemed a bit overdone, I thought, for such a simple announcement . . . until I replayed the conversation in my head and realized that I had given my wife's age not as *quarante*, forty, but as *quatorze*—fourteen.

*Conclusion
reinforces the
thesis: the
complexity of
communication*

Joining the laughter, I bowed deeply, gave my best imitation of a Gallic shrug, and, flourishing my glasses overhead, made my red-faced exit.

Facebook in a Crowd

HAL NIEDZVIECKI

Hal Niedzviecki (b. 1971) is a Toronto-based writer and culture critic. He is co-founder and (until 2002) fiction editor of *Broken Pencil*, a guide to zine culture and underground arts (brokenpencil.com). Among his many books are *Smell It* (1998, short fiction); *Ditch* (2001, novel); *Hello, I'm Special: How Individuality Became the New Conformity* (2004); *The Big Book of Pop Culture: A How-to Guide for Young Artists* (2006); and *The Peep Diaries: How We're Learning to Love Watching Ourselves and Our Neighbors* (2009). His articles have appeared in *Adbusters*, *Utne Magazine*, *The Walrus*, *This Magazine*, *Geist*, *Toronto Life*, *The Globe and Mail*, and the *National Post*. For more about his work, visit his website at www.smellit.ca.

One day this past summer, I logged on to *Facebook* and realized that I was very close to having 700 online "friends." Not bad, I thought to myself, absurdly proud of how many cyberpals, connections, acquaintances and even strangers I'd managed to sign up.   1

But the number made me uneasy as well. I had just fallen out   2
with a friend I'd spent a lot of time with. I'd disconnected with a few other ones for the usual reasons—jobs in other cities, family life limiting social time. I was as much to blame as they were. I had a 2-year-old kid of my own at home. Add to that my workaholic irritability, my love of being left alone and my lack of an office environment or mysterious association with the Masons° from which to derive an instant network of cronies. I had fewer friends to hang out with than I'd ever had before.

So I decided to have a *Facebook* party. I used *Facebook* to create   3
an "event" and invite my digital chums. Some of them, of course, didn't live in Toronto, but I figured, it's summer and people travel. You never know who might be in town. If they lived in Buffalo or Vancouver, they could just click "not attending," and that would be that. *Facebook* gives people the option of R.S.V.P.'ing in three categories—"attending," "maybe attending" and "not attending."

After a week the responses stopped coming in and were ready   4
to be tabulated. Fifteen people said they were attending, and 60 said maybe. A few hundred said not, and the rest just ignored the invitation altogether. I figured that about 20 people would show up. That sounded pretty good to me. Twenty potential new friends.

---

5   On the evening in question I took a shower. I shaved. I splashed on my tingly man perfume. I put on new pants and a favorite shirt. Brimming with optimism, I headed over to the neighborhood watering hole and waited.

6   And waited.

7   And waited.

8   Eventually, one person showed up.

9   I chatted with my new potential friend, Paula, doing my best to pretend I wasn't dismayed and embarrassed. But I was too self-conscious to be genuine. I kept apologizing for the lack of attendance. I looked over my shoulder every time the door opened and someone new came in. Paula was nice about it, assuring me that people probably just felt shy about the idea of making a new friend. She said she herself had almost decided not to come.

10   "And now you have me all to yourself," I said, trying to sound beneficent° and unworried. We smiled at each other awkwardly.

11   We made small talk. I found out about her job, her boyfriend, her soccer team. Paula became my *Facebook* friend after noticing I was connected to a friend of hers. She thought it would be interesting to drop by and meet me.

12   Eventually we ran out of things to say. Anyway, she had to work in the morning. I picked up the tab on her Tom Collins and watched as she strode out into the night, not entirely sure if our friendship would grow.

13   After she left, I renewed my vigil, waiting for someone to show. It was getting on 11 o'clock and all my rationalizations—for example, that people needed time to get home from work, eat dinner, relax a bit—were wearing out.

14   I would learn, when I asked some people who didn't show up the next day, that "definitely attending" on *Facebook* means "maybe" and "maybe attending" means "likely not." So I probably shouldn't have taken it personally. But the combination of alcohol and solitude turned my thoughts to self-pity. Was I really that big of a loser? Or was it that no one wants to get together in real life anymore? It wasn't *Facebook's* fault; all those digital pals were better than nothing. For chipping away at past friendships and blocking honest new efforts, you really have to blame the entire modern world. People want to hang out with you, I assured myself. They just don't have the time.

15   By now it was nearing midnight. My head was clouded by drink, and it was finally starting to sink in: no one else was coming. I'd have to think up some other way to revitalize my social life. I ordered one more drink.

The beer arrived, a British import: Young's Double Chocolate   16
Stout. I raised my glass in a solitary toast and promised myself
I'd spend less time online. Then I took a gulp: the beer was delicious but bittersweet. Seven hundred friends, and I was drinking
alone.

Words and Meanings

Paragraph

Masons	an international men's organization; famous for secret rituals and for charity work (particularly on behalf of children)	2
beneficent	kindly, charitable	10

Structure and Strategy

1. What kind of introductory strategy does the author use to begin this essay?
2. Why does the author put quotation marks around the word "friends" in the first sentence?
3. Why are paragraphs 6, 7, and 8 so short and repetitive? What effect do they have on the reader?
4. How would you describe the TONE of the essay?
5. In the CONCLUSION of the essay the author issues a kind of challenge to himself—or at least gives himself some advice. What is it?

Content and Purpose

1. What is the significance of the essay's title?
2. How many friends does Niedzviecki have on *Facebook*? How did most of them become his "cyberpals"?
3. Why does the author decide to have a *Facebook* party (see paragraph 2)?
4. How do people respond to a party invitation on *Facebook*? How many responses does Niedzviecki get in each category? What does he learn that these clicks mean?
5. Who comes to the party? Why? How does the conversation at the party go?
6. In paragraph 14, Niedzviecki considers the question why "no one wants to get together in real life anymore." What answer does he come up with? Do you agree with him?
7. How does Niedzviecki feel about the experience of his *Facebook* party? What is the IRONY in the final paragraph?

Suggestions for Writing

1. If you use *Facebook* or another social network, write an essay explaining your relationship with your virtual friends. How many are you in regular contact with? How many are also real-life friends? Would your "friends" come to your party? Would you go to theirs?
2. How much of your social life takes place online? Write an essay that argues for or against the idea that social media bring people together in a satisfying way.
3. What is a friend? Write an essay that explains the characteristics of a good friend, based on your own experience.
4. A 1937 movie called *Stella Dallas* (a tearjerker starring Barbara Stanwyck) has a famous scene of a party that no one comes to, giving rise to the phrase "Stella Dallas party." Watch the movie, and compare Stella's experience to that described in "*Facebook in a Crowd.*" Why don't people come to Hal's or Stella's party? How do the no-shows make the party-givers feel?

Clinging to The Rock

RUSSELL WANGERSKY

Russell Wangersky is an award-winning journalist and fiction writer. Born in New Haven, Connecticut, but raised in Canada, Wangersky was educated at Acadia University. He is currently the editorial page editor of *The Telegram* in St. John's, as well as a columnist and magazine writer. His book *Burning Down the House: Fighting Fires and Losing Myself*—a non-fiction memoir of his twenty years as a volunteer firefighter—was published in 2008. His first novel, *The Glass Harmonica*, was released in the spring of 2010.

1   There's life yet in gritty, tightly knit outport° communities. In Reefs Harbour on Newfoundland's Northern Peninsula, a handful of fishing sheds, their sides weathered to a uniform silver-grey, stand like forgotten teeth on a half-buried lower jaw. Lobster markers hang from coils of yellow rope inside their dusty windows. A single boat curves in towards the harbour, its engine the only sound in the still air, a solitary fisherman at the stern. Every few seconds, a small wave breaks over the shoals° in the

Reprinted by permission of the author.

harbour, loud enough to drown out the vessel's approach. You can't shake the feeling that Reefs Harbour is asleep, asleep like Rip Van Winkle°, breathing slowly through a nap that could last for years.

Up and down the island's west coast, with the end of the lobster season, traps are standing in regimented rectangular stacks deep back in the woods, hunkered down as if already waiting for winter—even though it's only early August. In North Harbour, St. Mary's Bay, the small convenience store has closed, the sign gone and a basketball net is put up in the parking space. The store used to be connected to a family home looking out over the wide, flat bay. Coming in the door at suppertime, you'd smell cabbage and gravy; you'd have to wait a few minutes while someone pushed back from the table and came into the store to ring in your chips and Coke.

It's not just North Harbour: it's Sandringham, on the Eastport peninsula nearing central Newfoundland, and Swift Current on the south-reaching Burin Peninsula and many, many more. With shrinking populations in communities, the stores, often known as the "Groc and Conf"—shorthand for their wares in groceries and confectionery—have smaller and smaller margins, their owners working more hours because they can't afford staff. So the signs come down and the inventory goes back. But when it comes to forecasting the demise of outport Newfoundland, you'll meet people in a hurry to tell you that rumours of its death have been greatly exaggerated.

Where and when there's a fishery—less frequently now that there's so little cod—it works with such frenzy that people who have never seen it can hardly imagine. Big fish trucks with grey, yellow and blue fish boxes piled along their flat backs roar down rural roads belching black diesel smoke, heavy with loads of capelin or snow crab. Plants race through shrimp hauls, trying to keep up with the vessels, intent on catching their share before quotas are reached. There are long hours and multiple shifts, with an aging, diminishing workforce.

Comment about the struggle of keeping a fish processing plant going, and up above the fine grey sand of the beach at Eastport, a businessman will make a point of almost physically turning you towards the speck in the distance to point out the small town of Salvage and its vibrant fish plant. Go to the town on a Sunday and it's hard to keep from being hit by a forklift on the main street. Comment on the unworldly quiet of the empty side streets in Cape Broyle, just south of St. John's, and you'll get an angry retort telling you that three babies have been born in the last few weeks.

What no one should forget is that there are still thousands of outport Newfoundlanders, and these are resilient, hard-working

2

3

4

5

6

people. It's just that there are fewer of them. Scores° have left for greener pastures, to the point that the number of school-aged children in the province has fallen by 30 per cent—or 27,000—in the past decade alone. The stories the travellers send back about drugs and violence and gangs are sometimes daunting, but money can provide an irresistible lure.

7   Outport communities are shaking themselves like a dog, shaking themselves into a new arrangement and then lying down again, changed in fundamental ways. But giving up doesn't really seem to be in their vocabulary: communities are driven, as always, by their people.

8   There are more and more tourists along the Northern Peninsula and across the Avalon, tourists struck by the bare vistas and raw, rugged beauty of the place. If stunning aesthetics are the skin that covers Newfoundland and Labrador, then its people are the sinew. Sometimes they even look the part, strung together with twine and leather, their faces the image of being the next best thing to indestructible.

9   Without cod and with fewer people, the outports are changing forever. Not a requiem° yet, perhaps—but still a different, desperate song, sung by fewer voices. They'll admit that in an honest instant at the convenience store—so long as you find one that's still open.

Words and Meanings

Paragraph		
1	outport	small, isolated communities along the coasts of Newfoundland
	shoals	shallow waters near the shore
	Rip Van Winkle	character in a famous American short story who fell asleep for twenty years
6	scores	large numbers
9	requiem	religious song or service for the dead

Structure and Strategy

1. What is the TOPIC SENTENCE of paragraph 1? How is the paragraph developed?
2. Identify two SIMILES in paragraph 1. Now consider them in the context of the whole essay. Why are they effective?
3. What EXAMPLES does the author use in paragraphs 2 and 3 to illustrate the decline of Newfoundland's outport communities?

4. Highlight two places in the essay where the description appeals to the sense of smell, and another two that appeal to the sense of hearing.
5. Why does Wangersky address the reader directly in paragraph 5 (e.g., "Comment about. . ."; "Go to. . ."; "Comment on. . . and you'll get. . .")?
6. What method of paragraph development does the author use in paragraph 6?
7. Explain the METAPHOR developed in paragraph 8. Is it effective?

Content and Purpose

1. On what economic activity do Newfoundland's outports depend? How does the author emphasize this activity in paragraph 4?
2. Why do you think Wangersky compares the outports to Rip Van Winkle? (See paragraph 1.)
3. The last sentence in paragraph 3 is an allusion to a famous quotation. Can you identify the quotation and the person who first said it?
4. How does Wangersky characterize the people of the outport communities? What have many of them done in the past decade or so? What are the risks they encounter when they do so?
5. What new industry may keep the area economically viable? Do you think this hope is realistic?
6. Do you think Wangersky is ultimately optimistic or pessimistic about the fate of Newfoundland's outport communities? Support your answer with specific references to the text.

Suggestions for Writing

1. If you are from Newfoundland or if you have spent any time there, write an essay that argues for or against Wangersky's view of the outport communities. Provide ample description and enough examples to give your reader a vivid sense of the place.
2. Using description, narration, and example, explain the way the people of a specific community, neighbourhood, or other group you belong to and know well are shaped by their environment. (Consider any influences that contributed to the place as it is today: history, geography, economics, demographics, etc.)

Mongolian Invasions

DAVE BIDINI

Home-grown musician, journalist, playwright, film writer, and just-plain-author Dave Bidini (b. 1963) is a founding member of the rock band the Rheostatics. He has published a number of books, mostly about music, sports, or both: *Baseballissimo* (2004), *The Best Game You Can Name* (2005), and *Around the World in 57½ Gigs* (2007). Bidini wrote and hosted the Gemini Award–winning small-screen adaptation of *Tropic of Hockey* (2001), called *Hockey Nomad,* which was first broadcast in January 2003. In addition to playing both music and sports, Bidini writes regularly for *Maisonneuve* magazine and the *National Post.*

1   My friend Pujee is a hockey player from Ulaan Baator, Mongolia. His real name is Choijiljav Purevdavaa (and you thought "Tverdovsky" was hard to say). When I first met him in 2003 he drove a nearly destroyed Jeep whose side and rear-view mirrors were long ago pillaged and sold for scrap. It was the perfect ride for the rubble-filled craters and dead-brick mountains that give the Mongolian capital its post-apocalyptic look. But this torn gray canvas was Pujee's home, and as we steered through the city's tilted streets and dirt hills—I was there making a movie for the CBC about my hockey travels abroad—he pointed out the highlights: the deep bright snow ringing the edge of the city; the Skylab and Let it Be discotheques (built after Mongolia's liberation from the Soviets); Buddhist monasteries; soldiers patrolling on snorting horses; and two outdoor hockey rinks.

2   There was no plaque affixed to Pujee's wreck, so you'd be excused for not recognizing him as the father of Mongolian hockey. But Pujee—who was inducted into the International Hockey Hall of Fame in 2007—has done as much as anyone to professionalize the sport in his country. He devotes his waking hours to coaching the city's youth teams, organizing tournaments, fund-raising, and building outdoor rinks. Like other Mongolian boys, he fell in love with the game as a child. From the balcony of his family's apartment, he would watch Russian factory workers play on natural ice, and then would tape together the broken sticks they left at rink-side. At forty-five, Pujee enjoys slightly better access to equipment. One afternoon, I accompanied him to the train station, where he passed a fistful of American dollars to a friend bound for the region's nearest sporting goods store in Irkustk, Siberia, ten hours away. The friend would return two weeks later with a bouquet

Reprinted by permission of the author.

of thirty new Sher-Woods, the tools with which the Mongolian National Hockey League would start its eighth season.

Prior to the Internet and Mongolia's democratization after 3 seventy years as a Communist satellite state, Pujee's only exposure to professional hockey had been through a Russian translation of Bobby Hull's *I Live to Play*. He'd also tried Ken Dryden's *The Game* in Czech, but didn't get far. Later, he procured an NHL rulebook, which he translated into Mongolian. It became clear during my stay, however, that the country's isolation and limited resources hadn't slowed down the game's phenomenal popularity. Pujee wanted to take us to Banghanor, a small, industrial town where, he told us, spectators gather on horseback to watch local mining teams play shinny. But time and the weather prevented us from going. Instead, joined by Bobby and Battaan—two of the country's split-toothed hockey veterans—Pujee relished telling stories about what it was like to play in the dead of Mongol winter. The wind coming off the Gobi desert, he said, was so strong it would knock you off your skates. He remembers coming in on a breakaway, and being blown sideways to the ice. Other times, the puck would split into three pieces and skate blades would crack.

It was this kind of bloody-mindedness that led to Mongolia 4 finally competing internationally at the 1999 Asian Games in South Korea. Their inaugural game was against Kazakhstan. Because it was also their first time playing indoors—there still isn't a single covered rink in the country—the team wasn't used to the warmth of the arena. Pujee remembers how unsettling it was to be playing while swimming in one's sweaty armour. Also, since their skates had been sharpened to suit the rough, bumpy outdoor rinks of home, they slipped and slid once they hit the smooth, fast ice. Pujee said that none of the organizers had told them that the referees would speak English, and because they only knew Mongolian, they ignored icings° that weren't, and skated through off-sides° that were. For much of the game, it was like they were playing to the wrong end of the ice.

The Mongol goalie faced 127 shots in his first game. Pujee 5 brought a videotape to our hotel room and we saw how, midway through the final period, he could barely stand, playing the last ten minutes from his knees. The Kazakhs won 42–0. Nik Antropov, the Toronto Maple Leafs' draft pick, scored ten goals. He scored from centre ice, the blue line, the slot. (I met Antropov in Kazan, Russia, a few years later, and told him that I'd seen this tape. He glowered above me in the hallway of the rink. "No," he said. "It was twelve.")

The Mongolians lost their next game against Japan, but as 6 they prepared to face Thailand, Pujee was determined not to see his team finish in last place. The Thais came out flying, but the Mongols held steady. They answered each Thai goal and as the game moved into the third period, Thailand led 4–3. The Mongolian National Team found themselves in a place they'd never been before, with a chance to win their first international hockey game.

7   Pujee led the comeback, tying it four all. Then, late in the third period, he moved towards the high slot, gathered in a pass, and lifted the puck over the goalie's shoulder: 5–4, Mongolia.

8   It was the greatest moment in Mongol hockey history. The team's photo appeared in every newspaper back home. The kid with the broken sticks became his country's first hockey hero.

9   I heard most of these stories on my first night in UB, as if Pujee had been waiting for years in his hockey hinterland to tell them. That night, Pujee had taken me to a shack that doubled as the team's clubhouse, where many of the game's elders hung out. With a wood-burning stove pushing heat around the clapboard walls, we cracked bottle after bottle of Mongolian vodka and listened to the old men talk about Mongol pride. Bobby—who tradition-ally booked off his job at the copper mine in the winter to play hockey—swore that, one day, Mongolia would conquer Asia as Genghis Khan had done before. With the light of the stove's fire playing upon his face, he reminded us that the Chinese had built the Great Wall to keep the Mongols out, and that it wouldn't be long before they'd need that Wall again.

10   It was also thanks to Pujee that I crossed paths with the Dalai Lama. A few days before my encounter, Pujee had brought me to Mongolia's largest monastery—one of the few that hadn't been razed° by the Soviets—where I was guided by a half-dozen monks in their gold and red robes up a long staircase to gaze over their sixty-foot bronze Buddha, bejewelled in light and colour. While standing on the landing, they mentioned that the Dalai Lama was returning for his first visit in more than thirty years. I asked if he might play a little hockey while he was here. One of the monks grinned and stepped a few feet back, making swishing sounds while pretending to stickhandle a puck around the sacred floor, remembering the cold winter days of his youth while playing on the city's rogue ponds.

11   A few evenings later, Pujee and I were wandering through a half-built apartment block when we came upon a small crowd of people gathering for an appearance by the very deity himself°, who, like me, was bunking in one of UB's small, newish, Western-style hotels.

12   After hearing that the Holy Man was about to make an appear-ance, Mike Downie—my friend and director of the CBC hockey documentary—pushed me from behind to the head of the line yelling "Buddhism! Number One!" and "star quality" and "taking shots on the Dalai Lama!" Before consenting to this, I asked if I could hold my stick while waiting in the line-up. "Brilliant idea!" Mike said, imagining, no doubt, that the Lama would stop

in his tracks, fit my gleaming Easton° between his hands, and impulsively work a cracked brick puck through the city streets. Mike disappeared, then returned with my Excalibur°.

The Lama strode out of the hotel flashing his smile before being whisked off to a waiting Town Car. As the driver inched down the driveway and cruised towards us, a pulse of joy travelled through the crowd. The car moved slowly so that everyone could take in the great man, who sat in the passenger side, tipping his head, waving and smiling. It was really quite a scene, with the sky darkening into a low blue-black, brightened only by the thick falling snow. 13

As the Lama passed me, I did what any red-blooded Canadian hockey player would have done: I thrust my stick at him. My opponents, many of whom have been on the wrong end of a spear° or cross-check°, might suggest that this reaction was instinctive, but I wasn't actually attempting to jab the Lama (or his car). I was simply hoping that the Holy One might offhandedly bless my graphite one-piece. As the blade curved across his sight line, I saw him lower his head and, I sensed, incant a small prayer: a canticle° to an Easton. For the next few months back home, I carried my stick with a blessed-by-God permanence, pretty much shooting at the net every chance I got. And then, one day, the stick exploded at the heel. Maybe it wasn't a prayer that the Lama had incanted after all. 14

Words and Meanings

		Paragraph
icings, off-sides	violations of hockey rules	4
razed	destroyed	10
the very deity himself	the Dalai Lama (see "Many Faiths, One Truth," page 178)	11
Easton	a brand of hockey stick	12
Excalibur	the sword King Arthur pulled out of a stone; thus, a legendary weapon	
spear, cross-check	violations of hockey rules	14
canticle	holy song	

Structure and Strategy

1. Highlight three or four of the descriptive details in paragraph 1 that give the reader a sense of Ulaan Baator, Mongolia.
2. What comparison does the author use in paragraph 9 to communicate to the reader the passionate drive of Mongolian hockey players?
3. What concluding strategy does the author use? Is it effective?

Content and Purpose

1. Why is Bidini in Mongolia? Who is his guide there? Why?
2. How did boys in Mongolia learn about and come to love hockey, the quintessentially Canadian game?
3. What does the author tell us about the game of hockey in Mongolia? How and where is it played?
4. Why is Pujee known as "the father of Mongolian hockey" (paragraph 2)?
5. How did the Mongolian team do in the 1999 Asian Games? Why?
6. What famous person does Bidini meet in Mongolia? What is this person's relationship to hockey? How does Bidini greet this famous person?

Suggestions for Writing

1. Explain why the game of hockey has such a strong hold on the Canadian imagination.
2. Have you ever played a sport in another country? Or learned to play a sport, such as soccer or cricket, that is more prominent in other countries than it is in Canada? Write an essay that explains the relationship between a sport and the part of the world in which it dominates.
3. Compare two different popular sports and the athletes who play them.

My Father and the Baby Seal

TOMMY AKULUKJUK

Originally from Pangnirtung, Nunavut, and an alumnus of the Nunavut Sivuniksavut program, Tommy Akulukjuk (b. 1983) currently lives in Ottawa. He maintains a blog, *Kuniks and Kakivaks* (http://kuniksandkakivaks. blogspot.com), which often explores issues of cultural prejudice with a dash of wit and a healthy dose of humour. Akulukjuk is a part-time journalist and a part-time hunter.

1   My father is in Ottawa for surgery. He's been down there for weeks now. It's hard for me to think of him like this. When I was growing up in Pangnirtung, Nunavut, he

Reprinted by permission of the author.

knew what to do all the time. Only when I was older did I start seeing him as being weaker, as having doubts.

When I was a child, he was good to me and my six siblings. He would take us hunting and always made sure we caught some-thing—any animal, any food. When it came time for me to catch my first seal, he consulted my brothers and talked to my mother and then came to me. He said, "Angakuluk, this is the trail of a seal that's strayed away from its hole. The seal will have no place to go, so you can easily kill it." And that's what I did, killing the seal with my father at my side.

I went with him and his cousin on a seal hunt once. The sea-ice that year was not formed evenly, so instead of heading out onto the ocean, we went overland. The weather turned bad and we were stuck on the land for a whole week, with not much more to eat than tea and bannock°. We were hungry. Finally the weather cleared and we headed for the hunting grounds. On the way, my father said he felt we had to stop. His cousin suggested we make tea, so my father went to get snow for water.

That's when he heard a whimpering sound. He listened closer and it was a baby seal, right by his side, hidden under a foot of snow. He grabbed it with his hands and killed it. It had a snow-white coat and dark eyes. It was the first real food we'd had in a week. My father told me he knew that this seal was a gift from God. He knew he needed to stop there and it was for a reason that the baby seal whimpered loud enough for my father to hear. In that way, I feel I can say my father heard the voice of God.

On that same trip, on our way back home, we decided to take a risk and travel on the sea-ice that my father had earlier deemed unsafe. Inuit hunters are always careful, checking what they think is dangerous. Along the way we tested the thickness of the ice with a harpoon. At one point, when my father got off the snowmobile to do this, he said to me, "Don't follow. Stay here." I felt apprehension in his voice, an uncertainty I'd never heard before.

Walking away from the snowmobile, he fell through the ice up to his waist. I stood up to run to where he was, but his cousin stopped me and told me not to risk it. I was shaking all over. I had adrenaline running through me like it was being pumped from a hose. I was almost in tears. Just a couple days before, he had heard the voice of God, and now his life was in danger.

But like any good Inuk hunter, my father didn't panic. He got out of the hole by himself. Still dripping wet from the frigid sea-water, he led us down a different, safer trail.

That night we slept at an outpost camp, and the strange thing is, we laughed about the ordeals of that week—about how different it

2

3

4

5

6

7

8

had been from our day-to-day life, and how refreshing it was to have a little bit of a scare. To my father, especially, this was part of life: The good can often turn out not-so-good, even at the best of times.

9   And now he's in hospital in Ottawa. It's not the best of times. My father says he's amazed by the doctors and what they're planning to do. He says they have a lot of confidence. But all I can think about is [that] I want to be as humble and compassionate as he is.

Words and Meanings

Paragraph

3   bannock

a bread made of wheat flour, baking powder, and water; the dough may be fried or wrapped around a stick and cooked over a fire

Structure and Strategy

1. What is the framing device of this narrative? Where do the INTRODUCTION and CONCLUSION take place?
2. How many episodes does the author narrate from his childhood?
3. Identify three descriptive details in paragraph 4. How do they affect you as a reader?

Content and Purpose

1. As a child, how does the author feel about his father? What kind of a man is he?
2. How does the author communicate the idea that killing his first seal is an important rite of passage in his community?
3. What event leads the author to believe his father heard "the voice of God"?
4. How does the father risk his life on the hunting expedition? What is his son's reaction to this event?
5. What is the converse (the opposite) of the father's outlook on life expressed in paragraph 8? How does it apply to the situation described in paragraph 9?
6. As a grown man, how does the author feel about his father?

Suggestions for Writing

1. Have you ever gone hunting? Write an essay about your experience. What did you learn about yourself by killing a bird or animal?
2. Most young children think that their parents know everything and are, in general, quite wonderful. (Of course, most

teenagers think precisely the opposite.) Write a narrative essay about the first time you discovered that one of your parents was human: in other words, mistaken, fearful, or otherwise less than perfect.

3. Write an essay that focuses on the illness and/or hospitalization of one of your parents. How did the family cope with the crisis? How did it make you feel?

4. Write an essay about the politics of seal hunting, a contentious issue in Newfoundland. Should anyone be allowed to hunt seals? If so, who? Why?

First

RYAN VAN METER

Ryan Van Meter holds an MA in creative writing from DePaul University and an MFA in non-fiction writing from the University of Iowa. His essays have been widely published in literary magazines and anthologies, including *The Best American Essays 2009*. Van Meter's first collection of creative non-fiction, *If You Knew Then What I Know Now*, was published in 2011. Originally from Missouri, he currently lives in California, where he teaches creative writing at the University of San Francisco.

B en and I are sitting side by side in the very back of his 1 mother's station wagon. We face glowing white headlights of cars following us, our sneakers pressed against the back hatch door. This is our joy—his and mine—to sit turned away from our moms and dads in this place that feels like a secret, as though they are not even in the car with us. They have just taken us out to dinner, and now we are driving home. Years from this evening, I won't actually be sure that this boy sitting beside me is named Ben. But that doesn't matter tonight. What I know for certain right now is that I love him, and I need to tell him this fact before we return to our separate houses, next door to each other. We are both five.

Ben is the first brown-eyed boy I will fall for but will not be the 2 last. His hair is also brown and always needs scraping off his forehead, which he does about every five minutes. All his jeans have dark squares stuck over the knees where he has worn through the denim. His shoelaces are perpetually undone, and he has a magic

---

"First" by Ryan Van Meter. Reprinted by permission of the author.

way of tying them with a quick, weird loop that I study and try myself, but can never match. His fingernails are ragged because he rips them off with his teeth and spits out the pieces when our moms aren't watching. Somebody always has to fix his shirt collars.

3   Our parents face the other direction, talking about something, and it is raining. My eyes trace the lines of water as they draw down the glass. Coiled beside my legs are the thick black and red cords of a pair of jumper cables. Ben's T-ball bat is also back here, rolling around and clunking as the long car wends its way through town. Ben's dad is driving, and my dad sits next to him, with our mothers in the back seat; I have recently observed that when mothers and fathers are in the car together, the dad always drives. My dad has also insisted on checking the score of the Cardinals game, so the radio is tuned to a staticky AM station, and the announcer's rich voice buzzes out of the speakers up front.

4   The week before this particular night, I asked my mother, "Why do people get married?" I don't recall the impulse behind my curiosity, but I will forever remember every word of her answer— she stated it simply after only a moment or two of thinking— because it seemed that important: "Two people get married when they love each other."

5   I had that hunch°. I am a kindergartener, but the summer just before this rainy night, I learned most of what I know about love from watching soap operas with my mother. She is a gym teacher, and during her months off she catches up on the shows she has watched since college. Every summer weekday, I couldn't wait until they came on at two o'clock. My father didn't think I should be watching them—boys should be outside, playing—but he was rarely home early enough to know the difference, and according to my mother, I was too young to really understand what was going on anyway.

6   What I enjoyed most about soap operas was how exciting and beautiful life was. Every lady was pretty and had wonderful hair, and all the men had dark eyes and big teeth and faces as strong as bricks, and every week, there was a wedding or a manhunt or a birth. The people had grand fights where they threw vases at walls and slammed doors and chased each other in cars. There were villains locking up the wonderfully haired heroines and suspending them in gold cages above enormous acid vats. And, of course, it was love that inspired every one of these stories and made life on the screen as thrilling as it was. That was what my mother would say from the sofa when I turned from my spot on the carpet in front of her and faced her, asking, "Why is he spying on that lady?"

7   "Because he loves her."

In the car, Ben and I hold hands. There is something sticky on his fingers, probably the strawberry syrup from the ice cream sundaes we ate for dessert. We have never held hands before; I have simply reached for his in the dark and held him while he holds me. I want to see our hands on the rough floor, but they are visible only every block or so when the car passes beneath a streetlight, and then for only a flash. Ben is my closest friend because he lives next door, we are the same age, and we both have little brothers who are babies. I wish he were in the same kindergarten class as me, but he goes to a different school—one where he has to wear a uniform all day and for which there is no school bus. 8

"I love you," I say. We are idling, waiting for a red light to be green; a shining car has stopped right behind us, so Ben's face is pale and brilliant. 9

"I love you too," he says. 10

The car becomes quiet as the voice of the baseball game shrinks smaller and smaller. 11

"Will you marry me?" I ask him. His hand is still in mine; on the soap opera, you are supposed to have a ring, but I don't have one. 12

He begins to nod, and suddenly my mother feels very close. I look over my shoulder, my eyes peeking over the back of the last row of seats that we are leaning against. She has turned around, facing me. Permed hair, laugh lines not laughing. 13

"What did you just say?" she asks. 14

"I asked Ben to marry me." 15

The car starts moving forward again, and none of the parents are talking loudly enough for us to hear them back here. I brace myself against the raised carpeted hump of the wheel well as Ben's father turns left onto the street before the turn onto our street. Sitting beside my mom is Ben's mother, who keeps staring forward, but I notice that one of her ears keeps swiveling back here, a little more each time. I am still facing my mother, who is still facing me, and for one last second, we look at each other without anything wrong between us. 16

"You shouldn't have said that," she says. "Boys don't marry other boys. Only boys and girls get married to each other." 17

She can't see our hands, but Ben pulls his away. I close my fingers into a loose fist and rub my palm to feel, and keep feeling, how strange his skin has made mine. 18

"Okay?" she asks. 19

"Yes," I say, but by accident my throat whispers the words. 20

She asks again. "Okay? Did you hear me?" 21

"Yes!" this time nearly shouting, and I wish we were already home so I could jump out and run to my bedroom. To be back here in the dark, private tail of the car suddenly feels wrong, so Ben and 22

I each scoot off to our separate sides. "Yes," I say again, almost normally, turning away to face the rainy window. I feel her turn too as the radio baseball voice comes back up out of the quiet. The car starts to dip as we head down the hill of our street; our house is at the bottom. No one speaks for the rest of the ride. We all just sit and wait and watch our own views of the road—the parents see what is ahead of us, while the only thing I can look at is what we have just left behind.

Words and Meanings

Paragraph
5

hunch   vague feeling about something; intuition

Structure and Strategy

1. Highlight six or seven descriptive details that set the scene: the specific time and place of this incident. What is the cumulative effect of these details?
2. Trace the sequence of events in the narrative.
3. Identify two or three details that characterize (a) the boy; (b) his mother; and (c) his father.
4. What is the climax of the story? How is the narrator different at the end of the story than at the beginning? What are his feelings about himself?
5. Identify three or four examples of literary language in this essay. (There are many: select the ones that you think are most powerful.)
6. An essay (as distinct from a short story) is supposed to be based in fact. How factual do you think "First" is? Does it matter to you if the story is "fact" or "fiction"? Why?

Content and Purpose

1. How old are the little boys? What does the narrator say he knows "for certain" in paragraph 1?
2. What details in "First" indicate the significance of conventional gender roles in the narrative? The narrator of this essay is an adult recounting an experience from his childhood. Do you think the gender roles he describes have altered in the intervening years? If so, how?
3. What is significant about the answer the mother provides to her son's question in the first flashback (paragraph 4)?
4. What does the little boy enjoy about the soap operas he shares with his mother? What do the soap operas teach him about "love"?

5. What do the narrator and Ben have in common? What does the narrator ask Ben? (Paragraphs 8 through 12)
6. What happens in the car after the narrator makes his declaration of love?
7. Just before the mother responds to her son, the narrator says "for one last second, we look at each other without anything wrong between us." What goes "wrong" in the next second?
8. Is there anything in "First" that suggests that the author's sexual orientation has remained constant since he was five years old? Why do you think the author chose the title?

Suggestions for Writing

1. Write a creative non-fiction essay that recounts an event from your childhood that made you realize something about yourself or your family that changed you. Develop the scene, plot, and characters, but base your narrative in fact; in other words, it should be about something that really happened.
2. When does a creative non-fiction essay become a short story? What is the difference? Explore the writing of a few people (e.g., Dave Eggers, Tom Wolfe, Margaret Atwood, and Wayne Johnston) who write in both genres: fiction and non-fiction. Do you prefer one genre to the other? Why?
3. Research the case of James Frey and his memoir *A Million Little Pieces*. He appeared on *Oprah* to publicize his book, and then it was discovered that he had fabricated many of the episodes he wrote about as fact. On a later show, *Oprah* took Frey to task for lying. What do you think about the issues raised in this controversy?

Me Want More Square Footage!

CHARLES MONTGOMERY

Charles Montgomery (b. 1968) is an award-winning writer and photojournalist whose articles examine science, culture, myth, and cities. His first book, *The Last Heathen* (published internationally as *The Shark God*), won the 2005 Charles Taylor Prize for literary non-fiction. *Happy City,* an exploration of cities and the science of happiness, was published in Canada by Doubleday in 2011. Montgomery shares a big house with four people in East Vancouver.

1   We live in a basement suite, my guy and I. At five foot two, he isn't bothered by the low ceiling, while I am mercifully developing calluses on my forehead from collisions with door frames and low-hanging lights. Now that we've squeezed the futon into the storage nook, it's almost like having a bedroom. If we keep the floor clear of books (mine), hiking gear (ours), and dirty laundry (his), we cope just fine.

2   Still, we suspect we could be happier. In fact, we're betting on it. Along with our friend Keri, we're shovelling a quarter of a million dollars into the renovation of an old house a few blocks away. By the time you read this, we should be enjoying 2,600 square feet of floor space, nine-foot ceilings, reconditioned fir floors, and not one but two living rooms. Like most people, we're guided by the instinctive sense that a bigger nest is a happier nest. Though we know maxing out our ecological footprint might involve picking up some bad carbon karma°, we feel somewhere deep in our guts that we *need* this house in order to be happy.

3   Unfortunately, it has recently been revealed that our guts may be fooling us. The psychological matrix° that fuels our desire for more square footage also ensures that we will be thoroughly unsatisfied once we settle into our new place. This bad news comes from a growing army of economists, psychologists, and evolutionary biologists obsessed with happiness. The field offers plenty of insight into how our cities and our emotional lives shape each other, as well as a rudimentary map of the minefield laid around the walls of the happy house. To my chagrin, I didn't discover any of this until I had already signed my first mortgage.

4   My education began with an obscure treatise° written by a pair of University of Chicago economists. Luis Rayo and his Nobel Prize-winning colleague, Gary S. Becker, poured evolutionary theory into an algorithm° that could be used to prove, among other things, that the big-home urge is woven right into our genes, a hand-me-down from our hunter–gatherer ancestors. Imagine the caveman on a good day: He and his pals have managed to whack a deer and drag its bloodied carcass back to the clan. He feels terrific. Now he's faced with a couple of options. He can sit around and bask in his success, or, compelled by the idea of what he might catch next, he can head out on the hunt once again. The hunter–gatherer who is oriented to dissatisfaction, who compulsively looks ahead in order to kill more game than he did yesterday, or more than the Joneses in the cave next door caught today, is more likely to pass on his genes.

5   This is part of the reason we've come to assess material success in relative terms. Like eyes, which perceive colour and luminosity

relative to surrounding objects, the brain constantly adjusts its idea of what it needs to be happy. We compare what we have now to what other people have, and what we might possibly get next, and then we recalibrate our measure of happiness. In Rayo and Becker's model, happiness is less an ideal state than a tool our genes use to get us working harder and grasping for more stuff, whether we enjoy the struggle or not.

This shifting happiness function served our ancestors well. But it has been less useful in the age of affluence. Most of us don't need to worry about freezing or starving to death. Yet our happiness barometer continues to compare our living rooms and countertops and backyard barbecues with a constantly modified ideal. "We are victims of that evolutionary hunting strategy," Rayo explained when I called him to discuss my real estate challenge. "There's a difference between what's natural and what's good."

This conundrum° is particularly urgent in Vancouver, the country's most expensive real estate market. The average price of a detached house on the city's affluent west side has hit $726,000°. People seeking big homes have to chase that dream right out to the edge of suburbia. But life in the sprawlscape punishes them in ways that rarely make it into the home-buying calculus.

Take commuting, for example. You would think that people would only put up with a long commute if that pain was balanced out by, say, the pleasure of living in a finer home. This behaviour would agree with the golden rule of economics that stipulates humans make rational choices to maximize utility°. However, a landmark study of German commuters found that those who suffer long drives to work and back are not maximizing utility at all. In fact, the longer their commutes, the less happy they are with life in general. Rayo says this is because while we become dulled to the wonders of our new houses over time, we never get used to ongoing irritations, like tailgaters, or gridlock, or missing dinner with the family. And there is plenty of irritation to be had: the average Canadian now spends nearly twelve full days a year travelling between work and home.

I've been tempted by the suburbs myself. With their wide lawns and cul-de-sacs°, they seem to offer a rough approximation of the pastoral landscapes that made our ancestors feel safe. This is an illusion. In the US, at least, people who live in low-density sprawl are more likely to die violently than their inner-city cousins—thanks mostly to car accidents. Meanwhile, a Columbia University study found that suburban kids are far more likely to get hooked on drugs and booze. Why? Not enough chill-out time with their parents, for one thing. And where are suburban parents in those crucial after-school hours? Drumming their dashboards on marathon commutes home from distant offices. We are fooled by the suburbs' verdant° disguise, even as they lock us into more dangerous lives.

10   Not that it's hard to fool us. The happiness economists have come to believe that people are almost always wrong when predicting how content today's choices will make them in the future.

11   Even though my new house sits well inside the commuter's divide, this revelation has been cause for some anxiety these past months. The contractors lifted our old house off its crumbling foundations in June. They poured concrete, built new walls, and lowered the thing in July. Windows arrived in August. In September, we were convinced we needed a new roof and vaulted ceilings over the kitchen. We wrote more cheques, and I fretted into October. Was this house going to be an expensive machine for unhappiness? Was it even on the right street? This last question, I soon found out, is just as important as the shape of the house, and the answer is tied to how we feel about the Joneses.

12   During twenty years of research among baboons in the Serengeti, woolly Stanford biologist Robert Sapolsky found that low-ranking baboons got stressed out under the constant, threatening frowns of alpha males°. Their bodies responded by pumping out hormones that were terrific for powering short sprints away from aggressors but terrible for long-term health. Sapolsky pointed out to me that humans are just as affected by status as other primates. For example, a study of thousands of British civil servants found that bureaucrats with lower social ranking died younger than their superiors. In the US, the poor are sickest in cities where income disparity is widest, suggesting that merely *feeling poor* can hurt us.

13   Sapolsky believes his baboons might have something to teach us about how to deal with status anxiety. Average baboons mitigate° the stress of subordination by hanging out, picking and eating parasites from one another's fur—in other words, by spending quality time with friends. It's the same with humans. We have evolved to be social. Think again of our hunter–gatherer ancestors: when they worked together, they fared much better against enemies and toothy beasts. Our bodies still reward us for playing well with others. When we co-operate or have trusting interactions, our brains pump out oxytocin, a neurotransmitter that makes us feel good. The best part about this is that we never get used to these positive interactions the way we get used to money or more stuff.

14   Trust, then, offers a fast track to happiness, but what does it have to do with real estate? Tons, as it turns out. Economists at the University of British Columbia mashed up Canadian survey and census data and found that the happiest neighbourhoods in big

cities tend to be those where trust is highest. Here in Vancouver, feelings of trust flow most freely in wealthy neighbourhoods. In other words, folks in spiffy West Vancouver are unlikely to panic if they drop their wallet while walking the dog. They know a neighbour will return it. Folks in the city's beleaguered Downtown Eastside don't share the same confidence.

Given the importance of trust, maybe I'd be better off owning the humblest shack on the best street in West Vancouver. Chris Barrington-Leigh, one of the UBC study authors, admitted that a superficial reading of his work might support that conclusion. Along with the high trust apparently swirling around wealthy neighbourhoods, the data reveals a twist on the status equation: while we do keep tabs on how the Joneses are faring, we actually absorb their successes. If Mrs. Jones buys a Ferrari, I may feel comparatively impoverished, but if she parks it out front I will also feel a certain ownership of her status. "You end up caring about your neighbours," Barrington-Leigh told me. "I'm not just talking about empathy. I'm talking about considering your neighbours as part of your identity, and then comparing your neighbourhood to others." We don't just measure our success against our neighbours' success, we measure it against that of everyone else in the city. 15

However, Barrington-Leigh urges caution about using the wealth/trust matrix as a reference guide for home buying. Sure, living among rich neighbours might crank up my sense of status more than it would corrode it. But buying a more expensive house in a fancier neighbourhood would also commit me to an even heftier mortgage, which would lock me into working harder, which means I'd have less time to hang out and scratch my friends' backs. This back-scratching, or potlucking, or poker-nighting, or block-watching is the most efficient way of all to increase long-term well-being. "A slight boost in neighbourly trust has a greater effect on happiness than doubling your income," Barrington-Leigh assured me. And here's the clincher: it's the trust we feel in our friends and neighbours that makes us happy, not the trust they happen to feel for one another. It's easier to cultivate trust among the pals we've got than to try to catch a free ride by moving into a trusting neighbourhood. 16

It's hard to put happiness theory to work in a personal real estate strategy, especially when you are part of a species programmed to make the wrong decisions. But policy-makers have begun to pick up the slack. Britain's Labour government used it to reform that country's unemployment system. The city of Bogotá used research on status to underpin a restructuring of its road system, taking prime space away from cars and giving it to buses, bikes, and pedestrians so poor commuters could feel more equal. Optimism shot up. 17

18   How would the lessons from well-being research inform a happier home policy? Would we tax big house lots as we do booze and cigarettes? Slap tolls on highways to push people into denser neighbourhoods? Combine old folks' homes with child care centres? The theory may actually support such measures, but it could just as easily be used to justify herding the poor into low-income ghettos such as the Downtown Eastside—after all, the jobless feel markedly better when they hang out with other unemployed people. The territory is as risky and uncertain as my own big-house conundrum°.

19   But the market may have been kind to my man and me, in a roundabout way. We weren't employing happy economics when we chose our new abode. We just couldn't afford a house of our own. That's how we came to buy a third of Keri's 100-year-old creaker in a quiet, leafy nook of East Vancouver, the cheap side of town. The house was cramped, but interest rates were low. It seemed natural to borrow more cash and invest it in a renovation. Everyone else was doing it. Now the place has grown three extra bedrooms. It's bigger than the neighbours' houses, bigger than all our friends' houses, too, and our mortgage payments have grown apace.

20   According to the arithmetic of well-being, this financial maxing out is a recipe for misery, especially if we decide to feed our monster mortgage by working harder or longer for more money. Instead, we have chosen not to let our house become proof of Rayo's unhappiness formula. No, we're not selling it. We're filling all those spare rooms with renters.

21   I never imagined I'd be living with a gaggle of roomies when I hit forty. From a distance, the prospect has the appearance of a kind of half-assed slackerism, a failure to maintain a respectable status trajectory°. Yet on good days, I have glimpsed in the half-framed shell and flapping plastic of our house a model straight from the hedonic° textbooks. We will fill those rooms with four, five, six bodies. We will all cross paths in the unfinished kitchen. Since we won't have the money to eat out, we will share meals on an old table alongside our recycled cabinets. There will be wine, too. Lots of wine. Our voices will carry over the arm's length to our neighbours' windows, and they will come over to borrow cups of sugar.

22   Our acquisitive, status-hungry genes may wish for a life more grand, more private, more sweepingly elegant and expansively lonely. But scarcity will have relegated us to a life of conviviality and trust. It will be hard to avoid the shared moments that drench baboons, cavemen, and even middle-aged slackers in feel-good neurotransmitters. If the economists are right, this big house just may render us happy, in spite of our unrealized desires.

Words and Meanings

karma	the idea that a person's actions affect his or her ultimate fate	2
matrix	structure within which something develops	3
treatise	a formal written analysis	4
algorithm	a set of calculations, a formula	
conundrum	intricate and difficult problem	7, 18
$726,000	average price in 2007	7
stipulates . . . utility	states that people choose whatever will most benefit them	8
cul-de-sacs	streets with no through-traffic; they end in a circle	9
verdant	green surroundings (lawns and gardens)	
alpha males	the dominant males in a group of animals	12
mitigate	relieve	13
status trajectory	path tracing one's wealth and position	21
hedonic	pleasure-seeking	

Structure and Strategy

1. This essay contradicts the commonly held belief that a larger, fancier house will make us happier. Where is this contradictory theory introduced? How does the author support the argument?
2. How does the example developed in paragraph 4 support the idea that human beings are genetically programmed to be dissatisfied, unhappy?
3. Why is paragraph 10 so short? What transition does it signal for paragraph 11 and the long example developed in paragraphs 12 and 13?
4. Montgomery develops his points with research. Identify the sources and assess their effectiveness in paragraphs 12 through 17.
5. Why do you think Montgomery returns to discuss his own housing situation near the conclusion of the essay (paragraphs 19–22)?
6. Why do you think Montgomery chose his ungrammatical title? Is it effective?

Content and Purpose

1. Where do the author and his partner currently live? Where are they going to move and why?
2. According to the Rayo and Becker model discussed in paragraphs 4–6, how do people tend to define happiness? What does this definition encourage people to do?
3. Why do people sometimes choose to live in suburbs that are far from their jobs? Identify two objections to this choice that the author presents in paragraphs 8 and 9. Do you agree or disagree?
4. What does the Sapolsky research into baboon life in the Serengeti tell us about status behaviour? How do the boss baboons intimidate lower-ranking baboons, and how does this affect the underlings? How do the lower-ranking baboons compensate for their inferior status? Do you think these observations have any validity in terms of human behaviour?
5. Trust in one's neighbours, according to the author, is an important index of happiness. Where does Montgomery suggest that this kind of trust is most likely to flourish? Do you agree or disagree?
6. The author is troubled by his own acquisitiveness and by the debt incurred by taking out a large renovation mortgage, especially after considering research that suggests bigger homes and mortgages don't make us happier. How does he reconcile his decision at the end of the article? Is he happy or unhappy about his choice? Why?

Suggestions for Writing

1. Does where we live make us happy? Do big, fancy, expensive mansions necessarily house happier people? Write an essay that explores the connection between people's accommodations and their satisfaction in life. Use your own experience to support your thesis, together with some background research from Montgomery's essay, or the sample essay in the Introduction ("What Makes You Happy?" page 20), or both.
2. What makes people happy? What are the qualities that provide people with satisfaction and contentment in life? Write an essay that details your own feelings about this important question.
3. Read Shaun Pett's "The Happiness Project" (page 230) and write an essay comparing Pett's objective view of human happiness with Montgomery's more subjective view. Are their views of happiness similar or dissimilar? How do they accord with your own idea of the meaning of happiness?

What Stays in the Family

LORNA CROZIER

Poet Lorna Crozier (b. 1948) was born in Swift Current, Saskatchewan. She attended the Universities of Saskatchewan, Regina, and Alberta, and earned her M.A. in 1980. She has published more than ten poetry collections and two non-fiction collections, and contributed to a number of anthologies. Crozier has taught in prestigious creative writing programs and been writer-in-residence at a number of universities. She won the 1992 Governor General's Award for poetry for *Inventing the Hawk*. Married to another poet, Patrick Lane, Crozier now lives near Victoria, where she is teaching in the writing department at the university.

"It's too late," my mother said when my father wanted her by his 1
side when he fell ill. For the first time in forty years, he stayed
home in the evenings. They ate their supper together, and
then he sat in the La-Z-Boy beside her smaller chair to watch TV.
Sometimes he was well enough to sip a beer, sometimes not. Even
before he was hospitalized in the palliative ward°, the tumours in
his throat from lymphatic cancer made swallowing a chore. Often
what he tried to drink dribbled from his nose.

It was difficult to watch him try to satiate° his hunger or walk 2
the few steps from the kitchen to the bathroom; difficult to watch
him sit so small behind the wheel of his car and drive around the
block just for the sake of getting out. But my mother's distress
went beyond these things. His sudden need of her company, his
new-found domesticity°, didn't sit well with her. At seventy, she
had spent the best part of their marriage making a life of her own,
one that didn't depend on him for companionship or money. In
the past, he'd spent his nights at the Legion or in the Imperial and
Healy hotels, drinking beer and playing shuffleboard or pool. He'd
had no problem paying for his games, his gambling and his drinks,
but when Mom would ask for grocery money, he'd hand her a one-
dollar bill with the attitude of a patron bestowing great gifts—and
for that, she'd almost have to beg.

When I was eight Mom found a job at the outdoor swimming 3
pool, lifting heavy baskets stuffed with shoes and clothing to their
numbered places on the four-tiered shelves, lifting them down
again when the swimmers plunked their metal tags on the counter
and claimed their belongings to get dressed. It was hard and
menial work, but it was a paying job, and she finally had money of
her own. She also did "day work," the name then given to cleaning

---

Reprinted by permission of the author.

other people's houses, and in the winter she sold tickets at the Bronco hockey games. After her first pay-cheque, I don't think she ever asked my father for grocery money again.

4   In her social life, she developed the same independence. I can't remember her getting together with women friends for a night on the town, but she curled and bowled in afternoon ladies' leagues, and she met her neighbours for coffee once a week. If she wasn't working, she'd be home with me, keeping Dad's supper warm on the back of the stove, knitting, reading, watching television. After my older brother left home when I was eleven, she and I spent Christmas Eves alone, Dad finding somewhere else to go after the bars shut down. Who can blame her for not welcoming him with open arms when he wanted to cling to her the last months of his life? It was too damn late.

5   My father was a drunk. It brings me great relief to say that now because his drinking was the biggest secret of my childhood. My mother never spoke about it to anyone but me, and I was warned not to tell my friends. His drinking was our skeleton in the closet, our mad child hidden in the attic. The bones rattled, the feet banged on the floor above our heads, but if someone else was around, we pretended not to hear.

6   Mom's attitude was small-town and pragmatic°. What went on in the family stayed in the family and was no one else's business. It wasn't that she was hiding any kind of physical or sexual violence—no matter how much my father drank, he never hit her or me or my brother. He never abused us. She was simply covering up embarrassing behaviour, like the time he woke up in the middle of the night and peed in his shoe. Why tell anyone about that? Or the time he tripped on an imaginary branch on the sidewalk and came home with his nose scraped and bleeding and his glasses broken. Or the nights he spent in jail. Or the summer evening we caught the train to Winnipeg for my brother's wedding and he kept everyone in the car awake with his shouting and singing, my mother and I hunched mortified in our seats as the porter threatened to throw him off. Her insistence on privacy had something to do with pride. She was honest and hardworking and she wanted, in spite of our family's poverty and her husband's bad behaviour, to hold her head up high. Although I respect and love her and understand her need to conceal our family troubles, I suffered terribly from our silence.

very embassed [margin annotation]

7   What our secret meant in small and practical terms was that I couldn't ask a girlfriend to sleep over if Mom thought Dad was on a toot. I couldn't tell anyone the real reason that Mom and I walked everywhere—Dad was too inebriated to drive, or he'd already lost his licence and then his job operating heavy

inebriated / drunk [margin annotation]

machinery in the oil patch. I couldn't tell my high-school boy-friend why I didn't ask him to spend Christmas with my family when he was left alone, his parents responding to a distant relative's emergency. When Dad didn't come home the night before my grade twelve graduation, Mom sent me to tell the teacher advisor that he'd been called out of town for work. I had to let the teacher know of Dad's absence because I was the valedictorian, and my parents were to sit at the head table beside the principal. As the gymnasium doors at the school banged shut behind me, I walked towards the teacher who stood at the far end by the stage, the distance I had to cross seemingly endless, the crepe-paper graduation streamers and balloons swaying above me. A few steps away, I stammered the excuse I had been rehearsing. I'll never forget the look of pity in his eyes. I turned around and walked back across that long shining floor, the soles of my runners squeaking with every step, the back of my neck burning. Later, when I was dressed in my first long gown and Mom and I were about to leave the house, Dad showed up. He couldn't even tie his shoes. I walked ahead of my parents to the gym, told the same teacher that the job had ended early, my father would sit at the head table after all. Beside the principal he took his place. Soon his head was nodding over the jellied salad and slices of ham, his mouth drooping open as I stood up to speak.

[margin handwriting: person high school graduate w̄ high mark]

Perhaps the worst effect of our secret was that it forced me to hide my sadness. I buried it beneath an exterior that had little to do with what was going on at home and with how I saw myself. My cheerful, outgoing double sang in the operettas, captained the cheerleading team, served on the executive of Teen Town, taught swimming lessons, acted in drama nights, went steady with boys, worried about how far a good girl should go, delivered the valedictorian address and never spoke of anything that mattered. On the surface I was well-adjusted, popular, optimistic. Inside I burned with shame. My father's drinking was such a disgraceful thing that it couldn't be talked about. It had to be carried invisibly like a terrible disease that had no name.

[margin: 8]

[margin handwriting: double = significant]

By the time I went to university, the only one in my extended family to do so, the shame over my father's drinking went hand in hand with the fear that I, as well as he, would be found out. It would be discovered that I was the daughter of the town drunk, and that I came from the kind of working-class poverty where not one good book, not one piece of art graced the shelves or walls of our run-down rented house. The fear that I have been tricking people has been with me almost all my life. One day someone will rise from an audience and say, "You're not good enough to read,

[margin: 9]

to make
impact ↗

publish, teach, write, pass those exams, get those promotions, win those awards. I'm going to tell everyone how dumb and bad you really are. I'm going to tell everyone where you come from."

10   When I went back to my home town at twenty-four to teach in the high school, I returned with my husband's name, not my father's, which had felt like such a burden. Most of my colleagues didn't know who my father was. One Friday night I joined a group of fellow teachers at the Legion for a beer. An older man came to our table and asked me to dance. I rose to his outstretched hand and he whirled me around to a country tune. A few songs later he returned and I danced with him again. He slurred his words, but he moved with grace across the floor, his arm around my waist guiding me through a two-step. The teacher beside me when I sat down the second time said, "That old drunk really likes you." I paused. I was tempted to say "Yes" and laugh it off, but instead I replied, "That old drunk is my father." As I hesitated before replying, I had to muster some courage. It would have been so easy to deny him. That moment of honesty loosened something inside as if my breath had been held in a fist that was slowly beginning to open.

11   It took ten years before I dropped my married name and reclaimed my father's. In 1983, "Crozier" appeared for the first time on a book of my poetry. Not until 1990, when I was over forty, did I write about my father's drinking in a poem. My mother still hadn't spoken of this area of her life with any of her friends. Since my poems would be the first public acknowledgement of it, I warned her they were coming and excused myself by insisting I had the right to my own version of my childhood. She wasn't pleased, but she didn't pressure me to stop. Some days I think I should be more concerned with privacy, or at least with my mother's sense of what should remain confidential in the past we shared. But the harm our silence caused continues to compel me to speak as openly as possible about those old family wounds.

12   At the same time I feel almost driven, now that my father has died, to put him on the page, to give him life in the music of my lines, not out of anger or shame but out of love, for the censorship of my childhood damaged him as well as me and my mother. It made him smaller because we let his drinking loom above everything else he brought to our lives. The shame I felt made me deny the other things he was—the young man who lost the farm, the hard worker, the one who believed things would always work out okay, the curler who won all the local bonspiels, the old-time fiddler who loved to dance, the man my mother loved and married. It's too late now for me to make amends to

him, but it's not too late to tell our family secrets, to find words for what could not be spoken. My father was a drunk. What a relief to say that! And what a delight to know there is so much more I need to say.

Words and Meanings

palliative ward	hospital unit reserved for patients who are near death	1
satiate	satisfy	2
domesticity	devotion to home life	
pragmatic	practical, realistic	6

Structure and Strategy

1. Where in the chronological sequence of events does Crozier begin her essay? Where does the narrative go from there? Where does it end?
2. Which paragraphs detail the author's mother's reaction to her husband's alcoholism?
3. What metaphors does Crozier use in paragraph 5 to describe her father's drinking? What meaning do the metaphors have in common?
4. Why do you think Crozier uses the word "drunk" to describe her father instead of "alcoholic" or "addict" or "substance abuser"?
5. How would you describe the TONE of the essay?
6. What is the significance of the title? How does the narrator's interpretation of the phrase "keep it in the family" differ from her mother's?

Content and Purpose

1. What is Crozier's father suffering from as the essay begins? What is her mother's reaction? Why?
2. How did the mother manage to build a life for herself during her marriage? What was their home life like when Crozier was young?
3. Why does Crozier's mother insist that the father's drinking remain a secret? How does this secrecy affect her daughter? What is the narrator's attitude toward school and academic achievement? How does she feel about herself?

b/c embarassed
man : responsible for family

4. Was the author's mother successful in hiding her shameful "family secret" from the community? Identify two or three examples to support your answer.

5. What is the "moment of honesty" that begins to set the author free from the effects of the family secret?

6. What name does the author use as a writer? When can she finally write about her father's drinking?

7. What has the shame attached to the secret of the father's drinking caused the author to deny about her father (see paragraph 12)? Do you think that a family should attempt to conceal from public knowledge the behaviour of one of their members that they consider shameful?

Suggestions for Writing

1. Have you experienced "secrets" in your own family or a family you know, a situation where the reality of a problem is denied or simply ignored? Write an essay about the effects of the secrecy on the people involved. Are there situations where the truth is too damaging or too embarrassing to be shared openly, and where secrets must be kept?

2. The word "co-dependent" is often used to describe the people in an addict's family who enable or hide the addict's destructive behaviour. What are the causes and/or effects of co-dependency? Do you think that this model applies to the situation Crozier writes about in "What Stays in the Family"?

3. Write an essay that defines the point where a person crosses the line from social drinking to problem drinking. What can family and friends do to get the person on a more productive path?

4. Read Gabor Maté's "Embraced by the Needle" (page 254), a causal analysis about addiction. Do you think he and Crozier would agree about the causes and/or effects of alcoholism on the drinker? On the family?

5. Read Amber Hayward's short story "Shelterbelt" (page 392). Using that story and Crozier's essay as evidence, write an essay explaining how a parent sometimes—without meaning to—harms a child.

Deficits

MICHAEL IGNATIEFF

Michael Ignatieff (b. 1947) is leader of the Liberal Party of Canada. Before entering politics in 2005, he served as director of the Carr Centre for Human Rights at Harvard University and taught at leading universities around the globe. Born and raised in Toronto, the son of a Russian émigré diplomat and a Canadian mother, Ignatieff is considered an expert on democracy, human rights, and international affairs. He is a versatile writer, having written plays, movies, and award-winning works of fiction and non-fiction. His recent works include *The Lesser Evil: Political Ethics in an Age of Terror* (2004) and *True Patriot Love* (2009).

It begins the minute Dad leaves the house. 1

"Where is George?" 2

"He is out now, but he'll be back soon." 3

"That's wonderful," she says. 4

About three minutes later she'll look puzzled: "But George . . . " 5

"He's away at work, but he'll be back later." 6

"I see." 7

"And what are you doing here? I mean it's nice, but . . . " 8

"We'll do things together." 9

"I see." 10

Sometimes I try to count the number of times she asks me these 11
questions but I lose track.

I remember how it began, five or six years ago. She was 66 12
then. She would leave a pot to boil on the stove. I would discover it
and find her tearing through the house, muttering, "My glasses, my
glasses, where the hell are my glasses?"

I took her to buy a chain so that she could wear her glasses 13
around her neck. She hated it because her mother used to wear
her glasses on a chain. As we drove home, she shook her fist at the
windscreen.

"I swore I'd never wear one of these damned things." 14

I date the beginning to the purchase of the chain, to the silence 15
that descended over her as I drove her home from the store.

The deficits, as the neurologists call them, are localized. She can 16
tell you what it felt like when the Model T Ford ran over her at the
school gates when she was a girl of seven. She can tell you what
her grandmother used to say, "A genteel° sufficiency will suffice°,"
when turning down another helping at dinner. She remembers the

Canadian summer nights when her father used to wrap her in a blanket and take her out to the lake's edge to see the stars.

17   But she can't dice an onion. She can't set the table. She can't play cards. Her grandson is five, and when they play pairs with his animal cards, he knows where the second penguin will be. She just turns up cards at random.

18   He hits her because she can't remember anything, because she keeps telling him not to run around quite so much.

19   Then I punish him. I tell him he has to understand.

20   He goes down on the floor, kisses her feet, and promises not to hit her again.

21   She smiles at him, as if for the first time, and says, "Oh, your kiss is so full of sugar."

22   After a week with him, she looks puzzled and says, "He's a nice little boy. Where does he sleep? I mean, who does he belong to?"

23   "He's your grandson."

24   "I see." She looks away and puts her hand to her face.

25   My brother usually stays with her when Dad is out of town. Once or twice a year, it's my turn. I put her to bed at night. I hand her the pills—small green ones that are supposed to control her moods—and she swallows them. I help her out of her bra and slip, roll down her tights, and lift the nightie over her head. I get into the bed next to hers. Before she sleeps she picks up a Len Deighton and reads a few paragraphs, always the same paragraphs, at the place where she has folded down the page. When she falls asleep, I pick the book off her chest and I pull her down in the bed so that her head isn't leaning against the wall. Otherwise she wakes up with a crick in her neck.

26   Often when I wake in the night, I see her lying next to me, staring into the dark. She stares and then she wanders. I used to try to stop her, but now I let her go. She is trying to hold on to what is left. There is a method in this. She goes to the bathroom every time she wakes, no matter if it is five times a night. Up and down the stairs silently, in her bare feet, trying not to wake me. She turns the lights on and off. Smooths a child's sock and puts it on the bed. Sometimes she gets dressed, after a fashion, and sits on the down-stairs couch in the dark, clutching her handbag.

27   When we have guests to dinner, she sits beside me at the table, holding my hand, bent forward slightly to catch everything that is said. Her face lights up when people smile, when there is laughter. She doesn't say much any more; she is worried she will forget a name and we won't be able to help her in time. She doesn't want anything to show. The guests always say how well she does. Some-times they say, "You'd never know, really." When I put her to bed afterward I can see the effort has left her so tired she barely knows her own name.

She could make it easier on herself. She could give up asking   28
questions.

"Where we are now, is this our house?"   29

"Yes."   30

"Where is our house?"   31

"In France."   32

I tell her: "Hold my hand, I'm here. I'm your son."   33

"I know."   34

But she keeps asking where she is. The questions are her way of 35
trying to orient° herself, of refusing and resisting the future that is
being prepared for her.

She always loved to swim. When she dived into the water,   36
she never made a splash. I remember her lifting herself out of the
pool, as sleek as a seal in a black swimsuit, the water pearling off
her back. Now she says the water is too cold and taking off her
clothes too much of a bother. She paces up and down the poolside,
watching her grandson swim, stroking his towel with her hand,
endlessly smoothing out the wrinkles.

I bathe her when she wakes. Her body is white, soft, and with-   37
ered. I remember how, in the changing-huts, she would bend over
as she slipped out of her bathing suit. Her body was young. Now I
see her skeleton through her skin. When I wash her hair, I feel her
skull. I help her from the bath, dry her legs, swathe her in towels,
sit her on the edge of the bath and cut her nails: they are horny and
yellow. Her feet are gnarled°. She has walked a long way.

When I was as old as my son is now I used to sit beside her at   38
the bedroom mirror watching her apply hot depilatory° wax to her
legs and upper lip. She would pull her skirt up to her knees, stretch
her legs out on the dresser, and sip beer from the bottle, while
waiting for the wax to dry. "Have a sip," she would say. It tasted
bitter. She used to laugh at the faces I made. When the wax had
set, she would begin to peel it off, and curse and wince, and let me
collect the strips, with fine black hairs embedded in them. When it
was over, her legs were smooth, silky to touch.

Now I shave her. I soap her face and legs with my shaving   39
brush. She sits perfectly still; as my razor comes around her chin
we are as close as when I was a boy.

She never complains. When we walk up the hill behind the   40
house, I feel her going slower and slower, but she does not stop
until I do. If you ask her whether she is sad, she shakes her head.
But she did say once, "It's strange. It was supposed to be more fun
than this."

I try to imagine what the world is like for her. Memory is what   41
reconciles° us to the future. Because she has no past, her future

rushes toward her, a bat's wing brushing against her face in the dark.

42   "I told you. George returns on Monday."

43   "Could you write that down?"

44   So I do. I write it down in large letters, and she folds it in her white cardigan pocket and pats it and says she feels much less worried.

45   In half an hour, she has the paper in her hand and is showing it to me.

46   "What do I do about this?"

47   "Nothing. It just tells you what is going to happen."

48   "But I didn't know anything of this."

49   "Now you do," I say and I take the paper away and tear it up.

50   It makes no sense to get angry at her, but I do.

51   She is afraid Dad will not come back. She is afraid she has been abandoned. She is afraid she will get lost and never be able to find her way home. Beneath the fears that have come with the forgetting, there lie anxieties for which she no longer has any names.

52   She paces the floor, waiting for lunch. When it is set before her, she downs it before anyone else, and then gets up to clear the plates.

53   "What's the hurry?" I ask her.

54   She is puzzled. "I don't know," she says. She is in a hurry, and she does not know why. She drinks whatever I put before her. The wine goes quickly.

55   "You'll enjoy it more if you sip it gently."

56   "What a good idea," she says and then empties the glass with a gulp.

57   I wish I knew the history of this anxiety. But I don't. All she will tell me is about being sprawled in the middle of Regent Street° amid the blood and shop glass during an air raid, watching a mother sheltering a child, and thinking: I am alone.

58   In the middle of all of us, she remained alone. We didn't see it. She was the youngest girl in her family, the straggler in the pack, born cross-eyed till they straightened her eyes out with an operation. Her father was a teacher and she was dyslexic°, the one left behind.

59   In her wedding photo, she is wearing her white dress and holding her bouquet. They are side by side. Dad looks excited. Her eyes are wide open with alarm. Fear gleams from its hiding place. It was her secret and she kept it well hidden. When I was a child, I thought she was faultless, amusing, regal. My mother.

60   She thinks of it as a happy family, and it was. I remember them sitting on the couch together, singing along to Fats Waller records. She still remembers the crazy lyrics they used to sing:

There's no disputin'
That's Rasputin
The high-falutin loving man.

I don't know how she became so dependent on him, how she lost so many of the wishes she once had for herself, and how all her wishes came to be wishes for him.

She is afraid of his moods, his silences, his departures, and his 61 returns. He has become the weather of her life. But he never lets her down. He is the one who sits with her in the upstairs room, watching television, night after night, holding her hand.

People say: it's worse for you, she doesn't know what is hap- 62 pening. She used to say the same thing herself. Five years ago, when she began to forget little things, she knew what was in store, and she said to me once, "Don't worry. I'll make a cheerful old nut. It's you who'll have the hard time." But that is not true. She feels everything. She has had time to count up every loss. Every night, when she lies awake, she stares at desolation.

What is a person? That is what she makes you wonder. What 63 kind of a person are you if you only have your habits left? She can't remember her grandson's name, but she does remember to shake out her tights at night and she never lets a dish pass her by without trying to clean it, wipe it, clear it up, or put it away. The house is littered with dishes she is putting away in every conceivable cupboard. What kind of a person is this?

It runs in the family. Her mother had it. I remember going to see 64 her in the house with old carpets and dark furniture on Prince Arthur Avenue. The windows were covered with the tendrils of plants growing in enormous Atlas battery jars, and the parquet° floors shone with wax. She took down the giraffe, the water buffalo, and the leopard—carved in wood—that her father had brought back from Africa in the 1880s. She sat in a chair by the fire and silently watched me play with them. Then—and it seems only a week later—I came to have Sunday lunch with her and she was old and diminished and vacant, and when she looked at me she had no idea who I was.

I am afraid of getting it myself. I do ridiculous things: I stand 65 on my head every morning so that the blood will irrigate my brain; I compose suicide notes, always some variant of Captain Oates's: "I may be gone for some time." I never stop thinking about what it would be like for this thing to steal over me.

She has taught me something. There are moments when her 66 pacing ceases, when her hunted look is conjured away° by the stillness of dusk, when she sits in the garden, watching the sunlight stream through all the trees they planted together over 25 years in this place, and I see something pass over her face which might be serenity°.

67   And then she gets up and comes toward me looking for a glass to wash, a napkin to pick up, a child's toy to rearrange.

68   I know how the story has to end. One day I return home to see her and she puts out her hand and says: "How nice to meet you." She's always charming to strangers.

69   People say I'm already beginning to say my farewells. No, she is still here. I am not ready yet. Nor is she. She paces the floor, she still searches for what has been lost and can never be found again.

70   She wakes in the night and lies in the dark by my side. Her face, in profile, against the pillow has become like her mother's, the eye sockets deep in shadow, the cheeks furrowed° and drawn, the gaze ancient and disabused°. Everything she once knew is still inside her, trapped in the ruined circuits—how I was when I was little, how she was when I was a baby. But it is too late to ask her now. She turns and notices I am awake too. We lie side by side. The darkness is still. I want to say her name. She turns away from me and stares into the night. Her nightie is buttoned at the neck like a little girl's.

Words and Meanings

Paragraph		
16	genteel	polite, well-bred
	suffice	be enough, satisfy
35	orient	Find one's bearings; figure out where one is in time and space
37	gnarled	knobby, crooked
38	depilatory	hair remover
41	reconciles	enables us to accept; resigns us
57	Regent Street	street in central London, England
58	dyslexic	having a reading disability
64	parquet	wood floor laid out in a square design
66	conjured away	made to disappear magically
	serenity	inner peace
70	furrowed	deeply wrinkled
	disabused	undeceived, under no illusion

Structure and Strategy

1. Look up the word "deficits" in a good general dictionary. What meanings of the word apply to Ignatieff's title?
2. Using both NARRATION and DESCRIPTION, Ignatieff describes the effects of Alzheimer's disease on its victims, and on those who care for them. What function does the opening dialogue (paragraphs 2 through 10) serve?
3. This essay contains several passages of dialogue. Each is included because it supports Ignatieff's THESIS in some way. Consider how each of the following passages contributes to the PURPOSE or intended effect of the essay: paragraphs 29 through 34; paragraphs 42 through 49; paragraphs 53 through 56.
4. Paragraphs 37 through 39 present the ironic contrast between Ignatieff's boyhood relationship with his mother and their current relationship. Identify the specific details that you think are most effective in conveying this contrast.
5. How does the author's own fear of contracting Alzheimer's disease affect the TONE of the essay?
6. The THESIS of Ignatieff's essay is implied rather than explicitly stated. Sum up the thesis in a one-sentence thesis statement.

Content and Purpose

1. What was the initial reaction of the mother when the first signs of the disease appeared? Does she maintain this feeling as her confusion and loss of memory increase?
2. Ignatieff includes a number of poignant descriptive details: the toenails, the gnarled feet, the depilatory wax, the bath. Why does he include these intimate aspects of his mother's life and condition? What emotional effect do they have on the reader?
3. What is the fundamental IRONY underlying the relationship between mother and son? Reread paragraphs 25, 27, and 70 for clues.
4. What experiences in the mother's life may be responsible for the "fear [that] gleams from its hiding place" in her eyes?
5. Is Ignatieff comfortable with the task of caring for his mother? Identify specific passages in the essay that point to the writer's personal conflict.

Suggestions for Writing

1. Modelling your essay on the combination of descriptive and narrative techniques that Ignatieff uses in "Deficits," write a paper on the physical and psychological impact of a serious

illness on someone you know and on that person's immediate family.

2. Using "Deficits" and Judy Stoffman's "The Way of All Flesh" (page 159) as background material, write an essay explaining how our society can enable the elderly to live in dignity, despite physical or psychological limitations.

3. Traditional societies such as the Chinese respect and venerate the old, but progressive Western societies increasingly see the aged as an unwelcome burden. Write an essay in which you identify and explain two or three significant reasons why our society excludes or rejects the elderly.

ADDITIONAL SUGGESTIONS FOR WRITING: NARRATION AND DESCRIPTION

Choose one of the topics below and write a thesis statement based on it. Develop your thesis statement into an essay by choosing descriptive and/or narrative details to support it.

1. A dangerous activity that you have engaged in
2. A humorous story that has become part of your family's history
3. A place that was special to you as a child
4. Your first day (*or* week) at college or university
5. A comforting place (*or* a scary place *or* a sacred place)
6. Your worst (*or* best) date ever
7. A family secret
8. A first impression that was mistaken or misleading
9. The importance of *Facebook* in your life
10. A celebration that you would like to forget
11. The birth of a child
12. The stupidest mistake that you ever made
13. A wedding that did not turn out as planned
14. The honeymoon from hell
15. I could not live without my _____

UNIT 2

Example

WHAT IS AN EXAMPLE?

An example is something selected from a class of things that is used to show the nature of all of them. For instance, if you didn't know what a *mammal* was, you could look in the dictionary and find this definition: "any vertebrate class of animal that brings forth live young, nourishes them with secretions of the female mammary glands, and is more or less covered with fur or hair." But you still might be confused until you learned from *examples*: a gorilla (not an insect), a puppy (not a newly hatched turtle), a nursing child (not a chick), and a grizzly bear (not a snake). Examples do the explaining.

Examples give concrete form to abstract ideas; that is, they enable the reader to visualize the concept you are explaining. In "What I Have Lived For" (page 199), Bertrand Russell writes that he feels "unbearable pity for the suffering of mankind." What does he mean by "the suffering of mankind"? Before we can fully understand Russell's idea, we need examples: "Children in famine, victims tortured by oppressors, helpless old people a hated burden to their sons, and the whole world of loneliness, poverty, and pain make a mockery of what human life should be." In one sentence, Russell gives us three concrete examples that enable us to picture exactly what he means by human suffering.

Examples may be short or long. You may use a few briefly stated instances of people, places, or things to support a key idea, as Bertrand Russell does. In "I Believe in Deviled Eggs," Angela Long provides many examples of the childhood sights, sounds, and tastes that she associated with her religious belief. Or you may construct longer examples, known as *illustrations,* to clarify and develop your ideas. For example, Margaret Wente's essay "The Way We Live Now" employs a number of extended examples of the kind of "bafflegab" she deplores. In "Victory," Claudia Casper narrates a long example of girl-on-girl violence from her own childhood to make a larger point about female rivalry.

WHY DO WE USE EXAMPLES?

Good writing is a blend of ABSTRACT and CONCRETE, of GENERAL statements and SPECIFIC examples. It's difficult to imagine *any* kind of writing that doesn't need examples to communicate its KEY IDEAS clearly and effectively.

Examples help to clarify complex ideas so that readers can understand them. In "Good Seeing" (page 244), Alan Wilson compares science to poetry in an abstract statement: "science in general, and astronomy in particular, are alluringly poetic." Then he grounds the abstraction with three concrete examples of scientific theories that approximate poetry for him:

> Einstein's view of gravity as a kind of geometry . . . is as unexpected and viscerally compelling as the gut-wrenching imagery in Sylvia Plath's best poetry. The ghostly world of particle physics can send a shiver up the spine as surely as Charles Simic's contemplations of everyday objects. And the indigestible scale of the universe, hinted at in a starry night, can be as overwhelming as a great epic.

Writers also use examples to support or back up their generalizations. In "Why Cree Is the Funniest of All Languages" (page 236), Tomson Highway explains an untranslatable phrase in Cree by providing English examples to show the reader what he means:

> Let's start with the syllable *neee*. As with many cultural concepts, the word is untranslatable, but we could come close with English expressions such as "oh dear" or "oh my goodness" or "good grief" or "yeah, right" or "you little slut" (in the affectionate, teasing sense) or "you little bastard" (ditto).

Examples are used to support key ideas in all kinds of essays. Bertrand Russell's essay, for instance, is organized according to the principle of **division**; the organizing principle of Wilson's essay and Highway's essay is **comparison and contrast**.

It is also possible to use **example** as the organizing principle of an essay. In this case, the examples are usually described at some length and are called **illustrations**. In "The End of the Wild" (page 112), for example, Wade Davis organizes his plea for the environment around three key ideas, each of which is developed as a long example: an animal extinguished by human greed (the passenger pigeon), an animal decimated by human short-sightedness (the buffalo), and an ecosystem threatened by the logging industry (the rainforest of British Columbia). Davis supports his THESIS with other examples, description, and several narratives, but the main organizing principle of his essay is three carefully arranged illustrations.

HOW DO WE USE EXAMPLES?

Writers use examples taken from research sources, their personal experience, or the experiences of others. Here are three guidelines for choosing good examples:

1. Be sure that any example you use is representative of your topic. Choose typical examples, not unusual or wacky ones.

2. Use examples that are relevant to your topic. There is a good reason why Wade Davis, in "The End of the Wild," did not include species—such as the dinosaurs—that were extinct before humans appeared on Earth. Davis's thesis is that human beings are recklessly destroying the natural world, and he has chosen examples that directly support this thesis.

3. Limit the number and range of your examples. Include only those examples that directly and effectively support your key ideas. If you include too many examples, you will reduce their effectiveness. Readers need the highlights, not the whole catalogue.

The essay below illustrates how three different kinds of examples can be used to develop a thesis.

A Manner of Speaking

Introduction (a scenario)

Consider this scenario: you are in the bank, applying for a loan that will gain you the car of your dreams. There you are, neatly dressed, seated opposite the loans manager, who scrutinizes you across her desk. In front of her is a pile of forms: your application, your account records, and your credit history, all of which are in order. But will the loans manager decide that you are a good credit risk? Will she believe what you have to say in support of your application? Her decision will depend not only on the information you give her in response to her questions but also on the information your body communicates during the interview.

Definition of topic

Body language is one kind of non-verbal communication that affects the message we send when we are speaking with someone face to face. Most of our body language is determined by the culture in which we were brought up; the gestures and expressions that are considered appropriate vary from place to place. The French and Italians, for instance, tend to use more hand gestures and facial expressions when they talk than do the English or the Japanese. What is important to understand is that body language can reinforce or undermine speech. While our mouths are saying one thing, our head, hands, and feet can be saying something else, and if there is a disconnect between the two messages, the listener is likely to put more trust in the nonverbal one.

Examples

Thesis statement (three examples)

Return to scenario and development of first example (head)

Let's go back to the bank. During your interview, the loans manager will focus most on your head—its positions and movement—and especially on your face. Your eyes and mouth speak volumes, even before you utter a word. Facial expressions reveal whether you are confident and comfortable or nervous and stressed. What conclusion do you think the loans manager is likely to draw if you keep your head lowered, avert your eyes whenever she asks you a question, and do not smile during the meeting? In North American culture, not looking people in the eye is often considered evasive. Her job requires that she be fair, so if you are stony-faced or don't look at her throughout the interview, she will turn to your hands and feet for clues to your trustworthiness.

Development of second example (hands)

Everyone knows people who "talk with their hands." We all use our hands to some degree as a natural reinforcement of our speech. Hand gestures relate to what we are saying at the moment. For instance, if you sit with your hands tightly clenched in your lap, you may unconsciously communicate that you are nervous, defensive—perhaps that you have something to hide. On the other hand, pointing a finger at someone, or—worse—wagging a finger may be seen as aggressive, even threatening. It's safe to confidently emphasize a point in your conversation with your hand extended, palm up, as if you were "underlining" your point. Fussing with your hair or clothing silently sends a message of uneasiness because people may assume that you are trying to conceal something, that you're not being entirely honest.

Development of third example (feet)

Although the loans manager may not be able to see your feet as clearly as she does your head and hands, she will quickly become aware of them if you tap your foot incessantly against her desk or jiggle one leg. Your nervousness would be literally audible. How you sit—whether you cross your legs or place your feet on the floor—also sends a message. (You've probably noticed that when they're relaxed, men tend to sit with one foot up on the opposite knee, and women tend to cross their legs at the knee.) If you sit with one foot tucked beneath you on the chair, you send a different signal from the one you send if you sit with both feet planted in front of you. Are you relaxed? Open? Looking to control? Set in your opinion? Insecure? These are just some of the feelings and attitudes that the positions of your legs and feet can reveal.

Conclusion (completes scenario introduced in first paragraph)

An experienced loans manager will know that it is dangerous to interpret a single nonverbal cue as an isolated message. Body language, as the term implies, involves the whole body, and she will base her decision on your whole presentation, together with the financial information you have provided. If your head, hands, and feet communicate the same message as the words you speak in support of your application, you have gained your goal. Her friendly smile and outstretched hand as she gets to her feet tell you—even before she speaks—that you have won her confidence. The loan and that dream car are yours!

I Believe in Deviled Eggs

ANGELA LONG

Angela Long completed a B.A. in creative writing at the University of British Columbia in 2006. Her first collection of poems, *Observations from Off the Grid*, was released in 2010. Her non-fiction, poetry, and fiction have appeared in the *Toronto Star*, *The Globe and Mail*, *Utne Reader*, *The Sun*, *Poetry Ireland Review*, *Carousel*, *The New Quarterly*, *Prairie Fire*, *Canadian Literature*, *The Antigonish Review*, and *The Dalhousie Review*. She lives in a log cabin on Haida Gwaii, where she runs her laptop on wind power.

1   I confess, I don't know much about religion. I grew up Protestant with a grandfather who was a minister, and I still don't know much about religion. I stopped going to church at the age of 12 when my grandfather died, and up until that point, religion was waking up every Sunday morning to get ready for the 10 o'clock service.

2   Religion was my mother delivering a freshly ironed dress to my bedroom door, and the smell of shoe polish in the kitchen. It was something that interfered with watching cartoons. It was a dark, windowless room in a basement where preteens drew scenes from the life of Jesus with crayons on paper plates. I didn't know much about Jesus except that I could never get his beard right.

3   Religion was the Banquet Burger Combo afterward at the Bo-Peep Restaurant, sometimes accompanied by red Jell-O, sometimes chocolate pudding. It was begging my parents to ask the Bo-Peep hostess if we could sit in the banquet section where the chairs were padded with red faux leather attached by brass studs, the walls covered with dark wood paneling and the stern expressions of British dukes in full hunting regalia°.

4   Religion was picnics at the park—deviled eggs, macaroni salad, potato salad, and Dixie Lee chicken. It was escaping the adults when the food was packed away and exploring the perimeters of the forestry station's "experimental forest," a thicket of scraggly trees that invited games of Truth or Dare. Religion was Grandpa giving my two older brothers a dollar to go to the arcade and telling me to help Grandma in the kitchen.

5   I never quite realized that only the kneeling, praying, and hymn singing counted as actual religion. I thought they were just things that we did before the real religion—the business of living—began. Don't get me wrong, I knew they were important; I did

---

Reprinted by permission of the author. First published in *Geez* magazine, Summer 2008.

them voluntarily, with relish° even. I even had a favorite hymn—"Onward, Christian Soldiers"—that I'd sing while I walked to school. But the actual words of the hymns were as meaningless to me as my grandfather's sermons. I looked for a catchy tune underlying the words in both. I discovered it by watching the stained-glass windows blaze in the late morning sunshine. I saw how the artist had perfected the curls of a sheep's wool, the gentle gaze of a cow. I discovered it observing the actions of the congregation: the nose picking, the napping, the fondling couples. It was during these moments that I found enlightenment.

I wasn't aware that my ignorance of the true meaning of religion was disrespectful or irreverent. The only time I seemed to breach° the contract I apparently signed with my baptism was when my grandfather scolded me for exclaiming something remotely blasphemous ("Holy cow!") or too close to the Lord's name ("Geez!"). If you had asked my 12-year-old self if I believed in God, I would have replied yes without a moment's hesitation. Of course I believed in God. At that time, I believed in everything.   6

I especially believed in Sunday—those spring Sundays when crocus shoots appeared, robins pecked at ground still damp from snowmelt, and the scent of rural Ontario filled the air. I believed in the look on my mother's face when I walked down the carpeted stairs in something other than corduroys and a sweatshirt. I believed in the hostess at Bo-Peep as she lifted the barrier to the banquet room and laid five heavy faux-leather-bound menus, one by one, upon the round table. I believed in sitting there, uncomfortable in my dress, passing around the ketchup and not wanting to be anywhere else. And when my older brother, after a week of torturing me in a subtle, big-brotherly fashion, laid his prized slice of dill pickle on the edge of my plate, like an offering, I even believed in miracles.   7

Words and Meanings

Paragraph

regalia	formal dress	3
relish	enthusiasm	5
breach	break	6

Structure and Strategy

1. Highlight five descriptive passages that appeal to the senses. Identify the sense(s) each passage appeals to.

2. Paragraphs 2–4 begin with the same phrase: "Religion was . . . ." Identify four different settings that the author associated with religion as a child. Are these settings usually associated with religious practice? Why do you think Long uses these EXAMPLES?

3. Food plays a significant role in Long's memories of her childhood religion. Why do you think she chose her title? What do "deviled eggs" have to do with the essay?

4. How would you describe the TONE of this essay?

Content and Purpose

1. This essay is about a child's experience, told from the point of view of an adult. Approximately how old was the author when the events she narrates took place? Where did she live?

2. In what religion was the author brought up? What is her family connection to her religion? When did she stop practising this religion?

3. How did the author, as a child, respond to the experience of being in church? What does she notice? (See paragraph 5.) What is she supposed to be experiencing?

4. What did Long think was "real religion" (paragraph 5)? Is there any conflict between it and the memories she has of her childhood religion?

5. What did Long believe in as a child? Why does Sunday play such an important role in these beliefs? What is the "miracle" that takes place in the Bo-Peep restaurant?

6. How do you think Long, as an adult, feels about the religion of her youth?

Suggestions for Writing

1. If you have been brought up inside a faith community, write an essay that relates your childhood memories of your religious upbringing. Develop your narrative with descriptive details and examples that make clear your feelings about your faith and your family's involvement in it.

2. Write an essay arguing for or against the idea that religious observance is important in a person's life.

3. Write an essay that details childhood memories of a secular (i.e., nonreligious) place, and/or person, and/or ritual that was deeply significant to you when you were young.

The Way We Live Now

MARGARET WENTE

Margaret Wente (b. 1950) has enjoyed a successful career in Canadian journalism as both a writer and editor. Born in Chicago, she moved to Toronto in her teens and holds a B.A. from the University of Michigan and an M.A. in English literature from the University of Toronto. Since 1992 she has been a columnist for *The Globe and Mail* and has twice won the National Newspaper Award for her writing. Her first book was the bestseller *An Accidental Canadian* (2004); her latest book is *You Can't Say That in Canada!* (2009).

Mark is the helpful fellow at the car dealer who sold us our Forester. Mark is not a car salesman. He is a Senior Subaru Brand Specialist. That's what they call car salesmen now. When we looked at the new cars we also asked if they had any used ones. They didn't. But they did have some that were pre-owned. 1

In a world where people who serve takeout coffee are rebranded as baristas, no one has a menial job any more. My nephew worked as a Customer Care Specialist, which means he made $11 an hour for talking to people in Florida who called to gripe about their cable. Job titles have become so refined that you have no idea what jobs they describe. 2

Because of outsourcing—which means, "we found cheaper people to do this"—these specialists seldom work for the same company from which you bought the cable service. Instead, they work for firms that specialize in Customer Care Solutions. If a business offers Proactive Customer Solutions, you can be pretty sure it does telemarketing. 3

Now that the word *sell* is a bad word, the customer must be extra wary°. I remember the first time I got a "courtesy call" from my bank. How nice, I thought. They're phoning to make sure everything is okay! But no. They were courteously offering me the chance to take advantage of new solutions for all my banking needs at a very reasonable fee. 4

In case you didn't know, hospitals don't have patients any more. They have clients. Think of that the next time you get impatient in Emerg with your broken ankle. The funny thing about health care is, the worse things get, the loftier the language. Health-care bureaucrats love talking about "seamless care," even 5 though the holes in the system are big enough to drop your granny through. You also may have noticed that everybody's now talking about "wellness." Alberta has rebranded its health ministry as Alberta Health & Wellness, in hopes, perhaps, that people will take up jogging and stop getting sick.

6   Just as title inflation is often devised as a substitute for money, euphemisms are designed to cover up the unpleasant facts of life. Residents of old-age homes are sometimes known as guests, as if they've dropped in for a vacation. Actually, there are no old-age homes any more; they're called assisted-living residences. And the Alzheimer's ward has been rebranded as the Memory Wing.

7   Today, we no longer have disturbing emotions such as grief and anger, separation and loss. Now we have healing and closure. I am not sure when these terms began to leak from the world of therapy into real life. But now they are ubiquitous°. No sooner does some catastrophe strike than people begin declaring that the healing has begun.

8   I'm not really sure what "closure" is. It seems to be something that occurs once you've healed. It is a highly optimistic concept, because it suggests that with the appropriate interventions all tragedy can be overcome, all grief surmounted, all the raw and bitter parts of life soothed away. It reflects the particularly North American belief that you can get over it and move on.

9   Healing and closure can often be facilitated by the government. After a group of students died in an avalanche in Alberta a few years ago, someone opined° that only a government inquiry could bring closure to the grieving parents. After the premier of Ontario apologized for abuses inflicted many years ago at a training school for teenage boys, several teary victims declared, "This brings closure for me." In B.C., a cabinet minister vowed to bring closure and healing to those who had been abused at an institution for the mentally disabled.

10   Professional facilitators help, too. No sooner does a sparrow fall from the sky than a grief counsellor arrives to help you express your feelings about it. Some people are old enough to remember the bad old days without these experts. Take the case of the man who, as a boy, witnessed a terrible drowning accident in which twelve other kids died. Fifty years later, he confessed, the memory still bothers him. "The healing process could have taken place a lot sooner," he said, "but we didn't have grief counsellors or therapists or self-help groups back then."

11   In the brave new world of bafflegab°, however, I hate management-speak the most. No area of public life today is safe from the language of the marketplace. Politics succumbed long ago.

We no longer have political parties. We have brands, which have images to be either polished or tarnished, and policy platforms that, like toothpaste, are carefully tested beforehand on focus groups. Citizens are treated as consumers who either do or don't like the flavour of the candidate, also known as product.

You might not expect better from politics. But what about good   12
works? The charitable world also has a terminal case of management-speak. The global CEO of Foster Parents Plan (now known as Plan Canada, for marketing simplicity) likes to talk about the importance of "brand awareness" in the voluntary sector. He's got ideas for better ways to "leverage dollars" and "compete for market share." As someone whose market share has been successfully captured by this group, I was relieved to learn that the little girls I sponsor in far-off lands are not simply passive recipients of aid. They are "development actors."

Every civic institution, arts organization and charity is obliged   13
to use management-speak nowadays. That's because they need to reassure their multiple stakeholders that they operate on a businesslike model. They must demonstrate that they are effective and efficient, as well as accountable and transparent. It's not enough to help kids who live in poor countries, or treat sick people, or teach students. Every homeless shelter and hospital, every museum and university and branch of the civil service must have a vision, a mission and a strategic plan. Their managers are made to go on long retreats with professional facilitators in order to come up with these things, which are then enshrined on plaques, highlighted in the annual report and hung prominently in the main entrance of the institution for everyone to see.

Since everybody's vision and mission statement winds up   14
sounding pretty much the same, this exercise may strike you as a phenomenal waste of time. And there's more. Everyone must also come up with tangible deliverables that have measurable outcomes. They must commit themselves to partner with their donors. They commit themselves to empower their clients, customers and, presumably, development actors. Above all, their institutions must be leaders, preferably world-class ones.

The decline of public language into sludge is the subject of a   15
passionate polemic° called *Death Sentences*, by Australian writer Don Watson. Mr. Watson thinks words ought to matter. He argues that the narrow, cliché-ridden vocabulary of managerialism has robbed the public language of elegance and gravity. "We use language to deal with moral and political dilemmas, but not this language," he fumes. "This language is not capable of serious deliberation. It could no more carry a complex argument than it could

describe the sound of a nightingale. Listen to it in the political and corporate landscape, and you hear noises that our recent ancestors might have taken for Gaelic or Swahili, and that we ourselves often do not understand."

16   The language of management-speak has created a dark and impenetrable thicket. And once it gets into a place, it spreads like duckweed. "All kinds of institutions now cannot tell us about their services, including the most piddling change in them, without also telling us that they are contemporary, innovative and forward-looking, and committed to continuous improvement," he points out. Much of this abuse originates with management consultants, who, far from being jailed or sued for it, are richly rewarded. By far the worst offenders are HR practitioners°, followed by those people who concoct recruitment ads. Like mission statements, all job ads sound the same. Everybody wants a "leader" who is "strategic," and preferably "visionary."

17   Anyone who cares about language, about meaning, about clarity, should revolt. Citizens are not customers, and democracy is not a product. If Barbra Streisand had sung "Customers . . . customers who need customers," would anyone have cared? If Martin Luther King had said, "I have a vision statement," would anyone have listened? As some wise man once said, what does it profit you if you gain market share but lose your soul? Or something like that.

Words and Meanings

Paragraph		
4	wary	cautious, careful
7	ubiquitous	everywhere
9	opined	stated an opinion
11	bafflegab	language designed to confuse; jargon
15	polemic	controversial argument
16	HR practitioners	human resources experts

Structure and Strategy

1. Wente structures her essay around examples of "the brave new world of bafflegab" (paragraph 11). Into which categories of "bafflegab" does she sort her examples?
2. In addition to exposition, what other rhetorical mode does the author use in this piece?

3. What is the topic sentence in paragraph 11? What areas of public life have been affected by the kind of bafflegab exemplified here? Identify at least five examples cited in the essay.
4. What kind of support does Wente provide in paragraphs 15 and 16?
5. What is the TONE of this essay?
6. Identify the ALLUSIONS in the final paragraph. Are they effective as a conclusion?
7. Do you think the title of this essay is effective? Why or why not?

Content and Purpose

1. Who is Mark in paragraph 1? What does he do for a living? Is Mark referred to anywhere else in the essay? Why do you think Wente begins her essay with him?
2. Identify the examples of "title inflation" cited in paragraphs 2–5. What do the jobs have in common?
3. What is a "euphemism" (paragraph 6)? Why does Wente object to them?
4. According to Wente, what has happened to "disturbing emotions" (paragraph 7) occasioned by loss or grief? Do you agree or disagree with her? Why?
5. Whom do Wente and her "expert witness" blame for much of the proliferation of bafflegab in institutional settings?

Suggestions for Writing

1. Write an essay that illustrates the use of bafflegab in a field that you are familiar with; for example, technology, sales, education, or fitness. Does the jargon help or hinder communication?
2. Have you ever participated in a corporate or institutional exercise designed to come up with a "vision" or "mission statement"? Write an essay about the experience, detailing the reasons why your group undertook the exercise and explaining the results.
3. Have you or has anyone you know ever been "downsized"? Write an essay about the experience.

My Life as a Cleaner

NOREEN SHANAHAN

Noreen Shanahan is a freelance journalist, poet, and housecleaner in Toronto. She has published a variety of work including obituaries and academic articles on lesbian mothering.

1 It was a bright spring afternoon when Suzanne* told me she wouldn't need me anymore. I had just finished my four-hour cleaning shift—tearing up and down the stairs of her three-storey Parkdale home, scraping crayon goo from broadloom and freeing Cheerios snagged in the kitchen sink. She was wearing jeans and a fluffy Gap sweatshirt, sitting at the pine table I had recently polished, a pile of papers scattered around her. "My husband is expecting a 30 per cent pay cut," she said. "We're trying to live as if it's already happened." I felt sorry for her—how could I not? But I also felt a piercing sense of loss. I almost started to cry.

2 I had been cleaning Suzanne's house for five years and had developed an unexpected attachment to her, her husband and their two girls, a 10-year-old and a seven-year-old. It wasn't just that I had become an expert on every dirt-attracting crack in their hardwood floor. Or that I knew the most tedious job in the house was wiping down a thin ledge in the bathroom where seashells and sand dollars perched precariously. Or that I had learned exactly how to position stuffed teddy bears, dogs, dolls, whales and frogs on the girls' beds. It was more than that. I felt I had become a part of the fabric of their lives.

3 Suzanne stayed home with the kids, so in the morning I'd often see her taking them through the alley behind the church to school. And I'd be there when they came home at lunch for grilled cheese sandwiches and piano practice. I had watched them grow up. Now I was being fired, and the weird thing was I really wanted to keep scraping away at the dirt and dusting the girls' rooms. I also felt a little wounded: didn't I deserve some small token of appreciation? A plate of Girl Guides cookies? A hand-drawn card from one of her daughters?

4 I left Suzanne's house that day wondering about the nature of my relationship with my clients. Who am I to them? On one

---

*Some names and details have been changed.

Noreen Shanahan, "My Life as a Cleaner," *Toronto Life*, March 2005. Reprinted with permission from the author. Noreen Shanahan's forthcoming book is entitled, *Dirt: A Writer's Survival Guide*.

level, I'm merely an employee—the lowest kind of employee, actually. The toilet bowl scrubber, the garbage taker-outer, the mirror Windex-er. But I'm also a trusted member of the household. I work inside people's homes, the place where they sleep, make love; the place where they become the person they rarely show any other person; the place where they lounge in their dressing gowns, picking popcorn kernels out of their teeth. I am the person who vacuums up those kernels. Stains are removed, pillows are fluffed. I appear and disappear. But while washing, dusting, polishing, lifting, sweating—and sometimes cursing—I can't help but be drawn into the dramas unfolding around me.

I made the decision to become a cleaner five years ago, when   5
I was a 40-year-old child-care worker and a single mother of a bright and hungry seven-year-old boy. When I found out that my friend Gloria, who cleaned houses, earned more money than I did taking care of young children in my house, I invited her out for coffee and quizzed her: How much did she charge? Did she declare the income or collect it under the table? How flexible can you be with your hours? (I wanted more time to work on my writing during the day.) Over the years, I'd had many different jobs—as a union organizer, as an activist with feminist collectives and as a teacher—and to my surprise, cleaning started to sound pretty good. It would allow me close proximity to my son, the freedom to dress casually and listen all morning to Shelagh Rogers° and, most important, lots of time on my own.

The only problem was that I didn't know much about the job.   6
My mother didn't have time to teach me housekeeping skills: she was busy raising five daughters and three sons on one unpredictable income. (My father, who usually wore his bathrobe till noon, had a million entrepreneurial schemes, some successful and others less so. Today, he earns a living as a locator of missing heirs.) The last time I had given cleaning serious thought, I was a seven-year-old Brownie, leaning over Tawny Owl's bathtub with Mr. Clean, trying to earn my housekeeping badges while Tawny Owl herself perched on the ledge, inspecting my work.

Gloria gave me tips: always work from top to bottom;   7
remember to dust between venetian blinds. Prepared to learn the rest on the job, I thumbtacked a sign to the notice board at Alternative Grounds coffee shop on Roncesvalles. It read "Strong-like-bull dyke: lesbian poet-cum-cleaner wants to dust your books and valuables." I used a pseudonym in my ad, unsure of what I was getting into, a little ashamed to be offering my services as a washerwoman.

8   Suzanne was my first client. On the phone, we agreed to four-hour shifts every second Wednesday for $75. When she first opened her front door, we recognized each other immediately. We'd seen each other around the neighbourhood and at the park. We had even stood next to each other, pushing our kids on the swings. There was an initial awkwardness, partly because it was my first cleaning job—I didn't yet know how to relax and just be professional—but also because of our past association. She knew me as a neighbourhood mom. Now I was her cleaning lady. It didn't take long, however, before I was given my list of tasks and sent on my way.

9   Cleaning proved to be harder than I expected. I sweated, groaned and, at times, regretted my decision. I also made mistakes. On my first day, I accidentally flushed a sodden pile of cleaning rags down the toilet, clogging it. Suzanne's husband—who happened to be home—rescued me with a plunger. Still, despite the mishap, I felt oddly elated at the end of my shift, pleased to have survived my first day. The instant cash also came in handy. I owed $20 to the corner greengrocer and paid him on my walk home.

10   My business grew, partly through word of mouth, partly through ad postings. Within a year, I had 10 clients for whom I worked every other week—all from Parkdale, along the Roncesvalles strip—which added up to a 20-hour workweek. In a good year, my total income would be roughly $20,000, no benefits or sick pay. (I always declare my earnings, which is unusual in my trade.) On any given day, I juggle 15 keys securely strapped to my knapsack and almost as many burglar alarm codes in my head. But my clients aren't wealthy. They tend to be the IKEA crowd, perhaps just one rung up the income ladder from me (I'm more the pick-IKEA-from-the-trash type). They drink $12 chardonnay and leave the dregs in bottles perched on top of the refrigerator, glasses by the side of the bed. Most of them are good about payment (only one cheque ever bounced), and one client even gave me a $10 raise unbidden. I learned pretty quickly that I was a luxury in the economy of these households—and, as such, I was vulnerable to the ups and downs of a family's financial life. When one couple I was working for had a second child, faced with the additional strain on their budget, they got rid of me.

11   After a while, I got into a routine. I'd arrive, peel off my street clothes and slip into my cleaning garb: purple Adidas shorts, with pockets large enough to stuff fistfuls of garbage or vacuum attachments, and a grey T-shirt. While I'd get ready, my client and I would chat about things like how the kids are doing at school,

plans for Halloween, whether to get a new puppy. Then I'd be left alone.

There is great emotional complexity in the dusty kingdoms my clients entrust to me. When I posted my sign, I had no idea I would be so drawn into their lives. But I see everything when I clean. I watch seasons pass through shoes and boots, coats and umbrellas. I watch holidays come and go through children's artwork spread across surfaces: hearts, wreaths, shamrocks, marigold seedlings in egg cartons, which leave bits of dirt that I wipe away. I know when birthdays happen, when relatives visit. As I dust family photos, I watch children grow beneath the glass.

Sometimes, however, I see more than I'd like. I can detect when marriages are in trouble: an overnight bag waiting by the front door, a half-empty box of tissues by the bed. There's a kind of barometer to every home. One day, at the apartment of a client named Rachel, who is roughly my age, I discovered a bag bulging with books on women and depression at the bottom of the stairs. Rachel has twin toddlers and two puppies. On her bedroom wall, in her wedding pictures, she wears a huge smile. I worried about her, but I never found out why she had those books. Nor could I ever ask.

Another woman I worked for on the same street was going through a divorce and had just returned to work. One morning as I was mopping the floor, I found a sleeping bag unceremoniously stuffed behind the sofa. I imagined late-night arguments, rages while the children huddled in their rooms. Her bedside books were about spirituality, as if she was trying to find calm in the chaos.

Clients sometimes open up to me, confessing stuff they can't easily tell anybody else. The first time it happened, I was shocked. I had been on the job for about a year and was halfway through my shift in a lovely semi-detached Parkdale house. I asked my client where the vacuum bags were kept, but instead of directing me to them, he burst into a tirade against his wife. Only she knew where the bags were kept, but she hadn't yet returned home from a date with her new boyfriend. "How the hell am I expected to keep it all together, get the kids to school and remember to make their damned lunches while she's still out with this guy?" he howled.

Standing by the stove, he refilled his coffee cup, describing the sordid details of his troubled life. I awkwardly mumbled something about how this too shall pass, then hightailed it out of the room in search of a sink to scour. But I never saw the man again. Two weeks later, his wife told me that he had moved out. I revealed nothing to her about our conversation.

17   Once, a client told me about her pregnancy scare. She was in her mid-30s, already the mother of three children under 10, and was re-entering the workforce after years away. "My period's late," she told me in a shaky voice, a look of horror on her face. I listened sympathetically—what else could I do? Then I pretended the conversation never took place. I don't know whether she was pregnant and, if so, what she did about it. I could hardly ask. When you're a cleaner, you're sucked into other people's plot lines and, just as quickly, you're ejected from them. You rarely get closure.

18   Another time, an exhausted new mother, who'd been up all night with a croupy baby, greeted me at the door at nine a.m. in her wildflower-patterned flannel nightgown and immediately burst into tears. I sat beside her on the couch for a few minutes, wanting nothing more than to hold her hand or draw her soothingly into my arms. "Tell me it's gonna get better," she said in a desperate whisper. I assured her it would, sharing early-motherhood stories of my own. Then I encouraged her to crawl back into bed while the baby slept, knowing how much easier it would feel when she got up, less exhausted, to a clean house.

19   There are things I love about cleaning: the satisfying shoosh and clink as a sizable something slides up the vacuum hose; digging up loose change beneath sofa cushions (which I place in a visible spot for my client to find); discovering a new cleaning product that finally erases grease smeared across the kitchen range. I'm often the only person at a house when a courier pulls up; I'll sign for the package. Or if Grocery Gateway drops off its crates, I'll put the perishables away and add the waybill to the growing mountain of little slips of paper gathered while tidying up. I'm the cleaner; these others are the deliverers. Together, we keep this family functional, well fed, sane, organized and clean. I don't usually do windows, but on a bright day, I might leap into action and wash the window upstairs in the baby's room, so my nursing client can look outside and watch the trees turn, the leaves fall, the snow arrive. I like to imagine she notices my little gift to her.

20   Most of my clients have children—curious, bright little things that jump over my cleaning bucket or obligingly run to the third-floor bathroom if I'm working on the second-floor one. Lifting my head out of the toilet bowl, I'll hand them their toothbrushes and send them on their way. I sometimes wonder what these children make of me, watching me fly by with my feather duster, sudsy red bucket and yellow gloves. I settle stuffed animals on their beds and dust under kid-made clay figurines their parent can't bear to throw out.

One five-year-old girl named Claire leaves me notes under her pillow, and the occasional drawing—a dog in the park, her baby brother eating breakfast, a stick-people sketch of the whole family. I write little messages back, describing an exchange I've had with her dolls or suggesting a costume change for Barbie. In a recent note, I thanked Claire for letting me use the new toilet bowl brush she had helped her mom pick out from Wal-Mart. 21

In a Tudor-style house I clean, there's a 10-year-old boy named Ethan, the youngest of five. When he was about seven, he dug out his art supplies and sketched me while I worked. He sat before me with his legs crossed, eyes fixed on my every gesture. I remember the purposeful way he watched me scoop up the plastic bones of Crayola markers and felt stickers, placing them in their proper boxes or drawers. I kept his sketch on my fridge for weeks. 22

I crossed a line once and told a client to get rid of the puzzle under her daughter Emily's bed. For months, I had been pulling out this abandoned puzzle, dusting it off, then sliding it back under. Emily also has no fewer than six dollhouses of varying sizes, equipped with tiny plates, beds, chairs and pets. Some days, when the pieces crunched underfoot, I hated them all. My client commiserated and agreed, but the next time I cleaned, the puzzle was still there, tugging at the end of my mop. 23

There's an unspoken agreement in the client–cleaner partnership that I'll pretend to know nothing about them. My job is to erase, scrape up and brush away all signs of messy life. I've thrown out used condoms, scrubbed down shit-streaked toilets (I privately refer to one house as belonging to the "diarrhea family"), but we all observe a distant decorum. I am not to know these people have sex in the sheets, which I straighten, making sure all four corners are even along the stitching; that they drool on the pillows I shake out and plump up. I certainly feign ignorance when I run into a client at the IGA, Granowska's deli or the High Park library. Usually, the client will barely recognize me, then stumble and stammer awkwardly past, avoiding eye contact. It reminds me of how I felt, in my early 20s, running into one-night stands. 24

I used to see Suzanne frequently at Alternative Grounds café. We'd sit at different tables. I'd usually be alone, writing, and she'd be somewhere near the back with a gathering of other at-home moms. Or if the café was crowded, we'd end up at tables beside each other. We'd smile but keep our distance. 25

One of the things you sacrifice when you become a housekeeper is the cleanliness of your own home. The last thing I want to do is 26

27   return from scrubbing someone else's house to clean mine. What I really want to do is soak in a lavender bath and eat chocolate. So, too often I shut the door to the glistening splendour of one of my clients' homes, then open the door to my dusty rented bungalow.

Friends and acquaintances ask advice on dealing with their cleaners: how to get them to vacuum dog hair from the sofa ("Just talk to them," I counsel), whether to tip at Christmas and, if so, how much ("Sure," I say, "why not?"). Sometimes I imagine running workshops on how to negotiate life with cleaners. Here's what I'd instruct: De-clutter the house the night before, so the cleaner can scrub the cupboards and dust the picture frames instead of wasting your time and money putting away dishes. Keep supplies well stocked. Trade in your upright vacuum for a canister one. Leave clear instructions on the priority of tasks. Offer her a cup of tea once in a while. And, most important, remember to raise her pay from time to time, because a pound of butter costs the same for your cleaner as it does for you.

28   First clients, like first lovers, are hard to part with. But Suzanne, of course, was not my lover. She wasn't even a friend. I saw her, as I see all my clients, in the raw—their smatterings of scattered things, their detritus, their leftover signs of life. But because they are usually absent in the flesh, they don't see me. I am, in many ways, an invisible presence in their lives—part of what it takes to have a sparkly clean kitchen sink and all the toys finally, finally put away. At the same time, my existence triggers associations with grunge and grime and the endlessness of wiping counters. I remind them of the shame of having a messy house. And I trigger their middle-class guilt about getting someone else to do their dirty work.

Words and Meanings

Paragraph

5   Shelagh Rogers   Canadian writer and radio broadcaster, former host of CBC One's *Sounds Like Canada*

Structure and Strategy

1. Paragraphs 1–3 serve as the INTRODUCTION to the essay. What strategy does Shanahan use to engage readers' interest? How does it set up the essay's CONCLUSION?
2. Which paragraphs of the essay explain how Shanahan got into cleaning as a career?
3. In paragraph 4, identify three or four examples of the kinds of tasks Shanahan does for her employers and the kinds of things she learns about them.

4. Choose a paragraph that you think is effective because of its DESCRIPTION. Identify several descriptive examples that you think are particularly striking. What is the dominant impression that these details leave with the reader?
5. Paragraph 27 is a short process ANALYSIS. What is its purpose?
6. What is the THESIS of this essay? Is it implied or stated?

Content and Purpose

1. The names given to Shanahan's clients are presumably false. How do you know this? Why do you think the author changes the names of people she works for?
2. Why did the writer decide to become a housecleaner? How did she set up her business?
3. What do we learn about Shanahan's personal life?
4. What details in the narrative suggest that Shanahan is a fundamentally honest person?
5. What income class do Shanahan's clients belong to: wealthy, upper-middle class, or middle class? Where do we learn about their financial lives?
6. How does Shanahan learn about the emotional ups and downs in her clients' lives?
7. What does the writer like about her career?
8. What is the "unspoken agreement" (paragraph 24) between cleaner and client? Why does it exist?
9. What is the IRONY in paragraph 26?
10. What is the "middle-class guilt" that Shanahan refers to in the final paragraph? Why does it exist?

Suggestions for Writing

1. Have you ever worked in someone's home as a cleaner, handyperson, baby-sitter, or other job? Write an essay describing what you learned about the people for whom you were working.
2. Have you or would you ever hire a person to clean up after you or perform another kind of personal service job (e.g., driver, maid, cook, nanny, trainer, shopper)? Write an essay about the nature of the relationship between you and the hired person.
3. Read Judy Brady's "Why I Want a Wife," and write an essay that compares Brady's and Shanahan's attitudes toward housework.

Victory

CLAUDIA CASPER

Claudia Casper (b. 1957) has been writing novels, short stories, and screenplays since the 1980s. She was born in Toronto, and studied at the University of Toronto. Her first novel, *The Reconstruction* (1996), has been optioned for a feature film. Her second novel, *The Continuation of Love by Other Means*, was published in 2004. Her shorter work has appeared in *The Globe and Mail*, *Geist*, and *Best Canadian Stories*.

1   It was the year of go-go boots, white mid-calf boots that zipped up the side. It was Centennial Year, the one-hundredth anniversary of Confederation, and my grade four classmates all returned from Expo '67 in Montreal with miniature red-and-gold Chinese lanterns. Goldie Hawn's giggle was new, miniskirts were in, the Beatles reigned, images of the Vietnam War were burned in people's minds. We knew nuclear bombs might end the world.

2   It was that year that Sharon Fink asked to see a bracelet I had stolen. The bracelet was made of neon pink and green plastic lozenges threaded with elastic to fit snugly on the wrist. I'd seen it attached to cardboard backing hanging from a chrome pin in Kresge's and recognized that it possessed qualities I wanted: it was cool, modern, grown up. If I took it and wore it, I could transfer those qualities to myself.

3   Sharon kept the bracelet all morning, through recess, then handed it back at lunchtime, broken.

4   "It's a stupid bracelet. Besides, you stole it anyway."

5   I sat. My hands and legs felt suddenly hot.

6   "You broke it on purpose, didn't you?"

7   "You want to make something of it?"

8   "Yes," I said, surprised.

9   Sharon had been one of the girls who'd dragged a slightly plump classmate, Debbie, to a lane off school grounds the week before. Two of the girls had held Debbie by the wrists and pulled her taut, while a third, Nancy, ran and kicked her in the stomach. They did this until Debbie had an asthma attack.

10   Our fight was set for the next day after school, just outside school grounds so the teachers couldn't break it up. I got my stepfather to give me a boxing lesson. I expected to lose.

11   At the appointed time kids gathered by the fence. Sharon and I faced each other awkwardly, then Sharon stepped back, rushed

forward and pushed me by the shoulders. I reeled, regained my balance, pushed back. She grabbed my shirt and tried to throw a punch, but I twisted away and punched her in the stomach, and she fell down. She got up crying and said she was going home to get her big brother. I couldn't believe it was so easy.

The next day I wore my favourite outfit: go-go boots, a pink corduroy miniskirt with a wide shiny white belt, and a white turtle-neck T-shirt. I went to school feeling victorious. 12

Another girl in our class, Cathy, claimed she was a model. She always had the latest fashions first, and she lived in a new apartment building with her mother, who was young and pretty. Cathy announced that she was going to be in the new Simpson Sears catalogue. Every season my friend Susan and I pored over this catalogue, deciding which outfits we were going to beg our mothers for. 13

When it arrived we couldn't find Cathy in it anywhere. Still basking in the glow of my victory, I challenged her: "You're lying. You're not in that catalogue." 14

"Yes, I am. I'm on pages 24 and 27." 15

Susan and I went home and looked. Those pages only had pictures of skinny girls from the waist down modelling underwear. The next day I challenged Cathy to a fight. 16

After school Cathy came out the girls' entrance with her friend Debbie and they hovered at the top of the stairs. I was down in the schoolyard. I started walking toward her. 17

All the kids in the schoolyard spontaneously gathered behind me and began to chant, "Go Claudia go!" My eyes sparkled as I marched forward. I thought, this must be what war feels like. I walked up the stairs feeling powerful, dominant, confident. When I reached the top Debbie said, "Cathy doesn't want to fight. Anyway, you can't fight here. It's school grounds." 18

I thought about that, then gave Cathy a contemptuous shove and walked back down the stairs. 19

Recently the media have been focussing on the so-called new phenomenon of increasing violence among girls. Subtextual questions lurk in these pieces: Is this what feminism has brought us? Are girls today adopting male behaviour? Et cetera. Whenever the media begin discussing a behaviour as new, I suspect it's something old in a marginally new form. The same old thing doesn't sell papers. 20

21   Scientists are just beginning to study hierarchies and dominance displays among females. Jane Goodall is still one of the first scientists to systematically examine dominant behaviour among female chimpanzees. Among women writers there has been discourse about the experience of being dominated, and of evading domination, but rarely of being dominant. For good reason. Confessions in this area arouse hostility and make friends suspicious.

22   In the story of my schoolyard scraps, clothes are an important conveyor of dominance. The coveted° object, the stomped-on object, the object that bestowed power on its owner, was a bracelet. The response to victory was display—not with the bracelet, which was beyond repair, but with a treasured pink corduroy miniskirt and go-go boots—display in the manner of a peacock, gorilla or seahorse, a silent, colourful, textile roar.

23   When I went to write this story I couldn't remember why I had picked a fight with Cathy. I didn't dislike her; she was never mean to me. I figured there must have been a precipitating incident I had forgotten. Now I understand why it was her I challenged. She had the best clothes in the class. I was challenging her for her crown. She was the princess.

24   I don't know if I actually gained ascendency through the confrontation, but I probably tarnished the sheen of her feathers. I remember her still looking great in a way I couldn't, but more nervously.

25   I was proud of beating Sharon, but not of diminishing Cathy, if I did. Yet a smile escapes as I write, unmasking too earnest a tone, because, although I'd censure behaviour like that in my own children, I still wouldn't trade that moment when, with the sea of classmates behind me, I marched up the girls' staircase.

26   What I wear is frequently a matter of indifference, but there are occasions when clothes express and augment° my confidence, or lack thereof. There are the nights when I eviscerate° my closet finding nothing to wear; the image reflected in the mirror too exposed or too dowdy, too flashy or drab. These are nights when I am not content to be meek but a failure of nerve prevents me from strutting. I retreat to the little black dress and medium-heeled pumps, or the dark pantsuit with low-heeled boots, coasting, waiting for the next sensation of mastery in anything—my work, governing my own impulses, playing squash or purchasing a new garment to give me that transforming little rush of power.

27   On those glory nights, a frisson° reminiscent of the thrill of battle returns as I don clothes—suggestive of royalty, with expensive tailoring, saturated colours or luxurious textures: velvet, satin, silk, leather, fine wool. I put on high heels, red lipstick, scent; I polish and sharpen my nails, highlight the gleam in my eyes, deepen the flush in my cheeks and step out, dressed to kill.

As an adult one hopes to experience a more diffuse sense of dominance—not triumph over an individual but a sense of triumph vis-à-vis a collective benchmark. Furthermore, one hopes to remember that all measurement is illusion. Yet even in enlightened moments, when the base pleasures and pains of measurement have faded away, the thrill of dressing up and stepping out on the town remains primitive, fun and never entirely harmless. 28

Words and Meanings

Paragraph

coveted	desired; longed for	22
augment	increase	26
eviscerate	tear apart	
frisson	little shiver of excitement	27

Structure and Strategy

1. Between paragraphs 19 and 20 is a small symbol that divides the essay into two parts. How do the two sections differ?
2. What purpose is served by the specific EXAMPLES in paragraph 1?
3. The first part of the essay uses dialogue to convey much of the author's message. Why? Do you think this technique is effective?
4. Highlight four or five of the descriptive details in paragraph 27 that help to create the author's image of herself as she dresses for a night on the town. What do these details convey about the author's sense of self?
5. The final sentence of this essay contains a double negative, an unusual stylistic device used for emphasis. Identify the phrase and comment on its significance in the context of the piece.

Content and Purpose

1. What is the cause of the fight between Claudia and Sharon (paragraphs 2 through 11)? Who wins? How does young Claudia respond the next day?
2. Why does Claudia challenge Cathy, the child with whom she has her second fight? What is the outcome of this conflict?
3. How do the author's feelings about her fight with Sharon (paragraph 10) differ from her feelings about taking on Cathy (paragraph 18)? What caused this change? What does it suggest about violence generally in our society?
4. Does the author think that violence among girls is a new phenomenon? According to Casper, how do the media explain girl-on-girl violence or bullying?

5. Why does Casper think there has been so little analysis of the experience of girl bullies, the dominant females, compared to the experience of the victims of bullying?
6. How would Casper react if her own children got into fights? Is she a hypocrite?
7. As an adult, how does Casper achieve the "sensation of mastery" that she got from fighting as a child (paragraph 26)?
8. What association between clothing and power does the author discuss in the last two paragraphs of the essay?

Suggestions for Writing

1. Think of a bullying incident in which you were involved. Write an essay describing the incident and its effects on the victim and on the perpetrator(s).
2. Write an essay about the rivalry that occurs between girls/women (or boys/men) over clothing and accessories.
3. In your experience, which sex is more violent: girls or boys? Write an essay explaining your opinion, exploring the reasons and providing evidence for your argument.

Dispatches from the Poverty Line

PAT CAPPONI

Author and activist Pat Capponi (b. 1949) has written two books in her mystery series, *Last Stop Sunnyside* (2006) and *The Corpse Will Keep* (2008), featuring her sleuth Dana Leoni. She has also written non-fiction works, including a searing memoir, *Upstairs in the Crazy House* (1992), and *Bound by Duty: Walking the Beat with Canada's Cops* (2000). A survivor of psychiatric illness and long periods of unemployment, Capponi has served on numerous agency and hospital boards. She is a recipient of the Order of Ontario and the C. M. Hincks Award by the Canadian Mental Health Association. Ms. Capponi became a leading advocate for the mentally ill with the mantra of "a home, a job and a friend."

1   We live in a time when manipulation of public opinion has been elevated to a science, when stereotypes are accepted as true representatives of their segment of the population.

And, as always, stereotypes cause a great deal of pain to those tarred with the same brush . . . .

I am not innocent as far as taking refuge in stereotypes goes. As much as I try to catch myself at it, on occasion I'm forced to admit to myself, and sometimes to others, that I've fallen prey to its comforting lure.

I've served on many committees, task forces, working groups and boards in my seventeen years of mental health advocacy°. Before consumer involvement became more widely accepted, I was often the only ex-patient at the table, trying to deal with hospital administrators, bureaucrats, psychiatrists, nurses and family groups. I didn't think any board could scare me again, or silence me through intimidation.

I was, however, being forced to admit that one hospital board in particular was giving me a great deal of angst°. It left me feeling as though I'd been flung back through time . . . . I used to tell audiences of consumers and mental health staff that one of our biggest problems was that there was no consensus in the system concerning the value of involving clients in the management and delivery of services. One day I'd be working with an agency that possessed the equivalent of New York sophistication around the issues, and the next I'd feel as though I were in Alabama before the civil rights movement got under way. It wasn't unusual for these opposites to be within a few city blocks of each other.

That was part of my problem with this board, that it was Alabama-like while believing itself to be cutting edge. But there was more. There were deep and obvious class distinctions, and even though I was, at the time, gainfully employed, a published author, someone who possessed the respect of my community, I felt intimidated, looked down on, stereotyped and all the rest. It got so that I had to force myself to attend.

The board was a status board, composed of high-powered bankers, lawyers, publishers and consultants, as well as hospital executives. I was the only one in jeans, in a hat. I was the only one from my particular class and background. I was the only voice expressing criticism of the liberal establishment we were running . . . . Meetings were corporate°; when I would leave for a cigarette I felt I should be bowing and backing up to the door. Nobody laughed, it seemed, ever. Nobody talked out of turn.

Then, one afternoon when I had screwed up my courage to attend, I bumped into the "fat cat" lawyer in the hallway. He made a joke, and I made one back before I had time to think about it. We both laughed, and . . . we both stared at each other, surprised at the unlikely evidence of a sense of humour beneath the stereotype. Ice got broken. Then the banker who had offered me lifts home before, which I'd declined—what would I have to talk to him about in the car?—offered again, and I accepted. I even teased him about his brand new BMW and the pervasive smell of leather from the seats. He demonstrated how his car phone responded to voice orders to dial numbers, and I confess I got a kick out of the gimmickry . . . .

8   I remember another kind of breakthrough event at that board. I was trying once again to explain why I needed more people like me (from my class and experience) around the table. How easy it was to get intimidated in the setting we were in if you didn't find the corporate air invigorating. How easy it was to dismiss the views I was putting forward because it was only me they were hearing them from. How our class differences, our life experiences, created gulfs between us.

9   My banker friend took umbrage°. He was sure, he said, that he was quite capable of relating to me as a person, as another human being. He felt we were operating on a level playing field°, and that I wasn't giving them enough credit.

10   My lawyer friend then made a remarkable statement.

11   "That's not true," he said. "Pat didn't start out on a level playing field with me. I took one look at her and summed her up. It wasn't until later that I started to see her differently."

12   "And I," I said, "did the same thing, summed up you guys at a glance, and what I felt was your attitude towards me. It got easier to walk around with a chip on my shoulder than to try and relate to you."

13   Even the publisher chimed in: "I understand what you mean about intimidation. I never saw myself as intimidating, I like to think I'm an easygoing, friendly guy. But some of my staff have been pointing out to me that people who work for me don't have that same picture, because I have power over them. It's not easy or comfortable to realize that you may scare people, but a lot of times it's true."

14   Only the banker held out for the level playing field precept, but of course the conversation was ruled out of order and we were on to the next item on the agenda°.

15   A month or two later, I decided to transfer my bank account to a branch nearer my residence. To get an account in the first place had been a challenge. I don't have credit cards, or a driver's licence: therefore, I don't have a system-recognized identity. This is a very common dilemma for those who make up the underclass, and it accounts for the prevalence° and huge success of Money Mart cheque-cashing services in poor areas. As long as I've been an advocate, various groups of workers have tried to break through

the banking system, to work out generally acceptable ways of identifying clients to tellers through letters of introduction, or special cards, with no real success . . . .

In order for me to get an account in the first place, my publisher, Cynthia Good, had to take me into her branch, where we met with her "personal banking representative," and on the basis of Cynthia's knowledge of me, I got an account in time to deposit the cheque I'd received for the movie rights to my book.   16

I confess I felt quite mainstream for a while, with my PIN number and cheques and account book, as though I'd arrived. It was enough to make me overconfident. I decided it was silly to travel forty minutes to that branch when there was one a few blocks from me. I still had a balance of a little over $5,000, so I didn't anticipate any problems. I walked into my local branch and was soon seated across from yet another "personal banking representative."   17

"What I can do for you today?" she asked, pleasantly.   18

"I'd like to transfer my account to here, please," I responded, handing over my account book and bank card.   19

"I see, um, would you have some identification?"   20

I was puzzled.   21

"Nothing you guys seem to accept. But I only want to transfer, not open, an account."   22

She persists: "A major credit card? A driver's licence?"   23

I have a birth certificate. I remember trying to rent a video using it, and the owner of the store turning the card over and saying, "Your signature's not on it."   24

I shake my head. I give her the card of the other personal banking representative, the one in whose presence I had been validated. She phones. She shakes her head. That person is on vacation. She purses her lips, not liking to create difficulties for me, but there are rules.   25

"I'm sorry, we really do need identification."   26

I'm getting angry, and I suspect she feels it, which accounts for her visible nervousness. It won't help to get snippy with her. I could just pack it in and leave—it wouldn't be the end of the world, after all. But the battle for reason is under way. It would feel too much like defeat to withdraw now.   27

I try for a reasoned, measured tone.   28

"I don't want to withdraw anything. I have $5,000 in my account. You have my card, my cheques, my account book."   29

I hear steps behind me, I'm sure the security guard is getting ready to pounce.   30

"It's a different branch of the same bank. C'mon, be reasonable."   31

"Don't you even have your Indian Status Card?"   32

33   "I'm not Indian!"

34   Ordinarily, I would take it as a compliment, being mistaken for one of the First People, but in this context, I know there's some heavy stereotyping, and quite possibly some heavy attitude, going on.

35   I get a flash. I'm terrible about names, remembering names. I can recall the most minute° details of conversations, mannerisms, backgrounds and clothing but not names. But I do remember the division my BMW banker is president of. And I do remember it's this same corporation.

36   I ask her to look up the name of the guy in charge of ———.

37   "Why?" she asks, immediately suspicious.

38   "I know him, he can tell you I exist."

39   Perhaps to humour me, she flips open a book and recites some names.

40   "That's him," I cry, vindicated°. "Give him a call, will you?"

41   I suppose it's like telling a private to ring up a general at the request of a possible lunatic, an aboriginal impersonator: it's not done.

42   She excuses herself to consult with a superior. Long minutes pass. I feel myself being examined from the glassed-in cubicles where the decision-makers sit. I feel the breath of the security officer. I feel renewed determination.

43   She's back.

44   "I'm sorry for the delay. His secretary had some difficulty reaching him, he's in a meeting. But he is available now."

45   My understanding smile is as false and strained as her apology.

46   She picks up the phone and annoyingly turns her chair away from me while she speaks in low tones into the receiver. A few heartbeats, then she passes the phone to me.

47   Not waiting for his voice, I say: "I told you there's no level playing field."

48   He laughs, loudly and honestly.

49   In under ten minutes, I have my new account, my new card, cheques and a small degree of satisfaction.

50   Chalk up one for the good guys.

51   I take refuge in a nearby park, liking and needing the sun and a place to enjoy it. I've checked out the four or five in my neighbourhood, and on days when I need to walk, I go up to the one opposite the Dufferin Mall. I love the solitude, the birds, the green—a perfect setting for reading and tanning. Picking an empty bench, away from small clumps of people dotting the large park, I open my paperback and disappear into it.

It doesn't seem very long (my watch died a few months ago)   52
before an old fellow, tottering on his cane, shuffles towards me.
I look up at his approach, smile briefly and dive back into P. D.
James. I am dismayed when he chooses to perch on the other end
of my bench, and I try to ignore his presence while my conscience
starts bothering me. Now, I only smiled at him because I am aware
that some folks think I look a bit tough, and I didn't want him
worrying, but he might have mistaken the gesture for a come-chat-
with-me invitation. He's probably lonely, isolated, this is probably
his big daily outing. Would it kill me to spend a couple of minutes
talking to him? Damn.

I close my book, look over at him looking over at me expect-   53
antly.

"Beautiful day, isn't it?"   54

I can barely make out his reply, cloaked in a thick accent, but   55
his head bobbing up and down is pretty clear. I'm stuck for the next
sentence, but he keeps going enthusiastically. I make out his name,
repeating it triumphantly: "Victor! Hi, I'm Pat."

One arthritic hand grasps mine briefly, then goes back to rest   56
on his cane with the other one.

"I'm retired." He's getting better at speaking clearly, maybe   57
it was just a lack of opportunity that made him rusty. "I was an
engineer."

"You live around here?"   58

He turns painfully, pointing vaguely over his shoulder.   59

"Right over there, a beautiful place. Very beautiful place."   60

"Good for you."   61

I offer him a cigarette, which he accepts, and we sit in compan-   62
ionable silence in the sun. I'm thinking after the smoke I will move
on, find another park, maybe nearer my home.

He's talking again, and when I realize what he's saying my jaw   63
drops open.

"If you come see my place, I will give you twenty dollars."   64

"Jesus Christ! Are you crazy?" I'm so annoyed, and shocked,   65
and thrown off balance by his offer, that I'm blustering. I want to
whack him, except he'd probably fall over, like the dirty-old-man
character on *Laugh-In*.

"Listen to me," I lecture, as I shake my finger in his face. "First   66
off, you're committing a crime. Secondly, it's stupid and dangerous
for you. You can't go around offering money to people you don't
know for things I don't want to think about. You've insulted me.
I could have you arrested! Do you understand?"

Now I'm pretty sure what his daily tour of the park is about,   67
and I worry about the school-age girls that hang out at lunch time.

68   "If I see you doing this to anyone else, I will report you, do you get that? I'll be watching you!"

69   He's stuttering out an apology, which I don't believe, and I refrain from kicking his cane, though I really want to.

70   On my way home, in between feeling outraged and feeling dirtied, I start to laugh at my own stereotyping of a lonely old man in need of conversation in juxtaposition° with his own stereotyping of me.

71   People ought to wear summing-up signs sometimes, just so you'd know what to expect.

Words and Meanings

Paragraph

3	mental health advocacy	working for improvement in the lives of people with mental illnesses
4	angst	anxiety
6	corporate	formal, businesslike
9	took umbrage	objected
	operating on a level playing field	business jargon for "equal"
14	agenda	list of topics to be discussed at a meeting
15	prevalence	widespread existence
35	minute	tiny, insignificant
40	vindicated	justified, cleared of suspicion
70	in juxtaposition	occurring close together

Structure and Strategy

1. This piece consists of two distinct narrative ILLUSTRATIONS. The first takes place in paragraphs 1 to 50, the second in paragraphs 51 to 71. What links the two examples?
2. Identify the author's thesis statement.
3. Why does Capponi introduce her discussion of stereotyping with a CLICHÉ ("tarred with the same brush," paragraph 1)? What does this cliché mean?
4. Why do you think the author describes her experience as a mental health advocate in Canada in terms of a contrast between "New York sophistication" and "Alabama before the civil rights movement" (paragraph 4)? Are these comparisons meaningful to the Canadian audience she is writing for? Are they original or are they STEREOTYPES?

5. Capponi relies primarily on dialogue to tell her story. Why do you think she chooses to re-create her experiences for the reader through dialogue rather than to summarize them through DESCRIPTION and NARRATION?

Content and Purpose

1. Based on the hints given in the essay, what do you think Capponi looks like? Now do an Internet search and find a photo of her; several are readily available. Given her appearance and behaviour, how might people STEREOTYPE her?
2. Paragraph 7 contains two examples of stereotyping. What are they, and who is responsible for them? What succeeds in breaking through these stereotypes? What other "breakthrough events" does Capponi relate in this essay?
3. How does Capponi succeed in opening her first bank account? Why is banking a problem for her? Does she think it is a problem for others? If so, why and for whom?
4. Why does the "personal banking representative" not want to transfer Capponi's account to her branch? In what ways does this woman stereotype Capponi?
5. How is the standoff with the banking representative resolved? How does Capponi feel about the resolution? What solutions do you think might be available to other victims of stereotyping?
6. In the second ILLUSTRATION (paragraphs 51 to 71), what does Capponi think the old man in the park is looking for? What is he really looking for? How does Capponi react to the misunderstanding? Does she learn anything from this experience?

Suggestions for Writing

1. Have you ever experienced stereotyping because of the way you look? Write an essay that recounts your experience and your response to it.
2. Have you ever wrongly stereotyped someone based on his or her appearance or behaviour? Write an essay that tells the story of your experience and indicates what you learned from it.
3. Read Brent Staples' "Just Walk On By: A Black Man Ponders His Power to Alter Public Space" on page 263 and Thea Lim's "Take Back Halloween" on page 329. Choose one of these essays and compare its treatment of stereotyping with that of "Dispatches from the Poverty Line."

The End of the Wild

WADE DAVIS

A native of British Columbia, Wade Davis (b. 1953) is an anthropologist, biologist, botanical explorer, and photographer; much of his work has focused on indigeneous cultures and their uses of psychoactive plants. He holds a degree in ethnobotany from Harvard. His travels have taken him from the forests of the Amazon to the mountains of Tibet, from the deserts of Africa to the high Arctic. His books include *The Serpent and the Rainbow* (1985), later released as a feature film; *One River* (1996), nominated for the Governor General's Award; *The Clouded Leopard* (1998); *Light at the Edge of the World* (2002); and *Shadows in the Sun: Travels to Landscapes of Spirit and Desire* (2010). Davis's television credits include *Earthguide*, a series on the environment, and *Ancient Voices/Modern World* (National Geographic Channel).

1   Some time ago at a symposium° in Barbados, I was fortunate to share the podium with two extraordinary scientists. The first to speak was Richard Leakey, the renowned anthropologist who with his mother and father drew from the dust and ashes of Africa the story of the birth of our species. The meeting concluded with astronaut Story Musgrave, the first physician to walk in space. It was an odd and moving juxtaposition of the endpoints of the human experience. Dr. Musgrave recognized the irony and it saddened him. He told of what it had been like to know the beauty of the earth as seen from the heavens. There he was, suspended 200 miles above the earth, travelling 18,000 miles per hour with the golden visor of his helmet illuminated by a single sight, a small and fragile blue planet enveloped in a veil of clouds, floating, as he recalled, "in the velvet void of space." To have experienced that vision, he said, a sight made possible only by the brilliance of human technology, and to remember the blindness with which we as a species abuse our only home, was to know the purest sensation of horror.

2   Many believe that this image of the earth, first brought home to us but a generation ago, will have a more profound impact on human thought than did the Copernican revolution of the 16th century, which transformed the philosophical foundations of the western world by revealing that the planet was not the center of the universe. From space, we see not a limitless frontier nor the stun-

ning products of man, but a single interactive sphere of life, a living organism composed of air, water, and earth. It is this transcendent vision which, more than any amount of scientific data, teaches us the earth is a finite place that can endure our foolish ways for only so long.

In light of this new perspective, this new hope, the past and present deeds of human beings often appear inconceivably cruel and sordid. Shortly after leaving Barbados, while lecturing in the midwest of the United States, I visited two places that in a different, more sensitive world would surely be enshrined as memorials to the victims of the ecological catastrophes that occurred there. The first locality was the site of the last great nesting flock of passenger pigeons, a small stretch of woodland on the banks of the Green River near Mammoth Cave, Ohio. This story of extinction is well known. Yet until I stood in that cold, dark forest, I had never sensed the full weight of the disaster, the scale and horror of it. 3

At one time passenger pigeons accounted for 40% of the entire bird population of North America. In 1870, at a time when their numbers were already greatly diminished, a single flock a mile wide and 320 miles long containing an estimated 2 billion birds passed over Cincinnati on the Ohio River. Imagine such a sight. Assuming that each bird ate half a pint of seeds a day, a flock that size must have consumed each day over 17 million bushels of grain. Such sightings were not unusual. In 1813, James Audubon° was travelling in a wagon from his home on the Ohio River to Louisville, some sixty miles away, when a flock of passenger pigeons filled the sky so that the "light of noonday sun was obscured as by an eclipse." He reached Louisville at sunset and the birds still came. He estimated that the flock contained over 1 billion birds, and it was but one of several columns of pigeons that blackened the sky that day. 4

Audubon visited roosting and nesting sites to find trees two feet in diameter broken off at the ground by the weight of birds. He found dung so deep on the forest floor that he mistook it for snow. He once stood in the midst of a flock when the birds took flight and then landed. He compared the noise and confusion to that of a gale, the sound of their landing to thunder. 5

It is difficult now to imagine the ravages of man that over the course of half a century destroyed this creature. Throughout the 19th century, pigeon meat was a mainstay of the American diet and merchants in the eastern cities sold as many as 18,000 birds a day. Pigeon hunting was a full time job for thousands of men. The term "stool pigeon" derives from a standard killing technique of the era. A hunter would sew shut the eyes of a living bird, bind its feet to a pole driven into the ground, and wait in the surrounding grass for 6 the flocks to respond to its cry. When the birds came, they arrived in such numbers that the hunter could simply bat them out of the air with a club. The more affluent classes slaughtered birds for recreation. It was not unusual for shooting clubs to go through 50,000 birds in a weekend competition; hundreds of thousands of live birds were catapulted to their death before the diminishing supply forced skeet shooters to turn to clay pigeons.

7   By 1896, a mere 50 years after the first serious impact of man, there were only some 250,000 birds left. In April of that year, the birds came together for one last nesting flock in the forest outside of Bowling Green, Ohio. The telegraph wires hummed with the news and the hunters converged. In a final orgy of slaughter over 200,000 pigeons were killed, 40,000 mutilated, 100,000 chicks destroyed. A mere 5,000 birds survived. The entire kill was to be shipped east but there was a derailment on the line and the dead birds rotted in their crates. On March 24, 1900, the last passenger pigeon in the wild was shot by a young boy. On September 1, 1914, as the Battle of the Marne consumed the flower of European youth, the last passenger pigeon died in captivity.

8   When I left the scene of this final and impossible slaughter, I travelled west to Sioux City, Iowa, to speak at Buena Vista College. There I was fortunate to visit a remnant patch of tall grass prairie, a 180-acre preserve that represents one of the largest remaining vestiges of an ecosystem that once carpeted North America from southern Canada to Texas. Again it was winter, and the cold wind blew through the coneflowers and the dozens of species of grass. The young biology student who was with me was familiar with every species in that extraordinary mosaic—they were like old friends to him. Yet as we walked through that tired field my thoughts drifted from the plants to the horizon. I tried to imagine buffalo moving through the grass, the physics of waves as millions of animals crossed that prairie.

9   As late as 1871 buffalo outnumbered people in North America. In that year one could stand on a bluff in the Dakotas and see nothing but buffalo in every direction for thirty miles. Herds were so large that it took days for them to pass a single point. Wyatt Earp described one herd of a million animals stretched across a grazing area the size of Rhode Island. Within nine years of that sighting, buffalo had vanished from the Plains.

10   The destruction of the buffalo resulted from a campaign of biological terrorism unparalleled in the history of the Americas. U.S. government policy was explicit. As General Philip Sheridan wrote at the time, "The buffalo hunters have done in the past two years more to settle the vexed Indian Question than the regular army has

accomplished in the last 30 years. They are destroying the Indians' commissary°. Send them powder and lead, and let them kill until they have exterminated the buffalo." Between 1850 and 1880 more than 75 million hides were sold to American dealers. No one knows how many more animals were slaughtered and left on the prairie. A decade after native resistance had collapsed, Sheridan advised Congress to mint a commemorative medal, with a dead buffalo on one side, a dead Indian on the other.

I thought of this history as I stood in that tall grass prairie near   11
Sioux City. What disturbed me the most was to realize how effort-
lessly we have removed ourselves from this ecological tragedy. Today the people of Iowa, good and decent folk, live contentedly in a landscape of cornfields that is claustrophobic in its monotony. For them the time of the tall grass prairie, like the time of the buffalo, is as distant from their immediate lives as the fall of Rome or the battle of Troy. Yet the destruction occurred but a century ago, well within the lifetime of their grandfathers.

This capacity to forget, this fluidity of memory, is a frightening   12
human trait. Several years ago I spent many months in Haiti, a country that as recently as the 1920s was 80% forested. Today less than 5% of the forest cover remains. I remember standing with a Vodoun priest on a barren ridge, peering across a wasteland, a desolate valley of scrub and half-hearted trees. He waxed eloquent as if words alone might have squeezed beauty from that wretched sight. He could only think of angels, I of locusts. It was amazing. Though witness to an ecological holocaust that within this century had devastated his entire country, this man had managed to endure without losing his human dignity. Faced with nothing, he adorned his life with his imagination. This was inspiring but also terrifying. People appear to be able to tolerate and adapt to almost any degree of environmental degradation. As the farmers of Iowa today live without wild things, the people of Haiti scratch a living from soil that will never again know the comfort of shade.

From a distance, both in time and space, we can perceive these   13
terrible and poignant events as what they were—unmitigated eco-
logical disasters that robbed the future of something unimaginably precious in order to satisfy the immediate and often mundane needs of the present. The luxury of hindsight, however, does nothing to cure the blindness with which today we overlook deeds of equal magnitude and folly.

As a younger man in Canada I spent a long winter in a logging   14
camp on the west coast of Haida Gwaii, or the Queen Charlotte Islands as they were then commonly known. It was a good life and it put me through school. I was a surveyor, which meant that

I spent all of my time far ahead of the loggers in the dense uncut forest, laying out the roads and the falling boundaries, determining the pattern in which the trees would come down. At the time I had already spent more than a year in the Amazon and I can tell you that those distant forests, however immense and mysterious, are dwarfed by the scale and wonder of the ancient temperate rainforests of British Columbia. In the valleys and around the lakes, and along the shore of the inlet where the soil was rich and deep, we walked through red cedar and sitka spruce, some as tall as a 25-storey building, many with over 70 million needles capturing the light of the sun. Miracles of biological engineering, their trunks stored thousands of gallons of water and could be twenty feet or more across at the base. Many of them had been standing in the forest for more than a thousand years, the anchors of an extraordinarily complex ecosystem° of mountains and rain, salmon and eagles, of squirrels that fly, fungi that crawl, and creatures that live on dew and never touch the forest floor. It is a world that is far older, far richer in its capacity to produce the raw material of life, and far more endangered than almost any region of the Amazon.

15   To walk through these forests in the depths of winter, when the rain turns to mist and settles softly on the moss, is to step back in time. Two hundred million years ago vast coniferous° forests formed a mantle across the entire world. Then evolution took a great leap and the flowers were born. The difference between the two groups of plants involves a mechanism of pollination and fertilization that changed the course of life on earth. In the case of the more primitive conifers, the plant must produce the basic food for the seed with no certainty that it will be fertilized. In the flowering plants, by contrast, fertilization itself sparks the creation of the seed's food reserves. In other words, unlike the conifers, the flowering plants make no investment without the assurance that a viable seed will be produced. As a result of this and other evolutionary advances, the flowering plants came to dominate the earth in an astonishingly short period of time. Most conifers went extinct and those that survived retreated to the margins of the world, where a small number of species managed to maintain a foothold by adapting to particularly harsh conditions. Today, at a conservative estimate, there are over 250,000 species of flowering plants. The conifers have been reduced to a mere 700 species and in the tropics, the hotbed of evolution, they have been almost completely displaced.

16   On all the earth, there is only one region of any size and significance where, because of unique climatic conditions, the

conifers retain their former glory. Along the northwest coast of North America the summers are hot and dry, the winters cold and wet. Plants need water and light to create food. Here in the summer there is ample light for photosynthesis, but not enough water. In the winter, when both water and light are sufficient, the low temperatures cause the flowering plants to lose their leaves and become dormant. The evergreen conifers, by contrast, are able to grow throughout the long winters and since they use water more efficiently than broad-leafed plants, they also thrive during the dry summer months. The result is an ecosystem so rich, so productive, that the biomass° in the best sites is easily four times as great as that of any comparable area of the tropics.

Inevitably there was, at least for me, an almost surrealistic quality to life in our remote camp where men lived away from their families and made a living cutting down in minutes trees that had taken a thousand years to grow. The constant grinding of machinery, the disintegration of the forest into burnt slash and mud, the wind and sleet that froze on the rigging and whipped across the frozen bay, etched patterns into the lives of the men. Still, no one in our camp had any illusions about what we were doing. All the talk of sustained yield and overmature timber, decadent and normal forests we left to the government bureaucrats and the company PR hacks. We used to laugh at the little yellow signs stuck on the sides of roads that only we would ever travel, that announced that twenty acres had been replanted, as if it mattered in a clearcut that stretched to the horizon 17

Everyone knew, of course, that the ancient forests would never come back. One of my mates used to say that the tangle of half-hearted trees that grew up in the slash° no more resembled the forest he'd cut down, than an Alberta wheatfield resembled a wild prairie meadow. But nobody was worried about what they were doing. It was work, and living on the edge of that immense forest, they simply believed that it would go on forever. 18

If anyone in the government had a broader perspective, we never heard about it. Our camp was nineteen miles by water across an inlet from a backroad that ran forty miles to the nearest forestry office. The government had cut back on overtime pay, and, what with the statutory coffee and lunch breaks, the forestry fellows couldn't figure out how to get to our camp and back in less than seven and a half hours. So they didn't try. The bureaucracy within the company wasn't much better. The mills down south kept complaining that our camp was sending them inferior grades of Douglas fir, which was surprising since the species doesn't grow on the Charlottes. 19

20   There were, of course, vague murmurs of ecological concern that filtered through to our camp. One morning in the cookhouse I ran into a friend of mine, a rock blaster named Archie whose voice had been dusted by ten thousand cigarettes and the dirt from a dozen mine failures. Archie was in a particularly cantankerous mood. Clutching a donut he'd been marinating in caffeine, he flung a three-day-old newspaper onto the table. The headline said something about Greenpeace.

21   "Fucking assholes," he critiqued.

22   "What's wrong, Arch?" I asked.

23   "Sons of bitches don't know a damn thing about pollution," he said. Archie then proceeded to tell me about working conditions in the hard rock uranium mines of the Northwest Territories shortly after the Second World War. The companies, concerned about the impact of radioactivity, used to put the workers, including Archie, into large sealed chambers and release a gas with suspended particles of aluminum in it. The idea being that the aluminum would coat the lungs and, at the end of the shift, the men would gag it up, together with any radioactive dust.

24   "Now that," growled Archie, "was environmental pollution."

25   In truth, it is difficult to know how much the forest destruction actually affected the men. Some clearly believed blindly in the process and were hardened by that faith. Others were so transient, moving from camp to camp, sometimes on a monthly basis, that they never registered the full measure of the impact of any one logging show. Some just didn't care. The entire industry was so itinerant° that no one ever developed a sense of belonging to a place. There was no attachment to the land, nor could there be given what we were doing. In the slash of the clearcuts, there was little room for sentiment.

26   I knew of a veteran faller who, having cut down thousands of trees, finally came upon one giant cedar that was simply too magnificent to be felled. When he refused to bring it down, the bullbucker° threatened to fire him. The faller felt he had no choice. He brought it down and then, realizing what he had done, he sat on the stump and began to weep. He quit that afternoon and never cut another tree.

27   Like everyone else in our camp, I was there to make money. On weekends, when our survey crew was down, I picked up overtime pay by working in the slash as a chokerman°, wrapping the cables around the fallen logs so the yarders° could drag them to the landings° where they were loaded onto the trucks. Setting beads° is the most miserable job in a logging show, the bottom rung of the camp hierarchy.

One Saturday I was working in a setting high up on the 28
mountain that rose above the camp. It had been raining all day
and the winds were blowing from the southeast, dragging clouds
across the bay and up the slope, where they hung up in the tops of
giant hemlocks and cedars that rose above the clearcut. We were
working the edge of the opening, but the landing was unusually
close by. It took no time at all for the mainline to drag the logs
in, and for the haulback° to fling the chokers° back to us. We'd
been highballing° all day and both my partner and I were a mess
of mud, grease and tree sap. He was a native boy, a Nisga'a from
New Aiyansh on the Nass River, but that's all I knew about him.

Late in the afternoon, something got fouled up on the landing, 29
and the yarder shut down. Suddenly it was quiet and you could
hear the wind that had been driving the sleet into our faces all day.
My partner and I abandoned the slash for the shelter of the forest.
We found a dry spot out of the wind in a hollow at the base of an
enormous cedar and waited for the yarder to start up. We didn't
speak. He kept staring off into the forest. All hunched up with the
cold, we looked the same—orange hardhats, green-black rain gear,
rubber corkboots. We shared a cigarette. I was watching his face as
he smoked. It struck me as strange that here we were, huddled in
the forest in silence, two young men from totally different worlds.
I tried to imagine what it might have been like had we met but a
century before, I perhaps a trader, he a shadow in the wet woods.
His people had made a home in the forest for thousands of years.
I thought of what this country must have been like when my own
grandfather arrived. I saw in the forest around us a world that my
own children might never know, that Nisga'a children would never
know. I turned to my partner. The whistle blew on the landing.

"What the hell are we doing?" I asked. 30

"Working," he said. I watched him as he stepped back into 31
the clearcut, and then I followed. We finished the shift and, in the
falling darkness, rode back to camp together in the back of the company crummy. That was the last I saw of him.

Fifteen years have passed since I left that camp and I've often 32
wondered what became of the Nisga'a boy. It's a good bet he's no
longer working as a logger. Natives rarely get promoted beyond
the landing and, what's more, over the last decade a third of all logging jobs have been lost. The industry keeps saying that environ-
mentalists are to blame, but in reality all the conservation initiatives
of the last ten years in B.C. have not cost the union more than a few
hundred jobs, if that. Automation and dwindling timber supplies
have put almost 20,000 people out of work in this province alone.
And still we keep cutting. In Oregon, Washington and California

only 10% of the original coastal rainforest remains. In British Columbia roughly 60% has been logged, largely since 1950. In the mere 15 years since I stood in the forest with that Nisga'a boy, over half of all timber ever extracted from the public forests of British Columbia has been taken. At current rates of harvest, the next 20 years will see the destruction of every valley of ancient rainforest in the province.

33   We are living in the midst of an ecological catastrophe every bit as tragic as that of the slaughter of the buffalo and the passenger pigeon. Our government policies are equally blind, our economic rationales equally compelling. Until just recently, forestry policy in British Columbia explicitly called for the complete eradication of the old growth forests. The rotation cycle, the rate at which the forests were to be cut across the province, and thus the foundation of sustained yield forestry, was based on the assumption that all of these forests would be eliminated and replaced with tree farms. In other words, consideration of the intrinsic value of these ancient rainforests had no place in the calculus of forestry planning. Like the buffalo and the passenger pigeon, these magnificent forests were considered expendable°.

34   But while the passenger pigeons are extinct, and the buffalo reduced to a curiosity, these forests still stand. They are as rare and spectacular as any natural feature on the face of the earth, as biologically significant as any terrestrial ecosystem that has ever existed. If, knowing this, we still allow them to fall, what will it say about us as a people? What will be the legacy of our times?

35   The truth is, in an increasingly complex and fragmented world we need these ancient forests, alive and intact. For the children of the Nisga'a they are an image of the dawn of time, a memory of an era when raven emerged from the shadow of the cedar and young boys went in search of spirits at the north end of the world. For my own two young girls these forests echo with a shallow history, but one that is nevertheless rich in the struggles of their great grandparents, men and women who travelled halfway around the world to live in this place. Today all peoples in this land are drawn together by a single thread of destiny. We live at the edge of the clearcut, our hands will determine the fate of these forests. If we do nothing, they will be lost within our lifetimes and we will be left to explain our inaction. If we preserve these ancient forests they will stand apart for all generations and for all time as symbols of the geography of hope.

Words and Meanings

symposium	academic conference	1
James Audubon	Haitian-born U.S. scientist and artist who painted all the species of birds known in North America in the early nineteenth century	4
commissary	food supply	10
ecosystem	interdependent network of all living things	14
coniferous	pertaining to cone-bearing evergreen trees	15
biomass	weight (density) of all living things in a given area	16
slash	an open space in a forest resulting from logging	18
itinerant	travelling from place to place	25
bull-bucker, chokerman, yarders, landings, beads, haulback, chokers, highballing	The terms in these paragraphs are loggers' jargon to describe the act of getting trees out of the slash. The foreman (bullbucker) supervises the workers who hook the logs onto a cable (choker) that is operated by a machine (yarder). Once the logs reach the "landing," the site from which they are loaded onto trucks, another line (the haulback) returns the empty chokers (or beads) to the site to be reset. Performing these activities at top speed to ensure maximum production is "highballing."	26 to 28
expendable	something we can use up for short-term gain without serious consequences	33

Structure and Strategy

1. Davis introduces his essay with examples of two scientists who spoke, along with the author, at an international conference. Why did he choose to begin with Leakey and Musgrave? What is the "odd and moving juxtaposition" these two men represent?
2. What is the THESIS of this essay? Which sentence in paragraph 3 most clearly expresses it?
3. Which paragraphs detail the extinction of the passenger pigeon? Which deal with the decimation of the plains buffalo herds? What is the third ILLUSTRATION of Davis's point? In what ORDER has he arranged these three main sections of his essay?

4. Identify vivid descriptive details in paragraphs 5, 14, and 17. What is the purpose of the ANECDOTE in paragraph 26?
5. Identify the TOPIC SENTENCES in paragraphs 6, 10, 12, and 16; then determine what kind of support the author uses to develop his topic in each of these paragraphs.
6. How is the topic of paragraph 7 developed? Find another paragraph in the essay that uses the same kind of support to develop the topic. What effect do these paragraphs have on the reader?
7. What is the TONE of paragraph 19? How does the tone contribute to your understanding of the author's opinion of the government?
8. Why does Davis elaborate his third point in such detail, including dialogue and characterization?
9. Besides EXPOSITION, what other RHETORICAL MODE does Davis employ in "The End of the Wild"?
10. Who is the intended AUDIENCE for this piece? What is its overall TONE?

Content and Purpose

1. According to the essay, what does the earth look like from space? (See paragraph 2.) What IRONY is explored in paragraphs 2 and 3? According to Davis, what should we have learned from the image of earth as seen by space travellers?
2. What was the passenger pigeon population in North America in 1870? What happened to them? How? Why?
3. What is a "stool pigeon" (paragraph 6)? What is the meaning of the idiom today?
4. What has North America lost along with the buffalo? (See paragraphs 8, 10, and 11.) How do these paragraphs reinforce Davis's THESIS?
5. Explain in your own words the political purpose of the U.S. government in promoting the slaughter of the buffalo that makes this "biological terrorism" (paragraph 10) so horrific.
6. According to Davis, why are the rainforests of British Columbia even more remarkable and more endangered than those of the Amazon? (See paragraphs 14 through 16.)
7. According to the essay, what are the attitudes of the loggers, the logging companies, the government, and the Native peoples to clearcutting the rainforest?
8. Why do you think Davis includes the narrative involving "a rock blaster named Archie" (paragraphs 20 through 24) and "a native boy, a Nisga'a from New Aiyansh" (paragraphs 28 through 33)? What effect do these narratives have on the reader?

9. Summarize what has happened in the years since the author worked in the logging industry (see paragraph 32).

10. How does Davis unify his essay in the CONCLUSION (paragraphs 33 through 35)? How does he connect his three examples? Why does he want to preserve the rainforests?

Suggestions for Writing

1. Compare Davis's view of the ecosystem of British Columbia with that of Daniel Francis in "The Potemkin Province" (page 351). Do you think the two authors would agree or disagree about BC's management of its natural resources?

2. Using an example from the natural environment (but not pigeons, buffaloes, and rainforests), write an essay illustrating a specific damage that humans are doing to the natural world. Support your argument with carefully chosen quotations from David Beers's "Grounded" (page 268); Jane Rule's "The Harvest, the Kill" (page 362); or Daniel Francis's "The Potemkin Province" (page 351).

3. Davis refers to his experience in forest-denuded Haiti a number of years ago, before the devastating 2010 earthquake. Do some research, and write an essay about the relationship of rebuilding the country to reforesting its landscape.

Lost in Translation

EVA HOFFMAN

Born in Poland in 1945, Hoffman immigrated to Canada with her family in 1959. She went to school in Vancouver, then studied at Rice University, the Yale School of Music, and Harvard, where she completed her Ph.D. in English literature. She is the author of *Lost in Translation* (1989); *Exit into History* (1993); *After Such Knowledge: Memory, History and the Legacy of the Holocaust* (2004); as well as two novels. She lives in London.

Every day I learn new words, new expressions. I pick them up   1
from school exercises, from conversations, from the books I take out of Vancouver's well-lit, cheerful public library.

There are some turns of phrase to which I develop strange allergies. "You're welcome," for example, strikes me as a gaucherie°, and I can hardly bring myself to say it—I suppose because it implies that there's something to be thanked for, which in Polish would be impolite. The very places where the language is at its most conventional, where it should be most taken for granted, are the places where I feel the prick of artifice°.

2   Then there are words to which I take an equally irrational liking, for their sound, or just because I'm pleased to have deduced their meaning. Mainly they're words I learn from books, like "enigmatic" or "insolent"—words that have only a literary value, that exist only as signs on the page.

3   But mostly, the problem is that the signifier has become severed from the signified. The words I learn now don't stand for things in the same unquestioned way they did in my native tongue. "River" in Polish was a vital sound, energized with the essence of river-hood, of my rivers, of my being immersed in rivers. "River" in English is cold—a word without an aura. It has no accumulated associations for me, and it does not give off the radiating haze of connotation°. It does not evoke°.

4   The process, alas, works in reverse as well. When I see a river now, it is not shaped, assimilated by the word that accommodates it to the psyche—a word that makes a body of water a river rather than an uncontained element. The river before me remains a thing, absolutely other, absolutely unbending to the grasp of my mind.

5   When my friend Penny tells me that she's envious, or happy, or disappointed, I try laboriously to translate not from English to Polish but from the word back to its source, to the feeling from which it springs. Already, in that moment of strain, spontaneity° of response is lost. And anyway, the translation doesn't work. I don't know how Penny feels when she talks about envy. The word hangs in a Platonic° stratosphere, a vague prototype° of all envy, so large, so all encompassing that it might crush me—as might disappointment or happiness.

6   I am becoming a living avatar° of structuralist° wisdom; I cannot help knowing that words are just themselves. But it's a terrible knowledge, without any of the consolations that wisdom usually brings. It does not mean that I'm free to play with words at my wont°; anyway, words in their naked state are surely among the least satisfactory play objects. No, this radical disjoining between word and thing is a desiccating° alchemy°, draining the world not only of significance but of its colors, striations, nuances—its very existence. It is the loss of a living connection.

The worst losses come at night. As I lie down in a strange bed in 7
a strange house—my mother is a sort of housekeeper here, to the
aging Jewish man who has taken us in return for her services—I
wait for that spontaneous flow of inner language which used to
be my nighttime talk with myself, my way of informing the ego°
where the id° had been. Nothing comes. Polish, in a short time, has
atrophied, shriveled from sheer uselessness. Its words don't apply
to my new experiences; they're not coeval° with any of the objects,
or faces, or the very air I breathe in the daytime. In English, words
have not penetrated to those layers of my psyche from which a
private conversation could proceed. This interval before sleep
used to be the time when my mind became both receptive and
alert, when images and words rose up to consciousness, reiterating
what had happened during the day, adding the day's experiences
to those already stored there, spinning out the thread of my personal story.

Now, this picture-and-word show is gone; the thread has 8
been snapped. I have no interior language, and without it, interior images—those images through which we assimilate the
external world, through which we take it in, love it, make it our
own—become blurred too. My mother and I met a Canadian
family who live down the block today. They were working in
their garden and engaged us in a conversation of the "Nice
weather we're having, isn't it?" variety, which culminated
in their inviting us into their house. They sat stiffly on their
couch, smiled in the long pauses between the conversation, and
seemed at a loss for what to ask. Now my mind gropes for some
description of them, but nothing fits. They're a different species
from anyone I've met in Poland, and Polish words slip off them
without sticking. English words don't hook on to anything. I try,
deliberately, to come up with a few. Are these people pleasant
or dull? Kindly or silly? The words float in an uncertain space.
They come up from a part of my brain in which labels may be
manufactured but which has no connection to my instincts,
quick reactions, knowledge. Even the simplest adjectives sow
confusion in my mind; English kindliness has a whole system of
morality behind it, a system that makes "kindness" an entirely
positive virtue. Polish kindness has the tiniest element of irony.
Besides, I'm beginning to feel the tug of prohibition, in English,
against uncharitable words. In Polish, you can call someone an
idiot without particularly harsh feelings and with the zest of a
strong judgment. Yes, in Polish these people might tend toward
"silly" and "dull"—but I force myself toward "kindly" and

"pleasant." The cultural unconscious is beginning to exercise its subliminal° influence.

9   The verbal blur covers these people's faces, their gestures with a sort of fog. I can't translate them into my mind's eye. The small event, instead of being added to the mosaic of consciousness and memory, falls through some black hole, and I fall with it. What has happened to me in this new world? I don't know. I don't see what I've seen, don't comprehend what's in front of me. I'm not filled with language anymore, and I have only a memory of fullness to anguish me with the knowledge that, in this dark and empty state, I don't really exist . . . .

10   My voice is doing funny things. It does not seem to emerge from the same parts of my body as before. It comes out from somewhere in my throat, tight, thin, and mat—a voice without the modulations, dips, and rises that it had before, when it went from my stomach all the way through my head. There is, of course, the constraint and the self-consciousness of an accent that I hear but cannot control. Some of my high school peers accuse me of putting it on in order to appear more "interesting." In fact, I'd do anything to get rid of it, and when I'm alone, I practice sounds for which my speech organs have no intuitions, such as "th" (I do this by putting my tongue between my teeth) and "a," which is longer and more open in Polish (by shaping my mouth into a sort of arrested grin). It is simple words like "cat" or "tap" that give me the most trouble, because they have no context of other syllables, and so people often misunderstand them. Whenever I can, I do awkward little swerves to avoid them, or pause and try to say them very clearly. Still, when people—like salesladies—hear me speak without being prepared to listen carefully, they often don't understand me the first time around. "Girls' shoes," I say, and the "girls" comes out as a sort of scramble. "Girls' shoes," I repeat, willing the syllable to form itself properly, and the saleslady usually smiles nicely, and sends my mother and me to the right part of the store. I say "Thank you" with a sweet smile, feeling as if I'm both claiming an unfair special privilege and being unfairly patronized.

11   It's as important to me to speak well as to play a piece of music without mistakes. Hearing English distorted grates on me like chalk screeching on a blackboard, like all things botched and badly done, like all forms of gracelessness. The odd thing is that I know what is correct, fluent, good, long before I can execute° it. The English spoken by our Polish acquaintances strikes me as jagged and thick, and I know that I shouldn't imitate it. I'm turned

off by the intonations I hear on the TV sitcoms—by the expectation of laughter, like a dog's tail wagging in supplication, built into the actors' pauses, and by the curtailed, cutoff rhythms. I like the way Penny speaks, with an easy flow and a pleasure in giving words a fleshly fullness; I like what I hear in some movies; and once the Old Vic° comes to Vancouver to perform *Macbeth*, and though I can hardly understand the particular words, I am riveted by the tones of sureness and command that mold the actors' speech into such majestic periods°.

Sociolinguists° might say that I receive these language mes- 12 sages as class signals, that I associate the sounds of correctness with the social status of the speaker. In part, this is undoubtedly true. The class-linked notion that I transfer wholesale from Poland is that belonging to a "better" class of people is absolutely dependent on speaking a "better" language. And in my situation especially, I know that language will be a crucial instrument, that I can over- come the stigma° of my marginality°, the weight of presumption against me, only if the reassuringly right sounds come out of my mouth.

Yes, speech is a class signifier. But I think that in hearing these 13 varieties of speech around me, I'm sensitized to something else as well—something that is a matter of aesthetics°, and even of psy- chological health. Apparently, skilled chefs can tell whether a dish from some foreign cuisine is well cooked even if they have never tasted it and don't know the genre of cooking it belongs to. There seem to be some deep-structure qualities—consistency, proportions of ingredients, smoothness of blending—that indicate culinary achievement to these educated eaters' taste buds. So each language has its own distinctive music, and even if one doesn't know its sep- arate components, one can pretty quickly recognize the propriety of the patterns in which the components are put together, their harmonies and discords. Perhaps the crucial element that strikes the ear in listening to living speech is the degree of the speaker's self-assurance and control.

As I listen to people speaking that foreign tongue, English, I 14 can hear when they stumble or repeat the same phrases too many times, when their sentences trail off aimlessly—or, on the contrary, when their phrases have vigor and roundness, when they have the space and the breath to give a flourish at the end of a sentence, or make just the right pause before coming to a dramatic point. I can tell, in other words, the degree of their ease or disease, the extent of authority that shapes the rhythms of their speech. That authority—in whatever dialect, in whatever variant of the mainstream language— seems to me to be something we all desire. It's not that we all want to speak the King's English, but whether we speak Appalachian or Harlem English, or Cockney, or Jamaican Creole, we want to be at home in our tongue. We want to be able to give voice accurately and fully to ourselves and our sense of the world. John Fowles, in one of his stories in *The Ebony Tower*, has a young man cruelly violate an elderly writer and his manuscripts because the legacy of language has not been passed on to the youthful vandal properly. This seems to me an entirely credible premise. Linguistic dispossession° is a sufficient motive for violence, for it is close to the dispossession of one's self. Blind rage, helpless rage is rage that has no words—rage that overwhelms one with darkness. And if one is perpetually without words, if one exists in the entropy° of inarticulateness°, that condition itself is bound to be an enraging frustration. In my New York apartment, I listen almost nightly to fights that erupt like brushfire on the street below—and in their escalating fury of repetitious phrases ("Don't do this to me, man, you fucking bastard, I'll fucking kill you"), I hear not the pleasures of macho toughness but an infuriated beating against wordlessness against the incapacity to make oneself understood, seen. Anger can be borne—it can even be satisfying—if it can gather into words and explode in a storm, or a rapier-sharp attack. But without this means of ventilation, it only turns back inward, building and swirling like a head of steam—building to an impotent, murderous rage. If all therapy is speaking therapy—a talking cure—then perhaps all neurosis° is a speech disease.

Words and Meanings

Paragraph		
1	gaucherie	awkward, boorish expression
	artifice	effort; the work of carefully crafting something
3	connotation	See Glossary
	evoke	produce or call to mind (connotations)
5	spontaneity	immediacy, quickness
	Platonic	developed by the Greek philosopher Plato (c. 427–347 BCE)
	prototype	the original form of something; the standard from which copies or examples are made
6	avatar	incarnation; an idea given physical form
	structuralist	structuralism is a theory of language that emphasizes form (words) over function (meaning)

wont	habit	
desiccating	intellectually and emotionally withering; the opposite of nourishing	
alchemy	a pseudoscience that claims to transform one thing into another; e.g., copper into gold; words into meaning	
ego	in Freudian theory, the part of the personality that governs rational behaviour	7
id	in Freudian theory, the unconscious part of the personality that energizes the other parts of the psyche (ego and superego) and demands immediate gratification	
coeval	co-existent; occurring at the same time	
subliminal	subconscious; hidden below the surface of conscious awareness	8
execute	carry out; perform	11
Old Vic	well-known English theatre company	
periods	from the sixteenth to the nineteenth century, a period was a long, complex sentence composed of perfectly balanced main and subordinate clauses	
sociolinguists	academics who study the relationship between language and the way people are organized into social groups (e.g., different kinds of slang)	12
stigma	sign or mark indicating shameful behaviour	
marginality	living on the sidelines; not integrated into mainstream culture	
aesthetics	the study of what is beautiful as distinct from what is functional or useful	13
linguistic dispossession	loss of mastery over one's native language	14
entropy	the tendency toward disorder, chaos	
inarticulateness	inability to express oneself in words	
neurosis	psychological disorder	

Structure and Strategy

1. Which sentence in the first part of this essay (paragraphs 1 to 6) sums up the problem Hoffman is struggling with? What examples does she choose to illustrate her point?

2. Consider the DICTION of this essay. Identify three or four examples of complex, ABSTRACT vocabulary followed by CONCRETE examples or an illustration that clarifies the author's meaning.
3. Paragraphs 8 and 9 contain a short narrative that illustrates the difficulties the author experienced living in the "empty state" between Polish and English. Why is this illustration effective?
4. What examples does Hoffman use to illustrate the sounds and rhythms of spoken language? (See paragraph 11.)
5. What is the topic of paragraph 14? Which sentence in that paragraph most clearly states the topic?

Content and Purpose

1. Identify examples of the words and phrases Hoffman finds difficult as she makes the transition from Polish to English.
2. In paragraph 3, Hoffman says "the problem is that the signifier has become severed from the signified." Explain what she means by this statement.
3. What do you think Hoffman means when she says (paragraph 9) "I don't really exist"? What is the connection between language and identity?
4. In paragraph 10, the author changes her focus from the problems of thinking in a new language to the difficulties of speaking an unfamiliar language. Identify two or three examples Hoffman provides to illustrate her personal difficulties and how she felt about them.
5. Hoffman is concerned with more than the "correctness" of her pronunciation. What is her larger concern? (See paragraphs 11 to 13.) What ANALOGY does she use to illustrate her point?
6. What, according to this essay, is the link between "linguistic dispossession" and violence? (See paragraph 14.) Do you agree with the author?

Suggestions for Writing

1. Have you ever tried to learn a new language? Write an essay based on your experience. Provide examples of the difficulties you encountered while learning to listen to, speak, read, and/or write a new language.
2. Most students hate having their writing corrected; many writers hate being edited. Write an essay explaining how you feel when your "best work" is returned to you covered in red ink, and why you think professional correction makes you feel this way.

3. Explain by means of examples how your language changes depending on the person(s) you are talking/writing to, and what these differences may signify.
4. Explain how cultural assumptions are embodied in the idiom of a language. Show by examples how certain phrases simply do not translate literally from one language to another. What conclusions can you come to about the work of professional translators (e.g., in the courts, on TV broadcast news, for publishers of literary works)?

ADDITIONAL SUGGESTIONS FOR WRITING: EXAMPLE

Choose one of the topics below and write a thesis statement based on it. Develop your thesis statement into an essay by selecting specific examples or one extended example from your own experience to support your KEY IDEAS.

1. Social networking as a positive (*or* negative) force in your life
2. Travel teaches us about ourselves as well as about others.
3. Movies can teach us much about our culture.
4. You are (*or* are not) what you wear.
5. Media violence (e.g., video games) affects (*or* does not affect) the level of violence in our lives.
6. A sports figure who has had a positive (or negative) effect on the culture. (*Or:* Sports figures who have…)
7. Something that drives your parents crazy. (*Or:* Some things that drive…)
8. And example (*or* examples) of cultural differences that can lead to misunderstanding between people
9. A television show (*or* shows) that has influenced the way we look at the world
10. A threat (*or* threats) to democracy in Canada
11. "Good fences make good neighbours." (Robert Frost)
12. "You are not a gadget." (Jaron Lanier)
13. "I believe the world needs more Canada." (Bono)
14. "Tell me his friends and I'll tell you who he is." (Spanish proverb)
15. "The world is a dangerous place—not because of the people who are evil but because of the people who don't do anything about it." (Albert Einstein)

UNIT 3

Process Analysis

WHAT IS PROCESS ANALYSIS?

Process analysis is writing that explains how something happens. It explains the steps or phases of a particular process. For example, the model essay in this unit, "Metamorphosis," explains how a baby learns to talk. It charts the course of a baby's development from birth to eighteen months of age, explaining the stages that she goes through as she develops from a wailing infant to a talking toddler.

WHY DO WE USE PROCESS ANALYSIS?

Process analysis answers the question *how*. It is a familiar pattern of writing. Just think of the websites you consult and the how-to books that people rush to buy. They are full of instructions for improving your looks; your game; your house; your relationship with your spouse, children, parents, boss, pet—or anything else you can think of.

Process analysis is used for two purposes that lead to two different kinds of essays or reports. A **directional process analysis**—the "how-to-do-it" essay—gives readers the directions they need to perform a process themselves, whether it's building a robot or training a dog. One example of a directional process analysis in this unit is Paul Quarrington's "Home Ice," which tells you how to make a backyard ice rink. The other directional process analysis is Richard Poplak's "Loaves and Wishes," which comes complete with a recipe for the bread his father learns to bake.

The second kind of process analysis provides information about how something happens (or happened). Readers of an **informational process analysis** do not want to perform the process they are reading about; they just want to learn how it is (or was) performed. For example, Jeffrey Moussaieff Masson's "Dear Dad" (page 146) describes the fascinating role played by male penguins in the reproductive cycle. Information rather than "how-to" directions is the goal of this kind of process writing. Judy Stoffman's "The Way of All Flesh" explains how the human body ages; Jill Frayne's "Struck by Lightning" explains the natural phenomenon of lightning. Clearly, aging and lightning are occurrences that happen by themselves and, thus, are informational process analyses. (How to age gracefully or avoid being hit by lightning would be examples of directional process analyses.)

Some writers use process analysis as a vehicle for humour or social commentary. The conventional how-to-do-it essay can be funny if a writer provides instructions for something no one wants to do, such as become obese or fail in school. Sarah Walker's "How to Perform a Tracheotomy" (which explains how to save someone from choking by jabbing a hole in his throat) obviously belongs in this category.

HOW DO WE WRITE PROCESS ANALYSIS?

Here are five guidelines for writing an effective process analysis:

1. Think through the whole process carefully and write an outline detailing all the steps involved. If you are writing a directional process analysis, be sure to include any preparatory steps or special equipment the reader should know about.

2. Put the steps of the process into CHRONOLOGICAL ORDER.

3. Write a clear thesis statement. (You need not include a preview of the main steps unless your topic is complex or your instructor specifically requires it.)

4. Write your first draft. Define any specialized or technical terms that may be unfamiliar to your reader. Use TRANSITIONS, or time-markers, to indicate the progression through the steps or stages (*first, next, after,* and so on).

5. Revise your draft carefully. Clarify any steps that are incomplete or confusing, and revise until the whole paper is both clear and interesting.

The model essay that follows is an informational process analysis.

Metamorphosis

Introduction (*creates a scenario and introduces the central analogy*)

Meet newborn Jeanie. Weak and helpless as a caterpillar, Jeanie's only defence against hunger and pain is the one sound she can make at will: crying. Eighteen months later, Jeanie will be a busy toddler who asks questions, expresses opinions, and even makes jokes. From helplessness to assertiveness: how does this wondrous transformation take place?

Thesis
statement

First stage
(developed by
definition and
factual details
of speech
development)

Transition
(continues the
analogy)
Second stage
Note definitions
and examples

To discover how we learn to speak, let's follow Jeanie as she develops from infant to toddler, from caterpillar to butterfly.

Infancy, the first stage of language development, literally means "not able to speak." For the first six months of her life, Jeanie isn't able to talk, but she can respond to speech. Shortly after birth, she'll turn her head toward the sound of a voice. By two weeks of age, she will prefer the sound of a human voice to non-human sounds. Between two and four months, she will learn to distinguish the voices of her caregivers from those of strangers, and she knows whether those voices are speaking soothingly or angrily. By the time she is two months old, Jeanie will have learned to coo as well as cry, and she coos happily when people smile and talk to her. Now she can express contentment as well as discomfort. At around four months of age, Jeanie's happy sounds become more varied and sophisticated: she registers delight on a scale ranging from throaty chuckles to belly laughs. All this vocal activity is actually a rehearsal for speech. As Jeanie cries and coos and laughs, her vocal cords, tongue, lips, and brain are developing the coordination required for her to speak her first words.

At six or seven months of age, Jeanie is no longer an infant; she's moved on to the *baby* stage of language development. Like a pupa in its cocoon, Jeanie is undergoing a dramatic but (to all but her closest observers) invisible change. She looks at her mother when someone says "Mama." She responds to simple directions: she'll clap her hands or wave "bye-bye" on request. By the time she is a year old, Jeanie will recognize at least twenty words. The sounds Jeanie produces at this stage are called *babbling,* a word that technically describes a series of reduplicated single consonant and vowel sounds and probably derives its name from a common example: "ba-ba-ba-ba." About halfway through this stage of her development, Jeanie progresses to *variegated babbling,* in which sounds change between syllables. "Da-dee, da-dee, da-dee," she burbles, to the delight of her father (who doesn't know that Jeanie cannot yet connect the sounds she makes to the meaning they represent to others). But by the time Jeanie celebrates her first birthday, the variety, rhythm, and tone of her babbling have become more varied, and her family begins to sense consistent meaning in the sounds she makes. "Bye-bye!" is as clearly meant as it is spoken—Jeanie wants to get going!

Third stage (developed with description, examples, dialogue)

Jeanie's recognition of the link between sounds and meanings signals her entry into the *toddler* stage—twelve to eighteen months. At eighteen months, Jeanie will understand approximately 250 words—more than ten times the number she understood at twelve months. Most of what she says are single-word utterances: "kitty" for a cat in her picture book, "nana" for the bananas she loves to squish and eat. But even single words now function as complex communications depending on the intonation Jeanie gives them. "Kitty?" she inquires, looking at a picture of a tiger. She demands a "nana!" for lunch. About halfway through the toddler stage, Jeanie begins to link words together to make sentences. "Mama gone," she cries when her mother leaves for work. "Me no go bed," she tells her father. Though it marks the beginning of trouble for her parents, this development marks a triumph for Jeanie. She has broken out of the cocoon of passive comprehension into the world of active participation.

Reference to metamorphosis analogy contributes to unity

Conclusion (refers back to introduction and completes analogy)

In less than two years, Jeanie has metamorphosed from wailing newborn to babbling baby to talking toddler. Through language, she is becoming her own woman in the world. Now she can fly.

How to Perform a Tracheotomy°

SARAH WALKER

Sarah Walker is a New York City writer and comedian whose book *Really, You've Done Enough: A Parents' Guide to Stop Parenting Their Adult Child Who Still Needs Their Money But Not Their Advice* was published in 2007. She writes the "Sarah Walker Shows You How" column for *McSweeney's Internet Tendency*. She has written for *The Daily Show with Jon Stewart*, *Late Night with Conan O'Brien*, and *The Late Show with David Letterman*. She is also one-half of the sketch duo Walker and Cantrell (www.walkerandcantrell.com).

First, go to a fancy restaurant that has waiters with accents who   1
wear tuxedos and a rolling dessert table. Be with a significant
other and clink your glasses of red wine while staring lovingly at each other, across the single tapered white candle in the
middle of the table. Then, notice a person who is choking on food,
probably a fancy meat. This person should be a husky middle-aged
man, preferably balding, whose equally husky, curly-haired wife is
looking on, horrified, clutching her pearl necklace and screeching,
"Somebody help him! He's choking!"

Excuse yourself from your date, throw your white linen napkin   2
down on the white linen tablecloth, and rush over to the choking
man. Attempt to give him the Heimlich°, but when this fails, calmly
realize what must be done. The fancy meat is lodged in his throat and
this man requires a tracheotomy. Always address the wife as Susan.

"Susan, Earl requires a tracheotomy." Always address the   3
choking victim as Earl.

Assure Susan that you are a doctor and be sure to have made   4
up a doctor badge that you can show her. It should be made of
pure gold with something like five snakes engraved on it. You
probably aren't a doctor. If you are, good for you. That must've
taken a long time. You must be very proud and possibly wealthy.

Susan will nod her head in assent, too scared to speak. Place   5
the back of your hand on her cheek and say, "Don't worry, Susan. I
didn't go to doctor school for 11 years to let Earl die." Then lay Earl
on his back on the floral-carpeted floor.

Make sure a hushed silence falls over the restaurant as waiters   6
and diners and kitchen staff peeking out of the kitchen look nervously on. Remove from your breast pocket a custom-engraved
Tiffany sterling-silver pen, which was given to you on your 17th

---

First published at *McSweeney's Internet Tendency*: www.mcsweeneys.net. Reprinted
by permission of the author.

birthday and which you always carry around for such occasions. It should say something like "Happy Birthday, [*your name*]" and then the date of your birth.

7   Before you go to the restaurant, but only after you've secured your paisley ascot°, replace the pen tip with an X-Acto knife. Raise the pen above your head and click the button so that the X-Acto knife pops out and wait for a gasp from the crowd and for a young boy to drop his fork and have it clatter on his plate. Twist the "pen-knife" just so, so that the candlelight gleams off it. It would be nice if, when the light hits it, there could be a *ding* sound effect. Maybe you could arrange to have your significant other tap a wine glass with a fork at that moment.

8   Then, in one swift movement, jab the pen into Earl's neck, more or less around the throatish area. Earl will pop up, gasping, the pen dangling comically from his neck. Do not be distracted by this, as you will have to catch Susan, who, with her hand on her forehead, will be falling into a swoon.

9   Wait for applause, then pull the smelling salts out of your other breast pocket and revive Susan. Then signal to the waiter and say, "Check, please!" Pause for relieved laughter and applause from the crowd.

10   Be prepared for a bear hug from post-smelling-salts Susan. And for an endless pumping handshake from Earl, who will also give you $200 because he's a wealthy industrialist and carries hundred-dollar bills in his pockets. Wear an extra shirt so the hearty pats on the back from the kitchen staff and waiters don't hurt you too much. Develop calluses on your hands beforehand by doing a lot of pull-ups, so all the handshakes you receive from your fellow diners don't chafe your carefully manicured hands.

11   No need to bring your wallet, as dinner will obviously be on the house, so make sure you've ordered the most expensive things on the menu. Plus, you have two hundo from Earl. Don't forget to ask for your pen back.

Words and Meanings

Title	tracheotomy	an emergency procedure performed when someone has an obstruction in the throat and cannot breathe: the act of cutting through the trachea (tube that leads from the larynx to the lungs) to admit air
Paragraph 2	Heimlich	the Heimlich manoeuvre, an emergency technique used to dislodge a piece of food from the throat; involves a sudden upward

thrust just below the rib cage to force air from the lungs

ascot   a silk scarf tucked loosely into the neck of a   7
dress shirt; in North America, usually associated with affectation or showing off

Structure and Strategy

1. Into how many steps does this essay divide the process of performing a tracheotomy?
2. Where does the supposed tracheotomy take place? What kind of descriptive details give you this impression?
3. Why is the piece written in the second person (e.g., "Assure Susan that you are a doctor")?
4. What steps in this process are misplaced (that is, steps you are told about only after you would have had to complete them)? Why do you think the author "misplaced" these instructions?
5. What is the TONE of this essay?

Content and Purpose

1. How much of this essay did you read before you realized you were reading SATIRE? What is the author satirizing?
2. Who are "you" with in the first paragraph? What are the two of "you" doing?
3. Who are Susan and Earl? What happens to Earl?
4. What do "you" do to relieve Earl's problem?
5. What do the following details suggest: the pure gold "doctor badge" (para 4), the "custom-engraved Tiffany sterling-silver pen" (para 6), and "paisley ascot" (para 7)? What impression do they give you of the narrator?
6. Who is watching your heroic feat? What is their reaction?
7. What details in the piece give it a cinematic feel, making it sound like a skit from *Saturday Night Live* or other television comedy show?

Suggestions for Writing

1. Write a satirical process analysis that explains how to do a task that no one who is not a qualified professional would *ever* do.
2. Write a process analysis that provides directions about how to pass yourself off as something you're not (e.g., rich, stupid, a biker, a teacher, a gang member, a lawyer, a shopaholic).

Loaves and Wishes

RICHARD POPLAK

Richard Poplak was born in Johannesburg, South Africa, in 1973 and immigrated to Canada with his family a few short months before Nelson Mandela's release from prison in 1990. He trained as a filmmaker at Montreal's Concordia University and has produced and directed numerous short films, music videos, and commercials. Poplak's writing has been published in *The Walrus, THIS Magazine, Toronto Life, The Globe and Mail, CBC.ca Arts Online, Bicycling,* and *Maverick.* His books include *Ja, No, Man: Growing Up White in Apartheid-Era South Africa* (2007); *The Sheikh's Batmobile: In Pursuit of American Pop Culture in the Muslim World* (2009); and *Kenk: A Graphic Portrait* (2010), a graphic novel about a notorious Toronto bicycle thief.

1   "**D**on't bother asking," said my father before removing the tea towel from a hunched shape on his kitchen table. "This recipe dies with me." With a flourish I suspected he'd learned from a cooking show, he whipped away the veil, revealing a small brown oval, pocked at one end with what looked like furious acne, and scarred at the other by a vicious gash. With a mental lurch, I tried to reconcile the smell in the kitchen—the warm, earthy tang of active yeast—with the disfigured lump on the table. My father, the dentist, a man who back in the old country lacked the kitchen skills even to open a can of beans, mistook my bafflement° for awe. He stood straight, his hand pointing to the creation, his grey moustache stretched wide over a large, cocksure grin. "How about that, eh?"

2   For the better part of a decade—since my family's arrival in Toronto from Johannesburg in December 1989—my father had been on a desperate quest. It was a search that had produced 10 years' worth of dead ends, too many frustrations to count, the purchase of a bread-making machine in the late '90s, and now this. My father was looking for something so South African that it could not possibly be found anywhere else. My father was looking for Government Brown.

3   With its perfectly firm crust, slightly blackened base and nutty, downy-soft interior, Government Brown had few detractors. One could chase half a loaf with a bottle of cold Coca-Cola, as the local blacks did, or hollow out the dough by the fistful and stuff the crust with a curried meat concoction devised in the littoral° cafés (pronounced *keh*-fees) of Natal° and called—no one can say why—

Reprinted by permission of the author.

Bunny Chow. My aunt Velda organized martial rows of sardines on thin-sliced Government Brown; my mother's specialty was molten, gooey, toasted cheddar cheese and tomato sandwiches. Everyone in our household—our maid, Bushy; our gardener, Manson; even our dog, Chomps—ate at least a hunk a day. My father, however, was the bread's biggest acolyte°—so much so that he happily drove to the corner café every afternoon after work to buy our family's daily supply. (The only other victual°-related task he ever performed was the Sunday afternoon ritual of badly charring meat on the barbecue, or *braai*.) He never missed a day.

These humble porterman's° loaves were a staple in township shanty and suburban manse° alike, at least in part because of the price. In the 1980s, a loaf cost the equivalent of a quarter—this in a country where blacks earned a couple of dollars a day. The bread was heavily subsidized by the apartheid° regime, an act of largesse° justified with choice passages from the Bible and motivated by Machiavellian self-interest. The black labour class that did the country's heavy lifting required cheap, high-carbohydrate sustenance; our rulers had no choice but to provide the indigent° with the staff of life. And, in a strange twist, even though Government Brown was an industrially made food product used to sustain a bitterly exploited racial underclass, to this day it remains the best industrially made food product I have ever tasted. "Who needs fancy restaurants," my father would ask between bites smeared with Marmite°, "when you have this?" And it was this bread, imbued° with such bitter history and coated with the patina° of Biblical righteousness, that my father was searching for. His quest began almost as soon as the sliding doors of Pearson's Terminal 2 opened onto our icy new world. 4

There were long, dark years after we arrived, where my father trawled° the city's bakeries and grocery stores, hoping each time he walked into another shop that he might finally find the taste of home. But nothing came close. "No, man," he'd complain, "it's all too sweet." And after what felt like an eon° of frustrated searching, he realized he would never find Government Brown in his new world. So he was forced by circumstance to take matters into his own hands. Thus, the bread machine. "Now we'll see," he threatened no one in particular. 5

His first hurdle, after those early botch jobs°, was to approximate the look of an actual loaf of bread. He consulted reams of recipe booklets; he spent hours on the Internet, perusing bread-making sites for hints, suggestions. He read tips from hausfraus° in Manitoba, Arkansas, Chile, Spain and Pakistan. His loaves were living things—they grew taller, wider. They tasted nuttier, grainier, their dough became chewier. Sometimes they were wenge° dark, 6 occasionally they were pine blond. "We're getting there," he'd say. "We're getting there."

7   And yet, South African wheat, harvested under limpid° autumnal Orange Free State° skies, made for perfect whole-wheat flour. Hardy and par-bleached by the sun, it was key to Government Brown's trademark nuttiness. My father had no access to Free State flour, nor could he know the precise quantities of salt, water and flour Government Brown's bakers used (the apartheid regime was not a transparent one).

8   There was another problem, one that troubled me about so many of the vespers° of home that we chased in those early years. My father was, of course, trying to bake a comfort food—a way to link him and, by extension, us with our homeland. But nostalgia for apartheid-era South Africa—an impulse almost every white South African émigré succumbs to at some point—is imbued with uncomfortable implications.

9   It was a world, however, that was fading. Several years after that first misshapen loaf—and more than a decade removed from his last taste of Government Brown—my father was baking a steadily collapsing memory. Every bite of his own bread took him further from the taste he had originally set out to duplicate. Consistency in the kitchen, despite the rigorous scientific proportions baking demands, had never been his métier°. Slowly, without fully realizing what he was doing, he started to revel in his bread's caprice°. Where Government Brown was the same bread day to day, week to week, my father's bread changed with such variables as his mood, the barometric pressure, the general state of the universe; its taste ranged from yeasty robustness° to grainy understatement, its texture from bulletproof-dense to wispy fluffiness. All this had at first seemed so preposterous—my father, the baker?—but slowly, I came to understand that his enthusiasm was no mere passing derangement°. Every time he presented a loaf, whipping away its tea towel shroud, the smell emanating from it now almost entirely analogous with real bread, I'd well up with a surge of emotion. This bread, I now know, is a gift, and a link.

10   Seventeen years since we left South Africa, my father is still uninterested in leaving a culinary° legacy. His recipe dies with him. Stuffed with nuts, raisins and whole grains, his bread is now in line with the fashion of the day. Prunes, molasses, organic milled flour, wheat grass, maple syrup, beer—any damn thing! He'll send me home with a half loaf, packed alongside toasting instructions; he now feeds the family.

11   Government Brown, like so much of the old country, has faded almost completely from memory—and so has the freight° that came

with it. And after a lengthy quest for a bread he was never able to duplicate, my father knows his way around a kitchen all too well. "Here," my father, the baker, says to me, dousing a doorstop slice in thick goops of Marmite. "Eat! Have another slice."

Slice of Life
¼ cup raw almonds
¼ cup pitted prunes (about five)
2 tbsp wheat bran
2 tbsp oat bran
2 tbsp Red River cereal
2 tbsp large-flake oats

2 cups white flour
2 cups whole wheat flour
1 tsp salt
1 tbsp molasses
3 tsp active dry yeast
$1\frac{2}{3}$ cups warm (100–110°F) water
1 tbsp olive oil

1. Pulse almonds, prunes, wheat bran, oat bran and Red River in a food processor until coarsely ground. Stir in oats. Combine with flours and salt. Reserve.

2. Stir molasses and yeast into water. Let stand 10 minutes or until foamy. Pour into bowl of a stand mixer. Add two cups flour mixture and blend on low speed using paddle attachment. Continue adding flour mixture one cup at a time until dough is sticky but not overly wet. Add additional white flour, two tbsp at a time, only if dough is too wet.

3. Switch to dough hook attachment and knead on medium speed four to five minutes or until dough forms a smooth, elastic ball. Add olive oil and knead one more minute.

4. Scrape onto a floured countertop and knead 10 to 15 times. Shape into a ball and place in a large, lightly oiled bowl. Cover and set in a warm place to rise for 45 minutes or until doubled in bulk.

5. Punch dough and scrape onto a floured countertop. Knead 10 to 15 times, then divide the dough in half and knead each half 10 to 15 times. Shape dough balls into ovals and place well apart on a parchment-lined baking sheet. Cover loosely and set in a warm place to rise for 30 minutes or until doubled in bulk.

6. Preheat oven to 375°F. Brush each loaf with water; make three slashes in the top of each loaf with a sharp knife. Bake 25 to 35 minutes or until golden and bread sounds hollow when tapped on the bottom. Cool on a rack.

Makes 2 loaves.

Words and Meanings

Paragraph		
1	bafflement	state of being puzzled, bewildered
3	littoral	seaside
	Natal	a region in South Africa
	acolyte	devoted follower
	victual	food
4	porterman	worker
	manse	large home, mansion
	apartheid	policy of racial, social, and economic segregation in South Africa from 1948–1994
	largesse	generosity (meant ironically)
	indigent	extremely poor people
	Marmite	a spread made from yeast extract, as popular in Britain and South Africa as peanut butter is in North America
	imbued	stained, dyed, permeated
	patina	surface shine that results from long usage (usually associated with precious metals)
5	trawled	thoroughly searched through
	eon	long period of time; thousands of years
6	botch jobs	(usually "botched") poor jobs, spoiled by lack of skill
	hausfraus	(German) housewives
	wenge	very dark brown (the name of a heavy, dark wood)
7	limpid	clear
	Orange Free State	region of South Africa
8	vespers	reminders

métier	work for which one has special ability	9
caprice	unpredictability	
robustness	full-flavoured density	
derangement	madness	
culinary	having to do with cooking	10
freight	metaphorical baggage	11

Structure and Strategy

1. What strategy does Poplak use in his INTRODUCTION? Where else in the essay is this device used?
2. Identify three phrases used to describe the loaf of bread in the first paragraph (e.g., "vicious gash"). What kind of impressions do these descriptions give you?
3. What is the ALLUSION in the title?
4. Consider the directional process analysis that ends this essay, that is, the recipe. Is it clear and complete? Could you bake a loaf of Government Brown?

Content and Purpose

1. What is Poplak's father doing in paragraph 1? How long has he had an interest in this activity? What does he do for a living?
2. When did Poplak and his family arrive in Toronto? Where did they come from?
3. How did different populations in South Africa eat Government Brown? (See paragraph 3.)
4. What is the political shame that lurked behind the "heavily subsidized bread" sold during the apartheid regime in South Africa?
5. What is Poplak's attitude toward the country of his birth?
6. What process does Poplak's father undertake to try to find the Government Brown bread that he loves? Why does he miss the bread so much?
7. Why is it so difficult to find or duplicate Government Brown in the Poplak family's new home, in their "icy new world"?
8. What is the "freight" (paragraph 11) that came with Government Brown? What is happening to that "freight" twenty years after the end of apartheid?
9. Is Poplak's father satisfied with the bread he bakes? Does he intend to pass on the recipe to his family? Why or why not?

Suggestions for Writing

1. If you come from another culture—or have family members who do—write an essay about a special food or dish that you cannot find or duplicate in Canada. Describe the process of making the food, and include details that make it clear to the reader why the food is something that you or your family long for.

2. Write a directional process analysis that details the instructions for making a special comfort food.

Dear Dad

JEFFREY MOUSSAIEFF MASSON

Jeffrey Moussaieff Masson (b. 1941) taught Sanskrit and Indian Studies at the University of Toronto from 1969 to 1980. After graduating from the Toronto Institute of Psychoanalysis in 1978, he served as projects director of the Sigmund Freud Archives. He has demonstrated his fascination with animal psychology in such books as *When Elephants Weep* (1994), *Dogs Never Lie About Love* (1997), and *The Nine Emotional Lives of Cats* (2002). Writing *The Pig Who Sang to the Moon: The Emotional World of Farm Animals* (2003) turned him into a vegan, a topic he explores in *The Face on Your Plate: The Truth about Food* (2009). Masson currently lives with his family in New Zealand.

1   One reason that so many of us are fascinated by penguins is that they resemble us. They walk upright, the way we do, and, like us, they are notoriously curious creatures. No doubt this accounts for our fondness for cartoon images of penguins dressed up at crowded parties, but as fathers, penguins are our superiors.

2   Unlike mammals, male birds can experience pregnancy as an intimate matter, with the father in many species helping to sit (brood) the egg. After all, a male can brood an egg as well as a female can. But in no other species does it reach this extreme.

3   The emperors usually wait for good weather to copulate, any time between April 10 and June 6. They separate themselves somewhat from the rest of the colony and face each other, remaining still for a time. Then the male bends his head, contracts his abdomen,

Reprinted by permission of the author.

and shows the female the spot on his belly where he has a flap of skin that serves as a kind of pouch for the egg and baby chick. This stimulates the female to do the same. Their heads touch, and the male bends his head down to touch the female's pouch. Both begin to tremble visibly. Then the female lies face down on the ice, partially spreads her wings and opens her legs. The male climbs onto her back and they mate for 10 to 30 seconds.

They stay together afterward constantly, leaning against one another when they are standing up, or if they lie down, the female will glide her head under that of her mate. About a month later, between May 1 and June 12, the female lays a single greenish-white egg. French researchers noted that the annual dates on which the colony's first egg was laid varied by only eight days in 16 years of observation. Weighing almost a pound, and measuring up to 131 millimetres long and 86 millimetres wide, this is one of the largest eggs of any bird. The male stays by the female's side, his eyes fixed on her pouch. As soon as he sees the egg, he sings a variation of what has been called the "ecstatic" display by early observers, and she too takes up the melody.

She catches the egg with her wings before it touches the ice and places it on her feet. Both penguins then sing in unison, staring at the egg for up to an hour. The female then slowly walks around the male, who gently touches the egg on her feet with his beak, making soft groans, his whole body trembling. He shows the female his pouch. Gently she puts the egg down on the ice and just as gently he rolls it with his beak between his large, black, powerfully clawed feathered feet, and then, with great difficulty, hoists the egg onto the surface of his feet. He rests back on his heels so that his feet make the least contact with the ice. The transfer of the egg is a delicate operation. If it falls on the ice and rolls away, it can freeze in minutes or it might even be stolen. If it is snatched away by a female penguin who failed to find a mate, its chances of survival are slight because the intruder will eventually abandon the egg, since she has no mate to relieve her.

With the egg transfer successfully completed, the happy couple both sing. The male parades about in front of the female, showing her his pouch with the egg inside. This thick fold, densely feathered on the outside and bare inside, now completely covers the egg and keeps it at about 95 degrees Fahrenheit, even when the temperature falls to 95 degrees below zero.

The female begins to back away, each time a little farther. He tries to follow her, but it is hard, since he is balancing the egg. Suddenly she is gone, moving purposefully toward the open sea.

She is joined by the other females in the colony, who, by the end of May or June, have all left for the ocean almost 100 kilometres away. The females have fasted for nearly a month and a half, and have lost anywhere between 17 to 30 per cent of their total weight. They are in urgent need of food.

8   The female must renew her strength and vitality so that she can return with food for her chick. Going to the sea, she takes the shortest route to reach a polynya (open water surrounded by ice). Penguins appear to be able to navigate by the reflection of the clouds on the water, using what has been called a "water sky."

9   The male penguin, who has also been fasting, is now left with the egg balanced on his feet. The first egg was laid on the first of May; a chick will emerge in August. Since the seasons are reversed south of the equator, full winter has arrived, with many violent blizzards and the lowest temperatures of the year. Emperor penguins are well adapted to the almost unimaginable cold of these 24-hour Antarctic nights: Their plumage is waterproof, windproof, flexible and renewed annually. They may not need tents, but as soon as the bad weather starts, generally in June, the males need some protection from the bitter cold, and nearly all of them find it by forming a *tortue,* which is a throng of very densely packed penguins. When the storms come they move in close to one another, shoulder to shoulder, and form a circle. The middle of the tortue is unusually warm and one would think that every penguin fights to be at the epicentre of warmth. But in fact what looks like an immobile mass is really a very slowly revolving spiral. The constantly shifting formation is such that every penguin, all the while balancing that single precious egg on his feet, eventually winds up in the middle of the tortue, only to find himself later at the periphery.

10   What early French explorers noticed during the two- to three-month incubation period is an almost preternatural calm among the males. This is no doubt necessitated by the long fast that is ahead of them. Many of them have already fasted, like the females, for two months or more, and must now face another two months of fasting. And moving about with an egg balanced on one's feet is difficult at the best of times.

11   The only time a father will abandon an egg is if he has reached the maximum limit of his physiological° ability to fast, and would die if he did not seek food. Not a small number of eggs are left for this reason, and it would seem that in each case the female is late in returning.

12   In July or August, after being gone for almost three months, the female emperor returns from the sea, singing as she penetrates various groups of birds, searching for her mate and her chick

or egg. The males do not move, but make small peeping noises. When she finds her partner, she sings, she makes little dance steps, then she goes quiet and both birds can remain immobile for up to 10 minutes. Then they begin to move around one another. The female fixes her eyes on the incubatory pouch of her partner, while her excitement grows visibly. Finally, if it is the right bird, the male allows the egg to fall gently to the ice, whereupon the female takes it and then turns her back to the male, to whom, after a final duet, she becomes completely indifferent. The male becomes increasingly irritated, stares at his empty pouch, pecks at it with his beak, lifts up his head, groans, and then pecks the female. She shows no further interest in him and eventually he leaves for the open sea, to break his long fast. The whole affair has lasted about 80 minutes. . . .

The miracle is that the mothers usually return on the day their chicks hatch. How is it, one wonders, that the female emperor penguin is able to return just in time for the birth of her chick? As Alexander Skutch notes in his wonderful book, *The Minds of Birds*, it is improbable that she has consciously counted the 63 days or whatever the exact number is between the laying of her egg and the hatching of her chick. "Some subconscious process, physiological or mental, was evidently summing the days to prompt the birds to start homeward when the proper number had elapsed." 13

If the egg has hatched before her arrival and the male already has a chick between his legs, the female is even more excited to hear it peep, and quickly removes it from the male. She immediately regurgitates food to the chick. If she is late in coming, the male, in spite of his near starvation, has a final resource: He regurgitates into the beak of his peeping newborn a substance known as penguin milk, similar to pigeon's milk, or crop milk, which is secreted from the lining of his esophagus. The secretion is remarkably rich, containing essential amino acids, much like the milk of marine mammals such as seals and whales. These feedings allow the young birds to survive for up to two weeks after hatching. Many of these males have now fasted for four and a half months, and have lost up to half of their body weight. It is a sight to see the well-nourished, sleek, brilliantly feathered, healthy-looking females arrive, and the emaciated°, dirty, tired males leave. 14

How difficult it is for us to understand the emotions involved in these events. Yet it is hard to resist the anthropomorphic urge. Obviously the male emperor is aware of the loss of what has, after all, been almost a part of his body for two to three months. Is he disappointed, bewildered, relieved, or are his feelings so remote from our own (not inferior, mind you, just different) that we cannot 15 imagine them? We would groan, too, under such circumstances, but the meaning of a penguin's groan is still opaque° to us. Yet we, too, are fathers and mothers with babies to protect and comfort, negotiating meals and absences and other obligations, just like our Antarctic cousins. Sometimes, when we are overwhelmed by an emotion, we are hard-pressed to express ourselves. If penguin fathers could speak about this moment in their lives, perhaps they would be at a similar loss for words. Perhaps the songs and groans of the male penguin are all the expression they need.

Words and Meanings

Paragraph

11	physiological	having to do with the physical functioning of a living creature
14	emaciated	thin, starved
15	opaque	not transparent; difficult to figure out

Structure and Strategy

1. What kind of attention-getter does Masson use in the INTRODUCTION (paragraphs 1 and 2)?
2. What is Masson's THESIS? Is it implied or stated in the essay?
3. Which paragraphs are developed primarily by means of numerical facts and statistics? Why is this a useful strategy for explaining the KEY IDEAS of these paragraphs? Are there any factual details the essay doesn't provide that you would have been interested to learn about?
4. How is the key idea of paragraph 13 developed?
5. The DICTION of this essay combines scientific terms with words and phrases more commonly associated with human emotion, such as "happy couple" in paragraph 6 and "increasingly irritated" in paragraph 12. Find other examples of diction that Masson uses to support the ANALOGY he draws between penguins and humans. Why do you think he uses the penguin–human analogy to develop his process analysis? Do you find this analogy interesting or off-putting? Why?

Content and Purpose

1. In two or three sentences, summarize Masson's PURPOSE in this essay.
2. In this analysis of the emperor penguins' reproductive cycle, which parts of the process are described in paragraphs 3 through 8, 9 through 11, and 12 through 14?

3. How do emperor penguins mate? What physical characteristic makes it possible for the male to "experience pregnancy as an intimate matter" (paragraph 2)?
4. Why do the female penguins temporarily abandon their eggs and mates? What happens when the females return?
5. What kind of "male bonding" takes place among the males during the females' absence? What purpose is served by the *tortue*?
6. Identify three reproductive behaviours that penguins have in common with humans. Identify three behaviours that are significantly different.
7. What is the mystery at the core of the essay's CONCLUSION (paragraph 15)? What do you think is the source of "the songs and groans of the male penguin"?
8. What is the author's attitude toward the creatures he writes about? Identify three or four examples to support your opinion.
9. From an evolutionary perspective, how is the emperor penguin's mating and chick-rearing process adaptive? (See Helena Cronin's "The Evolution of Evolution," on page 275, for an explanation of this concept.)

Suggestions for Writing

1. Write an essay about the role of a father in his child's life. What are the essential tasks of fatherhood?
2. Write an essay about being a caregiver. Describe a situation in which you have cared for someone on an ongoing basis. What does this narrative reveal about you, the caregiver?
3. When people attribute human characteristics and feelings to animals or things they are engaging in *anthropomorphism*. Write an essay that provides one or more examples of anthropomorphism. Why do you suppose people anthropomorphize? Are there any dangers in attributing human feelings to animal behaviours? If so, what are they?

Home Ice

PAUL QUARRINGTON

Paul Quarrington (1953–2010) was an acclaimed novelist, playwright, screenwriter, journalist, filmmaker, songwriter, musician, and educator. He was a prolific writer, publishing ten novels, including *Whale Music,* for which he won the 1989 Governor General's Literary Award, *King Leary* (1987), *The Spirit Cabinet* (1999), *Galveston* (2004), and *The Ravine* (2008). His non-fiction writing runs to more than five books, as well as numerous plays, screenplays, and magazine articles. He was frontman, vocalist, and rhythm guitarist for the band Porkbelly Futures. His final book, *Cigar Box Banjo,* published posthumously, is a moving memoir of a life lived in music and words.

1   Think of it as wintry gardening. Better yet, think of it as nocturnal thaumaturgy°. Focus on the magical aspects, for on a more worldly level, we are about to discuss standing outside on the most bitter of nights with a spurting garden hose in your hand, likely frozen there forever. We are about to discuss making a backyard skating rink.

2   It seems to me that the backyard rink ranks right up there with frozen duck ponds and ice-locked rivers. Which is to say, they have a home not only on the earth but also in our frostbitten imaginations. Dreams of Stanley Cups and figure-skating championships are born there. Local arenas are nice enough places, I suppose, but the important thing is the sense of community. When I think of local arenas, I think of the benches, the snack bars, the people huddled together eating cold hot dogs and blowing on cups of hot chocolate. The ice itself is nothing special—it is quiet and subdued, not like the unruly ice you find in the backyard rink. Curlers and assorted Celts call the outdoor variety "roaring ice." The blades of skates produce sharp-edged howls. The ice of a backyard rink is welted and scarred and unable to smooth the wrinkled face of the planet. It is elemental, having as much claim to the land as rocks or wind.

3   That is why the process is not really so much "making" or "constructing" a backyard rink; it is more along the lines of allowing one to come into being, a sort of shivering midwifery. Some people conceive of the process as imposing the rink on the ground, which results in that most mundane and dreary objection to the backyard skating rink: it will ruin the grass. That is not true. You don't have to take my word for it. I went and asked Peter Hayward, a landscaper/gardener here in Orillia, Ontario, where

"Home Ice" by Paul Quarrington. Reprinted by permission of The Cooke Agency.

the backyards are huge and backyard rinks commonplace. "No, it won't ruin the grass," he assured me, although after a moment of judicious and professional musing, he added, "Might make it grow a bit *funny*." What he meant was that the grass may grow in opposing directions in the spring—but only for a time.

Funny grass is a small price to pay. This is something you can do for your children, something meaningful. The magic will not be lost upon them. They will be delighted that a field of ice has bloomed during the night. They will stare at it and think, "Geez, Dad [or Mom] must have frozen his [or her] butt off!" They will be right. There is little point sugarcoating this truth. If you can't stand the cold, stay in the kitchen. 4

I propose to pass on the recipe for the definitive, the quintessential, the perfect backyard skating rink. I did not arrive at such a recipe without a lot of help. I turned to my friend Peter Hayman (not to be confused with Peter Hayward, although this, perhaps, cannot be helped), a Toronto filmmaker and father of three young boys. He was led to make a rink mostly because he remembered one from his childhood: "Also, there's a rink at the end of our street that the city is supposed to keep up, and, of course, they never do. A little thaw, and it's wiped out." I have skated on Hayman's rink and know it to be first-class. (I have a simple test: any ice that does not immediately flip me onto my dustcover is first-class.) I also received a lot of information from Ronn Hartviksen, an art teacher who lives in Thunder Bay. Hartviksen is the creator of perhaps the most ambitious and beautiful backyard rink in the world, a huge thing (about 65 by 110 feet) that has achieved almost legendary status in the hockey-playing community. The rink is called the "Bean Pot," a nod to Boston and the Boston Bruins, Hartviksen's favourite hockey team. An ice artist, he has put the team's distinctive "B" at centre ice. 5

When Dave King was preparing the Canadian team for the 1988 Olympics, he made sure the players found time to visit Hartviksen's place and skate on the Bean Pot. Similarly, he had the team skate on the Ottawa Canal. Coach King, a man who takes pains to seem reasonable and sedate°, sometimes talks about "the romance of the backyard rink" and hints there is something very important to be discovered out on that ice. 6

"The indoor rink," opines King, "is a good place to develop technical skills. But the outdoor rink is the place to acquire a real love for the game. In the new generation of hockey players, this is missing." Despite unpredictable chinooks° in Calgary, where King lives, he continues to make his own backyard rink. Lastly, I went to the guru of the backyard rink, the man who made what is surely the most famous backyard rink in the world, Walter Gretzky°. 7

8   If you are going to make a backyard rink, decide early in the season, well before winter is actually in sight. This is the easy part, walking outside and choosing the likeliest site. It may be that you have a smallish backyard and are therefore simply going to flood the whole thing. Others may be faced with a larger expanse and should select some portion of it. The guiding principle should arise from the fact that you are going to have to shovel, resurface and otherwise groom your backyard rink, so you should keep it to a manageable size. Twenty by forty feet seems reasonable: large enough for skaters to manoeuvre, even to play a spirited, if congested, game of shinny, but small enough to care for.

9   A prime consideration is flatness. It is not necessary that the ground be perfectly smooth (you will be surprised at how hilly and full of cavities your lawn really is), but there is no getting around the fact that it must be level. Some depressions can, of course, be built up with snow, and small rises will just become part of the rink (I can recall a section of a rink long ago that would supply me with a quick burst of speed, alarming, not to mention astounding, everyone else on the ice), but a slope, even a gentle one, will undermine all your best efforts.

10   The last consideration is proximity° to a water source. Tapping into an inside source is best. If you can run a hose into the basement, for example, and hook up with the washing-machine taps, you will reap a number of benefits. Remember that no nozzle/hose connection is perfect, and imagine some of the nasty things that could happen at an outside connection—such as finding the thing encased in a block of ice. Even if you avoid nightly chipping and hacking, any outside terminal is going to require a bucket or two of hot water just to get the tap cranked. So if you can get to the water inside, so much the better, especially because, in the maintenance stages, you can employ the hot water for resurfacing, a technique I call "the poor man's Zamboni" (a machine used to resurface the ice in arenas). My own experience has taught me the value of hot water to promote a smooth ice surface. Curiously, none of the authorities I talked to used the method.

11   But let's not worry about maintenance right now; let's get the thing started. Just a couple of quick points here: you probably lack enough hose, because you are used to pulling it up the centre of the lawn. It is now necessary to pull the hose around the outside of a 20-by-40-foot rectangle (you must be able to stand at any point around the perimeter°, hose in hand), so go out and buy another section. It must be a good-quality, thick, heavy rubber hose, because plastic ones are likely to crack open when the world is hung about with ice spikes.

Having selected the site, make sure the ground is properly tended, which means mowing and raking. If you don't, you might face what proved to be the bane of my childhood backyard rinks: errant° blades of grass popping through the ice surface. I know this does not seem likely or even possible, but believe me, little green Ninjas will sprout up and flip you onto your backside. So give your lawn a marine cut late in the fall. 12

Here is an optional step, depending on where you live. Ronn Hartviksen—who, you will recall, resides in Thunder Bay—says that sometimes in late fall, he will hose down the naked earth. It's cold enough to freeze, and he has a layer of black ice for his rink's foundation. In other, more southerly places, watering your lawn late fall serves no purpose except to demonstrate to your neighbours that you are fairly strange, so they will not think twice the first time you are out there at midnight and 40 below. 13

Now you wait. 14

You wait for cold temperatures. "It would be lovely to do all this, say, over the Christmas holidays," says Hayman, "but that's usually just not possible here in Toronto. You're more likely going to have to wait until the middle of January." So you wait for the requisite cold temperatures, and you wait for snow. Wait until there is a whole lot of snow, maybe two or three good dumpings. Then clear some of it away from your rectangle, leaving behind anywhere from four to six inches. This clearing supplies you with a little border, something to aid in water retention while flooding. It also gives a comfortable sense of containment and might even keep a puck on the ice, although you and I both know that the puck will hit your little ridge of snow, pick up torque° and be gone into the neighbour's yard. 15

It is best to flatten the snow. Hartviksen sends out a troop of kids to play what he calls "boot hockey." He also possesses a heavy piece of wood that he can drag behind him, smoothing the surface. This is not as crucial a step as some people believe. I recall from childhood when someone—I think maybe Mr. Michaels (the kind of man who locked his garage doors)—rented one of those huge industrial drum rollers. The problem is that snow sticks to things like that; also, those rollers are fairly useless unless you fill them with water, which can cause problems. For instance, it can deprive you of your coffee breaks, lest the water inside the drum freeze. The process of backyard rink building raises the market value of coffee breaks considerably; they soon seem as important as reaching Base Camp while scaling K2°. 16

The foundation of the base is snow. Snow plus water and the chilly, chilly air. I am going to advocate the "slush" approach to 17 base building, which differs slightly from, say, Hartviksen's "sugar-cube" approach. (Hartviksen's approach is really more of an aid to visualization. He gives the snow a heavy watering and imagines each section of snow as a large sugar cube. The darkening on the surface gives a good indication of the degree of saturation.)

18   I am a proponent of the most active sort of base building, getting out there with a hose and creating slush, which is then smoothed flat. You want the slush to be more solid than a Slurpee, just watery enough that snowball construction is out of the question. Do small sections at a time. Hayman's technique is effective here: water the ground, work it into slush with a snow shovel, use the back of the snow shovel to smooth it out, move along, do it again. Work lanes, walking backward across the rink-to-be. Once you get that done, have someone carry you inside to thaw you out in a dry, warm corner.

19   In the morning, it will be slightly hilly—well, let's face it, your rink at this point would baffle most topographical° mapmakers. But that's all right. You have done most of the heavy human work now; it is time to turn things over to Mother Nature and let her smooth everything out. The next night . . . oh, let's clear that up. It is not absolutely necessary to do this at night, although a fierce sun can slow things down even on the coldest day. In my experience, however, backyard rink building is always done at night for various practical reasons (a job being the chief one) and for one very impractical one: Did the elves ever show up at the shoemaker's before midnight?

20   The next night, go out there armed with your hose. Just the hose, no fancy nozzles or sprayers: you have to have the open-ended hose because you want to get as much water on the ground in as short a time as possible. "People are always offering me gadgets to put on the end of my hose," says Hartviksen, "but I find they clog and drip and freeze my pant legs. I always end up with just the hose and my thumb. I alternate thumbs. I'm thinking of getting them insured." You should be able to hit most places without stepping on the ice surface, but if you can't, go ahead and step on it. Your foot will go through, but the footprints will be filled in as you build layer by layer, and that is a better option than depriving your rink-to-be of an even flooding. Depending on how cold it is, you might be able to do two, even three, floodings that first night. When you have finished do yourself an enormous favour: coil the hose up, and take it inside the house with you.

21   The next morning, you will find a vaguely flat sheet of ice, although it might be alarmingly pitted, cracked and ravined. Now, in Peter Hayman's words, you "make like a referee." No, he doesn't

mean that you get small-minded and petty and order your children to bed early for no good reason (just joking); he means that you get out there on hands and knees—as referees often do during games—grab handfuls of snow and start stuffing the cracks and holes. Stuffing and tamping, tamping and stuffing. It's amazing how much snow even the smallest crack can hold, so don't imagine this is the work of a few moments. However, the more patching you do, the better your rink is going to be.

Now, the ice might look uniformly strong, but it is very doubtful that it is. The roll of the lawn has a lot of influence here, and usually there are air pockets undermining the structure. I hold to the view that it is best to know about them at this stage of the game—when they can be corrected. So as you do your flood that evening, get out there. Flood the rink, drink cognac and wait until it freezes, flood the rink, drink cognac, drink cognac. . . . 22

In the morning, you have something that looks like a skating rink. This cheers you up, because you drank too much cognac the night before and are feeling a little poorly. There is still some patching to do, but it seems less fundamental—more like polishing than anything else—and after another couple of floodings that evening, you will have, if not a proper skating rink, what Hayman refers to with caution as "a skateable situation." 23

Put the lightest family member out there. Hold your breath. Watch as he or she makes a couple of circuits around the outer edges. There will be some creaking, maybe a little cracking—make like a referee, and flood again that evening. And the next. And the next. You need an ice thickness of perhaps six inches to survive sudden thaws. If it should snow, it must be cleared away almost immediately, because a thick blanket can result in an ice–snow commingling° that will ruin the surface. 24

In time, you will not have to flood every night, or even every other night, but many nights will find you out there, hose in hand, practising a little wintry gardening, a little nocturnal thaumaturgy. 25

Words and Meanings

nocturnal thaumaturgy	nighttime magic	1
sedate	calm, composed, thoughtful, steady	6
chinooks	warm winter winds that blow eastward across the Rocky Mountains into Alberta and Saskatchewan	7
Walter Gretzky	father of hockey great Wayne Gretzky	

10	proximity	closeness
11	perimeter	outer boundary, the edge around the rink
12	errant	uncontrolled, growing in all directions
15	torque	speed and spin
16	scaling K2	climbing the world's second-highest mountain
19	topographical	showing the surface features of a place or region; for example, mountains or rivers
24	commingling	mixture, blending together

Structure and Strategy

1. What METAPHORS does the author use in the opening paragraph? Do they recur later in the essay? (*Hint:* Are there any other references to magic?) Why does the author choose such sophisticated DICTION ("nocturnal thaumaturgy") to identify his subject?
2. Paragraph 2 is based on a contrast. What is it and why does the author introduce it here? (See paragraph 3.)
3. After the INTRODUCTION (paragraphs 1 through 4), Quarrington moves to the preparation stage (paragraphs 5 through 7). What three "experts" did he consult? What are their qualifications to act as authorities on this topic?
4. In which paragraph does the author's process analysis actually begin? Trace the ten steps involved in creating a backyard rink. Are Quarrington's instructions clear and easy to follow? Do they adhere to the principles described in the introduction to this unit?
5. Quarrington employs several FIGURES OF SPEECH to develop his ideas; for example, "more solid than a Slurpee" (paragraph 18), and "make like a referee" (paragraph 21). Find other examples of figurative language. (*Hint:* Look first at the title.)
6. Quarrington tries to encourage his readers by using humour to modify the impression that making a backyard rink is a long, tedious, and even painful process. Identify three or four examples of humour in this essay.

Content and Purpose

1. What objection to backyard rink building does paragraph 3 refute? What objection cannot be refuted, and how does the author suggest the reader deal with it (paragraph 4)?
2. Identify three significant reasons why anyone would go through the trouble and discomfort of making a backyard rink.

3. The first step in the process, deciding where to put the rink, depends on what three factors? (See paragraphs 8 through 10.)
4. How does the author suggest you check to see whether your rink is ready for skating?

Suggestion for Writing

Write a directional process analysis for a multi-step project: for instance, DJ-ing, detailing a car, getting into college, building a deck, designing a webpage, making sushi, doing a body piercing. Make sure that your essay not only explains how to complete the process but also suggests why the process is worthwhile.

The Way of All Flesh: The Worm Is at Work in Us All

JUDY STOFFMAN

Judy Stoffman, currently book review editor of the *Toronto Star*, was born in Budapest, Hungary, and arrived in Vancouver as a refugee in 1957. She has degrees in English from the University of British Columbia and from Sussex University in England. She has also lived and studied in Aix-en-Provence, France. Stoffman's articles and editorials have appeared in *Canadian Living*, *The Globe and Mail*, and *Weekend* magazine, where "The Way of All Flesh" was originally published.

W hen a man of 25 is told that aging is inexorable°, inevitable, universal, he will nod somewhat impatiently at being told something so obvious. In fact, he has little idea of the meaning of the words. It has nothing to do with him. Why should it? He has had no tangible evidence yet that his body, as the poet Rilke said, enfolds old age and death as the fruit enfolds a stone.

The earliest deposits of fat in the aorta, the trunk artery carrying blood away from the heart, occur in the eighth year of life, but who can peer into his own aorta at this first sign of approaching debility°? The young man has seen old people but he secretly

1

2

believes himself to be the exception on whom the curse will never fall. "Never will the skin of my neck hang loose. My grip will never weaken. I will stand tall and walk with long strides as long as I live." The young girl scarcely pays attention to her clothes; she scorns makeup. Her confidence in her body is boundless; smooth skin and a flat stomach will compensate, she knows, for any lapses in fashion or grooming. She stays up all night, as careless of her energy as of her looks, believing both will last forever.

3   In our early 20s, the lung capacity, the rapidity of motor responses and physical endurance are at their peak. This is the athlete's finest hour. Cindy Nicholas of Toronto was 19 when she first swam the English Channel in both directions. The tennis star Bjorn Borg was 23 when he triumphed . . . at Wimbledon for the fourth time.

4   It is not only *athletic* prowess° that is at its height between 20 and 30. James Boswell, writing in his journal in 1763 after he had finally won the favors of the actress Louisa, has left us this happy description of the sexual prowess of a 23-year-old: "I was in full flow of health and my bounding blood beat quick in high alarms. Five times was I fairly lost in a supreme rapture. Louisa was madly fond of me; she declared I was a prodigy°, and asked me if this was extraordinary in human nature. I said twice as much might be, but this was not, although in my own mind I was somewhat proud of my performance."

5   In our early 30s we are dumbfounded to discover the first grey hair at the temples. We pull out the strange filament and look at it closely, trying to grasp its meaning. It means simply that the pigment has disappeared from the hair shaft, never to return. It means also—but this thought we push away—that in 20 years or so we'll relinquish° our identity as a blonde or a redhead. By 57, one out of four people is completely grey. Of all the changes wrought by time this is the most harmless, except to our vanity.

6   In this decade one also begins to notice the loss of upper register hearing, that is, the responsiveness to high frequency tones, but not all the changes are for the worse, not yet. Women don't reach their sexual prime until about 38, because their sexual response is learned rather than innate. The hand grip of both sexes increases in strength until 35, and intellectual powers are never stronger than at that age. There is a sense in the 30s of hitting your stride, of coming into your own. When Sigmund Freud was 38 an older colleague, Josef Breuer, wrote: "Freud's intellect is soaring at its highest. I gaze after him as a hen at a hawk."

7   Gail Sheehy in her book *Passages* calls the interval between 35 and 45 the Deadline Decade. It is the time we begin to sense

danger. The body continually flashes us signals that time is running out. We must perform our quaint deeds, keep our promises, get on with our allotted tasks.

Signal: The woman attempts to become pregnant at 40 and finds she cannot. Though she menstruates each month, menstruation being merely the shedding of the inner lining of the womb, she may not be ovulating regularly.   8

Signal: Both men and women discover that, although they have not changed their eating habits over the years, they are much heavier than formerly. The man is paunchy around the waist; the woman no longer has those slim thighs and slender arms. A 120-pound woman needs 2,000 calories daily to maintain her weight when she is 25, 1,700 to maintain the same weight at 45, and only 1,500 calories at 65. A 170-pound man needs 3,100 calories daily at 25, 300 fewer a day at 45 and 450 calories fewer still at 65. This decreasing calorie need signals that the body consumes its fuel ever more slowly; the cellular fires are damped and our sense of energy diminishes.   9

In his mid-40s the man notices he can no longer run up the stairs three at a time. He is more easily winded and his joints are not as flexible as they once were. The strength of his hands has declined somewhat. The man feels humiliated: "I will not let this happen to me. I will turn back the tide and master my body." He starts going to the gym, playing squash, lifting weights. He takes up jogging. Though he may find it neither easy nor pleasant, terror drives him past pain. A regular exercise program can retard some of the symptoms of aging by improving the circulation and increasing the lung capacity, thereby raising our stamina and energy level, but no amount of exercise will make a 48-year-old 26 again. Take John Keeley of Mystic, Connecticut. . . . [W]hen he was 26, he won the Boston marathon with a time of 2:20. . . . [At] 48, [he was] as fiercely competitive as ever, yet it took him almost 30 minutes longer to run the same marathon.   10

In the middle of the fourth decade, the man whose eyesight has always been good will pick up a book and notice that he is holding it farther from his face than usual. The condition is presbyopia, a loss of the flexibility of the lens which makes adjustment from distant to near vision increasingly difficult. It's harder now to zoom in for a closeup. It also takes longer for the eyes to recover from glare; between 16 and 90, recovery time from exposure to glare is doubled every 13 years.   11

In our 50s, we notice that food is less and less tasty; our taste buds are starting to lose their acuity°. The aged Queen Victoria was   12 wont to complain that strawberries were not as sweet as when she was a girl.

13   Little is known about the causes of aging. We do not know if we are born with a biochemical messenger programmed to keep the cells and tissues alive, a messenger that eventually gets lost, or if there is a "death hormone," absent from birth but later secreted by the thymus or by the mysterious pineal gland, or if, perhaps, aging results from a fatal flaw in the body's immunity system. The belief that the body is a machine whose parts wear out is erroneous, for the machine does not have the body's capacity for self-repair.

14   "A man is as old as his arteries," observed Sir William Osler. From the 50s on, there's a progressive hardening and narrowing of the arteries due to the gradual lifelong accumulation of calcium and fats along the arterial walls. Arteriosclerosis eventually affects the majority of the population in the affluent countries of the West. Lucky the man or woman who, through a combination of good genes and good nutrition, can escape it, for it is the most evil change of all. As the flow of blood carrying oxygen and nutrients to the muscles, the brain, the kidneys and other organs diminishes, these organs begin to starve. Although all aging organs lose weight, there is less shrinkage of organs such as the liver and kidneys, the cells of which regenerate, than there is shrinkage of the brain and the muscles, the cells of which, once lost, are lost forever.

15   For the woman it is now an ordeal to be asked her age. There is a fine tracery of lines around her eyes, a furrow in her brow even when she smiles. The bloom is off her cheeks. Around the age of 50 she will buy her last box of sanitary pads. The body's production of estrogen and progesterone which govern menstruation (and also help to protect her from heart attack and the effects of stress) will have ceased almost completely. She may suffer palpitations°, suddenly break into a sweat; her moods may shift abruptly. She looks in the mirror and asks, "Am I still a woman?" Eventually she becomes reconciled to her new self and even acknowledges its advantages: no more fears about pregnancy. "In any case," she laughs, "I still have not bad legs."

16   The man, too, will undergo a change. One night in his early 50s he has some trouble achieving a complete erection, and his powers of recovery are not what they once were. Whereas at 20 he was ready to make love again less than half an hour after doing so, it may now take two hours or more; he was not previously aware that his level of testosterone, the male hormone, has been gradually declining since the age of 20. He may develop headaches, be unable

to sleep, become anxious about his performance, anticipate failure and so bring on what is called secondary impotence—impotence of psychological rather than physical origin. According to Masters and Johnson, 25 percent of all men are impotent by 65 and 50 percent by 75, yet this cannot be called an inevitable feature of aging. A loving, undemanding partner and a sense of confidence can do wonders. "The susceptibility° of the human male to the power of suggestion with regard to his sexual prowess," observe Masters and Johnson, "is almost unbelievable."

After the menopause, the woman ages more rapidly. Her bones start to lose calcium, becoming brittle and porous. The walls of the vagina become thinner and drier; sexual intercourse now may be painful unless her partner is slow and gentle. The sweat glands begin to atrophy° and the sebaceous glands that lubricate the skin decline; the complexion becomes thinner and drier and wrinkles appear around the mouth. The skin, which in youth varies from about one-fiftieth of an inch on the eyelids to about a third of an inch on the palms and the soles of the feet, loses 50 percent of its thickness between the ages of 20 and 80. The woman no longer buys sleeveless dresses and avoids shorts. The girl who once disdained cosmetics is now a woman whose dressing table is covered with lotions, night creams and makeup. 17

Perhaps no one has written about the sensation of nearing 60 with more brutal honesty than the French novelist Simone de Beauvoir: "While I was able to look at my face without displeasure, I gave it no thought. I loathe my appearance now: the eyebrows slipping down toward the eyes, the bags underneath, the excessive fullness of the cheeks and the air of sadness around the mouth that wrinkles always bring. . . . Death is no longer a brutal event in the far distance; it haunts my sleep." 18

In his early 60s the man's calves are shrunken, his muscles stringy looking. The legs of the woman, too, are no longer shapely. Both start to lose their sense of smell and both lose most of the hair in the pubic area and the underarms. Hair, however, may make its appearance in new places, such as the woman's chin. Liver spots appear on the hands, the arms, the face; they are made of coagulated melanin, the coloring matter of the skin. The acid secretions of the stomach decrease, making digestion slow and more difficult. 19

Halfway through the 60s comes compulsory retirement for most men and working women, forcing upon the superannuated worker the realization that society now views him as useless and unproductive. The man who formerly gave orders to a staff of 20 now finds himself underfoot as his wife attempts to clean the house or get the shopping done. The woman fares a little better 20 since there is a continuity in her pattern of performing a myriad of essential household tasks. Now they must both set new goals or see themselves wither mentally. The unsinkable American journalist I.F. Stone, when he retired in 1971 from editing *I.F. Stone's Weekly*, began to teach himself Greek and is now reading Plato in the original. When Somerset Maugham read that the Roman senator Cato the Elder learned Greek when he was 80, he remarked: "Old age is ready to undertake tasks that youth shirked° because they would take too long."

21   However active we are, the fact of old age can no longer be evaded from about 65 onward. Not everyone is as strong minded about this as de Beauvoir. When she made public in her memoirs her horror at her own deterioration, her readers were scandalized. She received hundreds of letters telling her that there is no such thing as old age, that some are just younger than others. Repeatedly she heard the hollow reassurance, "You're as young as you feel." But she considers this a lie. Our subjective reality, our inner sense of self, is not the only reality. There is also an objective reality, how we are seen by society. We receive our revelation of old age from others. The woman whose figure is still trim may sense that a man is following her in the street; drawing abreast, the man catches sight of her face—and hurries on. The man of 68 may be told by a younger woman to whom he is attracted: "You remind me of my father."

22   Madame de Sévigné, the 17th-century French writer, struggled to rid herself of the illusion of perpetual youth. At 63 she wrote: "I have been dragged to this inevitable point where old age must be undergone: I see it there before me; I have reached it; and I should at least like so to arrange matters that I do not move on, that I do not travel further along this path of the infirmities, pains, losses of memory and the disfigurement. But I hear a voice saying: 'You must go along, whatever you may say; or indeed if you will not then you must die, which is an extremity from which nature recoils.'"

23   Now the man and the woman have their 70th birthday party. It is a sad affair because so many of their friends are missing, felled by strokes, heart attacks or cancers. Now the hands of the clock begin to race. The skeleton continues to degenerate from loss of calcium. The spine becomes compressed and there is a slight stoop nothing can prevent. Inches are lost from one's height. The joints may become thickened and creaking; in the morning the woman can't seem to get moving until she's had a hot bath. She has osteoarthritis. This, like the other age-related diseases, arteriosclerosis and diabetes, can and should be treated, but it can never

be cured. The nails, particularly the toenails, become thick and lifeless because the circulation in the lower limbs is now poor. The man has difficulty learning new things because of the progressive loss of neurons from the brain. The woman goes to the store and forgets what she has come to buy. The two old people are often constipated because the involuntary muscles are weaker now. To make it worse, their children are always saying, "Sit down, rest, take it easy." Their digestive tract would be toned up if they went for a long walk or even a swim, although they feel a little foolish in bathing suits.

In his late 70s, the man develops glaucoma, pressure in the   24
eyeball caused by the failure of aqueous humour° to drain away; this can now be treated with a steroid related to cortisone. The lenses in the eyes of the woman may thicken and become fibrous, blurring her vision. She has cataracts, but artificial lenses can now be implanted using cryosurgery°. There is no reason to lose one's sight just as there's no reason to lose one's teeth; regular, lifelong dental care can prevent tooth loss. What can't be prevented is the yellowing of teeth, brought about by the shrinking of the living chamber within the tooth which supplies the outer enamel with moisture.

Between 75 and 85 the body loses most of its subcutaneous fat.   25
On her 80th birthday the woman's granddaughter embraces her and marvels: "How thin and frail and shrunken she is! Could this narrow, bony chest be the same warm, firm bosom to which she clasped me as a child?" Her children urge her to eat but she has no enjoyment of food now. Her mouth secretes little saliva, so she has difficulty tasting and swallowing. The loss of fat and shrinking muscles in the 80s diminish the body's capacity for homeostasis, that is, righting any physiological imbalance. The old man, if he is cold, can barely shiver (shivering serves to restore body heat). If he lives long enough, the man will have an enlarged prostate which causes the urinary stream to slow to a trickle. The man and the woman probably both wear hearing aids now; without a hearing aid, they hear vowels clearly but not consonants; if someone says "fat," they think they've heard the word "that."

At 80, the speed of nerve impulses is 10 percent less than it was   26
at 25, the kidney filtration rate is down by 30 percent, the pumping efficiency of the heart is only 60 percent of what it was, and the maximum breathing capacity, 40 percent.

The old couple is fortunate in still being able to express physi-   27
cally the love they've built up over a lifetime. The old man may be capable of an erection once or twice a week (Charlie Chaplin fathered the last of his children when he was 81), but he rarely has

the urge to climax. When he does, he sometimes has the sensation of seepage rather than a triumphant explosion. Old people who say they are relieved that they are now free of the torments of sexual desire are usually the ones who found sex a troublesome function all their lives; those who found joy and renewal in the act will cling to their libido°. Many older writers and artists have expressed the conviction that continued sexuality is linked to continued creativity: "There was a time when I was cruelly tormented, indeed obsessed by desire," wrote the novelist André Gide at the age of 73, "and I prayed, 'Oh let the moment come when my subjugated° flesh will allow me to give myself entirely to. . . .' But to what? To art? To pure thought? To God? How ignorant I was! How mad! It was the same as believing that the flame would burn brighter in a lamp with no oil left. Even today it is my carnal self that feeds the flame, and now I pray that I may retain carnal desire until I die."

28   Aging, says an American gerontologist°, "is not a simple slope which everyone slides down at the same speed; it is a flight of irregular stairs down which some journey more quickly than others." Now we arrive at the bottom of the stairs. The old man and the old woman whose progress we have been tracing will die either of a cancer (usually of the lungs, bowel or intestines) or of a stroke, a heart attack or in consequence of a fall. The man slips in the bathroom and breaks his thigh bone. But worse than the fracture is the enforced bed rest in the hospital which will probably bring on bed sores, infections, further weakening of the muscles and finally, what Osler called "an old man's best friend": pneumonia. At 25 we have so much vitality that if a little is sapped by illness, there is still plenty left over. At 85 a little is all we have.

29   And then the light goes out.

30   The sheet is pulled over the face.

31   In the last book of Marcel Proust's remarkable work *Remembrance of Things Past*, the narrator, returning after a long absence from Paris, attends a party of his friends throughout which he has the impression of being at a masked ball: "I did not understand why I could not immediately recognize the master of the house, and the guests, who seemed to have made themselves up, in a way that completely changed their appearance. The Prince had rigged himself up with a white beard and what looked like leaden soles which made his feet drag heavily. A name was mentioned to me and I was dumbfounded at the thought that it applied to the blonde waltzing girl I had once known and to the stout, white haired lady now walking

just in front of me. We did not see our own appearance, but each like a facing mirror, saw the other's." The narrator is overcome by a simple but powerful truth: the old are not a different species. "It is out of young men who last long enough," wrote Proust, "that life makes its old men."

The wrinkled old man who lies with the sheet over his face was once the young man who vowed, "My grip will never weaken. I will walk with long strides and stand tall as long as I live." The young man who believed himself to be the exception.   32

Words and Meanings

		Paragraph
inexorable	relentless, unstoppable	1
debility	weakness	2
prowess	courage, skill	4
prodigy	person capable of extraordinary achievement	
relinquish	give up	5
acuity	sharpness	12
palpitations	irregular heartbeats	15
susceptibility	sensitiveness	16
atrophy	wither	17
shirked	neglected	20
aqueous humour	fluid in the interior chamber of the eyeball	24
cryosurgery	surgical technique involving freezing of the tissues	
libido	sexual desire	27
subjugated	conquered, subdued	
gerontologist	expert on aging	28

Structure and Strategy

1. How does the first paragraph reinforce the title and subtitle of this essay?
2. Into how many stages does Stoffman divide the aging process? Identify the paragraphs that describe each stage.
3. Why do you think Stoffman uses so many direct quotations in her essay? Select two of these direct quotations and explain why they are particularly effective.

4. How does the last paragraph unify or bring together the whole essay? Why do you think Stoffman ends her essay with a sentence fragment?

Content and Purpose

1. The title of this essay is a biblical ALLUSION ("I am going the way of all the earth. . . ." 1 Kings 2:2). Why do you think Stoffman chose this title?
2. What is "the worm" referred to in the subtitle?
3. Summarize the changes, both internal and external, that occur during one's fifties (paragraphs 12 through 17).
4. On his eightieth birthday, Morley Callaghan, the celebrated Canadian novelist, declared that "everyone wants to live to be 80, but no one wants to *be* 80." Do you think Stoffman would agree or disagree with Callaghan?

Suggestions for Writing

1. Write a directional process essay explaining how to enjoy the experience of aging.
2. Write an informational process on how to keep yourself as young (and/or as young-looking) as possible as you age.
3. As a result of the Charter of Rights and Freedoms in Canada, many vigorous 65-year-olds are challenging the principle of compulsory retirement. Do you agree or disagree that workers should be required to retire at 65? Why?

Struck by Lightning

JILL FRAYNE

Jill Frayne lives near Ontario's Algonquin Park. She has worked as a therapist and writer. The daughter of writers June Callwood and Trent Frayne, she has written for *explore* magazine, *The Walrus*, *Canadian Geographic*, and *Up Here*. Her travel memoir *Starting Out in the Afternoon* (2002) is a meditative look at life and landscape through the prism of a journey from Ontario to the Yukon.

1   In the summer of 2002, I was camped at the mouth of the French River, lying on my Therm-a-Rest waiting out a thunderstorm, when my tent was struck by lightning. It was over before

Reprinted by permission of the author.

I knew what had happened, before adrenalin had any role to play, before fear took over. My tent poles took the charge and I was spared, completely. The narrow escape got me asking around. How often does this happen? It turns out everybody has a lightning story.

Floyd Woods, a retired truck driver from Ardbeg, Ontario, was twelve years old in 1943 when his house was hit. The strike shot through the radio antenna, exploded in the living room into a blue fireball that roared down the hall, lifting up the linoleum runner by the tacks, ripping the nails out of the floor, splintering the house walls as fine as kindling before it ran off over the bedrock outside and died. Woods' guitar was hanging on the wall over his bed. Sixty-five years later, he still shakes his head: "That strike burned the guitar strings off, *bing, bing, bing,* threw me right out of bed and across the room so I ached for a month. Nothin' will move you faster than lightning. Nothin'."

· · · · ·

The ball of blue fire that rolled through Floyd Woods' house was a rare example of a phenomenon that is anything but rare. The planet ripples with lightning. According to Environment Canada, at any given time there are 1,500 to 2,000 active thunderstorms on earth, and tens of millions of lightning points touch ground each year—some 2.7 million across Canada alone. If viewed from space, earth would appear to be pulsing with storms. Of all the forces of nature, lightning is peerless in its intensity, in the magnitude of its release in a single instant. It is the ravishing dagger, the fire bolt joining earth and heaven, part of the original chemical soup. It might not be too great a leap to suppose lightning supplied the electric jolt that kindled organic life. It is Frankenstein in a galactic laboratory.

Like every force of nature, lightning gives and takes away. Its great boon° is that it exudes nitrogen, crucial to plants. But its touch is also deadly: lightning scorches whatever it strikes. It chars, explodes, sears. We are thrilled by its terrible beauty, pulsing in and from the clouds, jagging out of a riven sky, but lightning strikes cause huge crop damage, ignite forest fires, and can be lethal° to living creatures. The Canadian Lightning Detection Network estimates that lightning kills seven Canadians a year, and injures sixty to seventy. In the wake of a direct strike, most survivors suffer long-term neuropsychiatric effects and/or impaired brain function. Hearing and vision loss, numbness, chronic pain, concentration problems, and psychological disorders are all common results.

· · · · ·

5   We are rather susceptible° in Canada. Our country is mostly landscape, and we're often roaming around it, beyond broadcast areas, beyond cover. To prepare ourselves, we have to be our own Environment Canada: we have to learn the rudiments° of storms, know the terrain° we're travelling through, be able to tell a front from a squall line, a stratus cloud from a nimbus. Thunderstorms do give notice—wickedly short, usually, but always distinctive. After my brush on Georgian Bay, I boned up, taking myself to the You and Your World shelf at the library.

6   Storms rely on the rapid, sustained uplifting of air, especially warm, moist air. This is why they occur frequently in summer, when the ground has grown hot by late afternoon. Open fields heat faster than forests or water, rocky slopes faster than ground covered by vegetation; hence the sudden onrush of the storm we experienced, parked on the warm rock enfolding Georgian Bay, just at cocktail hour at the end of a hot day.

7   Convection° fuels thunderstorms, either from warm air rising off the ground, or from a drop in temperature in the atmosphere. Cheery, popcorn white clouds in the sky mean unstable air has stopped rising and has reached the dew point, when its temperature equals that of the surrounding air. These cumulus clouds can persist for days or they can dissipate°, but if warm thermal air keeps pushing up, they often develop into cumulonimbus clouds. When this happens, an aerial game of pinball begins. Droplets bounce around, collide, pick up grit, old volcanic ash, the detritus° of life below, all of it freezing into ice crystals in the troposphere°. Air travellers experience this as turbulence, their plane passing through cumulonimbus clouds, lurching in the chaos, the cabin windows dashed with rain or hail, until the aircraft emerges from the cloud.

8   On the ground, this intense interior action looks like a change from roly-poly clouds jogging in the sky to clouds darkening and mounting into towers. This formation means a storm is brewing. Inside the cloud, ice crystals and raindrops zing about in all directions, slamming into and fusing with one another, growing larger and heavier, until they start falling through the cloud as rain or snow or hail.

9   Lightning gets into the action through an electrical charge that builds during these high-wire collisions. When a beauty of a storm is brewing, a negative charge heats up at the base of the cloud. The earth's surface tends to be negatively charged, and since like charges repel, current at the bottom of the cloud draws away from the ground, leaving a positive charge in the air. This is that pre-storm sense one gets, the hair on the head lifting slightly, the air freighted with electricity.

It's in the nature of air to act as a buffer, to resist electrical   10
flow, and for a time it contains the mounting charge. But it can't
hold out forever. At a certain point, the negative charge from the
cloud expends itself, not all at once, which would be an atomic
reaction, but haltingly, in a "stepped leader" about as thick as a
pencil. This negative charge gropes° toward the ground, moving
in a searching way, like a lonely drunk in a bar looking for a connection. Eventually, it attracts a positive charge from something
tall on the ground—a tree or a tower, a farmer on a tractor. When
lightning strikes, the charges have connected in a streamer, a flood
of positive current that surges back up into the cloud, spectacularly
hot, so intensely superheating the surrounding air that a shock
wave bulges out, faster than the speed of sound.

Thunder is the sonic boom we hear when the percussive force   11
breaks the sound barrier. Once the stepped leader from the cloud
locks to the streamer from the ground, a channel opens for pulses
of electricity to pass through, producing several flashes. We see the
lightning before we hear the boom, but the thunder actually occurs
first; the speed of light outraces the sound of thunder to our senses.

In its defence, lightning is only doing its job. It's the celestial°   12
housekeeper, balancing an overcharged heaven and earth.

. . . . .

I continue to be baffled by why the strike that hit my tent was so   13
glancing. Was it side splash, the point coming to ground somewhere nearby, leaping a fallen log or tag alder and hitting my tent
somewhat tired out? Or was it the speed of the bolt that spared me,
current zooming through the poles at 220,000 kilometres an hour?
But if lightning's temperature is thousands of degrees, why didn't
my tent simply vaporize°?

I'll never know. What was plain in that particular storm, in   14
that particular place, is that my aluminum poles acted similar to
a Faraday cage° around me and took the heat. Another time, who
knows?

The more we learn, the more capricious and imponderable°   15
lightning becomes. It's the wild card, familiar but eternally a
wonder. How many imponderables do we have left? We have so
mastered, so paved over this world, but there is still something
ungovernable we must live with, a supremely random force of
nature, quite outside ourselves. . . .

Lightning's ultimate benefit, perhaps, is that it puts us in our   16
place, reminds us of nature's power, and suggests that the celestial
order of things has its own rules and should not be trifled with°.
Still, for tens of thousands of years humans have craved inspira-
tion, a state of awe. That lightning comes threaded with danger

makes us cautious, as it should, but we remain bound to seek it out, even at our peril.

Words and Meanings

4	boon	gift
	lethal	deadly
5	susceptible	vulnerable, likely to experience thunderstorms
	rudiments	basic facts
	terrain	landscape
7	convection	transfer of heat by movement of air currents from one region to another
	dissipate	gradually disappear
	detritus	debris, particles
	troposphere	the lowest region of the atmosphere, just above the earth's surface; the region in which most storms originate
10	gropes	reaches
12	celestial	belonging to the sky, the heavens
13	vaporize	evaporate; disappear in an instant
14	Faraday cage	an electromagnetic shield, such as a car or metal tent poles, that channels electrical charges into the ground
15	capricious and imponderable	unpredictable and mysterious
16	trifled with	treated lightly; dismissed without thought

Structure and Strategy

1. What INTRODUCTORY strategy is used in this essay?
2. Identify three METAPHORS in paragraph 3. Are they effective?
3. What is the topic sentence of paragraph 4? Summarize the effects of lightning, both positive and negative, as detailed in this paragraph.
4. What paragraphs provide the informational process analysis of how lightning happens?
5. Identify a SIMILE in paragraph 10. What comparison is at its root?
6. What CONCLUSION strategy does the essay rely on?

Content and Purpose

1. Why is Canada "rather susceptible" (paragraph 5) to lightning strikes? What does this susceptibility require us to do?
2. When are lightning storms most likely to occur? Why? What fuels them?
3. What is going on inside a cumulonimbus cloud? What does this activity have to do with lightning? (See paragraphs 8 and 9.)
4. What is thunder? Which occurs first in a storm—thunder or lightning?
5. How does Frayne explain why the lightning that hit her tent did so little damage (paragraph 14)?
6. What two benefits of lightning does the author identify at the end of the essay?

Suggestions for Writing

1. Write an informational process analysis about another dramatic act of nature; for example, an earthquake, tornado, tsunami, or hurricane.
2. Write a directional process analysis that explains how to avoid being hit by lightning.

ADDITIONAL SUGGESTIONS FOR WRITING: PROCESS ANALYSIS

I. Choose one of the topics below and develop it into an informational process ANALYSIS.

1. How a smartphone (or any other electronic device) works
2. How an animal is born or hatched
3. How a particular celebrity, musician, sports personality, or political figure appeals to the crowd
4. How to save Canada's universal health-care system (medicare)
5. How a company plans the marketing of a new product
6. How alcohol (or any other drug) affects the body
7. How a star is born
8. How the Internet has changed dating
9. How to survive on the streets
10. How a particular process in nature occurs—for example, how coral grows, a spider spins a web, salmon spawn, a snowflake forms, a specific crop is grown and harvested

II. Choose one of the topics below and develop it into a directional process analysis.

1. How to buy (or sell) something—for example, a used car, a house, a piece of sports equipment, a computer, or a work of art
2. How to get into a good college
3. How to play roulette, blackjack, poker, or some other game of chance
4. How to organize a successful party
5. How to create a scrapbook, blog, or digital record commemorating an event, a person, or a family
6. How to make or build something—for example, wine, bread, a kite, or a radio transmitter
7. How to survive English (or any other subject that you are studying)
8. How to get your own way
9. How to satisfy champagne tastes on a beer budget
10. How to talk your way out of a traffic ticket, a failing grade, a date, a conversation with a bore, a threatened punishment, or keeping a promise

Classification and Division

WHAT ARE CLASSIFICATION AND DIVISION?

ANALYSIS is the process of separating something into its parts in order to understand the whole. In Unit 3, we used the term *process analysis* to refer to a writing pattern in which a process (hatching a penguin, for example) is described in terms of the steps or stages performing in performing it. All forms of analysis involve sorting or dividing—breaking a complex whole into its stages, parts, or categories in order to understand it better.

In the rhetorical pattern called *classification,* the writer sorts a group of things or people into classes or categories on the basis of some shared characteristic. For example, in "The Term Paper Artist," Nick Mamatas classifies the three types of student clients who buy—rather than write—term papers. Dennis Dermody, in "Sit Down and Shut Up or Don't Sit by Me," classifies moviegoers on the basis of their behaviour in the movie theatre.

In *division,* on the other hand, a single thing (not a group of things) is divided into its component parts. For example, the model essay "Listen Up" divides the skill of listening into its three separate parts. In "Toothpaste," David Bodanis breaks down the everyday substance of toothpaste into its constituent ingredients and surprises us with the odd stuff that we put into our mouths every morning.

WHY DO WE USE CLASSIFICATION AND DIVISION?

Classification answers the question "What are the different kinds or types of X?" Division answers the question "What are the various parts or components of X?" Classifying or dividing a topic organizes it into logically related units that a reader can understand. These two strategies are essential ways of making sense of the world around us.

A **classification essay** uses a sorting mechanism to examine a group of similar things that have meaningful differences among them. A **division essay** looks at a topic in terms of its constituent parts; it examines each part to discover its distinctive features and its function within the whole. Sometimes writers use both strategies. For example, in "What I Have Lived For," Bertrand Russell divides his life's purpose—his reason for living—into what he calls "three passions": the longing for love, the search for knowledge, and pity for the suffering of mankind. Then he classifies his search for love into three different kinds of love, for knowledge into three kinds of knowledge, and his pity for humanity's ills into three different kinds of suffering.

Besides giving form and focus to unorganized chunks of information, division and classification are useful for evaluation purposes. When a writer's purpose is to evaluate the relative merits of several items or ideas, classification and division can help to ensure a clear, coherent piece of communication.

HOW DO WE WRITE CLASSIFICATION AND DIVISION?

Here are three guidelines for writing a good **classification** paper:

1. Identify a logical and consistent classifying principle.

2. Make sure that your categories do not overlap. Dennis Dermody's humorous classification of annoying moviegoers includes *latecomers, chatterers, krinklers,* and *popcorn people.* The addition of the category *talkers* would overlap with "the *chatterers* [who] comment blithely on everything that is happening on the screen."

3. Include a clear thesis statement. For example, Nick Mamatas states his thesis in "The Term Paper Artist": "In broad strokes, there are three types of term paper client."

Here are two guidelines for writing a good **division** paper:

1. Identify the principle of division. Bertrand Russell's division essay, "What I Have Lived For," divides the complex idea of his reasons for living into three passions that have ruled his life.

2. Construct a clear division thesis statement. For example: "Active listening results from the interaction of three related components: questioning, paraphrasing, and empathizing." (See "Listen Up," below.)

Classification and **division** are two of the most effective strategies you can use to explain a complex topic to your readers. The ability to analyze using classification and division is a valuable skill that every writer should acquire.

The model essay that follows divides the skill of *listening* into its component parts.

Listen Up

Introduction (a striking fact)

Most of us are surprised to learn that listening—not reading, not writing, not speaking—is the communication skill we use most frequently. Perhaps equally surprising is that listening is a skill that can be learned and improved. We can all become better listeners by becoming *active* listeners, people who not only "hear" but also "understand." Active listening is an interaction of three related activities: questioning, paraphrasing, and empathizing.

Thesis statement

First component of listening process (developed with an illustration)

One of the easiest ways to check whether you've "heard right" is to ask. By asking questions, you not only show interest, but also get additional details and clarification. For example, if your friend Sophie says she has to cancel the plans the two of you had made for Saturday night, you would be wise to ask why she is cancelling before you assume that she is angry with you.

Second component (supported by definition and an example)

Paraphrasing is another way to ensure that you "got it right." It is actually a form of feedback: restating in your own words in a summarized form what you think the speaker said. Perhaps Sophie cancelled by saying, "I've had a terrible week at work, and I don't think I'll be good company on Saturday. I'm really not in much of a mood to sit in a crowded theatre and watch a three-hour movie I haven't heard anything good about." It would be in both your and Sophie's best interests if you "checked" her message by paraphrasing it to make sure you understood her correctly; for example, "You're tired, so you don't feel up to the movie on Saturday. Would you like to get together on Sunday?"

Third component (defines term and further develops the example)

Empathizing—putting yourself in the other person's shoes, so to speak—involves a sincere interest in the speaker and his or her perceptions. If you empathize with Sophie, you will respect her feelings although you may not necessarily agree with what she says. You may think that Sophie doesn't have a particularly exhausting job, and you may know that the movie you had planned to see got rave reviews. But what matters is that Sophie isn't feeling up to going out on Saturday night as the two of you had originally planned. Whether you share Sophie's perspective or not isn't the point. The point is to understand what she is saying. Empathizing means listening to the story through the speaker's ears.

Conclusion (restates the thesis and asks a rhetorical question)

As you can see, in any conversation, questioning, paraphrasing, and empathizing are intertwined. It is not easy to separate them because they all stem from the same motive: a genuine concern for the speaker that inspires the listener to *want* to hear the message the way it was intended. Active listening improves not only your communication skills but also your ability to get along with the people around you. Are you listening?

Many Faiths, One Truth

TENZIN GYATSO, THE 14TH DALAI LAMA

Tenzin Gyatso was born in 1935 in the small Tibetan village of Taktser. Tibetan Buddhists traditionally believe that their leaders, known as Dalai Lamas, are the reincarnation of their predecessors. At the age of two, Tenzin (whose name was Lhamo Dhondup at that time) was recognized as the reincarnation of the 13th Dalai Lama and was taken from his family to be given a rigorous monastic education. Thus, he became the spiritual head of Tibetan Buddhism and, between 1951 and 1959, the temporal leader of Tibet. After the Tibetan uprising against the Chinese government in 1959, the Dalai Lama fled to India, where he established a Tibetan government in exile. Since that time, he has travelled the world as a proponent of Tibetan independence, as well as an advocate for international peace, nonviolent protest, interfaith dialogue, and environmental awareness. In 1989 he won the Nobel Peace Prize, and in 2006 he became one of only five people ever to have received honorary Canadian citizenship from the Governor General of Canada.

W hen I was a boy in Tibet, I felt that my own Buddhist   1
religion must be the best—and that other faiths were
somehow inferior. Now I see how naïve I was, and how
dangerous the extremes of religious intolerance can be today.

Though intolerance may be as old as religion itself, we still see   2
vigorous signs of its virulence°. In Europe, there are intense debates
about newcomers wearing veils or wanting to erect minarets and
episodes of violence against Muslim immigrants. Radical atheists
issue blanket condemnations of those who hold to religious beliefs.
In the Middle East, the flames of war are fanned by hatred of those
who adhere to a different faith.

Such tensions are likely to increase as the world becomes more   3
interconnected and cultures, peoples and religions become ever
more entwined. The pressure this creates tests more than our tolerance—it demands that we promote peaceful coexistence and understanding across boundaries.

Granted, every religion has a sense of exclusivity as part of   4
its core identity. Even so, I believe there is genuine potential for
mutual understanding. While preserving faith toward one's own
tradition, one can respect, admire and appreciate other traditions.

An early eye-opener for me was my meeting with the Trappist   5
monk Thomas Merton in India shortly before his untimely death in
1968. Merton told me he could be perfectly faithful to Christianity,
yet learn in depth from other religions like Buddhism. The same is
true for me as an ardent Buddhist learning from the world's other
great religions.

A main point in my discussion with Merton was how central   6
compassion was to the message of both Christianity and Buddhism.
In my readings of the New Testament, I find myself inspired by Jesus'
acts of compassion. His miracle of the loaves and fishes, his healing
and his teaching are all motivated by the desire to relieve suffering.

I'm a firm believer in the power of personal contact to bridge   7
differences, so I've long been drawn to dialogues with people of
other religious outlooks. The focus on compassion that Merton
and I observed in our two religions strikes me as a strong unifying
thread among all the major faiths. And these days we need to highlight what unifies us.

8   Take Judaism, for instance. I first visited a synagogue in Cochin, India, in 1965, and have met with many rabbis over the years. I remember vividly the rabbi in the Netherlands who told me about the Holocaust with such intensity that we were both in tears. And I've learned how the Talmud and the Bible repeat the theme of compassion, as in the passage in Leviticus that admonishes, "Love your neighbor as yourself."

9   In my many encounters with Hindu scholars in India, I've come to see the centrality of selfless compassion in Hinduism too— as expressed, for instance, in the Bhagavad Gita°, which praises those who "delight in the welfare of all beings." I'm moved by the ways this value has been expressed in the life of great beings like Mahatma Gandhi, or the lesser-known Baba Amte, who founded a leper colony not far from a Tibetan settlement in Maharashtra State in India. There he fed and sheltered lepers who were otherwise shunned. When I received my Nobel Peace Prize, I made a donation to his colony.

10   Compassion is equally important in Islam—and recognizing that has become crucial in the years since Sept. 11, especially in answering those who paint Islam as a militant faith. On the first anniversary of 9/11, I spoke at the National Cathedral in Washington, pleading that we not blindly follow the lead of some in the news media and let the violent acts of a few individuals define an entire religion.

11   Let me tell you about the Islam I know. Tibet has had an Islamic community for around 400 years, although my richest contacts with Islam have been in India, which has the world's second-largest Muslim population. An imam° in Ladakh once told me that a true Muslim should love and respect all of Allah's creatures. And in my understanding, Islam enshrines compassion as a core spiritual principle, reflected in the very name of God, the "Compassionate and Merciful," that appears at the beginning of virtually each chapter of the Koran.

12   Finding common ground among faiths can help us bridge needless divides at a time when unified action is more crucial than ever. As a species, we must embrace the oneness of humanity as we face global issues like pandemics°, economic crises and ecological disaster. At that scale, our response must be as one.

13   Harmony among the major faiths has become an essential ingredient of peaceful coexistence in our world. From this perspective, mutual understanding among these traditions is not merely the business of religious believers—it matters for the welfare of humanity as a whole.

Words and Meanings

Paragraph

virulence	poisonousness	2
Bhagavad Gita	sacred Hindu scripture	9
imam	a Muslim leader (religious, secular, or both)	11
pandemics	global epidemics	12

Structure and Strategy

1. What is the TOPIC SENTENCE of paragraph 2? How is the paragraph developed?
2. What is the "unifying thread" (paragraph 7), the classifying principle, that the Dalai Lama observes among the major faiths of the world?
3. What examples does the author use to support his classification according to the "unifying thread"?
4. Identify the scriptural quotations that the author uses to support his idea about the centrality of compassion to the world's major religious faiths.
5. Along with classification, this essay uses persuasion to convince its readers of an important point. What is its THESIS?

Content and Purpose

1. The Dalai Lama begins his essay by describing one of his religious beliefs when he was a boy. What was it? What personal details does the essay recount that indicate how he changed this belief over the years?
2. What is the tension that is a potential danger of religious faith (see paragraph 4)? What does the Dalai Lama prescribe as the antidote to this danger?
3. What does the Dalai Lama see as the most important way to "bridge differences" (paragraph 7) between people? Do you agree or disagree? Why?
4. What threats does the Dalai Lama see as imperiling the human race at this point in history?
5. According to him, what must the major religions do to counteract these perils? What are the implications for people of faith? For people who don't practise any religion?

Suggestions for Writing

1. Tenzin Gyatso, the 14th Dalai Lama, has become a revered figure in the world. Write an essay about his life and the influence he extends over people and governments.

2. Read Bertrand Russell's "What I Have Lived For" (page 199) and compare it with "Many Faiths, One Truth." Write an essay about the similarities between the ideas of self-declared atheist Lord Russell and Buddhist leader His Holiness the 14th Dalai Lama of Tibet.

Sit Down and Shut Up or Don't Sit by Me

DENNIS DERMODY

Dennis Dermody has lived in New York since he was actor Christopher Walken's manny (male nanny). When Walken's children outgrew him, he turned to writing to support his movie habit. Film critic for *Paper* magazine, he is the man to go to for witty, unpretentious takes on horror, cult, and exploitation films. He writes a blog, "Cinemaniac," on the *Papermag* site.

1   All right, I admit it: I'm a tad neurotic when it comes to making it to the movies on time. I have to be there at least a half hour before the feature begins. Not that I'm worried about long lines at the box office, either. The movies I rush off to see are generally so sparsely attended you can hear crickets in the audience. It's just a thing I do.

2   Of course, sitting for 30 minutes watching a theater fill up is pretty boring, but through the years I've amused myself with a Margaret Mead°-like study of the way people come in and take their seats and their antics during a movie. I felt I should share my impressions lest you find yourself succumbing to these annoying traits.

3   Right off the bat: Leave the kids at home. We're not talking about *Aladdin* or *Home Alone 2*—that I understand—but recently I went to see *Body of Evidence,* and it looked like a day-care center in the theater. Strollers were flying down the aisle, children were whining for candy, restless and audibly bored (especially during the hot-wax-dripping sequence), and eventually the day-care atmosphere caused fights among the adults. "Shut your kid up!" prompted a proud parent to slug a fellow patron, and before you knew it there were angry skirmishes all over the theater and the

police had to be brought in. So either leave them at home with a sitter or tie them up to a fire hydrant outside the theater.

For some people, choosing a seat takes on moral and philo-   4 sophical implications. Sometimes they stand in the middle of the aisle juggling coats, popcorn, and Cokes, seemingly overwhelmed by the prospect of choice. Should I sit down front, or will that be too close? Is this too far back? That man seems awfully tall; I bet I couldn't see the movie if I sat behind him. I'd love to sit somewhere in the middle but would I be too close to that group of teenagers shooting heroin into their necks? If I sit on this side, will the angle be too weird to watch the movie? Is that seat unoccupied because it's broken? Good Lord, the lights are dimming and I haven't made up my mind and now I won't be able to see where I'm going.

Many, upon choosing their seats, find they are unsatisfied   5 and have to move. I've watched many couples go from one spot to another more than a dozen times before settling down—it's like watching a bird testing different spots to build a nest.

As the lights begin to dim and the annoying theater-chain logo   6 streaks across the screen, lo and behold, here come the *latecomers*! Their eyes unaccustomed to the dark, in a panic they search for friends, for assistance, for a lonely seat. Just the other day, I watched an elderly woman come into the darkened theater 10 minutes after the movie had begun and say out loud, "I can't see anything!" She then proceeded to inch her way down the aisle, grabbing onto what she thought were seats but were actually people's heads. I saw her sit down right in the lap of someone who shrieked in shock. After the woman stumbled back into the aisle, chattering wildly, someone mercifully directed her to an empty seat. Then, after a great flourish of getting out of her bulky coat, she asked spiritedly of the grumbling souls around her, "What did I miss?"

I also must address the behavior of people *during* the movie.   7 The *chatterers* comment blithely on everything that is happening on the screen. Like Tourette's syndrome° sufferers unable to control what they blurt out, these people say anything that comes into their heads. "What a cute puppy," they say when they spy an animal ambling off to the side of the frame. "I have that lamp at home," they exclaim. And add, five minutes later, "But mine is red."

The *krinklers* wander down the aisle with a million shopping   8 bags and wait for a key sequence, then begin to forage° in their bags for the perfect and most annoying plastic wrap, which they use to make noise with sadistic relish. You try to focus on the screen but the racket starts up again with a wild flourish. I've seen grown men leap to their feet with tears streaming down their face and scream, "Will you stop shaking that motherfucking bag!"

9   The *unending box of popcorn* people sit directly behind you and start masticating during the opening credits. It's bad enough having the smell of cooked corn wafting around you, but the sound is enough to drive you mad. You tell yourself that eventually they'll finish, but they never do. They keep chewing and chewing and chewing and you're deathly afraid that next they'll start on a four-pound box of malted milk balls.

10   So in summary: Get to the movie theater early and scout out the territory. It's a jungle in there, filled with a lot of really stupid animals. Know the telltale signs and act accordingly. And then sit down and shut up.

Words and Meanings

Paragraph

2	Margaret Mead	U.S. anthropologist famous for her studies of people's behaviour in various "exotic" cultures
7	Tourette's syndrome	hereditary disease that causes uncontrollable physical twitching and bursts of speech in its sufferers
8	forage	search for food

Structure and Strategy

1. What is the function of paragraph 3? After all, not all movie-goers bring their children to the theatre.
2. Identify three SIMILES in paragraphs 3, 5, and 7. How would the impact of this essay be lessened if the author had not included these figures of speech?
3. When Dermody uses phrases such as "tie them up to a fire hydrant" (paragraph 3) or "teenagers shooting heroin into their necks" (paragraph 4), he obviously does not mean to be taken seriously. Identify two or three other examples of this kind of exaggeration and consider how it affects the TONE of the essay.
4. What METAPHOR does Dermody use in the CONCLUSION of this piece? How does it contribute to the UNITY of the essay?

Content and Purpose

1. What does Dermody mean when he admits, in his opening sentence, that he is a "tad neurotic"? How does this confession affect the reader's response to the judgments that follow?
2. What is the author's PURPOSE (see paragraph 2)? Do you think he achieves it?

3. This essay classifies moviegoers according to their pre-movie and during-movie behaviours. Identify the six categories of the author's classification system.

4. Would you like to go to a movie with the author? Why or why not?

Suggestions for Writing

1. Write an essay in which you classify partygoers, friends, relatives, neighbours, children, workers, supervisors, students, or any other group of people you choose. Be sure your classification is logical and consistent, and that the purpose of your classification is clear to your reader.

2. How do you spend your time? Write an essay identifying the categories into which you divide your time each week. What did you learn about yourself from this exercise?

Toothpaste

DAVID BODANIS

David Bodanis is an academic, business consultant, and author who publishes in both the United States and England. His books include non-fiction works of popular science such as *The Body Book: A Fantastic Voyage to the World Within* (1984), *The Secret House: The Extraordinary Science of an Ordinary Day* (1986), *E=mc²: A Biography of the World's Most Famous Equation* (2000), *Electric Universe: The Shocking True Story of Electricity* (2005), and a novel, *Passionate Minds: The Great Love Affair of the Enlightenment, Featuring the Scientist Emilie du Châtelet, the Poet Voltaire, Sword Fights, Book Burnings, Assorted Kings, Seditious Verse, and the Birth of the Modern World* (2006).

Into the bathroom [we go], and after the most pressing need is 1
satisfied it's time to brush the teeth. The tube of toothpaste is
squeezed, its pinched metal seams are splayed, pressure waves

Excerpted from *The Secret House: 24 Hours in the Strange and Unexpected World in Which We Spend Our Days and Nights*. New York: Simon & Schuster, 1986. 45–47. Copyright © 2003 by David Bodanis. Reprinted with permission of the Carol Mann Agency.

are generated inside, and the paste begins to flow. But what's in this toothpaste, so carefully being extruded° out?

2   Water mostly, 30 to 45 per cent in most brands: ordinary, everyday simple tap water. It's there because people like to have a big gob of toothpaste to spread on the brush, and water is the cheapest stuff there is when it comes to making big gobs. Dripping a bit from the tap onto your brush would cost virtually nothing; whipped in with the rest of the toothpaste the manufacturers can sell it at a neat and accountant-pleasing $2 per pound equivalent. Toothpaste manufacture is a very lucrative occupation.

3   Second to water in quantity is chalk: exactly the same material that schoolteachers use to write on blackboards. It is collected from the crushed remains of long-dead ocean creatures. In the Cretaceous° seas chalk particles served as part of the wickedly sharp outer skeleton that these creatures had to wrap around themselves to keep from getting chomped by all the slightly larger other ocean creatures they met. Their massed graves are our present chalk deposits.

4   The individual chalk particles—the size of the smallest mud particles in your garden—have kept their toughness over the aeons°, and now on the toothbrush they'll need it. The enamel outer coating of the tooth they'll have to face is the hardest substance in the body—tougher than skull, or bone, or nail. Only the chalk particles in toothpaste can successfully grind into the teeth during brushing, ripping off the surface layers like an abrading wheel grinding down a boulder in a quarry.

5   The craters, slashes, and channels that the chalk tears into the teeth will also remove a certain amount of built-up yellow in the carnage, and it is for that polishing function that it's there. A certain amount of unduly enlarged extra-abrasive chalk fragments tear such cavernous pits into the teeth that future decay bacteria will be able to bunker down there and thrive; the quality control people find it almost impossible to screen out these errant super-chalk pieces, and government regulations allow them to stay in.

6   In case even the gouging doesn't get all the yellow off, another substance is worked into the toothpaste cream. This is titanium dioxide. It comes in tiny spheres, and it's the stuff bobbing around in white wall paint to make it come out white. Splashed around onto your teeth during the brushing it coats much of the yellow that remains. Being water soluble it leaks off in the next few hours and is swallowed, but at least for the quick glance up in the mirror after finishing it will make the user think his teeth are truly white. Some manufacturers add optical whit-

ening dyes—the stuff more commonly found in washing machine bleach—to make extra sure that the glance in the mirror shows reassuring white.

These ingredients alone would not make a very attractive con- 7 coction°. They would stick in the tube like a sloppy white plastic lump, hard to squeeze out as well as revolting to the touch. Few consumers would savor rubbing in a mixture of water, ground-up blackboard chalk and the whitener from latex paint first thing in the morning. To get around that finicky distaste the manufacturers have mixed in a host of other goodies.

To keep the glop from drying out, a mixture including glyc- 8 erine glycol—related to the most common car anti-freeze ingre- dient—is whipped in with the chalk and water, and to give *that* concoction a bit of substance (all we really have so far is wet colored chalk) a large helping is added of gummy molecules from the seaweed *Chondrus crispus*. This seaweed ooze spreads in among the chalk, paint and anti-freeze, then stretches itself in all directions to hold the whole mass together. A bit of paraffin oil (the fuel that flickers in camping lamps) is pumped in with it to help the moss ooze keep the whole substance smooth.

With the glycol, ooze and paraffin we're almost there. Only two 9 major chemicals are left to make the refreshing, cleansing substance we know as toothpaste. The ingredients so far are fine for cleaning, but they wouldn't make much of the satisfying foam we have come to expect in the morning brushing.

To remedy that, every toothpaste on the market has a big 10 dollop of detergent added, too. You've seen the suds detergent will make in a washing machine. The same substance added here will duplicate that inside the mouth. It's not particularly necessary, but it sells.

The only problem is that by itself this ingredient tastes, well, 11 too like detergent. It's horribly bitter and harsh. The chalk put in toothpaste is pretty foul-tasting too for that matter. It's to get around that gustatory° discomfort that the manufacturers put in the ingredient they tout° perhaps the most of all. This is the fla- voring, and it has to be strong. Double rectified peppermint oil is used—a flavorer so powerful that chemists know better than to sniff it in the raw state in the laboratory. Menthol crystals and sac- charin or other sugar simulators are added to complete the camou- flage operation.

Is that it? Chalk, water, paint, seaweed, anti-freeze, paraffin 12 oil, detergent and peppermint? Not quite. A mix like that would be irresistible to the hundreds of thousands of individual bacteria lying on the surface of even an immaculately cleaned bathroom sink. They would get in, float in the water bubbles, ingest the ooze and paraffin, maybe even spray out enzymes to break down the chalk. The result would be an uninviting mess. The way manufacturers avoid that final obstacle is by putting something in to kill the bacteria. Something good and strong is needed, something that will zap any accidentally intrudant bacteria into oblivion. And that something is formaldehyde—the disinfectant used in anatomy labs.

13   So it's chalk, water, paint, seaweed, anti-freeze, paraffin oil, detergent, peppermint, formaldehyde and fluoride (which can go some way towards preserving children's teeth)—that's the usual mixture raised to the mouth on the toothbrush for a fresh morning's clean. If it sounds too unfortunate, take heart. Studies show that thorough brushing with just plain water will often do as good a job.

Words and Meanings

Paragraph

1	extruded	pushed
3	Cretaceous	relating to the last period of the Mesozoic era (135 million to 65 million years ago)
4	aeons	ages, an immensely long time
7	concoction	mixture
11	gustatory	having to do with taste
	tout	advertise; promote aggressively in order to attract customers

Structure and Strategy

1. This essay analyzes toothpaste by dividing it into its component parts. Identify each ingredient and the paragraph(s) in which it is described.
2. What is the function of paragraph 7? Paragraph 9? Paragraph 13?
3. Underline six or seven examples of the author's use of vivid DESCRIPTION to help communicate KEY IDEAS.
4. Part of the effect of this essay depends on Bodanis's description of toothpaste. He uses words that are very different from those we are familiar with in television commercials to describe the same product. For example, in paragraph 8 we read, "seaweed ooze spreads in among the chalk, paint and anti-freeze."

Find other examples of Bodanis's use of language that you would never hear in a product advertisement. What effect does his DICTION have on the reader?

Content and Purpose

1. What is toothpaste's main ingredient and what is its primary function? What is the purpose of the SIMILE used in paragraph 4 to describe this function?
2. What's the function of glycol in toothpaste? The seaweed and paraffin? The detergent? The formaldehyde?
3. Explain the IRONY in the last paragraph.
4. Did you have any idea what toothpaste was made of before you read this essay? Did any of the ingredients surprise you? Revolt you? Why?

Suggestions for Writing

1. Does Bodanis's ANALYSIS of toothpaste make you wonder about the composition of other familiar products? Do you know what goes into margarine? Lipstick? Kraft Dinner? A hot dog? Write an essay that identifies the surprising elements of a common substance.
2. Write an essay in which you classify the different kinds of grooming aids available to assist us in making ourselves irresistible (or at least attractive) to others.

Why I Want a Wife

JUDY BRADY

Judy Brady (b. 1937) is a veteran of the women's liberation movement of the 1960s and '70s. She lives in San Francisco, where she works in the environmental justice movement. She is interested in the link between environmental pollution and the erosion of human health, with an emphasis on the politics of cancer. "Why I Want a Wife" was published in the inaugural issue of *Ms* magazine, 1971, and quickly became a classic example of ironic writing.

1   I belong to that classification of people known as wives. I am A
Wife.

2   And, not altogether incidentally, I am a mother. Not too
long ago a male friend of mine appeared on the scene fresh from
a recent divorce. He had one child, who is, of course, with his ex-
wife. He is looking for another wife. As I thought about him while
I was ironing one evening, it suddenly occurred to me that I too,
would like to have a wife. Why do I want a wife?

3   I would like to go back to school so that I can become economically independent, support myself, and if need be, support those
dependent upon me. I want a wife who will work and send me
to school. And while I am going to school I want a wife to take
care of my children. I want a wife to keep track of the children's
doctor and dentist appointments. And to keep track of mine, too.
I want a wife to make sure my children eat properly and are kept
clean. I want a wife who will wash the children's clothes and keep
them mended. I want a wife who is a good nurturant° attendant
to my children, who arranges for their schooling, makes sure that
they have an adequate social life with their peers, takes them to
the park, the zoo, etc. I want a wife who takes care of the children
when they are sick, a wife who arranges to be around when the
children need special care, because, of course, I cannot miss classes
at school. My wife must arrange to lose time at work and not lose
the job. It may mean a small cut in my wife's income from time
to time, but I guess I can tolerate that. Needless to say, my wife
will arrange and pay for the care of the children while my wife is
working.

4   I want a wife who will take care of my physical needs. I want
a wife who will keep my house clean. A wife who will pick up
after my children, a wife who will pick up after me. I want a wife
who will keep my clothes clean, ironed, mended, replaced when
need be, and who will see to it that my personal things are kept in
their proper place so that I can find what I need the minute I need
it. I want a wife who cooks the meals, a wife who is a good cook.
I want a wife who will plan the menus, do the necessary grocery
shopping, prepare the meals, serve them pleasantly, and then do
the cleaning up while I do my studying. I want a wife who will care
for me when I am sick and sympathize with my pain and loss of
time from school. I want a wife to go along when our family takes a
vacation so that someone can continue care for me and my children
when I need a rest and change of scene. I want a wife who will not
bother me with rambling complaints about a wife's duties. But I
want a wife who will listen to me when I feel the need to explain
a rather difficult point I have come across in my course of studies.

And I want a wife who will type my papers for me when I have written them.

I want a wife who will take care of the details of my social life. 5 When my wife and I are invited out by my friends, I want a wife who will take care of the baby-sitting arrangements. When I meet people at school that I like and want to entertain, I want a wife who will have the house clean, will prepare a special meal, serve it to me and my friends, and not interrupt when I talk about things that interest me and my friends. I want a wife who will have arranged that the children are fed and ready for bed before my guests arrive so that the children do not bother us. I want a wife who takes care of the needs of my guests so that they feel comfortable, who makes sure that they have an ashtray, that they are passed the hors d'oeuvres, that they are offered a second helping of the food, that their wine glasses are replenished° when necessary, that their coffee is served to them as they like it. And I want a wife who knows that sometimes I need a night out by myself.

I want a wife who is sensitive to my sexual needs, a wife 6 who makes love passionately and eagerly when I feel like it, a wife who makes sure that I am satisfied. And, of course, I want a wife who will not demand sexual attention when I am not in the mood for it. I want a wife who assumes the complete respon-sibility for birth control, because I do not want more children. I want a wife who will remain sexually faithful to me so that I do not have to clutter up my intellectual life with jealousies. And I want a wife who understands that my sexual needs may entail more than strict adherence° to monogamy°. I must, after all, be able to relate to people as fully as possible.

If, by chance, I find another person more suitable as a wife than 7 the wife I already have, I want the liberty to replace my present wife with another one. Naturally, I will expect a fresh, new life; my wife will take the children and be solely responsible for them so that I am left free.

When I am through with school and have a job, I want my wife 8 to quit working and remain at home so that my wife can more fully and completely take care of a wife's duties.

My God, who wouldn't want a wife? 9

Words and Meanings

nurturant	providing care, food, and training	3
replenished	refilled	5

6   adherence   constancy, sticking to

monogamy   custom of marrying and being faithful to one
                          mate

Structure and Strategy

1. What is the function of the first two paragraphs? What TONE do they establish?
2. Into what main functions does Brady divide the role of a wife? Identify the paragraph(s) that focus on each. Then write a one-sentence summary of this essay (a thesis statement).
3. Why does Brady never use the pronouns "she" or "her" to refer to a wife? What purpose does the frequent repetition of the word "wife" serve?
4. What is the effect of having so many sentences begin with the words "I want"?

Content and Purpose

1. What is Brady's attitude toward the traditional roles assigned to men and women in our society? Identify two or three passages that clearly convey her feelings.
2. Is this forty-year-old essay dated or not? Consider the degree to which men's and women's roles have changed since Brady wrote her essay. Is her view of sex-differentiated social roles still valid in contemporary Canada?
3. What would be the effect of this essay if it had been written by a man in the early part of the twenty-first century? How would readers respond?

Suggestions for Writing

1. Write an essay organized, like Brady's, on the principle of division. Your first paragraph should contain the sentence, "I want a husband."
2. Read Noreen Shanahan's essay "My Life as a Cleaner" on page 92 and compare her job with that of the wife in Brady's essay. Identify the big difference between them. Is Shanahan the solution for Brady's dissatisfaction?
3. Read Margaret Wente's "The New Heavyweights of the Workplace" on page 338 and write an essay in which you argue that men should (or should not) take over household duties as their financial contribution to the family diminishes.
4. Write an essay in which you classify types of wives or husbands (or mothers, or fathers, or children).

5. Brady's essay was first published in 1971. Do you think expectations of wives have changed since then? Write an essay explaining your opinion about how a wife's role has or has not changed in the past 40 years.

The Term Paper Artist

NICK MAMATAS

Novelist, short story writer, and journalist, Nick Mamatas (b. 1972) funded his early writing career by producing term papers for college students. His novel *Mover Underground* (2006) was nominated for the Bram Stoker and the International Horror Guild awards. Mamatas followed up with the suburban nightmare novel *Under My Roof* (2007). Mamatas writes short stories and articles, which have appeared in *Razor, Village Voice, Spex, Polyphony,* and numerous other journals. Most recently, he published a collection of short fiction, *You Might Sleep* (2009), and co-edited with Ellen Datlow an original horror anthology, *Haunted Legends* (2010).

One great way to briefly turn the conversation toward myself at a party is to answer the question, "So, what do you do?" with, "I'm a writer." Not that most of the people I've met at parties have read my novels or short stories or feature articles; when they ask, "Have I seen any of your stuff?" I shrug and the conversation moves on. If I want attention for an hour or so, however, I'll tell them my horrible secret—for several years I made much of my freelance income writing term papers. 1

I always wanted to be writer, but was told from an early age that such a dream was futile°. After all, nobody ever puts a classified ad in the paper that reads "Writers Wanted." Then, in the *Village Voice,* I saw just such an ad. Writers wanted, to write short pieces on business, economics, and literature. It was from a term paper mill, and they ran the ad at the beginning of each semester. 2

Writing model term papers is above-board and perfectly legal. Thanks to the First Amendment, it's protected speech, right up there with neo-Nazi rallies, tobacco company press releases, and those "9/11 Was an Inside Job" bumper stickers. It's custom-made Cliff Notes. Virtually any subject, almost any length, all levels of education—indulgent parents even buy papers for children 3

The Smart Set (Drexel University) 10 Oct. 2008. Copyright © 2008 by Nick Mamatas.

too young for credit cards of their own. You name it, I've done it. Perhaps unsurprisingly, the plurality of clients was business administration majors, but both elementary education majors and would-be social workers showed up aplenty. Even the assignments for what in my college days were the obvious gut courses crossed my desk. "Race in *The Matrix*°" was a fashionable subject.

4   The term paper biz is managed by brokers° who take financial risks by accepting credit card payments and psychological risks by actually talking to the clients. Most of the customers just aren't very bright. One of my brokers would even mark assignments with the code words DUMB CLIENT. That meant to use simple English; nothing's worse than a client calling back to ask a broker—most of whom had no particular academic training—what certain words in the paper meant. One time a client actually asked to talk to me personally and lamented that he just didn't "know a lot about Plah-toe°." Distance learning meant that he'd never heard anyone say the name.

5   In broad strokes, there are three types of term paper clients. DUMB CLIENTS predominate. They should not be in college. They *must* buy model papers simply because they do not understand what a term paper is, much less anything going on in their assignments. I don't believe that most of them even handed the papers in as their own, as it would have been obvious that they didn't write them. Frequently I was asked to underline the thesis statement because locating it otherwise would have been too difficult. But that sort of thing was just average for the bottom of the barrel student-client. To really understand how low the standards are these days, we must lift up the barrel and see what squirms beneath. One time, I got an e-mail from the broker with some last-minute instructions for a term paper—"I told her that it is up to the writer whether or not he includes this because it was sent to me at the last minute. So if you can take a look at this, that is fine, if not I understand." The last-minute addition was to produce a section called "BODY OF PAPER" (capitals *sic*°). I was also asked to underline this section so that the client could identify it. Of course, I underlined everything but the first and last paragraphs of the three-page paper.

6   The second type of client is the one-timer. A chemistry major trapped in a poetry class thanks to the vagaries° of schedule and distribution requirements, or worse, the poet trapped in a chemistry class. These clients were generally lost and really did simply need a decent summary of their class readings—I once boiled the 1000-page *New Testament Theology* by Donald Guthrie into a 30-page précis over the course of a weekend for a quick $600.

Others are stuck on their personal statements for college appli-   7
cations, and turn to their parents, who then turn to a term paper
mill. One mother unashamedly summarized her boy and his goals
like so: "[My son] is a very kind hearted young man. One who will
make a difference in whatever he does. Barely can go unnoticed
because of his vivacious character, happiness, and joy in life. He
is very much in tune with his fortune and often helps the less fortunate." The kid planned to be a pre-med major if accepted, but
was applying to a competitive college as a Women's Studies major
because Mother was "told the chances of him getting into [promi-
nent college] under less desirable subjects (as opposed to Business)
was better." Finally, she explained to me the family philosophy—
"Since our family places great emphasis on education, [boy] fully
accepts that the only guarantee for a good and stable future can be
only achieved through outstanding education."

The third group is perhaps the most tragic: They are well-   8
educated professionals who simply lack English-language skills.
Often they come from the former Soviet Union, and in their home
countries were engineers, medical professionals, and scientists. In
the United States, they drive cabs and have to pretend to care about
"Gothicism° in 'A Rose For Emily' " for the sake of another degree.
For the most part, these clients actually send in their own papers
and they get an edit from a native speaker. Sometimes they even
pinch-hit for the brokers, doing papers on graduate-level physics
and nursing themselves.

Term paper writing was never good money, but it was cer-   9
tainly fast money. For a freelancer, where any moment of slack time
is unpaid time, term papers are just too tempting. Need $100 by
Friday to keep the lights on? No sweat. Plenty of kids need 10 pages
on *Hamlet* by Thursday. Finals week is a gold mine. More than once
the phone rang at midnight and the broker had an assignment. Six
pages by 6 a.m.—the kid needs three hours to rewrite and hand in
the paper by 9 or he won't graduate. "Cool," I'd say. "A hundred
bucks a page." I'd get it, too, and when I didn't get it, I slept well
anyway. Even DUMB CLIENTS could figure out that they'd be
better off spending $600 on the model paper instead of $2,500 to
repeat a course. Back in the days when a pulse and pay stub was
sufficient to qualify for a mortgage, term papers—along with gigs
for dot.com-era business magazines—helped me buy my first house.

Term paper work is also extremely easy, once you get the hang of   10
it. It's like an old dance routine buried in one's muscle memory. You
hear the tune—say, "Unlike the ancient Greek tragic playwrights,
Shakespeare likes to insert humor in his tragedies"—and your body
does the rest automatically. I'd just scan Google or databases like

Questia.com for a few quotes from primary and secondary sources, create an argument based on whatever popped up from my search, write the introduction and <u>underline the thesis statement</u>, then fill in the empty spaces between quotes with whatever came to mind.

11   Getting the hang of it is tricky, though. Over the years, several of my friends wanted in on the term paper racket, and most of them couldn't handle it. They generally made the same fundamental error—they tried to write term papers. In the paper mill biz, the paper isn't important. The deadline, page count, and number of sources are. DUMB CLIENTS make up much of the trade. They have no idea whether or not Ophelia committed suicide or was secretly offed by Gertrude, but they know how to count to seven if they ordered seven pages.

12   The secret to the gig is to amuse yourself. I have to, really, as most paper topics are deadly boring. Once, I was asked to summarize in three pages the causes of the First World War (page one), the major battles and technological innovations of the war (page two), and to explain the aftermath of the war, including how it led to the Second World War (page three). Then there was this assignment for a composition class: six pages on why "apples [the fruit] are the best." You have to make your own fun. In business papers, I'd often cite Marxist sources. When given an open topic assignment on ethics, I'd write on the ethics of buying term papers, and even include the broker's Web site as a source. My own novels and short stories were the topic of many papers—several DUMB CLIENTS rate me as their favorite author and they've never even read me, or anyone else. Whenever papers needed to refer to a client's own life experiences, I'd give the student various sexual hang-ups.

13   It's not that I never felt a little skeevy writing papers. Mostly it was a game, and a way to subsidize my more interesting writing. Also, I've developed a few ideas of my own over the years. I don't have the academic credentials of composition experts, but I doubt many experts spent most of a decade writing between one and five term papers a day on virtually every subject. I know something they don't know; I know why students don't understand thesis statements, argumentative writing, or proper citations.

14   It's because students have never read term papers.

15   Imagine trying to write a novel, for a grade, under a tight deadline, without ever having read a novel. Instead, you meet once or twice a week with someone who is an expert in *describing* what novels are like. Novels are long stories, you see, that depict a "slice of life" featuring a middle-class protagonist. Psychological realism is prized in novels. Moral instruction was once fairly common in novels, but is now considered gauche°. Novels end

when the protagonist has an epiphany°, such as "I am not happy. Also, neither is anybody else." Further, many long fictions are called novels even though they are really adventures, and these ersatz° novels may take place in a fantastical setting and often depict wild criminal behaviors and simplified versions of international intrigues instead of middle-class quandaries°. Sometimes there are pirates, but only so that a female character may swoon at their well-developed abdominal muscles. That's a novel. What are you waiting for? Start writing! Underline your epiphany.

There's another reason I never felt too badly about the job, though I am pleased to be done with papers. The students aren't only cheating themselves. They are being cheated by the schools that take tuition and give nothing in exchange. Last year, I was hired to write two one-page summaries of two short stories. Here are the client's instructions: "i need you to write me two different story in all these listed under. The introduction of the story, the themes, topic and character, please not from internet, Or any posted web sites, because my professor will know if from internet this is the reason why i'm spending money on it. Not two much words, because i will still write it back in clsss go straight to the point and write me the conclution at end of the two story, the second story different introduction, themes, topic and character. Thank you God Bless." 16

At the parties I go to, people start off laughing, but then they stop. 17

Words and Meanings

Paragraph

futile	a waste of time	2
The Matrix	a trilogy of science-fiction action films directed by Andy and Lana (formerly Larry) Wachowski between 1999 and 2003	3
brokers	agents or intermediaries who enable a transaction between willing buyers and providers of a service or product	4
"Plah-toe"	mispronunciation of Plato ("Play-to"), fourth-century BCE Greek philosopher and mathematician; founder of the Athens Academy; associated with Socrates and Aristotle	
sic	a Latin term meaning "thus," used to mark an error in an original document; the writer understands that it's an error and wants the reader to know he or she did not commit it.	5
vagaries	uncontrollable elements	6

8	Gothicism	a style of fiction that emphasizes the grotesque and mysterious
15	gauche	passé, awkward, not "with it"
	epiphany	a sudden, life-changing insight
	ersatz	fake
	quandaries	dilemmas, problems

Structure and Strategy

1. What INTRODUCTORY strategy does the author use in the essay? How does it relate to the CONCLUSION?
2. In paragraph 3, why do you think Mamatas chose the three examples of other kinds of "First Amendment . . . protected speech" to compare to his own work as a term-paper writer for money?
3. What group of people does Mamatas classify in this essay? Into how many categories does he classify them? Identify the paragraphs in which he discusses each category.
4. What is the IRONY in paragraph 7?
5. What is the basis of the ironic comparison in paragraph 15? Who is the author criticizing here?
6. Why do you think Mamatas chose his title? Is it an ALLUSION?

Content and Purpose

1. Who manages the "term paper biz" (paragraph 4), and what kind of risk does the manager assume? Is the writer ever in touch with the client?
2. What are the three types of term-paper clients? Which type makes up most of the clientele? Summarize the reasons why each type has to/chooses to buy essays for college courses.
3. How are term-paper writers paid: a flat fee? By the page? Are there factors that would affect the rate? Did Mamatas make much money at his "profession"? What is his other "real" job?
4. According to Mamatas, is it easy or difficult to write a paper for money? Summarize his essay writing process. What has his output been (see paragraph 13)?
5. What's important to the DUMB CLIENTS in their purchased papers? Why does the author consistently capitalize those words? What's important to Mamatas in his work?
6. How does Mamatas feel about his work as a hired-gun essay writer? Why does he think students don't know how to write term papers?

7. Why does Mamatas think schools are cheating students? Why does he choose to use a long quotation to make his point (paragraph 16)? Do you agree or disagree with him?
8. Why do you think people at parties start laughing when they hear about Mamatas' job, but then stop (paragraph 17)?

Suggestions for Writing

1. Have you ever handed in someone else's work as your own? Write an essay describing why you chose to do so and how the assignment turned out. Did you learn anything from this experience?
2. Write an essay arguing either for or against the contention that many students are not prepared for college or university work and thus find themselves unable to perform satisfactorily at a postsecondary level.

What I Have Lived For

BERTRAND RUSSELL

Bertrand Russell (1872–1970), philosopher, mathematician, and social reformer, was awarded the Nobel Prize for Literature in 1950. His progressive views on the liberalization of sexual attitudes and the role of women led to his dismissal from the University of California at Los Angeles in the 1920s. Russell was a leading pacifist and proponent of nuclear disarmament. Among his many books are *Principia Mathematica*, *Why I Am Not a Christian*, and *History of Western Philosophy*.

Three passions, simple but overwhelmingly strong, have governed my life: the longing for love, the search for knowledge, and unbearable pity for the suffering of mankind. These passions, like great winds, have blown me hither and thither, in a wayward° course, over a deep ocean of anguish, reaching to the very verge° of despair.

I have sought love, first, because it brings ecstasy°—ecstasy so great that I would often have sacrificed all the rest of life for a few hours of this joy. I have sought it, next, because it relieves loneliness—that terrible loneliness in which one shivering consciousness looks over the rim of the world into the cold unfath-omable lifeless abyss°. I have sought it, finally, because in the union of love I have seen, in a mystic miniature, the prefiguring° vision of the heaven that saints and poets have imagined. This is what I sought, and though it might seem too good for human life, this is what—at last—I have found.

3   With equal passion I have sought knowledge. I have wished to understand the hearts of men. I have wished to know why the stars shine. And I have tried to apprehend the Pythagorean° power by which number holds sway above the flux°. A little of this, but not much, I have achieved.

4   Love and knowledge, so far as they were possible, led upward toward the heavens. But always pity brought me back to earth. Echoes of cries of pain reverberate° in my heart. Children in famine, victims tortured by oppressors, helpless old people a hated burden to their sons, and the whole world of loneliness, poverty, and pain make a mockery of what human life should be. I long to alleviate° the evil, but I cannot, and I too suffer.

5   This has been my life. I have found it worth living, and would gladly live it again if the chance were offered me.

Words and Meanings

Paragraph

1	wayward	unpredictable, wandering
	verge	edge, brink
2	ecstasy	supreme joy
	abyss	bottomless pit, hell
	prefiguring	picturing to oneself beforehand
3	Pythagorean	relating to the Greek philosopher Pythagoras and his theory that through mathematics one can understand the relationship between all things and the principle of harmony in the universe
	flux	continual motion, change
4	reverberate	echo
	alleviate	relieve, lessen

Structure and Strategy

1. Identify Russell's thesis statement and the TOPIC SENTENCES of paragraphs 2, 3, and 4.

2. How does the structure of the second sentence in paragraph 1 reinforce its meaning?
3. The number three is the basis for the structure of Russell's essay. Three is an ancient symbol for unity and completeness and for the human life cycle: birth, life, death. Find as many examples as you can of Russell's use of "threes." (Look at paragraph and sentence structure as well as content.)
4. What is the function of the first sentence of paragraph 4?
5. How does Russell's concluding paragraph contribute to the UNITY of the essay?
6. Refer to the introduction to this unit and show how paragraph 1 sets up a division essay and how paragraph 4 is actually a classification.
7. Analyze the ORDER in which Russell explains his three passions. Do you think the order is chronological, logical, climactic, or random? Does the order reflect the relative importance or value that Russell ascribes to each passion? How?

Content and Purpose

1. For Bertrand Russell, love means more than physical passion. What else does he include in his meaning of love (paragraph 2)?
2. What are the three kinds of knowledge Russell spent his life seeking?
3. Which of Russell's three "passions" has he been least successful in achieving? Why?
4. Which passion is most important to Russell? How do you know?

Suggestions for Writing

1. What goals have you set for yourself for the next ten years? Write a short paper in which you identify and explain two or three of your goals.
2. In what ways are you different from other people? Write a short paper in which you identify and explain some of the qualities and characteristics that make you a unique human being.
3. Imagine that you are seventy-five years old. Write a short paper explaining what you have lived for.

ADDITIONAL SUGGESTIONS FOR WRITING: CLASSIFICATION AND DIVISION

Use classification or division, whichever is appropriate, to analyze one of the topics below into its component parts, or characteristics, or kinds. Write a thesis statement based on your analysis and then develop it into an essay that will interest a reader who doesn't necessarily share your point of view.

1. Part-time jobs
2. Marriages
3. Films
4. Media celebrities, such as movie stars, pop stars, politicians, media gurus
5. Computer games
6. Popular novels
7. Sitcoms
8. A family or families
9. Dreams
10. Colleges
11. Television commercials
12. Drivers/neighbours/bullies
13. Friendship or friends
14. Text messagers
15. Reality TV shows
16. Teachers/coaches
17. Shoppers or shopping malls
18. Vacation destinations
19. Internet scams
20. A religious or social ritual (such as a wedding, funeral, baptism, bar/bat mitzvah, birthday celebration)

UNIT 5

Comparison and Contrast

WHAT ARE COMPARISON AND CONTRAST?

To *compare* two things is to point out the similarities between them; to *contrast* them is to point out their differences. When we look at both similarities and differences, we are engaging in *comparison and contrast*. Often, however, people use the term "comparison" to describe both processes. "Comparison shopping," for example, means to discover significant differences among similar items. An **analogy** is a special kind of comparison that is useful in some kinds of writing; we explain it at the end of this introduction.

WHY DO WE USE COMPARISON AND CONTRAST?

Comparison and contrast answer the following questions: In what ways are two things alike? In what ways are they different? Comparing and contrasting things is a common mental process; it's something we do, consciously or unconsciously, whenever we encounter something new. Using such a pattern in written communication can be useful in two specific ways.

First, an essay or report structured to compare various items can provide a reader with helpful information. It can offer new insight into two topics by looking at them side by side. For example, Shaun Pett's "The Happiness Project" contrasts the purely quantitative economic index GDP (gross domestic product) with the more qualitative CIW (Canadian Index of Wellbeing) as ways to measure happiness.

Second, a comparison or contrast can evaluate as well as inform. It can assess the relative merits of two topics and explain the writer's preference for one over the other. In "Ottawa vs. New York," for example, Germaine Greer not only contrasts the two cities but also argues for the quality of life in Canada versus that in the United States.

HOW DO WE WRITE COMPARISON AND CONTRAST?

Here are four guidelines for organizing a paper according to the principles of comparison and contrast:

1. Make sure that your two topics are in fact comparable; they must have something significant in common even if you want to focus on differences.

2. Select terms of comparison that apply to both topics. For example, don't compare the age, height, and weight of one person with the intelligence, ambition, and personality of another. Use the same terms of comparison for both topics.

3. Decide on the most appropriate pattern of organization to use: block or point-by-point (see below).

4. Write a thesis statement that clearly identifies your topic, states or implies your terms of comparison/contrast, and indicates your organizational pattern.

Organizing a comparison according to the **block pattern** involves separating the two topics and discussing them one at a time, under the headings or categories you've chosen as your KEY IDEAS. If you were asked, for example, to compare Sarah Polley's movie *Away from Her* to the short story on which it was based, Alice Munro's "The Bear Came Over the Mountain," you might decide to focus your analysis on the characters, the setting, and the plot of the two versions. You would first discuss the story in terms of these three key ideas, and then you would do the same for the film. Here is a sample block outline for such an essay:

Paragraph 1   Introduction and thesis statement

Paragraph 2   The story
        a. characters in the story
        b. setting in the story
        c. plot in the story

Paragraph 3   The film
        a. characters in the film
        b. setting of the film
        c. plot of the film

Paragraph 4   Conclusion summarizing the similarities and differences and possibly stating your preference

The block pattern does not rule out discussing the two topics
in the same paragraph. In this example, particularly in your analysis of the film, some mention of the story might be necessary.
However, the overall structure of a block comparison should communicate the essentials about Topic 1 and then communicate the
essentials about Topic 2. The block style works best with fairly
short papers (essay questions on exams, for instance) in which the
reader does not have to remember many intricate details about
Topic 1 while trying to understand the details of Topic 2.

Structuring a comparison according to the **point-by-point
pattern** involves setting out the terms or categories of comparison, then discussing both topics under each category heading.
Organized by points, the essay comparing Munro's story with
Polley's film could communicate the same information as it does
in the block pattern, yet its shape and outline would be quite
different:

Paragraph 1   Introduction and thesis statement

Paragraph 2   Characters
  a. in the story
  b. in the film

Paragraph 3   Setting
  a. in the story
  b. in the film

Paragraph 4   Plot
  a. in the story
  b. in the film

Paragraph 5   Conclusion summarizing the similarities and differences and possibly stating your preference

A point-by-point structure makes the resemblances and differences between your two topics more readily apparent to the reader.
This structure is ideally suited to longer reports and papers in which
the terms of comparison are complex and demand high reader recall.

ANALOGY: A CREATIVE COMPARISON

Have you ever taken a test that had a question like this one?

racquet: tennis: club: (fill in the blank)

If so, you are being asked to solve an *analogy* question, to
figure out how two different things are alike. (The answer, by the

way, is golf.) An analogy is a comparison that shows similarities between two very different things; we use analogy to communicate an original and creative insight.

Usually, a comparison essay looks at two fundamentally similar things (e.g., two cities in "Ottawa vs. New York"; two cartoon family doctors in "D'oh!") and explores how they are alike and/or different. In an essay based on *analogy,* two *dissimilar* things are pulled together and the writer focuses on similarities. Here's an example: an analogy that draws an unexpected connection between students and oysters to make a point about what education—and teaching— should do.

> Pupils are more like oysters than sausages. The job of teaching is not to stuff them and then seal them up, but to help them open and reveal the riches within. There are pearls in each of us, if only we knew how to cultivate them with ardor and persistence. (Sydney J. Harris, "What a True Education Should Do")

Analogies are often used to emphasize a point. A successful analogy causes the reader to pause and consider a new and unexpected idea. A good analogy also helps the reader to understand complex or highly abstract ideas. For example, in "The Evolution of Evolution" in Unit 6, Helena Cronin creates an analogy to explore "the neatly-arrayed toolbox that is our mind." She sustains the analogy throughout the essay to make complicated ideas more accessible to readers. No matter how little we may know about the human mind or about evolution, we all know what a toolbox is.

Writers sometimes base an entire essay on analogy, as Richard Lederer does in "Writing Is . . . ." He compares writing to throwing a Frisbee. The reader is drawn in by the unlikely comparison and, in the process, learns that writing can be both playful and liberating.

Because analogies tie together two things from different categories, analogy cannot be used to prove a thesis, the way classification, division, or causal analysis—which depend on rigorous logic—can. Analogy can, however, provide readers with insight and enjoyment. Consider it a creative device that will enrich personal essays or humorous pieces.

The model essay that follows contrasts two topics and illustrates the point-by-point pattern of organization.

She Said, He Said

Introduction (a scenario)

It's Friday night. You and some friends have met at your favourite bar for a little relaxation. You all place your orders, and the conversation begins. If you watch and listen carefully, you'll notice patterns in this conversation. If you are a male in an all-male group or a female in an all-female one, the patterns

Thesis statement

you observe will not be the same. When men and women engage in that intrinsically human activity called "talking," there is much that is different in why they talk, the way they talk, and what they talk about.

First key idea (specific details highlight differences)

Men talk mainly to exchange information, accomplish a task, offer advice, or enhance their status. They see conversation as a tool and consequently tend to talk for a reason, often with a specific purpose in mind. Women, on the other hand, talk in order to nurture and support and empathize. Sometimes accused of "talking for the sake of talking," women in fact talk to establish and maintain relationships. Because conversation is a human connection, women perceive talking as an end in itself rather than as the

Analogy reinforces the differences

means to an end. In other words, men's social conversation takes the freeway from place A to destination B, sticking to the GPS-designed route for speed and efficiency. Women's conversation tends to take a more meandering journey on backroads, discovering unknown towns and perhaps a gallery or two along the way.

Second key idea (developed by facts and examples)

The way men and women talk also differs. Men more readily take charge of a conversation, and they are more assertive in expressing their opinions. They are more likely to interrupt another speaker or to argue with what someone else says. Men tend to make declarative statements—unlike women, who inject their conversation with numerous questions and often end their assertions with a vocal uptick as if their statements were questions. Men tend to state their opinions straight out: "The problem is. . . ." Women tend to soften their opinion statements with "I think that. . . ." Women also tend to preface their opinions with an apology: "Perhaps I don't understand the issue here, but I think that. . . ." The pronouns men use most often are *I* and *he*; the pronouns women use most often are *you* and *we*. Men tend to listen in silence, giving non-verbal signals of consent or disagreement; women tend to make positive sounds of encouragement as they listen ("Uh-huh," "Mm-hm"), even when they disagree with the speaker. Women are more willing to defer, are more emotional in their speech, and are more interested in keeping a conversation going than in controlling it.

Note transitional phrase
Third key idea (supported with examples)

Given the differences in why and how men and women talk, it should come as no surprise that what they talk about differs too. If you're a male in a group of males, you'll probably hear discussion of such things as the latest advance in smartphone technology, last night's hockey game, the price of gas, a proposed fishing trip, what their next car is going to be, and who drank the most beer the last time you were all together. The conversation tends to focus on things more than on people. If you're a female in a group of females, chances are you'll hear about quite different topics: a new boyfriend, the latest weight-loss program, or someone's argument with her mother, fiancé, husband, child, neighbour, boss, or any combination of the above. Female conversations tend to focus less on things than they do on relationships and people.

Conclusion (restates the thesis and issues a challenge)

Although it is dangerous to stereotype according to gender, research has shown that there are differences in the way men and women converse. Part of what makes male and female relationships so intriguing, if sometimes frustrating, is the divergence in their speech patterns. You're still not convinced? Then conduct your own research. Listen to your friends: why, how, and what they're saying.

Writing Is . . . .

RICHARD LEDERER

Richard Lederer (b. 1938) is the author of more than 30 books about language, its history and humour, including his best-selling *Anguished English*, *Crazy English*, *A Man of My Words*, and *The Miracle of Language*. Lederer's interests include uncovering word origins, exploring palindromes and anagrams, and exploiting puns. He and his wife live in San Diego, where they raised three children: one poet and two world-class professional poker players.

For me, writing is like throwing a Frisbee. 1

You can play Frisbee catch with yourself, but it's repeti- 2
tious and not much fun. Better it is to fling to others, to extend yourself across a distance.

At first, your tossing is awkward and strengthless. But, with 3
time and practice and maturity, you learn to set your body and brain and heart at the proper angles, to grasp with just the right force and not to choke the missile. You discover how to flick the release so that all things loose and wobbly snap together at just the right moment. You learn to reach out your follow-through hand to the receiver to ensure the straightness and justice of the flight.

And on the just-right days, when the sky is blue and the air 4
pulses with perfect stillness, all points of the Frisbee spin together within their bonded circle—and the object glides on its own whirling, a whirling invisible and inaudible to all others but you.

Like playing Frisbee, writing is a re-creation-al joy. For me, 5
a lot of the fun is knowing that readers out there—you among them—are sharing what I have made. I marvel that, as you pass your eyes over these words, you experience ideas and emotions similar to what I was thinking and feeling when, in another place and another time, I struck the symbols on my keyboard.

Like a whirling, gliding Frisbee, my work extends me beyond 6
the frail confines of my body. Thank you for catching me.

Structure and Strategy

1. What is the basis of the ANALOGY in this essay? How effective is it?
2. Identify the SIMILES in the introductory and concluding paragraphs.
3. What is the PUN in the last sentence?

Reprinted by permission of the author.

Content and Purpose

1. Is it possible to play Frisbee by yourself? Can you write for yourself alone? Is the analogy wholly accurate? Based on this essay, what would Lederer think about playing or writing alone?
2. What is the focus of paragraphs 3 and 4? What does it say about the way a skill develops with practice?
3. What do you think Lederer means by "re-creation-al joy" (paragraph 5)? What, to him, is a major satisfaction of writing?

Suggestions for Writing

1. What is writing like for you? Choose an activity and write a brief essay comparing it to writing.
2. Write an essay that draws an ANALOGY between two seemingly disconnected activities (not including writing) with which you are familiar.

The Blue Boy

GARY STEPHEN ROSS

Gary Stephen Ross (b. 1948) is an author and film writer (*Owning Mahoney*, 2003). Former editor of *Saturday Night*, he is currently editor-in-chief of *Vancouver* magazine and contributes to a variety of publications, including *The Walrus*.

1 My first memory of Vancouver, as a pubescent° kid in the early '60s: I'm stepping off the plane from Toronto with my father and brother into a foggy evening ripe with sulfurous emissions from the pulp mills along the Fraser River.

2 We check in to a place on Marine Drive called, oddly, the Blue Boy, after the eighteenth-century Gainsborough portrait that's cheaply reproduced in the lobby of the motor inn—or maybe it's not so odd, in a city named after the stern British Royal Navy captain who explored these shores at the end of the eighteenth century. While my brother and I fetch buckets of ice or run riot in the halls or shoot pool in the basement, Dad—employed by a union based in Pittsburgh—conducts

From "A Tale of Two Cities" by Gary Stephen Ross. Reprinted by permission of the author.

business from our room, plotting with a cast of characters out of
Damon Runyon°, ordering in Chinese food and, at strange hours,
arranging for a bottle of rye by asking for "Speedy Delivery."

I vividly recall, less than half a century ago, picking blueber-   3
ries and galloping horses just off No. 3 Road in Richmond, then a
country byway with open sewage ditches; it's now a retail mecca
of malls, franchise operations, and sleek Mercedes. Downtown, my
brother and I were stunned to realize you could step off the curb of
the busiest street and all traffic would halt—no crosswalk needed.
East Hastings, where Dad took us for seafood at the Only Café,
was more gruff pageant° than horror show, full of abject° loggers
and miners and stevedores° and what were then called, without
apology or embarrassment, drunken Indians. To us highly sophisticated easterners, the place felt like a frontier town.

It's easy to forget now, a quarter century after Expo 86 intro-   4
duced the world to Vancouver (and Vancouver to the world), easy to
forget after the exodus from Hong Kong in the '90s altered the city's
demographic profile and fuelled a real estate boom, easy to forget
now that Hermès and Coach and Gucci fill our shop windows—and
especially easy to forget during the klieg-lit invasion of the Winter
Olympics—what a small city this is. With a population of about
600,000, it's a quarter the size of Toronto proper. Edmonton, Calgary,
Montreal, and Ottawa have more citizens. Hell, Mississauga has
more. Winnipeg has more. Vancouver's American analogues are not
Chicago and New York, but Charlotte, Memphis, El Paso. Include
the metro area, and the population swells to 2.2 million, a third of
metropolitan Toronto's. If this city were an actor, it would acquit
itself beautifully in a supporting role—Philip Seymour Hoffman
before *Capote*. If it were a fighter, it would be a middleweight, albeit
one so slick and well marketed that you think of it as belonging
among the heavyweights—any of which would, in fact, clobber it.

Vancouver's youth, like its size, is easy to overlook. From the   5
air, the downtown commercial grid, circumscribed by salt water
and shining in the sun, calls to mind a sort of a mini-Manhattan, as
snugly fitted as a Lego project. But look closely, and you'll notice
that only recently have the central buildings started to poke dramatically upward; only now is a mature skyline taking shape, the
last of the baby teeth being displaced. Not so long ago, this thrum-
ming, cosmopolitan nexus° was little more than old-growth forest.
In 1881, three decades after St. Michael's College was founded
in Toronto, it was a rudimentary settlement of some 1,000 souls.
Unlike the principal cities of the East, Vancouver is only now
starting to take its place in the world, to understand the value of
heritage, to unfurl a history and plot a future.

6   One night at the Blue Boy, a union pal of my father's drunkenly informed me that he just might have found the cure for my virginity. He was an expert in such matters, and he figured a certain young woman in the coffee shop could be the ticket. "Partner," he said with a wink, "why don't you head down and give it a shot?" When he volunteered to come along for moral support, I made some excuse, but of course I headed downstairs by myself at the first opportunity.

7   I spotted her at once, as would anyone with a Y chromosome. She was stunningly endowed, effortlessly lovely; notepad in hand, she was absorbed in the task of taking an order. I sat at the counter, trembling and dry mouthed. Only when she came over and handed me a menu, brushing aside a tendril of blond hair, did I realize she was not a young woman at all. She was a girl, scarcely older than I. Her name was Lila; her name tag said so.

8   Ever since that stay at the Blue Boy, through many years in Toronto and stints of living abroad and a permanent move to the West Coast in 1989, I've associated Lila with Vancouver—younger than she seems, less sophisticated than she might like, undeniably radiant, proud to be attracting attention but not quite sure how to deal with it, a little self-conscious as the first complications of maturity settle upon her. You can't help but marvel at her good fortune, her beauty. You admire the earnestness of her endeavours. You envy the wealth of her possibilities.

9   You wonder what she'll become.

Words and Meanings

Paragraph

1	pubescent	in the early stages of puberty
2	Damon Runyon	New York journalist and short fiction writer (1880–1946), known for his colourful tales of gangsters, gamblers, and other social misfits
3	pageant	colourful display
	abject	unhappy, miserable
	stevedores	dock workers
5	nexus	centre, core

Structure and Strategy

1. An ANECDOTE from the author's memory serves as the INTRODUCTION to this essay. Where does the anecdote begin? Where does it end?

2. What feature of Vancouver is the topic of paragraph 4? How is the topic supported?
3. What examples in paragraph 4 provide illustrations of why it is "easy to forget" this important feature of Vancouver now?
4. What feature of Vancouver is the topic of paragraph 5? Identify the SIMILE and a METAPHOR in the paragraph. Why are they appropriate to the topic?
5. The essay develops an extended comparison or ANALOGY between Vancouver and a specific person. Who is the person? What features does this person share with the city, according to the author?
6. Why do you think the final paragraph is so short?

Content and Purpose

1. What kind of a hotel does the author remember staying in with his father in Vancouver? What do the details tell you about their accommodation?
2. Who is at the Blue Boy with the young Ross? When did the incident described take place?
3. What details in paragraph 3 suggest that Vancouver at the time was a backwater kind of place?
4. What is the problem that Ross's father's pal has a cure for in paragraph 6? What cure does he suggest?
5. Who is Lila? What does she look like? Do you think that Ross's "problem" was solved?

Suggestions for Writing

1. Write a descriptive essay that creates an analogy between a particular city and a specific person; for example, an actor, an athlete, a musician, an artist, or just someone you know.
2. Write an essay that compares two cities with which you are familiar. Using descriptive details, make it clear to your reader which one you prefer.

D'oh! An Analysis of the Medical Care Provided to the Family of Homer J. Simpson

ROBERT PATTERSON AND CHARLES WEIJER

Robert Patterson, who completed his M.D. at the University of Calgary, is a general surgeon in American Fork, Utah. Charles Weijer received his M.D. from the University of Alberta and Ph.D. in experimental medicine from McGill University. He is a professor of philosophy and medicine at the University of Western Ontario. His articles have appeared in leading bioethics, law, science, and medical journals. He has a wicked sense of humour.

1   These are hard times for physicians. Governments blame doctors for spiralling health care costs as they slash spending. Ethicists decry medical paternalism°. Our patients—sorry, our clients—demand to be treated like consumers. And political correctness has changed the way we speak. It's enough to give your average doctor an identity crisis. Who are we? Who should we aspire to be?

2   Working on the premise that life imitates art, we searched for and found a role model for physicians to follow in these difficult times. We found him in a long-running cartoon series, *The Simpsons*, and spent many hard hours in front of the television, collecting and collating data for analysis. We hope readers will give our conclusions the attention they deserve.

3   In the quiet town of Springfield,* noted for its substandard nuclear power plant and eccentric citizenry, Drs. Julius Hibbert and Nick Riviera frequently come in contact with Springfield's everyman, Homer J. Simpson, and his family. Homer, who works at the power plant, is known for his love of donuts and Duff's beer.

4   Like the forces of good and evil battling for the soul of medicine itself, these 2 physicians are polar opposites. Julius Hibbert is an experienced family physician with a pleasant, easygoing manner, while Nick Riviera is an ill-trained upstart who is more interested in money than medicine. Knowing that appearances can be deceiving (and first impressions rarely correct), we explored this

---

*It is unclear where Springfield is located. According to *Webster's Ninth New Collegiate Dictionary*, it could be in Illinois, Massachusetts, Ohio, Missouri, or Oregon.

question: Which of these 2 physicians should Canada's future physicians emulate?

We briefly entertained Hibbert as a potential role model. He is a 5
trusted family physician who provides care not only to Homer but also to his spouse Marge and their 3 children: Bart, Lisa and Maggie. He delivered all of the children and has weathered many a Simpson medical crisis, from Bart's broken leg to Lisa's primary depression.

Generally the quality of care he provides is solid, although 6
there was an incident when he accidentally left the keys to his Porsche inside a patient. We decided to ignore this incident, since such a mishap can befall any physician.

Hibbert has diagnostic acumen° of Oslerian° proportions. 7
He uses this regularly to identify a variety of baffling conditions, from Marge's alopecia areata° to Homer's unique form of hydrocephalus°.

"Don't worry, it's quite beneficial," he told Homer about 8
the latter condition. "Your brain is cushioned by a layer of fluid one-eighth of an inch thicker than normal. It's almost as if you're wearing a football helmet inside your own head. Why, I could wallop you all day with this surgical 2-by-4, without ever knocking you down."

Another positive trait is Hibbert's sense of humour, which he 9
uses to put patients and their families at ease. When Homer was critically injured and rushed to hospital after opening a can of beer that spent some time in a paint mixer thanks to Bart, Hibbert's levity° helped relieve an otherwise tense situation.

"Mrs. Simpson, I'm afraid your husband is dead," he said. 10

"Oh my god!" Marge responded. 11

"April Fools!" 12

Deeper analysis, however, reveals that Hibbert is no 13
Semmelweis°. He treats the health care system like his personal cash cow by taking time to talk to his patients and distributing lollipops to children. No wonder the US system is so expensive. Worse yet, he stocks his office with patient education materials that either contain value judgements or are poorly written.

When Homer first courted his bride-to-be, Hibbert gave a pam- 14
phlet entitled *So You've Ruined Your Life* to a pregnant but unmarried Marge. Fair enough. But later on, when Homer was poisoned after eating an incorrectly prepared blowfish at a Japanese restaurant, Hibbert handed him another brochure, *So You're Going to Die.* By giving away the conclusion in the title, Hibbert ruined the surprise ending. What fun is that?

Another gross violation of ethics occurred when Bart stuck 15
various objects to his skin with Crazy Glue. In a scene reminiscent of the Spanish Inquisition, Dr. Hibbert showed him the instruments

of surgery, thereby frightening the poor youngster so badly that he began to sweat, causing the objects to fall off.

16   Obviously, informed consent and truth-telling mean little or nothing to this medical Machiavelli. Any ethicist worth her salt would flail him for such an act of unbridled paternalism. Perhaps worst of all, Hibbert shows about as much sensitivity to politically correct language as Howard Stern°, as demonstrated by this conversation with Lisa.

17   "Yes, I remember Bart's birth well," he said. "You don't forget a thing like Siamese twins!"

18   "I believe they prefer to be called 'conjoined twins,'" Lisa replied.

19   "And hillbillies prefer to be called 'sons of the soil,'" Hibbert responded, "but it ain't gonna happen."

20   No, the true medical hero for whom we search is Julius Hibbert's foil, the enterprising Dr. Nick Riviera, an international medical graduate who attended the Club Med School. He practises with an enthusiasm that is matched only by his showmanship. Unfortunately, this has led to 160 complaints from Springfield's narrow-minded Malpractice Committee, but artists like Riviera are rarely understood in their time. Dr. Nick, as he is known, may be a tad weak on anatomy. "What the hell is that?" he asked after making the incision for Homer's coronary artery bypass. However, he does possess all the requisite traits for the doctor of tomorrow: he is resource conscious and he gives the customer what she wants.

21   Ever resourceful, Dr. Nick finds innovative new uses for under-utilized medical materials, such as cadavers. By placing several of them in his vehicle, he can drive in the car-pool lane and get to work more quickly. This commendable behaviour is also environmentally conscious.

22   And he's no shill° for the medical establishment. Knowing that physicians' fees are the real cause of the health care funding crisis, Dr. Nick produced a TV ad in which he offered to do any surgical procedure for just $129.95 (Can$193.95 at time of writing). Cost-effective and consumer conscious, Riviera would never let quality of care interfere with discount-rate fees.

23   His greatest asset, though, is his willingness—no, his mission—to satisfy every whim and fancy of his patients.

24   He is acutely aware that many patients actually want to be sick and, like Albert Schweitzer°, he compassionately helps them. When Bart was run over by a car but appeared unhurt, his parents considered a lawsuit against the driver. Dr. Nick was very eager to assist them. "Your son is a very sick boy," he said. "Just look at these

x-rays! You see that dark spot there? Whiplash. And this smudge here that looks like my fingerprint? That's trauma."

In another touching moment, Homer discovered that he would qualify for disabled benefits and be able to work at home if he weighed more than 300 pounds, and immediately sought a way to increase his weight. Dr. Nick was there in his time of need.   25

"You'll want to focus on the neglected food groups, such as the whipped group, the congealed group and the choc-o-tastic," he advised. "Be creative. Instead of making sandwiches with bread, use Pop-Tarts. Instead of chewing gum, chew bacon."   26

Being so burdened with his patients' wishes, Riviera often sacrifices his personal needs. Every now and then, however, he manages to think of his own well-being. "The coroner—I'm so sick of that guy," he told Homer as he prepared to perform cardiac surgery on him. "Now if something should go wrong, let's not get the law involved. One hand washes the other."   27

In these turbulent times, we need a hero to guide us into the next millennium. As a profession, we must shed the dark past embodied by Dr. Hibbert—a wasteful, paternalistic and politically incorrect physician. Instead, the physician of the future must cut corners to cut costs, accede to the patient's every whim and always strive to avoid the coroner. All hail Dr. Nick Riviera, the very model of a 21st-century healer.   28

"See you at the operating place!"   29

References
All quotations taken from our TV screens were checked against those from Richmond, R. (ed). *The Simpsons: A complete guide to our favorite family*. New York: HarperCollins Publishers; 1997.

Words and Meanings   Paragraph

medical paternalism	arrogance of doctors who assume they know better than anyone else how illness should be treated	1
acumen	shrewdness, penetrating wisdom	7
of Oslerian proportions	comparable to Sir William Osler (1849–1919), a Canadian medical pioneer and brilliant diagnostician	
alopecia areata	hair loss; baldness	
hydrocephalus	a medical condition that can cause enlargement of the head	

9	levity	tendency to make jokes
13	Semmelweis	Hungarian physician (1818–1865) who was called "the saviour of mothers" for his discovery that handwashing with disinfectants dramatically reduced maternal deaths during childbirth.
16	Howard Stern	raunchy radio talk show host
22	shill	someone who acts on behalf of a swindler by pretending to be enthusiastic about the product/service in order to dupe innocent bystanders into participating in the swindle
24	Albert Schweitzer	European physician (1875–1965) and Nobel Peace Prize-winning humanitarian

Structure and Strategy

1. What is the INTRODUCTION strategy in this essay?
2. Is this piece a comparison or a contrast? Who or what is being compared or contrasted?
3. How does the essay support most of its points about the two doctors?
4. Consider the authors' DICTION: the medical terminology (paragraph 7) and the ALLUSIONS (paragraph 7, 13, and 24). How do they contribute to the humour of the essay?
5. What is the TONE of this essay?

Content and Purpose

1. What are Springfield's Dr. Julius Hibbert's good qualities as a doctor, according to Patterson and Weijer? What are his not-so-good qualities?
2. Do you think Dr. Nick Riviera is a good physician? What does he provide for his patients, oops, consumers?
3. Which doctor do the authors praise? Why?

Suggestions for Writing

1. If you are a fan of *The Simpsons,* write an essay comparing and/or contrasting two of its many other characters.
2. What is it about *The Simpsons* that makes it so popular? Write an essay focusing on the enduring appeal of Homer, his family, and the hilarious citizens of Springfield.

Ottawa vs. New York

GERMAINE GREER

Controversial Australian feminist, author, and lecturer Germaine Greer (b. 1939) holds degrees from the universities of Melbourne, Sydney, and Cambridge. A regular contributor to periodicals and newspapers, she earned international recognition for her first book, *The Female Eunuch* (1970). Her later works include *The Obstacle Race* (1979), *Sex and Destiny* (1984), *The Whole Woman* (1999), *The Beautiful Boy* (2003), and *Shakespeare's Wife* (2007).

Waking up in Ottawa is not something I expect to do more 1 than two or three times in this lifetime, and two of those times have already happened. This is not solely because Ottawa coffee is perhaps the worst in Canada and Canadian coffee on the whole the bitterest and weakest you will ever encounter, though these truths have some bearing. The badness of the coffee could be directly related to the current weakness of the currency; there was certainly an air of poverty-strickenness about the once great hotel I woke up in. My room was huge; as long as it was lit only by the forty-watt bulbs in the four lamps that cowered by the walls I could not see the dispiriting dun colour of the quarter-acre or so of carpet, but I could smell its depressing cocktail of sixty years of food, drink, smoking, cosmetics and sex, overlaid by a choking amalgam of air-freshener, carpet-deodoriser, -dry cleaner and -shampoo. I slept with the window open as the first line of defence, and then leapt out of bed and into a shower that could not be regulated heatwise or pressurewise, and scooted off to an equally dun, dispiriting and malodorous dining room for breakfast, to wit, one bran muffin and juice made from concentrate. It is sybaritism°, rather than self-discipline, that has reduced me to the semi-sylph-like proportions that I at present display. Mind you, giving interviews and making speeches "over lunch" effectively prevents ingestion of anything solid. The Women of Influence lunches I spoke at in Canada featured cold noodle salad and polystyrene chicken thighs, suggesting more plainly than words could that Canadian business-women have at their command small influence and less money.

To escape from Ottawa . . . to New York and the Pierpont 2 Morgan Library, I took a plane to LaGuardia. Air Canada, as desperate to penny-pinch as all other Canadian operations, was sneakily folding the Newark flight into mine, which made me forty-five minutes late, and all the good people who needed to travel to New Jersey a great deal later. In that forty-five minutes the best-run hotel on the planet, or on Fifth Avenue, which comes to the same thing, let some interloper have my room.

3   The yingling at reception was so very, very sorry. Would I endure a night in a suite at the room rate instead of the statutory $3,000 a night, and let them move me to my own room tomorrow? I hummed and hawed and sighed for as long as I thought decent, then leapt at the chance. The yingling took me up himself, and threw open the door. I strode past him into a forty-foot mirrored salon hung with yellow silk damask; through the French windows a terrace hedged with clipped yew offered a spectacular view of aerial New York, as well as serried ranks of terracotta planters in which green and rose parrot tulips exhibited themselves. The east end of my salon was crowded with sofas and armchairs, all paying homage to a state-of-the-art music centre which, if I'd come equipped, I could have programmed for the whole evening. The west end featured a baronial fireplace and a ten-seater dining table. The yingling showed me my kitchen, my two bathrooms, and my seven-foot-square bed in my twenty-foot bedroom, and swept out before I could decide whether he should be tipped or not.

4   The only way to bring such magnificence into perspective was to take off all my clothes and skip about as naked as a jaybird, opening and shutting my closets, cupboards and drawers, turning all my appliances off and on, my phones, my faxes, my safe. If I had been anything more substantial than a nude scholar, I could have invited forty friends for cocktails, nine friends for dinner and a hundred for after-dinner drinks, and scribbled my signature on a room service check somewhere in the high six figures.

5   The salon soon felt less welcoming than vast, so I took a Roederer from the fridge and a salad into the bedroom, where, perched amid piles of pillows and bolsters stuffed with goose-down, I watched the fag-end of the Florida Marlins' batting order knock the Atlanta Braves' relief pitcher all over the park. The bed was meant for better things; under the television there was a VCR player. I could have ordered a selection of video-porn from room service, and had a cute somebody sent up to watch them with me.

6   Which is the great thing about New York. Anything, but anything, can be had for money, from huge diamonds of the finest water°, furs of lynx and sable, wines of vintages long said to have been exhausted, important works of art and rock cocaine, to toy-boys of the most spontaneous, entertaining and beautifully made, of any sexual orientation and all colours. Every day, planes land at JFK freighted with orchids from Malaysia, roses from

Istanbul, mangos gathered that morning from trees in Karnataka, passion-fruit from Townsville, limes from Barbados, truffles from Perigord, lobsters brought live from the coldest seas on the planet. Within twenty-four hours all will have been put on sale and consumed. The huge prices are no deterrent. The New York elite likes to be seen to pay them with nonchalance°, on the J. P. Morgan principle that if you need to know how much something costs you can't afford it. Nobody looks at the tab; the platinum credit card is thrown down for the obsequious salesperson to do his worst with.

That is what I don't like about New York. Below the thin upper 7 crust of high rollers there is a dense layer of struggling aspirants° to elite status, and below them dead-end poverty, which no longer aspires, if it ever did. The vast mass of urban New Yorkers are struggling to get by, in conditions that are truly unbearable, from the helots° who open the hair salons at six in the morning and lock them up at eight at night to the dry-cleaners who have worked twelve hours a day in the steam and fumes ever since they stepped off a boat from Europe sixty or even seventy years ago. It's great that I can get my hair washed at any hour of day or night and my clothes altered or invisibly mended within four hours of dropping them off, but it is also terrible. If I ask these people about their working lives they display no rancour°; they tell me that they cannot afford to retire and are amused at my consternation°. They would rather keep on working, they say. What else would they do? The pain in the hairdresser's feet and back, the listlessness and pallor of the dry-cleaner, can't be complained of. Everybody has to be up.

The power of positive thinking is to persuade people that the 8 narrative of their grim existence is a success story. Though New Yorkers have been telling themselves that story for so long that they have stopped believing it, they cannot permit themselves to stop telling it. Everywhere in New York, wizened ancients are drudging. The lift-driver who takes me up to my hotel room looks ninety if a day. Her bird-body balances on grossly distorted feet; the hands in her white gloves are knobby with arthritis; her skeletal face is gaily painted and her few remaining hairs coloured bright auburn and brushed up into a transparent crest. She opens and shuts the doors of her lift as if her only ambition had ever been to do just that. I want to howl with rage on her behalf. The covers of the bolsters I frolic on have all been laundered, lightly starched and pressed by hand; as I play at being a nabob°, I imagine the terribleness of the hotel laundry-room, all day, every day.

Though I love New York, I disapprove of it. Dreary as Ottawa 9 was, it was in the end a better place than New York. Canadians believe that happiness is living in a just society; they will not sing the Yankee song that capitalism is happiness, capitalism is freedom. Canadians have a lively sense of decency and human dignity. Though no Canadian can afford freshly squeezed orange juice, every Canadian can have juice made from concentrate. The lack of luxury is meant to coincide with the absence of misery. It doesn't work altogether, but the idea is worth defending.

Words and Meanings

Paragraph		
1	sybaritism	devotion to luxury
6	finest water	quality
	nonchalance	casual lack of concern or indifference
7	aspirants	people who seek or hope to attain something (in this case, status)
	helots	serfs or enslaved people
	rancour	bitter, deep-seated resentment
	consternation	bewilderment and dismay
8	nabob	a rich and powerful person

Structure and Strategy

1. Greer bases her contrast primarily on DESCRIPTION. Identify details that appeal to four physical senses in paragraph 1. What is the dominant impression created by these details? Now consider Greer's description of her second hotel room, in paragraph 3. What is the dominant impression created by these details?

2. In paragraphs 2 and 3, Greer tells an ANECDOTE to explain her sudden change of surroundings. Where does she go? What happens? Summarize the events.

3. The topic of paragraph 6 is developed by examples. Identify the TOPIC SENTENCE. Which of the examples do you recognize? Which are unfamiliar to you? Do these examples effectively support Greer's KEY IDEA?

4. The THESIS of this essay appears in the CONCLUSION. Summarize it in your own words.

Content and Purpose

1. Why is Greer in Ottawa as the essay begins? How does she feel about the city?
2. Who is "the yingling" in paragraph 3? What does he do? Why do you think she refers to him as a yingling? Define the term in your own words.
3. According to the author, what is "the great thing about New York"?
4. What doesn't Greer like about New York? What contrast is the basis of this dislike? (See paragraph 7.)
5. Summarize Greer's DESCRIPTION of the woman who operates the hotel elevator (paragraph 8). Why do you think this description is so detailed? How does it affect you?
6. How does Greer feel about life in Canada? In New York? Where do you think she would rather live? Do you agree with her? Why or why not?

Suggestions for Writing

1. Write an essay comparing or contrasting two cities that you are familiar with.
2. The contrast Greer draws between Ottawa and New York is based on her assessment of the attitudes toward wealth implicit in those cities. Write an essay that contrasts life in a wealthy family, city, or country with life in a less wealthy counterpart.
3. Read Shaun Pett's "The Happiness Project" on page 230 and write an essay that compares it with the view of Canada that Greer presents in "Ottawa vs. New York." Which country exemplifies qualities that could be measured in terms of the CIW as opposed to GDP? Which measurement do you think is more useful?

From Bikinis to Burkas

KAMAL AL-SOLAYLEE

Kamal Al-Solaylee is a former theatre critic for *The Globe and Mail* and has been widely published in newspapers and journals such as the *National Post, Eye Weekly, Elle Canada, Report on Business magazine, Chatelaine*, and *Canadian Notes & Queries*. Currently a professor at Ryerson University's School of Journalism, he holds a Ph.D. in Victorian literature from the University of Nottingham in England. He is co-editor of *The Best Canadian Essays 2010* and is currently working on a memoir, *Intolerable: A Memoir of Extremes*. Al-Solaylee loves to explore big cities such as Hong Kong, Sydney, Tokyo, Taipei, Beirut, and New York. Meanwhile he lives in midtown Toronto with his dog, Chester, in a building where the average resident's age is 80. He delights in being referred to by his neighbours as "the young man."

1   Shopping for bikinis with my four sisters in the summer of 1975 brought out the fashion beast in me, an 11-year-old living in exile with his family in Egypt. "The colour on this brown two-piece makes you look darker," I tell my sister Raja. She picks a lime-green bikini instead. "I love this one so much, I want to wear it myself," I blurt out to Ferial, clinching her choice of a black-and-white striped swimsuit.

2   The fruit of that shopping trip hangs on the office wall of my Toronto apartment—a photograph taken a few days later of myself, my four sisters and three brothers on a beach in Alexandria. The photo captures a moment of bourgeois° life in the Middle East, before the region became associated in the Western collective psyche with exporting terror or the subjugation° of women. It's an image of a large and admittedly privileged family, led by enlightened, secular° parents from southern Yemen.

3   Yes, the same Yemen that since Christmas Day° [2009] has been reintroduced to the world as a second Afghanistan or the third front in the war on terror—where my family still lives, in the capital, Sanaa. But the Yemen of today is nothing like the one where my older siblings came of age in the 1950s and 1960s. And when I speak to my family now, they have changed so much that it's hard to believe we are even related.

4   Yemen's new notoriety° doesn't surprise me; what does is how all the warning signs went unnoticed for so long. I saw it in my own flesh and blood: an open-minded family defined by its love

of arts and culture embraced hard-line interpretations of Islam and turned its back on social progress and intellectual freedom. Whatever happens next in Yemen, my family there, and no doubt millions of other middle-class Middle Eastern families, has been losing the war against extremism.

Our Camelot° was the ancient port city of Aden. There in 1945 my father, Mohamed, then 19, wed the 14-year-old Safia, a shepherdess from Hadramut, a part of Yemen now known as the birthplace of the bin Laden family. With his high-school education and some support from my grandparents, my father started a small real-estate business in what we would call flipping today: he would buy old buildings, renovate and sell them at a profit, as well as renting some units to the British expatriates° who "managed" Aden as a colony. His properties multiplied in number almost as fast as his progeny°, 11 in all, born from 1946 to 1964—the Yemeni version of the boomer generation. The youngest is me. 5

Today, Aden is home to a growing, violent southern secession movement, and the place where al-Qaeda hit the USS Cole with explosives in 2000 while it was in the harbour. But, according to my family, it was once a model of peace and harmony. "The Brits brought order," my father used to tell us. My sister Faiza talks of a cosmopolitan port where European ships would stop on the way from Europe to the Indian subcontinent, often bringing with them such coveted° merchandise as the latest fashions or, more thrillingly for my then-teenage sisters and brother, early Beatles albums. For some reason, Yemenis especially liked Ringo Starr. 6

But that security was rocked by guerrilla uprisings in the mid-1960s, and came to an end in the fall of 1967 when the nascent° nationalist movement declared independence from the British. That November, rebels kidnapped my father for two days and released him for a large sum of money, under one condition: We were to pack and leave Aden in 24 hours. Imagine having to find a new home for a family of 11 children in less than a day. Decades later, my sisters would still ask an aunt if she ever found the Beatles records my mother made them leave behind. 7

What followed were 15 years of exile between Beirut and Cairo. By the late 1970s, though, neither of those tension-filled cities felt safe or welcoming any more, and my father decided there was no choice but to return to Yemen—not to socialist Aden, but to pro-business Sanaa in the north, which was slowly making contact with the outside world after decades of insular, caste-based pseudo-monarchy°. 8

Sanaa? That medieval-looking city? As a young gay man still exploring his sexuality, I knew I couldn't spend the rest of my life in a place where hangings were still held in broad daylight as part 9 of *sharia* law°. But I had to go along, and lived there from 1983 to 1985. It was a jolt to the system: The streets came to a standstill at 9 p.m.—no one went out, and vans carrying uniformed security guards roamed the city as added security. It was too much silence for a teenager used to the bustle of Cairo.

10   My sisters' adjustment was more complex. Women were now expected to cover their heads and wear the burka° in public, and walk a few steps behind their husbands, fathers or brothers. When I was reunited with my cousin Yousra, who had been living in Sanaa for more than a decade, I reached out to give her a hug, but she pushed me away and shook my hand instead, within the bounds of propriety.

11   In 1985, I left to study in England, and later migrated to Canada, returning periodically to Sanaa for visits that became more distressing as the years passed, as the gap narrowed between my family and Yemen but widened between them and me.

12   Local events didn't help. One of the turning points in Yemen's recent history came in 1990, shortly after the Iraqi invasion of Kuwait in August. Yemen stood out for its support of Saddam Hussein's invasion, and paid a dear price. As hundreds of thousands of migrant Yemeni workers in Saudi Arabia and neighbouring Gulf countries were expelled in retaliation, many of them settled in Sanaa. A small capital city in an impoverished country, already ill equipped to serve its citizens, it cracked under the pressure. Streets teemed with the unemployed, particularly young men, many of whom succumbed to the Wahabi° brand of Islam that the exiled workers had picked up in Saudi Arabia and brought back.

13   At the co-ed Sanaa University, female students began to complain about harassment from repatriated° Yemenis who blamed women's education for the fast-rising unemployment. I don't recall seeing a single beggar in Sanaa during the early 1980s. Now, they stood at virtually every street corner. That medieval but safe city was now gritty—and still medieval.

14   I paid a visit to my family in the spring of 1992, my first in almost six years, and was shocked to see how just a few years changed us both so dramatically. There was a defeatist quality to their lives, while mine had hopes of a better future. My sisters seemed especially dispirited. Four of them worked for a living, but although their jobs gave them some economic independence, their lives remained limited. Beyond their commute to work, they rarely ventured anywhere other than grocery or clothing stores.

15   Returning again in the summer of 2001—my first visit since I had moved to Canada in 1996—I encountered a family that was a lot closer to the stereotype of regressive Muslim culture than I had ever known. The veils were in full view. Everybody prayed

five times a day. My brothers were unapologetically sexist in their dealings with their wives. Was this the same family that once took turns reading the great works of literature and subscribed to four newspapers daily, three in Arabic and one in English?

One of my brothers was actually suggesting that his eldest 16 daughter need not go to university because education wouldn't help her much as a housewife. One of my sisters, who is in the 1975 beach photo, now works as a librarian at Sanaa University and wears the full *niqab*°, covering her whole face except, just about, the eyes. One day, she followed me around town for half an hour, just for fun, to see if I would recognize her. I never did.

Collectively they have become television addicts. Satellite TV, 17 featuring hundreds of channels from the Arab world and beyond, has taken over from reading and socializing as the main form of entertainment. Why? Because among the many channels you can watch are the more Islamist ones (Hezbollah's Manar TV, for example) that promote a rigid version of the faith.

By the time I visited Sanaa again in 2006, anti-Western and pro- 18 Islamist sympathies intruded on virtually every conversation with friends, neighbours and family. The presence of al-Qaeda is never spoken of as positive, but it's not challenged or condemned either.

The real danger is the tacit° acceptance—an acceptance that has 19 been building slowly for more than two decades and has claimed even progressive families like mine. The government of President Ali Abdullah Saleh, in power for more than 30 years now, is too busy protecting its own interests from Yemen's relatively small oil wealth—businesses contributing to it include some Alberta oil companies—to show any real interest in the well-being of its middle-class citizens. Under his watch, Yemen has gone from a poor country to the most destitute in the Arab world. He fortified his stronghold on the country's larger cities in the north (Sanaa, Taiz, Houdeida), but lost control of the vast tribal terrains outside them. The result is a political culture where the cities are riddled with government red tape, while everywhere else is virtually lawless.

Comparisons to Afghanistan are not entirely warmongering on 20 the part of the U.S. media. My family is reasonably well connected, so it keeps surviving one crisis—food and water shortages, health scares—after another. But for how much longer?

In a black photo album tucked inside an old filing cabinet, I 21 keep more recent family photographs, from my visits to Sanaa, or ones they send in the mail. I don't believe that even my closest friends have seen them. The rare times I look at them, I see only a family that has betrayed its secular, intellectual history and has either chosen or been forced to accept intolerance instead.

22   One photograph from April, 2006, particularly infuriates me. My family's penchant for group photos never wavers, but this time my eldest brother voices his concern about my sisters being photographed in their "indoor" clothes. "What if the men who work at the photo-developing shop get to see your sisters in short sleeves or without a head scarf?" he asks, as if it's something I should have thought about myself. This is the same brother who is standing behind me in that 1975 picture I love so much. My sisters immediately see his point. I'm stunned. We reach a compromise. I can pose with my sisters and mother if they wear the *hijab*°, or at least long sleeves and skirts. I fake a smile as my heart breaks. The last thing I want is an argument on my last night in Sanaa.

23   I haven't seen my family since.

Words and Meanings

Paragraph

2   bourgeois   wealthy middle-class

     subjugation   control, dominance over

     secular   worldly, not religious

3   Christmas Day   On Christmas Day in 2009, "the underwear bomber," a young Nigerian man influenced by Yemeni jihadists, tried unsuccessfully to detonate a plastic explosive bomb en route from Amsterdam to Detroit

4   notoriety   negative reputation

5   Camelot   the legendary home of King Arthur and his court

     expatriates   people who have left their home country and chosen to live abroad

     progeny   children

6   coveted   longed for

7   nascent   growing

8   caste-based
     pseudo-monarchy   a hierarchical ruling system based on hereditary (often socio-economic) status

9   *sharia* law   Islamic law governing civil, criminal, and moral matters

10   burka   garment worn by some Muslim women, covering the body from head to foot

Wahabi	a Muslim sect known for its strict interpretation of the Koran, flourishing mainly in Saudi Arabia	12
repatriated	sent back to country of origin	13
niqab	a veil with a small aperture for the eyes	16
tacit	silent, unspoken	19
hijab	a scarf-like head covering that leaves only the face exposed	22

Structure and Strategy

1. What two contrasts does this essay focus on? (See paragraph 3.)
2. Identify a significant comparison in paragraph 5.
3. Part of the essay is structured around the author's visits to his family in Yemen. Identify the years of these visits and the paragraphs that describe them.
4. What common focus do the INTRODUCTION and CONCLUSION share? How is this focus picked up and carried throughout the essay?
5. What is the TONE of the essay?

Content and Purpose

1. When and where was the author born? How does he describe his family? Where was he brought up? Why?
2. According to the author's family, what was Yemen like in the 1950s and '60s? How had it changed by the early 1980s?
3. When and why did the author leave Yemen to study in England and then settle in Canada?
4. According to the author, how has life changed for his sisters and for women generally in Yemen?
5. How does Al-Solaylee feel about the changes in his family and in the country of his birth?

Suggestions for Writing

1. Families change over the generations, sometimes dramatically, sometimes incrementally. Write an essay that contrasts a family at one point in time with the same family a generation (or two) later.
2. Write an essay about wearing the *hijab, niqab,* or *burka.* Do such dress requirements free, protect, or repress women? Provide ample evidence to support your opinion.
3. Write an essay arguing for or against the view of "regressive Muslim culture" (paragraph 15) that al-Solaylee presents in this essay.

The Happiness Project

SHAUN PETT

Shaun Pett is a Montreal journalist who regularly contributes to *Maisonneuve*. His writing has also appeared in *The Globe and Mail*, the *Montreal Gazette*, and *Now Magazine*. Pett is currently working toward his Master of Fine Arts in creative writing at Concordia University.

1   "Happiness is love," says Mrs. Morris on an eponymous° track from Charles Spearin's *The Happiness Project*. Spearin, a member of Broken Social Scene, recorded his conversations with neighbours in the summer of 2008 and crafted songs from the accidental melodies of their voices. For content, he asked what made them happy.

2   According to Spearin, Mrs. Morris "genuinely loves the people around her and gets a lot of satisfaction from the simple things." Vanessa, born deaf, describes the first time she received a cochlear implant°: "All of a sudden I felt my body moving in sound." Then there's Mr. Gowrie, who talks glowingly about growing up poor in Trinidad and snorts, "Here, everything is commercial." For Spearin, these answers confirmed what research into the relationship between income levels and life satisfaction had already discovered. "Above a certain threshold, which is actually pretty low," he says, "wealth has very little to do with happiness."

3   Everyone knows this, or claims to. Yet the belief that money can buy happiness is pervasive°: a rise in a country's national income will, we're told, have a corresponding effect on collective well-being. Gross Domestic Product (GDP) tracks the ups and downs of a country's wealth. Expressed as a rate of growth, GDP keeps tabs on all goods and services produced within a country in a given period. A negative rate means the economy is producing less than it did the previous year, which would indicate higher unemployment and a lower standard of living. So influential is GDP—and the gospel of endless growth it encourages policy-makers to preach—the New York Times called it "a celebrity among statistics, a giant calculator strutting about adding up every bit of paid activity."

4   Yet this statistical superstar is getting some knocks. "GDP," says former Saskatchewan premier Roy Romanow, "has emerged as a surrogate° for well-being. But GDP doesn't distinguish between activities that are good and those that are bad for our society."

5   In other words, GDP doesn't care how happy we are. Misery-bringers like hurricanes are GDP boosters; survivors buy things to

replace all that they've lost. Cleaning up the 1989 Exxon Valdez oil spill added $4.5 billion U.S. to the economy. Another GDP winner? The crushing cost of treating preventable diseases—those caused by avoidable human behaviours like smoking. Why? Because money spent on cigarettes and health care grows the economy. To get really macabre°, Canada's high lung cancer death rate (nearly nineteen thousand men and women per year) could also be considered a gain for the marketplace: casket, funeral, cemetery workers. A healthy GDP, in other words, can be lethal°. Even the term's inventor, economist Simon Kuznets, has doubts: "the welfare of a nation can scarcely be inferred from a measure of national income as defined by the GDP."

What's needed, says Romanow, "is a more holistic view." 6 To that end, a new experiment, called the Canadian Index of Wellbeing (CIW)—which Romanow chairs—tries to counterbalance strictly economic measurements of prosperity. Launched [in June 2009] by the University of Waterloo-affiliated Institute of Wellbeing, the CIW intends to provide regular report cards on eight social indicators ignored by economists: our standard of living; our health; the quality of our environment; our education; how we use our time; the vitality of our communities; our participation in the democratic process; and the state of our culture.

What frustrates Romanow about all the emphasis the world's 7 governments place on GDP is that, even in terms of what it's supposed to do—gauge material well-being—it falls short. When the first CIW reports in the eight-part series were released at the launch, they revealed that Canada's GDP per capita rose steadily since 1981 while income inequality skyrocketed (the country's top 20 percent of earners did gangbusters) and salaries stagnated°. GDP's true value, Romanow suggests, is as a negative measurement: "What does it leave out? And what are the consequences of this omission?" That's where the CIW steps in. Its ambition is nothing less than to change how Canadians measure a good life.

Right now, your economic activity might be tallied this way: 8 How much did you spend on groceries? How much is your house worth? How expensive was your car? How much do you make at work? How successful is your employer? Here's how that looks through the CIW lens: Is the fruit you bought local or did it travel from afar? Do you feel a sense of community where you live? How much greenhouse gas does your car emit? Do you enjoy your job? How much free time does it give you? Does your company produce things that are good or bad for society? From the perspective of a card-carrying° GDPer, these questions might seem a tad naïve, but the CIW hopes to prompt a rethink of what John Ralston Saul has described as a "low-level, utilitarian°, narrow approach to economics."

9   GDP skepticism is far from new. In 1972, Jigme Singye Wangchuck, then King of Bhutan, wanted to build an economy focused on people rather than growth. He proposed the policy of Gross National Happiness (GNH). A newly minted parliamentary democracy—the King introduced democratic reform last year to add to his people's happiness—Bhutan has written GNH into its constitution. Dasho Karma Ura, head of the Centre of Bhutan Studies, which developed the new indicators based on extensive surveys ("How stressed are you?" "Have you ever thought of suicide?"), defines GNH as the "responsibility of the state to create a situation where individuals can pursue happiness."

10   What, according to the surveys, makes the Bhutanese sad? The dilution of their culture, loss of community and traditional values, and harm to the environment. To address this, GNH led to a ban on public smoking. Twenty-six percent of Bhutanese land is now under environmental protection, and no logging is allowed in old growth forests. The country also focuses on "high-value, low-impact" tourism (in a bid to chase off back-packers, tourists are charged a minimum daily tariff), and infrastructure° is constructed from traditional designs to preserve Bhutan's distinct cultural identity. "If a project or program is anti-GNH," says Ura, "then it has to be rejected or reviewed, depending on the severity of harm caused."

11   The CIW was inspired by Bhutan's experiment, but to see how it might work, we can look to another Canadian example: the Genuine Progress Index (GPI). The brainchild of Dr. Ron Colman, the GPI is the product of thirteen years of painstaking number-crunching on how Nova Scotians live and work. "If you don't count something, it doesn't get attention," Colman explained in 2008. He's right. A GPI report on chronic disease°, which showed that 25 percent of medical costs ($500 million) in Nova Scotia were attributable to preventable factors, motivated provincial policy changes. "Our reports were a fairly significant influence in the creation of the new Department of Health Promotion," says Colman.

12   Last summer, GPI Atlantic, the Halifax-based think tank Colman leads, released "New Policy Directions for Nova Scotia." Included in the 185-page report is an idea Colman's institute had been advocating° for years before it was made popular by the recent recession: work sharing. The report gathered information on several Nova Scotia companies that took advantage of a

decades-old federal government plan enabling employees to work a four-day week and receive EI benefits for the fifth day, thus avoiding layoffs and the societal damage they cause. GPI Atlantic discovered that work sharing had another unexpected benefit: it increased productivity. A 10 percent reduction in work hours could produce a 5 percent rise in productivity. According to GPI Atlantic, redistribution of work hours reduced work-related stress, enhanced well-being and acted as a job creation strategy.

Not everyone likes the idea of screening policy decisions according to their happiness-maximizing potential. Richard Kelly, senior economist at TD Bank Financial Group, contends that the CIW involves "qualitative features of life you couldn't quantify, because everyone is going to have a different opinion to how they would measure the quality of their well-being." However, Lynne Slotek, National Project Director of the CIW, says the CIW isn't about making value judgments but, rather, establishing a framework of values derived through intense consultations with Canadians. Far from fuzzy and feel-good, in other words, CIW reports are based in statistical analysis (data is, in part, taken from Statistics Canada and the CIBC employment quality index) and pass through a rigorous° review process conducted by national and international experts. "If you get the right framework," explains Slotek, "you create an environment where people can ask the right questions and the right people are at the table making good social policy." 13

What indices like the GPI and the CIW do, supporters say, is return complexity to our society. By highlighting the interconnected nature of problems like climate change and health care, they remind us there are no silver bullets. Happiness indexes also transcend partisanship° since they require broad agreement on goals—less crime, cleaner air—that call for multi-pronged approaches across various governments and departments. The Canada Well-Being Measuring Act, an early variant of the CIW, was co-authored by Liberal MP Joe Jordan and Green Party member Peter Bevan-Baker. ("We have to distinguish expenditures that truly benefit society," said Jordan at the time, "from those that signal trouble.") Introduced in 2001, it passed with most of the House's support but was forgotten in the following election. 14

The CIW could transform not only how policy is made, but also the public's sense of ownership over the issues. Slotek feels that by educating Canadians on what really makes their lives better, the CIW can give them what they've rarely had before: a vocabulary to shift political discourse°. "Talk to anybody on the street," Slotek told the Toronto Sun. "I guarantee you'll get people to say, 'it's not 15 just about the money in my pocket; it's about the health of myself and my family, my community and where I live.'"

16 With the final reports due in 2010, the CIW has already garnered° international interest from Israel, Australia and New Zealand. Romanow believes that getting serious about happiness could be "a great area for Canada to demonstrate global leadership." The Greens, however, were the only party to include the CIW in their 2008 election platform. And although Nova Scotia's NDP government has promised to use the GPI, Colman is still waiting for their call. He hopes it comes soon. "Either there is a major shift in direction in the coming ten years," Colman says, "or in many ways it will be too late."

Words and Meanings

Paragraph

1	eponymous	of the same name; i.e., the song is called "Mrs. Morris"
2	cochlear implant	hearing aid implanted in the inner ear
3	pervasive	everywhere present
4	surrogate	stand-in; substitute
5	macabre	gruesome; suggestive of death and decay
	lethal	deadly
7	stagnated	failed to grow
8	card-carrying	dedicated, committed
	utilitarian	practical
10	infrastructure	the facilities and services necessary for a community or society to function; e.g., roads, water and sewage systems, communication systems
11	chronic disease	long-lasting but not (usually) fatal diseases such as arthritis, depression, diabetes, obesity
12	advocating	promoting, supporting
13	rigorous	strict, demanding
14	transcend partisanship	go beyond political party affiliations
15	discourse	discussion
16	garnered	attracted, gathered

Structure and Strategy

1. What INTRODUCTION strategy is used in this essay? How many examples are provided in paragraphs 1 and 2 to illustrate the "happiness project" from the Broken Social Scene album? Why do you think the author chose Broken Social Scene to introduce a discussion of political and economic theory?
2. What is being contrasted in this essay? Is anything being compared?
3. What is the THESIS of this piece? What are the primary ways that the author supports his thesis?
4. Which paragraphs focus on a foreign country's experience with happiness indices? Which paragraphs focus on a specific Canadian province?
5. What is the ALLUSION in the second sentence of paragraph 14? Is it effective?

Content and Purpose

1. What is GDP? Why does the author think it is an unreliable measurement of human happiness?
2. What other indices of human happiness does the essay propose for measuring how happy people are in a specific country?
3. What are the indicators measured by the Canadian Index of Wellbeing? Would they adequately measure your personal level of happiness or well-being? Why or why not?
4. Where does the author present a counter-argument to the CIW? How does he refute the counter-argument?
5. What does the final paragraph suggest about the future of the CIW?

Suggestions for Writing

1. Charles Spearin's *The Happiness Project* won the Juno Award for Contemporary Jazz Album in 2010. Listen to the recording and write a review of it. What's it about? Do you like it? Why or why not?
2. How important is money to your own happiness? What are you willing to do—or give up—in order to acquire a lot of it? Write an essay that explores the connection between your financial well-being and your overall satisfaction with life.

Why Cree Is the Funniest of All Languages

TOMSON HIGHWAY

Tomson Highway (b. 1951) is the proud son of legendary caribou hunter and world-championship dogsled racer Joe Highway. Born in a tent pitched in a snow bank, he comes from the extreme northwest corner of Manitoba, where the province meets Saskatchewan and Nunavut. His family lived a nomadic life and spoke Cree. With no access to books, television, or radio, his parents told their children stories, and Tomson fell in love with storytelling. Today, he writes plays, novels, and music for a living. Among his best-known works are the plays *The Rez Sisters* (1986) and *Dry Lips Oughta Move to Kapuskasing* (1989), and the best-selling novel *Kiss of the Fur Queen* (1998).

1   Of the three to six thousand languages linguists have determined exist in the world—the prevalence of dialects° makes it impossible to pin down a number—each has its own special genius. I am fortunate enough to be familiar with three of these: English, French and the language I spoke to the exclusion of all others until age seven, Cree.

2   English is an intellectual, cerebral language. It comes from, and lives in, the head, and does so in a manner most brilliant. French, *par contre*°, is an emotional language, a language of the senses. It comes from, and lives in, the heart. *And* in the stomach. If you don't believe me, try calling your loved one "my cabbage, my lamb, my rabbit, my duck, my pussy, my pet, my casserole dish" with a straight face and see what kind of reaction you get. In French, it makes perfect sense to talk this sensually; in English, it is downright embarrassing. If you still don't believe me, try travelling back and forth between France and England and see what kind of food you find in each country. In one, the food is fantastic, utterly divine. If, as legend has it, the Inuit have forty words for snow, then the French have easily 350 words for cheese, some of which "orgasm" their way down your throat, which is the only way I have ever been able to describe the sensation in English. *Foie gras*? You die of the senses when you eat it and then float up to heaven. And then there is the wine. In England, by comparison, the food is decidedly *un*-fantastic, shall we say (that's putting it politely). But British Airways? Ho-la-la. The world's best, most efficient, most powerful airline, bar none. Works

"Why Cree is the Funniest of All Languages," by Tomson Highway, from the book *Me Funny*, edited by Drew Hayden Taylor, published 2005 by Douglas & McIntyre, an imprint of D&M Publishers Inc. Reprinted with permission from the publisher.

like a well-oiled engine. Two thousand planes, most of them the size of mansions, that reach all four corners of the world.

Cree, my mother tongue, is neither a language of the mind nor a language of the senses. It is a language of the flesh. A physical language. It lives in the human body not above the neck, as English does, not between the neck and the waist, as French does, but one step lower: between the waist and the thighs. Cree lives in the groin, in the sex organs. It lives, that is to say, in the most fun-loving, the most pleasurable—not to mention the funniest-looking—part of the human corpus°: a region of the body that has, for reasons I will posit° later, become so alienated from the head that speaking of it in English is a shameful, dirty, embarrassing, disgusting, dare one say evil thing to do.   3

Since I am writing this essay in English, the part of you that is most alive as you read is your brain. If I were writing in French, and you were reading it accordingly, the most alive parts of you would be your heart and your stomach. Try something as simple as this: *"Bonjour, Barbara, ça va?" "Oui, ça va. Et toi?" "Pas pire. Mais écoute, ma belle, je voudrais te dire quelque chose. . . ."°* You see? Your mouth even starts to water when your tongue and lips wrap themselves around those syllables! But if I were writing this in Cree, and you were reading it that way, then what you would be doing is laughing, laughing constantly, laughing so hard your sides would hurt. Somewhere deep inside of you, there would be a zany sensation perpetually on the simmer, perpetually on the verge of exploding into a wild cry of intoxicating, silly, giddy pleasure.   4

For instance, pronouncing the words syllable by syllable, and at the speed of lightning, say the following: "Winnipeg, Manitoba, Saskatoon, Saskatchewan, Mistassini, Chicoutimi, Chibougamou, Quebec, Temagami, Mattawa, Ottawa, Canada." That, in essence, is Cree. That is the natural rhythm and musicality of the language. Now, with the same feeling, rhythm and speed, say this: *"Neeee eeeeeeeeeeeeeeeeeeeeeeeeeeeeeeeeeeeeeeeeee, awinuk awa oota kaa-pee-pee-tig-weet?*[1] Practise it until you get it note perfect. You will find, very quickly, that even if you don't have a clue what you are saying, you are already smiling. If you practise it with friends, you will all be laughing. And laughing not lightly, but from the pit of your respective groins. The syllables sound comical not only in and of themselves but in the way they are strung together. It is as if a clown lives inside them. And a clown *does*, in fact, live inside those syllables, of which more in a minute.   5

---

[1] A note on pronunciation: The soft *g*—as in "George" or "gel"—does not exist in the Cree language. All *g*'s are hard, as in "girl" or "gig."

6   Thus far, you know the syllables to the above Cree sentence only with your tongue, your teeth, your lips, your palate and your windpipe. Now on to the meaning. Let's start with the syllable *neee*. As with so many cultural concepts, the word is untranslatable, but we could come close with English expressions such as "oh dear" or "oh my goodness" or "good grief" or "yeah, right" or "you little slut" (in the affectionate, teasing sense) or "you little bastard" (ditto). Then again, *neee* could mean something as simple as "hey." It could even be a combination of the above. You can, moreover, extend the sound for as long as you want to, depending on how you feel at any given moment, or how silly you want to act, or how you want to stress what you are about to say next. So this *neee*, realistically speaking, could be as short as *neee*. Or it could go on for as long as this (try it): Neeeeeeeeeeeeeeeeeeeeeeeeeeeeeeeeeeeeeeeeeeee eeeeeeeeeeeeeeeeeeeeeeeeeeeeeeeeeeeeeeeeeeeeeeeeeeeeeeeeeeeeee eeeeeeeeeeeeeeeeeeeeeeeeeeeeeeeeeeeeeeeeeeeeeeeeeeeeeeeeeeeeee eeeeeeeeeeeeeeeeeeeeeeeeeeeeeeeeeeeeeeeeeeeeeeeeeeeeeeeeeeeeee eeeeeeeeeeeeeeeeeeeeeeeeeeeeeeeeeeeeeeeeeeeeeeeeeeeeeeeeeeeeee eeeeeeeeeeeeeeeeeeeeeeeeeeeeeeeeeeeeeeeeeeeeeeeeeeeeeee. (Hope you remembered to take a great big breath beforehand!) There, I bet you ten dollars you're laughing again. Or at least smiling.

7   Now try the following at lightning speed: *Chipoo-cheech* (puppy). *Eemana-pitee-pitat* (he's pulling his tooth out). *Eemoo-mineet* (she's picking berries). *Neeeeeee, aspin eena-mateet* (oops, she's gone, disappeared, *pffft!*). Each syllable, each word is like a tickle in the *kipoo-chim* (blowhole, i.e., rectum); you sit there secretly squirming with visceral° pleasure at the same moment as your intellect is being scandalized, especially by the *kipoo-chim*—yikes! Try this on a friend or, better yet, your boss: "Get him in the *kipoo-chim*, bang him in the box." *That* is the Cree sense of humour—utterly ridiculous. It comes shooting out of the language natural as air.

8   Let's go back to our original sentence and translate it word for word into English. "*Neeeeeeeeeeeeeeeeeeeeeeeeeeeeeeeeeeeeeeeeeeeeeee, awinuk awa oota kaa-pee-pee-tig-weet?*" *Neee* we've discussed already. Next is *awinuk*, which means "who" (as it does in Ojibway, Blackfoot, Mi'kmaq, and at least thirty other Algonquian languages). The term *awa*, roughly speaking, turns the *awinuk* into a question, as in "who is this?" or "who is that?" *Oota* means "here." *Pee-tig-weet* means, roughly, "coming in"; in this case, by its context, "coming in the door," even though the door itself (*isk-wa-teem*) is not specified. ("*Pee-tig-wee!*" means "Come in!"—the greeting you call when someone comes knocking at your door.) And the *kaa-pee* in front of the *pee-tig-weet* turns the "coming in" into an immediate event, as in "coming in the door just now, right at this moment." So there you

go. What the sentence means in its entirety, in English, is: "Hey, who is coming in the door?"

Now I ask you: Is that sentence funny in English? As a fluent 9
English-speaker, permit me to answer the question for you: it is *not* funny, not in the least. Nothing inside you laughs for even a fraction of a second. But in Cree, the sentence is not only funny, it is hysterical; one might even say there is a cartoonish quality to it. It is as if Porky Pig° or Bugs Bunny° or Elmer Fudd° is about to enter through that door. And that is the visceral reality of the Cree language.

As I roam the world physically and intellectually and slide ever 10
so gracefully into my fifties, I find myself unravelling year by year the meaning of one truly fascinating piece of information. And that piece of information is this: When Christopher Columbus arrived in North America in October of the year 1492—a date arguably among the most important in our history as a people—probably the most significant item of baggage he had on his ship was the extraordinary story of a woman who talked to a snake in a garden and, in so doing, precipitated the eviction of humankind from that garden. This seminal° narrative has created severe trauma in the lives of many, many people and ultimately, one might argue, the life of our entire planet. I don't think it is any coincidence that the mythology/ theology this story comes from, Christianity, has at its centre the existence of a solo god who is male and male entirely.

Such a narrative—the eviction from a garden—most explic- 11
itly does *not* exist in Native North American mythology/theology (which also has not a monotheistic° but a pantheistic° superstructure or dream world). The Sinai Peninsula, at least as it appeared in Columbus's monotheistic world view, may have been a parched, treeless desert cursed by a very angry male god, but North America, our home and Native land, certainly was not. Quite the contrary: our land is blessed with the most extraordinary, lake-filled, forest-rich, food-filled, mind-boggling beauty. And North America is a landscape blessed most generously, most copiously, by a benevolent female god, one known to us, in the English language, as our Mother, the Earth.[2]

And then there is our Mother's son/daughter, that insane, 12
hermaphroditic progeny° of hers, so endlessly shape-shifting and malleable that *he*, if need be, can turn *herself*, amoeba-like, into

---

[2]As is true in all Native North American languages (all that I know of, anyway), Cree has no pronouns that distinguish between "he" and "she" or possessives that make a distinction between "her" and "his." The closest the language comes is a combined form: "he/she" and "her/his." In that sense, regardless of whether we are male biologically or female biologically, we are all "he/she's." As is God, one would think.

any number of different characters. I speak here, of course, of the Trickster, that cosmic clown, that laughing deity whose duty is to teach us a fundamental lesson: that the reason for our existence on this planet is not to suffer, not to wallow in guilt, but to celebrate the experience of living, to eat from the Tree of Knowledge as often, and with as much gusto°, as we can.

13   If languages, as I have come to believe, are shaped by mythologies, world views, collective dream worlds, then English is indelibly marked by that first eviction from the garden. And to this day, the language stops at the gate to that garden. It is forbidden, by an angel who guards the gate jealously with a large flaming sword, to *ever* re-enter. English speakers are *not* to partake of the Tree of Knowledge, laden with the most delicious fruit there is. Only God can do so; such pleasure as is to be found in the garden is reserved exclusively for His enjoyment. Cree, by comparison, did not give birth to a culture of jumbo jets that circumnavigate the globe with the efficiency of clockwork. Nor does it have a national literature that has helped to shape world history; not yet, anyway. But try speaking Cree in a virgin forest on some northern lake and you will find, very quickly, that it is pure genius.

14   In Cree, there is no gate blocking the entrance to—or the exit from—the garden. There is no angel with a flaming sword put there to thwart us. We are allowed into that garden of joy, that garden of beauty, to gambol about° as much as we want to. The Trickster—Weesageechak in Cree, Nanabush in Ojibway, Itkomi in Sioux, Raven on the West Coast, Glooscap on the East, Coyote on the Plains—also lives inside the garden. And lives there most pleasurably, sparking to life the syllables of a language that expresses the shudder of excitement that springs from the heart of that garden, from the very Tree of Knowledge itself, a tree that is, as we speak, being tweaked and tickled and pinched and . . . well . . . you don't even wanna *know*. In English, you can't. In English, you are not allowed to talk like that. You will go to Hell. (Or, at the very least, you will not get published.) So stop it!

15   Here, for purposes of comparison, is a creation myth that should knock the socks right off your English-speaking feet and, in the process, make you laugh until you're bent over double. There are many creation myths across Native North America, and many of them are untranslatable into English. Still, let me try this one on you. It comes to us from the Blackfoot Nation of southern Alberta/northern Montana. The Blackfoot are related to us Cree, not least in language, both tongues rising from Algonquian roots as they do. I choose this story because I think it illustrates, to perfection, the humour at the essence of the Trickster, whose energy spreads into all corners of the

Native North American dream world. One small request: Please pretend you are reading this story not in English but in Cree.

. . . . .

In the beginning there were only two human beings in this world, Old Man Coyote and Coyote Woman. Old Man Coyote lived on one side of the world, Coyote Woman on the other. By chance, they met. [16]

"How strange," said Old Man Coyote. "We are exactly alike." [17]

"I don't know about that," said Coyote Woman. "You're holding a bag. What's inside it?" [18]

Old Man Coyote reached into his bag and brought out a penis. "This odd thing." [19]

"It is indeed an odd thing," said Coyote Woman. "It looks funny. What is it for?" [20]

"I don't know," said Old Man Coyote. "I don't know what to use it for. What do you have inside your bag?" [21]

Coyote Woman dug deep into her bag and came up with a vagina. "You see," she said, "we are not alike. We carry different things inside our bags. Where should we put them?" [22]

"I think we should put them into our navels," said Old Man Coyote. "The navel seems to be a good place for them." [23]

"No, I think not," said Coyote Woman. "I think we should stick them between our legs. Then they will be out of the way." [24]

"Well, all right," said Old Man Coyote. "Let's put them there." So they placed these things between their legs. [25]

"You know," said Coyote Woman, "it seems to me that the strange thing you have there would fit this odd thing of mine." [26]

"Well, you might be right," said Old Man Coyote. "Let's find out." So Old Man Coyote stuck his penis into Coyote Woman's vagina. [27]

"Umm, that feels good," said Coyote Woman. [28]

"You are right," said Old Man Coyote. "It feels very good indeed. I have never felt this way before." [29]

"Neither have I," said Coyote Woman. "It's occurred to me that this might be the way to make other human beings. It would be nice to have company." [30]

"It certainly would," said Old Man Coyote. "Just you and me could become boring." [31]

"Well, in case doing what we just did should result in bringing forth more human beings, what should they look like?" said Coyote Woman. [32]

"Well, I think they should have eyes and a mouth going up and down." [33]

34   "No, no," said Coyote Woman. "Then they would not be able to see well, and food would dribble out of the lower corner of their mouths. Let's have their eyes and mouths go crosswise."

35   "I think that the men should order the women about," said Old Man Coyote, "and that the women should obey them."

36   "We'll see about that," said Coyote Woman. "I think that the men should pretend to be in charge and that the women should pretend to obey, but that in reality, it should be the other way around."

37   "I can't agree to this," said Old Man Coyote.

38   "Why quarrel?" said Coyote Woman. "Let's just wait and see how it will work out."

39   "All right, let's wait and see. How should the men live?"

40   "The men should hunt, kill buffalo and bears, and bring the meat to the women. They should protect the women at all times," said Coyote Woman.

41   "Well, that could be dangerous for the men," said Old Man Coyote. "A buffalo bull or a bear could kill a man. Is it fair to put the men in such danger? What should the women do in return?"

42   "Why, let the women do the work," said Coyote Woman. "Let them cook, and fetch water, and scrape and tan hides with buffalo brains. Let them do all these things while the men take a rest from hunting."

43   "Well, then, we agree upon everything," said Old Man Coyote. "Then it's settled."

44   "Yes," said Coyote Woman. "And now why don't you stick that funny thing of yours between my legs again?"

45   So there you go. In one group's collective world view, the act of creation is inseparable from an act of rage: revenge on human-kind for engaging in physical pleasure, the eating of fruit from a certain tree. In the other, the act of creation is an act of joy, a kick in the pants, one good fuck. In the language of the God—the language of the head—such a human act is gross and unnatural, the apogee° of evil. In the language of the goddess—the language of the groin, the womb—it is the most natural act imaginable. When creating the universe and everything in it, one god may have said, "Let there be light," but the other—his wife, the one we never hear of, the one He tried beating to her death with a big sledgehammer—begged to differ. What she said instead was, "Let there be laughter."

Words and Meanings

dialects	regional speech patterns	1
par contre	in contrast	2
corpus	body	3
posit	identify and defend	
"Bonjour. . . *quelque chose. . ."*	"Hi, Barbara, how're you doing? "Fine, thanks. And you?" "Not bad, but listen, dear, I want to tell you something."	4
visceral	gut; deep inner feelings (not intellect)	7
Porky Pig, Bugs Bunny, Elmer Fudd	animated characters from Looney Tunes	9
seminal	highly influential	10
monotheistic	believing in one God	11
pantheistic	believing in many gods	
hermaphroditic progeny	offspring that is both male and female	12
gusto	joyful energy	
gambol about	dance about playfully	14
apogee	the ultimate	45

Structure and Strategy

1. What is the basis of the contrast in paragraph 2? How is the contrast supported?
2. Paragraph 5 is developed through directional process analysis. What is the reader being told how to do?
3. What is the basis of the contrast developed in paragraphs 10, 11, and 12?
4. What is the TOPIC SENTENCE of paragraph 13? How is it supported?

Content and Purpose

1. According to Highway, what parts of the body are reflected in the English, French, and Cree languages?
2. Paragraphs 6–8 provide a digression to translate and explain a Cree phrase into English. What does the phrase mean? Do you think it's funny in English? In Cree?
3. What is Highway referring to when he identifies "probably the most significant item of baggage" (paragraph 10) that

Columbus had on his ship in 1492? According to Highway, what were the consequences of its arrival?

4. Who are the "only two human beings in this world" in the Blackfoot creation myth recounted in paragraphs 16–44? What happens between them? Who seems to be the smarter of the two? Do you find the story funny?

5. What is the difference between the two creation myths as developed in paragraph 45? What does each suggest about the "group's collective world view"?

Suggestions for Writing

1. Is accurate translation between languages ever possible? If you speak two or more languages, write an essay that uses examples to illustrate what may get lost in translation.

2. There are many creation myths. Identify two others and write an essay contrasting the world views on which they are based. Or contrast another creation myth (not the Blackfoot Old Coyote Man–Coyote Woman) with the traditional Adam and Eve story that begins the Bible.

Good Seeing

ALAN R. WILSON

Alan R. Wilson was born in New Brunswick and now lives in Victoria, BC. Wilson has an undergraduate degree in physics from the University of New Brunswick and a graduate degree in creative writing from the University of British Columbia. He has had several jobs, but the most memorable was his stint as a fire hydrant painter. He is the author of three books of poetry: *Animate Objects, Counting to 100,* and *Sky Atlas.* Wilson's first novel, *Before the Flood,* was shortlisted for both the Ethel Wilson Prize for Fiction and the Stephen Leacock Memorial Medal for Humour; it won the 2000 Books in Canada/Chapters First Novel Award. He is currently editing his next novel, *Lucifer's Hair,* and looking with his daughter through the astronomical telescope he bought in high school.

1   At first glance, science and poetry appear to have little in common. The former lays claim to the territory of objectivity and attempts to understand the intricacies of our

First published in *Canadian Notes and Queries,* Winter 2010. Reprint by permission of the author.

reality through the application of logic. Science has a reputation for orderliness, for doggedly pursuing the truth along unbending paths. Hypotheses are formed and then tested by observation or experiment. Lines of thought are followed with ruthless consistency. Beautiful irrelevancies are pared away like so much fat. But in the end, if nature throws one spanner into the works° by contradicting a predicted outcome, the theory is junked like a bad poem. The arts, and poetry in particular, investigate reality through the use of image and intuition. They employ the intricacy of language to open new pathways into the mystery of our existence, and rely on the idiosyncratic° particulars of an individual's feelings and experience to arrive at a general truth. Poetry's fuel is the synergy° of words, those unexpected combinations that can transform the mundane° into an event of sudden, even painful veracity°. These two endeavours are so seemingly distinct that there is a theory which legitimizes this cerebral apartheid° as the manifestation° of an inborn dualistic mental architecture. Science, and all things rational, supposedly dwell in the logical left side of the brain. On the other hand (or should I say other side), the arts emote° in the fervid° right hemisphere. The two solitudes inhabit one skull.

Even the practitioners of science and poetry appear to have little in common. In the favoured hang-outs of the two groups, such as universities, colleges, and cafes, they have minimal contact. Minimal also is each group's understanding or interest in what the other does. Scientists sometimes think of poets (when they think about them at all) as undisciplined, self-indulgent, trivial, and frivolous. Poets can view scientists as cold, unimaginative, self-limiting, and mechanistic. Even those few willing to venture into both realms can carry with them the prejudices and myopia° of their home group. Kim Maltman, a university mathematician who also writes poetry, has maintained that without the actual experience of being a research scientist, a poet cannot speak with authenticity about science, because it is "another mode of thinking" that is closed to the layman°. He emphasizes that, "without that intimate connection, use of such 'special' knowledge" can veer "toward the ornamental." To me, such a view veers dangerously close to ceding to° science the authority to limit the bounds of artistic imagination. The advocacy of such strictures° is as myopic (and perhaps as self-serving) as a Shakespearean scholar insisting that only an authority on the Bard can write a true and compelling sonnet. And it is as limiting as that exclusionary and pernicious° notion of cultural appropriation°, where the cultural tint of one's parents or the detailed structure of one's DNA is promoted to arbiter° of where your mind may go.

2

3   If such a perspective is to be accepted, then I am guilty on all counts. Although I am neither a working scientist nor working scholar, astronomy, physics, and mathematics figure prominently in both my fiction and my poetry. My most recent book, *Sky Atlas*, is a collection of 88 sonnets, each based on one of the 88 constellations. The sequence is blithe° with relativistic physics, exploding stars, particle decay, light pressure, time dilation, stellar evolution, and virtual particles, often cast in the form of fourteen lines with Petrarchan end rhyme—hardcore sonnets. For me, science in general, and astronomy in particular, are alluringly poetic. Einstein's view of gravity as a kind of geometry, which can be described (though perhaps not fathomed°) through the language of mathematics, is as unexpected and viscerally compelling° as the gut-wrenching imagery in Sylvia Plath's best poetry. The ghostly world of particle physics can send a shiver up the spine as surely as Charles Simic's contemplations of everyday objects. And the indigestible scale of the universe, hinted at in a starry night, can be as overwhelming as a great epic.

4   It is my suspicion that the rumoured duality of the human brain has been greatly exaggerated. I also suspect that the similarities between poetry and science far outweigh their differences. Both areas communicate through the use of language, facilitated, in the case of science, with mathematical equations. For reasons I have never been able to fathom, the language of the physical world is remarkably similar to the mathematics we have invented to describe it. In the case of poetry, communication is through the use of evocative°, weighted, or elliptical language and imagery. Like the equation, the poetic image is a means of linking entities that, on the surface, appear unrelated. It is a way to make sense of our experience by searching for connections and relationships that are not obvious. Astronomers use the term "good seeing" when referring to the transparency of the atmosphere. On such special nights, when the air is unusually clear and quiescent°, the structural details of distant galaxies or the presence of very faint stars can be discerned. Poets have good-seeing nights as well, when the turbulence° of everyday life goes still enough for the underlying connectivity of things to become visible.

5   There have always been those who have tried to draw boundaries around what others write, reveal, or say. I suspect it will ever be so. But the best science, like the best literature, is born of independence and daring. It is about the willingness to venture into unknown terrain in search of a better vantage point from which to view our world and ourselves. For the writer and poet, the only credential° needed is that most powerful and mysterious

one of all: the human imagination. You don't need to be a scholar, working scientist, degree holder, professor, mathematician, linguist, or psychologist to explore the imaginary landscape. Science itself is a set of human constructs created to make sense of the unfathomable. What exists in nature may approximate those constructs, but the limits of our mental geography decree we will never know for sure. It is these very limits, and not those imposed by ideology°, that give the human adventure its magic and excitement. They power both the urge to be more than we are and the hope that, in a moment of illicit° clarity, we will snatch insights from the laps of the gods that were never intended for us.

Words and Meanings

		Paragraph
throws one spanner into the works	disrupts a plan, messes things up	1
idiosyncratic	unique	
synergy	a complex whole (poem) whose effect is greater than the sum of its individual parts (words)	
mundane	common, uninteresting	
veracity	truth	
cerebral apartheid	intellectual separation	
manifestation	evidence	
emote	express themselves	
fervid	turbulent, passionate	
myopia	shortsightedness	2
layman	the non-professional	
ceding to	allowing, yielding to	
strictures	rigid rules	
pernicious	causing great harm, destructive	
cultural appropriation	belief that artists should not attempt to create characters or images that originate in a culture other than their own	
arbiter	one who has the power to judge or decide	
blithe	carefree, lighthearted	3

fathomed	understood
viscerally compelling	gut-wrenching, powerful
4 evocative . . . language	language that stimulates the imagination
quiescent	still
turbulence	violent confusion, disturbance
5 credential	qualification
ideology	rigid set of ideas or beliefs
illicit	outside the rules; inconsistent with the ideology; forbidden, wrong

Structure and Strategy

1. Is this essay a comparison or a contrast? Of what?
2. Identify a SIMILE in paragraph 1. How does it reinforce the topic of the paragraph?
3. Identify the paragraph that supports its point with a quotation from another expert. Does Wilson agree or disagree with the expert's opinion?
4. Identify the three comparison examples used in paragraph 3 to support the idea that science, especially astronomy, is "alluringly poetic."
5. Explain the title of the essay.

Content and Purpose

1. What is Wilson describing as "cerebral apartheid" in paragraph 1?
2. What kind of work does Wilson do?
3. Identify at least three similarities (there are six) that Wilson posits between science and poetry in paragraphs 4 and 5. Does the author convince you that poetry and science are more similar than they are different? Why?

Suggestions for Writing

1. Do you think that you are a "scientific" or a "poetic" person? Write an essay that explains why you would classify yourself as one or the other.
2. Have you ever been moved by a poem or the lyrics of a song? Did you feel that it provided you with an insight you had never had before? Or that it expressed an experience or emotion far better than you ever could? If so, write an essay identifying the poem or song lyrics and explaining why it affected you in a powerful way.

ADDITIONAL SUGGESTIONS FOR WRITING: COMPARISON AND CONTRAST

Write a comparison and/or contrast paper based on one of the topics below. Make sure that your thesis statement identifies the basis of your comparison or contrast, then develop it by providing relevant examples and details.

1. Contrast your present career goals with those you dreamed of as a child. How do you account for the differences between the two sets of goals?
2. Compare and/or contrast the way in which you and your parents view a particular issue: premarital sex, postsecondary education, same-sex marriage, raising children, children's obligations to their parents.
3. Compare and/or contrast living in Canada with living in another country.
4. Compare and/or contrast two types of contemporary music with which you are familiar.
5. Contrast two people of your acquaintance whose lifestyles reveal different attitudes toward life.
6. Compare and/or contrast two sports, teams, or players.
7. Compare and/or contrast men and women as consumers (or employees, supervisors, friends, roommates, students, etc.).
8. Compare and/or contrast two artists—painters, poets, film directors, musicians, or actors—with whose work you are familiar.
9. Compare and/or contrast men's and women's attitudes toward love, sex, and commitment.
10. "There is nothing like returning to a place that remains unchanged to find the ways in which you yourself have changed." (Nelson Mandela)

Causal Analysis

WHAT IS CAUSAL ANALYSIS?

In Unit 4, we defined ANALYSIS as the process of separating something into its parts in order to gain a better understanding of the
whole. The word "causal" (not to be confused with "casual,"
which means something else entirely) refers to "causes," so *causal
analysis* means identifying the causes or reasons for something; it
can also mean identifying effects.

   Causal analysis is a rhetorical pattern based on logical thinking.
A writer may explain *causes*—the reasons for something. For
example, the model essay in this unit, "The Trouble with Readers,"
explains the reasons for breakdowns in written communication.
Or a writer may analyze the *effects* of something. In his funny and
sad essay "The Telephone" (page 283), Anwar Accawi describes
the effects of the arrival of the first telephone in his small village in
Lebanon. Sometimes, a writer explores both causes and effects in a
longer, more complex analysis. In "Just Walk On By," on page 263,
Brent Staples looks at some of the causes of racism and explores
some of its effects on him.

WHY DO WE USE CAUSAL ANALYSIS?

Our natural human curiosity leads us to ask, "Why did this
happen?" and "What were the results?" We look for causes and
examine effects in an attempt to make sense of the flow of events
around us.

   Causal analysis is used to explain connections between ideas.
Complex historical, political, or scientific phenomena are often
best understood by looking at their causes. For example, in "The
Evolution of Evolution" (on page 275), Helena Cronin makes the difficult concept of Darwinian evolution accessible to readers by asking

simple questions about the causes of two different phenomena: sexual attraction and the craving for fast food.

Causal analysis is also used to get readers to think about new ideas and to argue the merits of a particular point of view. For instance, in "Embraced by the Needle" (page 254), Gabor Maté asserts that the cause of addiction is not an addict's behavioural choices but rather deficiencies in his or her upbringing.

HOW DO WE WRITE CAUSAL ANALYSIS?

Causal analysis is a challenging pattern of EXPOSITION. It is not easy to write because the thinking behind it must be rigorously logical. During the research and preparation stage, take the time to sort out your ideas before you begin to write. Here are six guidelines for writing a good causal analysis:

1. Be objective in your research. Don't oversimplify. Recognize that an event can be triggered by a number of causes.

2. Don't mistake coincidence for cause. The fact that one event happened before another does not mean the first event caused the second.

3. Analyze complex ideas carefully in order to sort out the *remote* (more distant, not immediately apparent) causes or effects and the *immediate* (direct, readily apparent) causes or effects.

4. Choose your focus and scope with care. In a short essay, you may have to focus on several immediate causes or effects, while omitting more remote or complicated ones.

5. Write a clear thesis statement. Usually, it will contain a preview of the causes or effects you intend to explain; these are your KEY IDEAS.

6. Support your causal analysis with sufficient, interesting, and well-chosen EVIDENCE (e.g., statistical data, examples, facts, definitions where required, and "expert witness" quotations). The purpose of this supporting material is to make the logic of your analysis clear to the reader.

The model essay that follows is a causal analysis of some of the causes of miscommunication between writers and readers.

The Trouble with Readers

Introduction
(a set of
questions)

Have you ever wondered why an e-mail you spent a long time composing was misunderstood by the recipient? Or why a report you submitted after careful research didn't have the impact you intended? Written language is vulnerable to misinterpretation, and the trouble with readers is that they read what you write, not what you mean. Clarity gives way to confusion if the writer fails to pay attention to the ambiguity of words, the mechanics of writing, or the organization of ideas.

English is notorious for its ambiguity—many English words have more than one meaning. The word *fan,* for instance, means a cooling device, an avid sports enthusiast, and a bird's tail. A *bank* may be a place to deposit money, the edge of a river, or the side-to-side slope of a racetrack. In addition to their dictionary meanings, words are subject to personal interpretation, and the more abstract the word, the more personal the interpretation becomes. Most readers can agree on what *cat* means but have different emotional reactions to words such as *abortion* or *euthanasia*, whose meanings resonate more deeply than their dictionary definitions imply. Even *cat* can stir feelings if used in one of its many slang senses or if the reader is allergic to cats.

If a writer has a shaky grasp of the mechanics of writing and cannot spell, punctuate, or construct grammatical sentences, clarity will be further eroded. Correctness goes beyond avoiding such obvious errors as "We could of done better." Even a single punctuation mark can dramatically alter meaning. Leave out the apostrophe in "The instructor called the students' names," and your reader will assume you have a provocateur, not a professor, in the classroom. Sometimes faulty word order causes misunderstanding: "Under the proposed plan, the elderly who now receive free prescription drugs will be abolished." Few readers will make the mistake of thinking that the writer of this sentence intended its "death panel" implications, but most readers will shake their heads ruefully. Of all the possible misunderstandings between writer and reader, perhaps the most painful is being laughed at when you didn't intend to be funny.

Finally, there is the matter of content: what to include and in what order. You need to include enough detail to give your reader the complete picture—in

Thesis statement

First cause (developed by definition and examples)

Second cause (developed by examples)

Third cause (developed by division and examples)

Note transition words (Finally, For example, Alternatively)

other words, all the information he or she requires. But different readers require different kinds of information. For example, if you are a computer programmer writing a report, you will not waste your supervisor's time by defining terms such as *operating system*, *interface*, or *debugging*. Alternatively, if your report is destined for someone who has little familiarity with computers, you will need to explain these terms and probably many more. You don't want to include anything irrelevant or redundant. If you do, you will create confusion, boredom, or frustration—or all three. The order in which you present your points makes a difference, too. In writing, as in life, humans need to perceive a sequence to events. When no order is apparent, readers become confused. If you're describing a process, for example, you will probably arrange your points chronologically. But if you are writing to convince, you will want to build to a strong conclusion and will likely arrange your points in climactic order. Never underestimate the importance of logic in writing!

Conclusion (highlights significance of topic; refers back to introduction)

Communicating clearly is not easy, and writing is the most demanding of all forms of communication. As a writer, you must pay close attention to words, mechanics, and organization. If you ignore even one of these obligations, your message may well be misinterpreted—because your readers will read what you wrote, not what you meant.

Embraced by the Needle

GABOR MATÉ

Gabor Maté was born in Hungary in 1944 and moved to Canada in 1957. He became a physician who specializes in the treatment of addiction and attention deficit disorder. He is a former medical columnist for *The Globe and Mail* and *the Vancouver Sun* and has written four books: *When the Body Says No: The Cost of Hidden Stress*; *Scattered Minds: A New Look at the Origins and Healing of Attention Deficit Disorder*; *Hold On to Your Kids: Why Parents Need to Matter More Than Peers*; and *In the Realm of Hungry Ghosts: Close Encounters with Addiction*. Dr. Maté has been in private practice in Vancouver; medical coordinator of the Palliative

Care Unit at Vancouver Hospital, caring for the terminally ill; and worked for a number of years in Vancouver's Downtown Eastside with patients challenged by hardcore drug addiction, mental illness, and HIV.

A ddictions always originate in unhappiness, even if hidden. 1
They are emotional anesthetics; they numb pain. The first question always is not "Why the addiction?" but "Why the pain?" The answer, ever the same, is scrawled with crude eloquence° on the wall of my patient Anna's room at the Portland Hotel in the heart of Vancouver's Downtown Eastside: "Any place I went to, I wasn't wanted. And that bites large."

The Downtown Eastside is considered to be Canada's drug 2 capital, with an addict population of 3,000 to 5,000 individuals. I am a staff physician at the Portland, a non-profit harm-reduction facility where most of the clients are addicted to cocaine, to alcohol, to opiates like heroin, or to tranquilizers—or to any combination of these things. Many also suffer from mental illness. Like Anna, a 32-year-old poet, many are HIV positive or have full-blown AIDS. The methadone I prescribe for their opiate dependence does little for the emotional anguish compressed in every heartbeat of these driven souls.

Methadone staves off the torment of opiate withdrawal, but, 3 unlike heroin, it does not create a "high" for regular users. The essence of that high was best expressed by a 27-year-old sex-trade worker. "The first time I did heroin," she said, "it felt like a warm, soft hug." In a phrase, she summed up the psychological and chemical cravings that make some people vulnerable to substance dependence.

No drug is, in itself, addictive. Only about 8 per cent to 15 per 4 cent of people who try, say alcohol or marijuana, go on to addictive use. What makes them vulnerable? Neither physiological predis- positions° nor individual moral failures explain drug addictions. Chemical and emotional vulnerability are the products of life experience, according to current brain research and developmental psychology.

Most human brain growth occurs following birth; physical and 5 emotional interactions determine much of our brain development. Each brain's circuitry and chemistry reflects individual life experi- ences as much as inherited tendencies. For any drug to work in the brain, the nerve cells have to have receptors—sites where the drug can bind. We have opiate receptors because our brain has natural

Originally published in *The Globe and Mail* 27 August 2001. © Gabor Maté M.D. Reprinted by permission of the author.

opiate-like substances, called endorphins, chemicals that partici-
pate in many functions, including the regulation of pain and mood.
Similarly, tranquilizers of the benzodiazepine class, such as Valium,
exert their effect at the brain's natural benzodiazepine receptors.

6   Infant rats who get less grooming from their mothers have
fewer natural benzo receptors in the part of the brain that controls
anxiety. Brains of infant monkeys separated from their mothers
for only a few days are measurably deficient° in the key neuro-
chemical, dopamine.

7   It is the same with human beings. Endorphins are released in
the infant's brain when there are warm, non-stressed, calm interactions with the parenting figures. Endorphins, in turn, promote
the growth of receptors and nerve cells, and the discharge of other
important brain chemicals. The fewer endorphin-enhancing experiences in infancy and early childhood, the greater the need for
external sources. Hence, the greater vulnerability to addictions.

8   Distinguishing° skid row addicts is the extreme degree of stress
they had to endure early in life. Almost all women now inhabiting
Canada's addiction capital suffered sexual assaults in childhood, as
did many of the males. Childhood memories of serial abandonment
or severe physical and psychological abuse are common. The histories of my Portland patients tell of pain upon pain.

9   Carl, a 36-year-old native man, was banished from one foster
home after another, had dishwashing liquid poured down his
throat for using foul language at age 5, and was tied to a chair in
a dark room to control his hyperactivity. When angry at himself—
as he was recently for using cocaine—he gouges his foot with a
knife as punishment. His facial expression was that of a terror-
ized urchin° who had just broken some family law and feared
Draconian retribution°. I reassured him I wasn't his foster parent,
and that he didn't owe it to me not to screw up.

10   But what of families where there was not abuse, but love,
where parents did their best to provide their children with a secure
nurturing home? One also sees addictions arising in such families.
The unseen factor here is the stress the parents themselves lived
under even if they did not recognize it. That stress could come from
relationship problems, or from outside circumstances such as economic pressure or political disruption. The most frequent source of
hidden stress is the parents' own childhood histories that saddled
them with emotional baggage they had never become conscious of.
What we are not aware of in ourselves, we pass on to our children.

11   Stressed, anxious, or depressed parents have great difficulty
initiating enough of those emotionally rewarding, endorphin-
liberating interactions with their children. Later in life, such

children may experience a hit of heroin as the "warm, soft hug" my patient described: What they didn't get enough of before, they can now inject.

Feeling alone, feeling there has never been anyone with whom to share their deepest emotions, is universal among drug addicts. That is what Anna had lamented on her wall. No matter how much love a parent has, the child does not experience being wanted unless he or she is made absolutely safe to express exactly how unhappy, or angry, or hate-filled he or she may feel at times. The sense of unconditional love, of being fully accepted even when most ornery°, is what no addict ever experienced in childhood—often not because the parents did not have it to give, simply because they did not know how to transmit it to the child.   12

Addicts rarely make the connection between troubled childhood experiences and self-harming habits. They blame themselves—and that is the greatest wound of all, being cut off from their natural self-compassion. "I was hit a lot," 40-year-old Wayne says, "but I asked for it. Then I made some stupid decisions." And would he hit a child, no matter how much that child "asked for it"? Would he blame that child for "stupid decisions"?   13

Wayne looks away. "I don't want to talk about that crap," says this tough man, who has worked on oil rigs and construction sites and served 15 years in jail for robbery. He looks away and wipes tears from his eyes.   14

Words and Meanings

Paragraph

eloquence	persuasive speech	1
physiological predispositions	physical tendencies, inclinations	4
deficient	lacking	6
distinguishing	marking, characterizing	8
urchin	street child	9
draconian retribution	harsh punishment	
ornery	stubborn, uncooperative	12

Structure and Strategy

1. What INTRODUCTION and CONCLUSION strategy does the author employ? Why do you think the author chose this strategy to open and close this essay?

2. What kind of support does the author use in paragraph 6? What does it illustrate? Is it effective?
3. Why do you think the author chose the title he did for this essay?
4. What is the TONE of the essay?

Content and Purpose

1. Who is the author? Where does he work? What expertise does he bring to the subject of addiction?
2. According to Maté, what causes people to become addicted to drugs or alcohol?
3. What experience do "skid row addicts" share that the author thinks causes their addictions? (See paragraph 8.)
4. How does Maté explain addiction among people who were loved, not neglected or abused, by their parents as children? How would his theory explain one addicted child in a family with non-addicted siblings?
5. In paragraph 12, Maté states clearly what he believes *all* addicts lacked during their infancy and childhood. Identify his assertion. Do you agree or disagree with him? Why?

Suggestions for Writing

1. Write an essay about what you feel are the causes of addictive behaviour. You can use examples from personal experience or media sources, such as Drew Pinsky's reality television show *Celebrity Rehab*. Do you agree with the idea that addiction is caused by emotional vulnerability resulting from early life experience? Or is there a measure of individual choice involved in chemical addictions?
2. Write an essay about the effects of addictive behaviour on the addict or on the addict's family and close friends.
3. Research the policy of "harm reduction" as a means of dealing with substance abuse, perhaps looking at a facility such as Vancouver's InSite, where addicts can inject heroin in a safe, medically supervised environment. Write a carefully reasoned essay that explains why you agree or disagree with the policy.
4. Read Lorna Crozier's "What Stays in the Family" on page 65 and apply Maté's theory to the experience she recounts in the essay.

Scaring Us Senseless

NASSIM NICHOLAS TALEB

Philosopher and former financial trader Nassim Nicholas Taleb was born in 1960 in Lebanon. He holds graduate degrees from the Wharton School of Business and the University of Paris, and teaches at the Polytechnic Institute of New York and Oxford. Taleb studies the philosophy of randomness and the role of uncertainty in society. Among his best-selling books are *Fooled by Randomness: The Hidden Role of Chance in Life and in the Markets* (2005) and *The Black Swan: The Impact of the Highly Improbable* (2007).

I was visiting London when a second wave of attacks hit the city, just two weeks after the traumatic events of July 7 [2005]. It is hard to avoid feeling vulnerable to this invisible enemy who does not play by known or explicit rules. Of course, that is precisely the anxiety that terrorists seek to produce. But its opposite—complacency—is not an option. 1

The truth is that neither human beings nor modern societies are wired to respond rationally to terrorism. Vigilance is easy to muster immediately after an event, but it tends to wane quickly, as the attack vanishes from public discourse. We err twice, first by over-reacting right after the disaster, while we are still in shock, and later by under-reacting, when the memory fades and we become so relaxed as to be vulnerable to further attacks. 2

Terrorism exploits three glitches in human nature, all related to the management and perception of unusual events. The first and key among these has been observed over the last two decades by neurobiologists and behavioral scientists, who have debunked a great fallacy that has marred Western thinking since Aristotle° and most acutely since the Enlightenment°. That is to say that as much as we think of ourselves as rational animals, risk avoidance is not governed by reason, cognition° or intellect. Rather, it comes chiefly from our emotional system. 3

Patients with brain lesions that prevent them from registering feelings even when their cognitive and analytical capacities are intact are incapable of effectively getting out of harm's way. It is largely our emotional toolkit, and not what is called "reason," that governs our capacity for self-preservation. 4

Second, this emotional system can be an extremely naïve statistician, because it was built for a primitive environment with simple dangers. That might work for you the next time you run 5

Nassim Nicholas Taleb "Scaring Us Senseless," *New York Times*, July 24, 2005. Reprinted with permission.

into a snake or a tiger. But because the emotional system is impressionable and prefers shallow, social and anecdotal information to abstract data, it hinders our ability to cope with the more sophisticated risks that afflict modern life.

6   For example, the death of an acquaintance in a motorcycle accident would be more likely to deter you from riding a motorcycle than would a dispassionate, and undoubtedly far more representative, statistical analysis of motorcycles' dangers. You might avoid Central Park on the basis of a single comment at a cocktail party, rather than bothering to read the freely available crime statistics that provide a more realistic view of the odds that you will be victimized.

7   This primacy of the emotions can distort our decision-making. Travelers at airports irrationally tend to agree to pay more for terrorism insurance than they would for general insurance, which includes terrorism coverage. No doubt the word "terrorism" can be specific enough to evoke an emotional reaction, while the general insurance offer wouldn't awaken the travelers' anxieties in the same way.

8   In the modern age, the news media have the power to amplify such emotional distortions, particularly with their use of images that go directly to the emotional brain. Consider this: Osama bin Laden continued killing Americans and Western Europeans in the aftermath of Sept. 11, though indirectly. How? A large number of travelers chose to drive rather than fly, and this caused a corresponding rise in casualties from automobile accidents (any time we drive more than 20 miles, our risk of death exceeds that of flying). Yet these automobile accidents were not news stories—they are a mere number. We have pictures of those killed by bombs, not those killed on the road. As Stalin° supposedly said, "One death is a tragedy; a million is a statistic."

9   Our emotional system responds to the concrete and proximate°. Based on anecdotal information, it reacts quickly to remote risks, then rapidly forgets. And so the televised images from bombings in London cause the people of Cleveland to be on heightened alert— but as soon as there is a new tragedy, that vigilance is forgotten.

10   The third human flaw, related to the second, has to do with how we act on our perceptions, and what sorts of behavior we choose to reward. We are moved by sensational images of heroes who leap into action as calamity unfolds before them. But the long pedestrian slog of prevention is thankless. That is because prevention is nameless and abstract, while a hero's actions are grounded in an easy-to-understand narrative.

11   How can we act on our knowledge of these human flaws in order to make our society safer?

The audiovisual media, with the ability to push the public's   12
emotional hot buttons, need to play a more responsible role. Of
course it is the news media's job to inform the public about the
risk and the incidence of terrorism, but they should try to do so
without helping terrorists achieve their objective, which is to ter-
rify. Television images, in all their vividness and specificity, have
an extraordinary power to do just that and to persuade the viewer
that a distant risk is clear and present while a pressing but under-
reported one is nothing to worry about.

Like pharmaceutical companies the news media should study   13
the side effects of their product, one of which is the distortion of
the viewer's mental risk map. Because of the way the brain is built,
images and striking narratives may well be necessary to get our
attention. But just as it takes a diamond to cut a diamond, the news
industry should find ways to use images and stories to bring us
closer to the statistical truth.

Words and Meanings

Paragraph

Aristotle	fourth-century BCE Greek philosopher, who developed the deductive method of logical reasoning on which much of Western thought was based	3
Enlightenment	eighteenth-century philosophical movement that emphasized the faculty of reason in studying questions of science, doctrine, and tradition	
cognition	the mental process of knowing (awareness, perception, reasoning, and judgment) based on factual evidence	
Stalin	(1879–1953) leader of the Soviet Union from 1941 to 1953. Notorious for its ruthlessness, Stalin's regime presided over the deaths of millions from starvation and terror.	8
proximate	very close in space, time, or order	9

Structure and Strategy

1. Write a sentence that summarizes the THESIS and KEY IDEAS of this essay.
2. How does the INTRODUCTION contribute to the author's credibility?

3. Identify three paragraphs that are developed primarily by means of examples.
4. What TRANSITIONS does Taleb use to move from one key idea to the next?
5. Which point is supported with a quotation? Why is this quotation IRONIC?
6. Why do you think that paragraph 11 consists of a one-sentence question?

Content and Purpose

1. According the author, which of the "three glitches" that "terrorism exploits" (paragraph 3) is most significant?
2. According to Taleb, are human beings essentially rational or emotional creatures when it comes to avoiding danger? How does this predilection affect our behaviour?
3. Why does Taleb consider our emotional reactions appropriate to a "primitive environment" (paragraph 5)?
4. Why do people tend to buy unnecessary—and expensive—insurance against terrorism at airports, rather than relying on their general insurance, which would cover them if they were attacked on a plane?
5. According to Taleb, how did the attacks of 9/11 continue to kill people indirectly in the weeks and months that followed?
6. Why do people tend to admire heroes who "leap into action" in a crisis more than they respect the people who endure the "long pedestrian slog" of preventing crises?
7. What answer does the author offer to the question he poses in paragraph 11? Do you agree or disagree? Why?

Suggestions for Writing

1. Have you ever experienced or been frightened by terrorist violence? Write an essay that describes the incident or threat and its effects on you.
2. Do people rely too much on emotion and anecdotal information and too little on reason and intellect in dangerous situations (e.g., crime, terrorism, accidents, storms)? Choose a situation, do some research into the chances of being injured or killed in that situation, and write an essay that realistically assesses the risks involved.

Just Walk On By: A Black Man Ponders His Power to Alter Public Space

BRENT STAPLES

Brent Staples (b. 1951) is an editorial writer for *The New York Times*, specializing in politics, culture, and race. He was born in Chester, Pennsylvania, and holds a Ph.D. in psychology from the University of Chicago. Staples is the author of *An American Love Story* (1999) and the award-winning memoir *Parallel Time: Growing Up in Black and White* (1994).

M y first victim was a woman—white, well dressed, probably in her early twenties. I came upon her late one evening on a deserted street in Hyde Park, a relatively affluent neighborhood in an otherwise mean, impoverished section of Chicago. As I swung onto the avenue behind her, there seemed to be a discreet, uninflammatory distance between us. Not so. She cast back a worried glance. To her, the youngish black man—a broad six feet two inches with a beard and billowing hair, both hands shoved into the pockets of a bulky military jacket—seemed menacingly close. After a few more quick glimpses, she picked up her pace and was soon running in earnest. Within seconds she disappeared into a cross street. 1

That was more than a decade ago. I was 22 years old, a graduate student newly arrived at the University of Chicago. It was in the echo of that terrified woman's footfalls that I first began to know the unwieldy inheritance I'd come into—the ability to alter public space in ugly ways. It was clear that she thought herself the quarry of a mugger, a rapist, or worse. Suffering a bout of insomnia, however, I was stalking sleep, not defenseless wayfarers. As a softy who is scarcely able to take a knife to a raw chicken—let alone hold it to a person's throat—I was surprised, embarrassed, and dismayed all at once. Her flight made me feel like an accomplice in tyranny. It also made it clear that I was indistinguishable from the muggers who occasionally seeped into the area from the surrounding ghetto. That first encounter, and those that followed, signified that a vast, unnerving gulf lay between nighttime pedestrians—particularly women—and me. And I soon gathered that being perceived as dangerous is a hazard in itself. I only needed to turn a corner into a dicey situation, or crowd some frightened, armed person in a foyer 2 somewhere, or make an errant° move after being pulled over by a policeman. Where fear and weapons meet—and they often do in urban America—there is always the possibility of death.

3   In that first year, my first away from my hometown, I was to become thoroughly familiar with the language of fear. At dark, shadowy intersections in Chicago, I could cross in front of a car stopped at a traffic light and elicit° the *thunk, thunk, thunk, thunk* of the driver—black, white, male, or female—hammering down the door locks. On less traveled streets after dark, I grew accustomed to but never comfortable with people who crossed to the other side of the street rather than pass me. Then there were the standard unpleasantries with police, doormen, bouncers, cab drivers, and others whose business it is to screen out troublesome individuals *before* there is any nastiness.

4   I moved to New York nearly two years ago and I have remained an avid° night walker. In central Manhattan, the near-constant crowd cover minimizes tense one-on-one street encounters. Elsewhere—visiting friends in SoHo, where sidewalks are narrow and tightly spaced buildings shut out the sky—things can get very taut indeed.

5   Black men have a firm place in New York mugging literature. Norman Podhoretz in his famed (or infamous) . . . essay, "My Negro Problem—And Ours," recalls growing up in terror of black males; they "were tougher than we were, more ruthless," he writes—and as an adult on the Upper West Side of Manhattan, he continues, he cannot constrain his nervousness when he meets black men on certain streets. Similarly, a decade later, the essayist and novelist Edward Hoagland extols° a New York where once "Negro bitterness bore down mainly on other Negroes." Where some see mere panhandlers, Hoagland sees "a mugger who is clearly screwing up his nerve to do more than just *ask* for money." But Hoagland has "the New Yorker's quick-hunch posture for broken-field maneuvering," and the bad guy swerves away.

6   I often witness that "hunch posture," from women after dark on the warrenlike° streets of Brooklyn where I live. They seem to set their faces on neutral and, with their purse straps strung across their chests bandolier style, they forge ahead as though bracing themselves against being tackled. I understand, of course, that the danger they perceive is not a hallucination. Women are particularly vulnerable to street violence, and young black males are drastically overrepresented among the perpetrators° of that violence. Yet these truths are no solace against the kind of alienation that comes of being ever the suspect, against being set apart, a fearsome entity with whom pedestrians avoid making eye contact.

7   It is not altogether clear to me how I reached the ripe old age of 22 without being conscious of the lethality° nighttime pedestrians

attributed to me. Perhaps it was because in Chester, Pennsylvania, the small, angry industrial town where I came of age in the 1960s, I was scarcely noticeable against a backdrop of gang warfare, street knifings, and murders. I grew up one of the good boys, had perhaps a half-dozen fist fights. In retrospect°, my shyness of combat has clear sources.

Many things go into the making of a young thug. One of those things is the consummation° of the male romance with the power to intimidate. An infant discovers that random flailings send the baby bottle flying out of the crib and crashing to the floor. Delighted, the joyful babe repeats those motions again and again, seeking to duplicate the feat. Just so, I recall the points at which some of my boyhood friends were finally seduced by the perception of themselves as tough guys. When a mark cowered and surrendered his money without resistance, myth and reality merged—and paid off. It is, after all, only manly to embrace the power to frighten and intimidate. We, as men, are not supposed to give an inch of our lane on the highway; we are to seize the fighter's edge in work and in play and even in love; we are to be valiant in the face of hostile forces. 8

Unfortunately, poor and powerless young men seem to take all this nonsense literally. As a boy, I saw countless tough guys locked away; I have since buried several, too. They were babies, really—a teenage cousin, a brother of 22, a childhood friend in his mid-twenties—all gone down in episodes of bravado played out in the streets. I came to doubt the virtues of intimidation early on. I chose, perhaps even unconsciously, to remain a shadow—timid, but a survivor. 9

The fearsomeness mistakenly attributed to me in public places often has a perilous flavor. The most frightening of these confusions occurred in the late 1970s and early 1980s when I worked as a journalist in Chicago. One day, rushing into the office of a magazine I was writing for with a deadline story in hand, I was mistaken for a burglar. The office manager called security and, with an ad hoc posse°, pursued me through the labyrinthine halls, nearly to my editor's door. I had no way of proving who I was. I could only move briskly toward the company of someone who knew me. 10

Another time I was on assignment for a local paper and killing time before an interview. I entered a jewelry store on the city's affluent Near North Side. The proprietor excused herself and returned with an enormous red Doberman pinscher straining at the end of a leash. She stood, the dog extended toward me, silent to my questions, her eyes bulging nearly out of her head. I took a cursory° look around, nodded, and bade her good night. Relatively speaking, however, I never fared as badly as another black male 11 journalist. He went to nearby Waukegan, Illinois, a couple of summers ago to work on a story about a murderer who was born there. Mistaking the reporter for the killer, police hauled him from his car at gunpoint and but for his press credentials would probably have tried to book him. Such episodes are not uncommon. Black men trade tales like this all the time.

12   In "My Negro Problem—And Ours," Podhoretz writes that the hatred he feels for blacks makes itself known to him through a variety of avenues—one being his discomfort with that "special brand of paranoid touchiness" to which he says blacks are prone. No doubt he is speaking here of black men. In time, I learned to smother the rage I felt at so often being taken for a criminal. Not to do so would surely have led to madness—via that special "paranoid touchiness" that so annoyed Podhoretz at the time he wrote the essay.

13   I began to take precautions to make myself less threatening. I move about with care, particularly late in the evening. I give a wide berth to nervous people on subway platforms during the wee hours, particularly when I have exchanged business clothes for jeans. If I happen to be entering a building behind some people who appear skittish°, I may walk by, letting them clear the lobby before I return, so as not to seem to be following them. I have been calm and extremely congenial° on those rare occasions when I've been pulled over by the police.

14   And on late-evening constitutionals° along streets less traveled by, I employ what has proved to be an excellent tension-reducing measure: I whistle melodies from Beethoven and Vivaldi and the more popular classical composers. Even steely New Yorkers hunching toward nighttime destinations seem to relax, and occasionally they even join in the tune. Virtually everybody seems to sense that a mugger wouldn't be warbling bright, sunny selections from Vivaldi's *Four Seasons*. It is my equivalent of the cowbell that hikers wear when they know they are in bear country.

Words and Meanings

Paragraph

Paragraph		
2	errant	unexpected
3	elicit	cause to happen
4	avid	keen, enthusiastic
5	extols	praises highly
6	warrenlike	crowded, narrow, dark—like a rabbit warren
	perpetrators	those who perform or commit a criminal action

lethality	deadliness	7
retrospect	hindsight, thinking about the past	
consummation	completion, fulfillment	8
ad hoc posse	group of people quickly assembled to catch a criminal	10
cursory	hasty, superficial	11
skittish	nervous	13
congenial	pleasant, friendly	
constitutionals	walks	14

Structure and Strategy

1. What strategy does Staples use in his INTRODUCTION? Identify the details that help the reader picture the scene described. Explain the IRONY in the first sentence.
2. What is the function of the paragraphs that include quotations from writers Norman Podhoretz and Edward Hoagland (paragraphs 5 and 12)? How would the impact of the essay differ if Staples had not included these supporting examples of racist thinking?
3. How is the TOPIC SENTENCE of paragraph 10 developed?
4. What is the TONE of this essay?

Content and Purpose

1. This essay considers the effects that the author, a black man, has on people in the street, merely by his presence. It also deals with the effects that this phenomenon has on him. What are they?
2. Explain what Staples means by his "unwieldy inheritance" and his feeling like "an accomplice in tyranny" (paragraph 2).
3. What does Staples acknowledge in paragraph 6? How does this acknowledgment prepare the reader for the next point he makes about street violence (in paragraphs 7 through 9)?
4. What measures does the author take to minimize his effect on other pedestrians as he walks at night?
5. In paragraph 7, the author observes that his own "shyness of combat has clear sources." What causes does he identify for his dislike of violence?
6. Paragraph 8 deals with the causes of another social tragedy, "the making of a young thug." What are these causes, as Staples sees them? How has this sad reality affected his own life?

Suggestions for Writing

1. It is often suggested that our society is more violent than it was a few decades ago. Others argue that we are simply more fearful, and that the incidence of violent crimes has actually decreased. Write an essay that explores the causes either for the increase or for the perception of an increase in violence.

2. Write an essay that explores the causes or effects of being an "outsider," someone who is seen not to "belong." Support your thesis from personal experience. How did your experience(s) affect you?

3. Read Pat Capponi's "Dispatches from the Poverty Line" on page 104 and Thea Lim's "Take Back Halloween" on page 329. Choose one of these essays and compare/contrast its treatment of stereotyping with Staples's.

Grounded: Imagining a World without Flight

DAVID BEERS

David Beers (b. 1957) grew up in San Jose, California, where his father worked for Lockheed as a satellite test engineer. He was senior editor of *Mother Jones* magazine until 1991, when he moved to Vancouver. There he became founding editor of an online publication called *The Tyee*. He has won national awards for his journalism, writing for *The Globe and Mail, Vancouver Magazine, The New York Times Magazine, Harper's, National Geographic,* and many other publications. Beers is author of *Blue Sky Dream,* a memoir about growing up in California suburbia during the Cold War. He is a lecturer at the University of British Columbia School of Journalism.

1   I remember being very young in the family backyard in California, looking skyward with my father at the passing airplanes. He helped me learn each shape, assigning names and purposes: transport, airliner, fighter. Before I was born, he had piloted a fighter jet, and he would tell stories of tearing up the heavens with his friends, of signing out a Grumman F9F-8 in the morning, flying more than 1,500 kilometres to have dinner with his

Reprinted by permission of the author.

parents, then climbing back into his cockpit the next morning and returning to base, six tonnes of kerosene fuel and a weekend well burned.

Air travel has lost most of its mystique in the half century 2 since, but that does not make the fact of mechanical flight any less impressive. On a sunny day, at the end of runway 26R at Vancouver International Airport, you may find a half-dozen people enjoying the spectacle of a 363,000-kilogram jumbo jet surfing the air. I show up on a misty and brooding morning, and because the wind is blowing out to sea, the airliners come and go on the other side of the airport. They sound like receding thunder. The tall grass whips and shivers. I am alone. It's easy to imagine a day, maybe not so far off, when the number of jets in the sky will have dwindled dramatically. A time when such huge birds might again seem exotic.

Could it happen? As the potential ravages of global warming 3 come more solidly into view, jet travel has been fingered as a dangerous emitter of greenhouse gases. And now the price of oil is said by various experts to be headed toward $200 (US) a barrel within the year, maybe five, a sign for many that we've entered a new age of fossil fuel scarcity. What if we come to decide jet travel has become too polluting to risk our children's future? Or just far too expensive to continue flying the kids to Disneyland? And if a million such decisions were to cause the jet age to end, how would we come back to earth? Softly, one would hope. Pleasantly. But maybe, instead, it will be a white-knuckle crash.

George Monbiot, *Guardian* columnist and author of the 2006 4 bestseller *Heat: How to Stop the Planet from Burning*, wants a forced landing—immediately. Jet travel, he states, is "the greatest future cause of global warming." And people who fly are "killers."

At present, aviation accounts for only about 2 percent of total 5 human carbon emissions, according to the Intergovernmental Panel on Climate Change. But because jets fly so high, their effect on global warming is near-tripled. Monbiot calculates that the industry is growing so fast that within decades jet travel will erase most potential climate-friendly gains in other sectors.

The European Union has responded by including aviation in its 6 carbon emissions trading scheme as of 2012. Next year, the United Kingdom will charge a carbon tax on all flights within and out of the country. Here in North America, neither approach is close at hand. British Columbia's "cutting-edge" carbon tax will apply to flights inside the province but not those with outside connections. And jet fuel itself can't be taxed by any nation; international trade agreements prevent it.

7   Some airlines will let you choose to spend more to buy carbon offsets, but such volunteer programs aren't likely to give the planet's thermostat much of a shove. After a year of offering the option, Air Canada reports its passengers bought a mere $131,529 in carbon offsets, worth a puny 1,644 trees. People might step up to buy a lot more carbon offsets if the "messaging" were better and "fully integrated into the ticket purchasing experience," says Joe Kelly, director of environmental services for InterVistas, a Canadian firm that consults for airline and tourism companies. His survey shows that "people need to feel confident their money is really going to make a difference." He adds, "Of course, a lot of people say one thing and do another."

8   [Kelly] also points out that Boeing will soon roll out its carbon-fibre-bodied 787 Dreamliner, said to be 20 percent more fuel efficient than its predecessors. And an April press release from the International Air Transport Association trumpeted "a historic commitment to tackle climate change" and a vision for "a carbon emission free industry."

9   Monbiot takes no solace° from any of it. The window on defeating global warming is closing rapidly, and governments must ground the fleets now. Like an angry preacher who has glimpsed hellfire, he spreads his gospel. "When I challenge my friends about their planned weekend in Rome or their holiday in Florida," he writes, "they respond with a strange, distant smile and avert their eyes°. . . . The moral dissonance° is deafening." He's not the only one championing the latest environmental commandment: thou shalt not fly. "Making selfish choices such as flying on holiday," preaches the bishop of London, Richard Chartres, is "a symptom of sin."

10   Yes, perhaps. But business is booming. As the middle classes of China and India take to the sky, the global airline industry expects passengers to double to 9 billion in twenty-five years. If this comes to pass, even aviation's most optimistic expectation of further carbon emission cuts, admits Kelly, will be more than wiped out by humanity's enthusiasm for air travel. It would seem Monbiot is pretty much on the money°.

11   Where [Monbiot] may be wrong, however, is in taking the air industry's growth projections seriously. Long before global warming punishes us for our sins, aviation will crash for a different reason: too little kerosene fuel. So say those who believe world oil production is very near, or at, its peak. On the other side of that peak, every barrel of oil becomes more expensive to pull out of the ground, even as demand rises. The result will be runaway fuel prices and, ultimately, the restructuring of our economies, whether we are ready or not.

Roger Bezdek—co-author of a famous 2005 report on peak   12
oil for the United States Department of Energy, and president of
Management Information Services, which consults with government agencies and power utilities—doesn't believe the aviation
industry's "sky's the limit" growth projections. "Officially, they
have to say that to protect their stock values and equipment sales."
But some airline execs have confided to him they are working on
Plan B: surviving the inevitable peak oil shakeout when fuel prices
go through the roof and the industry shrinks.

"If people have to decide between driving to their jobs or taking   13
a vacation, which will they choose?" Bezdek asks rhetorically. The
ripple effect, he predicts, will beggar° public treasuries and devas-
tate communities. "Across North America and worldwide, every
region, state, country, is betting the farm on the growth of the airline industry—financing infrastructure, business parks, convention
centres. That's hundreds of millions of dollars of infrastructure."

[Bezdek] expects, in twenty-five years, the "seedy" deteriora-   14
tion of hotel zones around overbuilt, underused airports. "Vegas is
going to grind to a halt. Orlando, Vail, Aspen—destination resort
areas will get a lot fewer customers." If you aren't rich, you won't
fly much, if at all. Priorities will be different, starker. More fossil
fuel will instead be burned to "handle social dissension, unrest."

The idea of a world without flight poses somewhat of a pre-   15
dicament to someone like Dr. Angus Friday of Grenada, a tiny
Caribbean island nation assumed to be below the main hurricane
belt—until two massive storms wracked the tiny nation, in 2004
and 2005. In his role as chair of the forty-four-member Alliance of
Small Island States, Friday flies around the world, urging action
against climate change, and aid for countries like his in bracing
for rising sea levels and increasingly violent storm surges. Yet the
day I catch up with him on the phone from somewhere in India, he
gently reminds me that jetliners bring the tourists to the beaches,
and that tourism is Grenada's main source of revenue, so he is in no
position to instruct sinners to stay home. "The real challenge is to
release some of the entrepreneurial forces that can create solutions
to climate change." And peak oil, presumably.

Friday prefers to place his faith in human ingenuity. He cites,   16
as many do, Virgin Atlantic Airways owner Richard Branson, who
recently proved one of his airliners could fly on 20 percent ethanol
blended with the usual kerosene, and who has invested $1 billion
(US) in developing alternative energy sources, including biofuels
from non-food plant waste.

Growing crops for biofuels is one of those green ideas that   17
seems to have come and gone in barely a year's time. The pressure

it was expected to put on agricultural land helped send food commodity prices soaring this spring. Studies reported in *The New York
Times* find biofuel cultivation would actually accelerate climate
change. At the far fringe of the field, some optimistic researchers
have proposed creating vast algae ponds in empty deserts to make
biodiesel from the muck. So far, Branson has been cryptic° about
what Virgin Fuel will be, except to boast, "It is 100 percent environmentally friendly, and I believe it's the future of fuel. Over the next
twenty or thirty years, I think it actually will replace the conventional fuel that you get out of the ground."

18   "Richard Branson," says James Howard Kunstler, author of
*The Long Emergency: Surviving the End of Oil, Climate Change, and
Other Converging Catastrophes of the Twenty-First Century*, "is suffering from the delusion of techno-triumphalism. In fact, he is close
to being off his rocker about this." No airline is going to escape the
"liquid fuels problem," he says, referring to the fact that US civil
aviation is expected to consume half the country's oil production
by 2030.

19   Kunstler suggests that Branson may have pulled off a small
"stunt," but that "it doesn't scale." Mass production of enough
biofuel to feed aviation is just not possible. In any case, in a few
years competition for access to every form of fuel will be chaoti-
cally fierce. Passing the global oil production peak will trigger, as
his book foretells, "an unprecedented economic crisis that will
wreak havoc° on national economies, topple governments, alter
national boundaries, provoke military strife, and challenge the continuation of civilized life.

20   "Commercial airlines will probably fail within the next five
years," Kunstler declares. Spiking fuel costs are already causing
carriers to cut other operating costs to the bone. "Look, we saw four
small airlines go out of business in just . . . ten days." If Kunstler
isn't buying what Branson is selling, many of us do yearn for it.
Sir Richard, with his boyish enthusiasm for balloons and jets and
private rocket ships, is the latest in a long line of public figures
who've exploited the obvious metaphor of flight as human ascent,
progress. He bids us not to lose faith in the heavens and our
dominion over them.

21   The airplane was the streamlined shape of the twentieth century, a war-spawned creation that, as Le Corbusier wrote, "mobi-
lized invention, intelligence and daring, imagination and cold
reason. It is the same spirit that built the Parthenon°." If so, what
new shapes, born of a similar spirit, might replace it?

22   On the Internet, I find images of helium-filled Zeppelins with
exotic curves, luxurious staterooms, haughty observation decks.

Their designers expect them to be propelled by combinations of fuel-efficient diesel motors, small jet turbines, the sun, and the wind. The Manned Cloud, designed by Jean-Marie Massaud with the French national aerospace research body ONERA, is intended to carry forty guests across 5,000 kilometres in about thirty hours, and is shaped like a beautiful white whale. There are also the sleek, electric-driven 250-kilometre-an-hour bullet trains already in operation in Europe and Asia; and, nearly twice as fast, the world's first superconducting magnetic levitation train, purchased for $1.2 billion (US) from German engineers to ferry travellers between Shanghai and its airport. Japan is planning to pour $100 billion (US) into an even faster maglev train to run between Tokyo and Osaka. Technically it will fly, if just a few inches above the ground.

But this is not the future envisioned by Kunstler, who I begin to   23
think enjoys picking the wings off humans. "It's a mistake to imagine that the years ahead are all about leisure and recreation and we can just substitute one form for another. We are going to be living in a far less affluent society." By then, one imagines, what's left of the legions of business warriors striding through airports today will instead be cooped up watching video screens in teleconferencing centres. But for must of us, the business at hand will be working the land. The way we produce and transport food now is extremely fossil fuel intensive. As peak oil makes air travel a remote luxury, says Kunstler, our eyes must revert downward, toward the soil.

To this child of the jet age, it all seems a terribly hard landing.   24
I phone my father, who retired from his aerospace engineering career long ago but still pilots a propeller-driven airplane he shares with a flying club. Can you imagine a world without air travel? I ask him. Do you think about it?

"Yes, I think about it often. And I can imagine you may see it in   25
your lifetime. What made the airplane and jet travel possible was oil, pure and simple. And now, as our oil supply inevitably diminishes, we are entering the end of a natural cycle. Right now, those people in those aluminum tubes at 30,000 feet are there because they can be, not because they need to be.

"We will adapt," he says, after a pause, "or not, I guess." And   26
he laughs.

Words and Meanings

solace	comfort
avert . . . eyes	look away
moral dissonance	clash between a person's values and actions

10	on the money	an idiom meaning *exactly right*
13	beggar	as a verb, means to exhaust, deplete
17	cryptic	puzzling, mysterious
19	wreak havoc	destroy
21	the Parthenon	temple to the goddess Athena built in the fifth century BCE; considered the supreme example of ancient Greek architecture

Structure and Strategy

1. What do the INTRODUCTION and CONCLUSION of the essay have in common?
2. Identify three descriptive details in paragraph 2. What is the main point of this paragraph?
3. Beers builds his analysis with "expert testimony," quotations from people presumably knowledgeable about commercial aviation. Identify the "experts" and their respective positions on the viability of mass air travel.
4. Identify a SIMILE in paragraph 9 and a METAPHOR in paragraph 23 to characterize two of the experts cited. What do these images suggest about the TONE of Beers' essay?
5. This essay explores the causes of the potential collapse of the aviation industry, so it is in part EXPOSITION. What other rhetorical mode does the author employ?

Content and Purpose

1. According to Beers, what are the causes of the potential collapse of commercial aviation? (See paragraph 3.)
2. What is "peak oil"? What does Beers think may be the results of peak oil on the aviation industry? What may happen to our huge airports and resort destinations?
3. Why are jets particularly bad for global warming? Are carbon offsets the answer, according to the essay?
4. Which of Beers' sources suggests that flying somewhere for a holiday has moral consequences? Do you agree or disagree?
5. What is the problem with growing crops for biofuels, according to this essay?
6. How is Virgin Atlantic Airways owner Richard Branson characterized in paragraphs 16–20?
7. What are some alternatives to mass air travel presented in paragraph 22? Do you think these ideas will work?

Suggestions for Writing

1. Write a narrative/descriptive essay about your first—or most memorable—plane ride. What was the flight like? How did it make you feel?
2. Research the concept of peak oil and write an essay that defines it, provides alternative timetables for it, and reflects your own opinion about the validity of the idea.
3. Research the potential impact of peak oil on another transportation industry; for example, automobiles, cruise ships, rail and/or truck cargo.
4. What effect would "being grounded" have on you and your family? How would you spend your holidays?

The Evolution of Evolution

HELENA CRONIN

A philosopher and natural scientist, Helena Cronin (b. 1942) is co-director of the Centre for Philosophy of Natural and Social Science at the London School of Economics. She is the author of the award-winning *The Ant and the Peacock*, an account of the debates that have surrounded evolutionary theory since Darwin published *The Origin of Species*. Cronin launched and runs Darwin@LSE and is co-editor of *Darwinism Today*. Her research interests include an evolutionary understanding of sex differences.

In one of my favorite cartoons, a hopeful patient asks his doctor, "Have you got something for the human condition?" One cannot but sympathize with the hapless physician. Or so I used to feel. Now my urge is to leap into action crying, "I'm a Darwinian°; perhaps I can help." For in the past decade or so evolutionary theory has yielded a mind-blowing discovery: it has pried open the neatly-arrayed toolbox that is our mind. Just as *Gray's Anatomy°* laid bare the human frame, so Darwinian scientists are beginning to write the owner-occupier's manual to that hitherto most recondite° of mysteries: human nature. Yes, human nature does exist and it is universal. Our minds and brains, just like our bodies, have been honed° by natural selection to solve the problems faced by our ancestors

1

"The Evolution of Evolution" by Dr. Helena Cronin, originally published in *Time Magazine*, Winter 1997–98. Reprinted with permission of the author.

over the past two million years. Just as every normal human hand has a precision-engineered opposable thumb for plucking, so every normal human mind enters the world bristling with highly special-ized problem-solving equipment. And these capacities come on stream during development as surely as the toddler's first faltering steps or the adolescent's acne and ecstasy.

2   This mind-and-body-building is orchestrated by genes. But we're not merely their slavish puppets. Certainly, genes can do their work single-mindedly. However, genes—responding to dif-ferent environments—also underpin the flexibility and variety that typify human behavior. All this apparent design has come about without a designer. No purpose, no goals, no blueprints. Natural selection is simply about genes replicating° themselves down the generations. Genes that build bodies that do what's needed—seeing, running, digesting, mating—get replicated; and those that don't, don't. All the more wondrous, then, to discover what natural selection has achieved with human nature. The Darwinian explora-tion is still a fledgling science. But already it is yielding answers that we didn't even know had questions: What's the winning figure for ratio of waist to hips? Why are mother and fetus locked in irre-solvable conflict? Why is fast food so addictive?

3   New though this science is, researchers are already pretty con-fident about some things. Fortunately, one of them is sex. Consider a familiar sex difference that emerged in a study of American col-lege students. Asked by a stranger for a date, 50% of both women and men agreed. But asked "Have sex with me tonight?" not one woman agreed—whereas men shot to 75%. And when stu-dents were asked "How long would you have to know someone before having sex?" the questionnaire had to be rescaled for males requiring only minutes or seconds. Not only are men willing to have sex with a perfect stranger; they're more than willing with an imperfect one too. Another American study found that, for brief encounters, men (but not women) were willing to drop their stand-ards as low as their trousers, ready to dispense with intelligence, humor, charm, honesty and emotional stability.

4   Why this difference between men and women? When natural selection shaped male–female differences, it didn't stop at muscles and naughty bits. It also shaped differences in our psychologies. Evolution made men's and women's minds as unalike as it made their bodies. Why? Think of it this way. Give a man 50 wives and he could have children galore. But a woman with 50 husbands? Huh! Generation after generation, down evolutionary time, natural selection favored the men who strove most mightily for mates—the most competitive, risk-taking, opportunistic. We are all the descendants of those winners. Females, meanwhile, faced nine

months hard labor, breast feeding, rearing. A woman had to be far more picky about whose genes ended up partnering hers. Faced with the prospect of highly dependent offspring, she'd be on the lookout for someone who was not only fit and healthy but also had access to resources. Nowadays a Rolex or designer trainers provide cues. But for our hunter–gatherer ancestors roving the Pleistocene° plains, what mattered were social resources—status, reputation, respect. Genes that built brains with tools for making these shrewd decisions were the ones that got themselves replicated.

Of course, natural selection doesn't download its strategic   5 plans straight into our consciousness. Its instruments are emotions, priorities, desires. Behind each of these everyday human feelings are the calculations of natural selection, millions of careful years in the making. So, for example, men, without knowing it, tend to prefer women with a waist-to-hip ratio (WHR) of 0.7—a waist that is 70% of the hips. Twiggy's skeletal form and Rubens' hefty muses share a 0.7 WHR; so do dumpy Paleolithic "Venuses," figurines shaped by our ancestors 28 000 years ago. Why? It's an ingenious fertility-detection mechanism. Waists and hips are shaped by sex hormones, estrogen in particular. And the optimal hormonal mix for fertility also sculpts that desired ratio.

Both sexes have a predilection° for symmetry. A body with   6 matching right and left sides is an honest signal (because it is hard to fake) that the genes that built it are robust against invading pathogens°. As for women's breasts, the larger they are, the more symmetrical they're likely to be. Why? Breast-building requires estrogen; the larger the breasts the more the developing body must have been awash with it. But estrogen suppresses immunity, making the woman vulnerable to pathogens. So breasts that are large and yet manage to be symmetrical signal that their owner's immune system is reliably robust. Facial symmetry, too, is highly attractive; beauty, far from being skin deep, is a Stone Age body scan, brimming with information about health and fertility. It's no surprise, then, that there's cross-cultural agreement on what consti- tutes a beautiful face; even two-month old babies concur.

Sherlock Holmes° read the personal column "because it is   7 always instructive." Yes, the instructions come straight from the Darwinian textbook. Turn to lonely hearts listings: man seeks young, good-looking woman; woman seeks older, financially stable man. Study sexual fantasies: men—anonymous multiple partners, thoughts of bare skin; women—someone familiar, tender emo- tions. Consider adultery (what Darwinians politely call "extra-pair copulations"): males go for quantity; females, having established resources within monogamy°, go for quality, particularly high- quality genes. Across all its manifestations, human sexuality bears

the stamp of evolved sex differences: always preferences diverge°
and always predictably. But it's not just sexuality. A funny thing
happened on the way to divergent mating strategies. Natural
selection created males and females so unalike that the differences
don't stop at how fast you'll jump into bed; they pervade our psychology, shaping our interests, our values, our ambitions, our skills.

8   It's often said, for example, that men lack social skills. Don't
believe it. It's just that their skills are, all too understandably, not
what we call sociable. They are masters at status-seeking, face-
saving, assessing reputation, detecting slights, retaliating against
insults and showing off. They are more persistent and competitive than females, more disposed to take risks. Who causes most
road accidents, climbs Everest, flies to the moon, commits suicide?
Who are the alcoholics, motor-bike riders, scientists, child-abusers,
CEOs, gamblers, smokers, bungee jumpers, murderers and computer nerds? Men, of course. Men outstrip women in deaths from
smoking, homicide and accidents. Social scientists view these
causes of death as "life-style" as opposed to "biology." But, in the
light of evolutionary theory, speeding to death in a flashy car is
enmeshed in men's biology.

9   Put males and females in the same environment and their
evolved psychologies trigger hugely different responses. Boys
thrive in competitive exams; girls could do without. Boys play competitive games, big on rules and winners; girls play co-operative
games with consensual° endings. Men buy records to complete the
set, women to enjoy the music. Rich, successful men go for ever-
younger "trophy" wives; top women go for men even richer, more
successful—and older—than themselves.

10   After the enlightenment of the personal column, Sherlock
Holmes would turn dutifully to the criminal news. This, he felt,
was not instructive. Darwinian detectives do better. Consider the
family. Criminologists° are fond of remarking that it is the most
dangerous place to be. If this were true, it would be a Darwinian
scandal. Why? Remember that evolution is about genes getting
themselves replicated. Sex is one way. Another is for genes to help
copies of themselves in other bodies. One reliable way is to help
kin—the closer the relationship, the more help is given. From this
genetic reckoning, calculated by the blind forces of natural selection
over millions of years, spring some of our most cherished human
values. Whenever a mother braves hazards to save her child from
drowning, whenever a brother donates a kidney for his sibling,
"kin selection" is at work. We are evolved to lavish altruism on
our kin, not to abuse or kill them. So it's no surprise to find that the
criminologists are wrong.

Take murder. For a start, most family victims are spouses—not 11
genetically related at all. But what about infanticide°? Children are
cargoes of their parents' genes, 50% each, sallying forth into future
generations. Infanticide is therefore a profound challenge to evo-
lutionists—so profound that it sent intrepid Darwinians trawling
through the statistics in Britain and North America to find out what
proportion of murdered children died at the hands of their genetic
parents. The researchers discovered that step-children are about
100 times more likely to be killed than genetic children. It's true
what they say about Cinderella: having a step-parent puts a child at
greater risk than any other known cause.

But where there is sharing, there also lies competition. When 12
your children insist indignantly that your decision is not fair; when
they squabble over a toy; when mother's keen to wean and baby
resists—then bear in mind the following calculus of kin selection.
A child's life is its sole bid for genetic immortality; and it values
itself more than it values its brothers and sisters. Indeed, it is 100%
related to itself but has only a 50% chance of sharing genes with
siblings. But for a parent each child has the same value, a 50% relationship. The child will therefore always value itself, relative to its
siblings, more than its parents do. The result is conflict. A child is
evolved to want more than parents are evolved to give.

Pregnancy puts its own peculiar twist on this conflict because, 13
at this point in the child's life, even the parents' interests diverge.
Indeed, the womb harbors strife between mother and father that
would make a divorce court look peaceable. "He only wants
me for my body," women have cried down the ages. Darwinian
analysis is now revealing that this is even more true after conception than before it. Fifty per cent of a fetus' genes come from its
father. Our species cannot boast a history of reliable monogamy;
so genes from that father might never borrow that womb again.
Therefore paternal genes in the fetus have evolved to exploit the
mother's body more than is optimal for her. The battleground is
the placenta°, an invasive network of plumbing that seizes control
of the mother's blood supply, enabling the fetus to grab more than
its (maternally calculated) fair share of nutrients. This has set off a
maternal–fetal arms race, escalating wildly over evolutionary time.
Occasionally, a mother succumbs to one of the typical illnesses
of pregnancy, such as diabetes. Only in the light of Darwinian
analysis have we at last been able to understand these recurrent
pathologies; they are glitches in an irresolvable conflict.

Darwinian science is also beginning to discover how our 14
ancient tool kit fares in the modern world. For 99% of human
existence we lived as hunter–gatherers. Ten thousand years

ago agriculture arrived. Our evolved bodies and minds were unchanged; but, placed in novel environments, triggered by cues they were not designed to cope with, how would they respond? For an inkling°, go no further than your local fast-food joint. It is a monument to ancient tastes, to our evolved preferences for sugar, fat and salt. In our past, these finds were so scarce that we couldn't eat too much. Now our instincts are misled, resulting in the first epidemic of obesity that humans have ever known.

15   And we are processing not only food but also information that we weren't designed to digest. We have initiated a huge inadvertent° experiment on human nature. Think of our devices for choosing mates—exquisitely fine-tuned but not, perhaps, to some of today's challenges. A recent study found that, when people were shown pictures of beautiful and high status people of the opposite sex, both women and men became more dissatisfied with their own partners. We were evolved to assess beauty and status, and to calibrate° our satisfaction against a few hundred people at most. Yet we are all now exposed daily to images of the world's most beautiful women and richest and most powerful men, more beguiling than any our ancestors ever saw. Global communications amplify these invidious° messages across the world.

16   Our species has been faced with unprecedented inequalities ever since agriculture enabled us to hoard resources. But in recent years the game has increasingly become winner-take-all. From the world's chess champion to the leading libel lawyer, the few places at the top command almost all the status; and, as rewards rise, the gap between top and bottom grows. Caught in this game are males who are evolved to value status. What impact might these novel inequalities be making on them? Might it be significant that throughout the developed world, countries with the greatest inequalities in income have the poorest health and earliest death?

17   What of the future? It is often claimed that human evolution has ended because technology cushions us from disease and death; and, equally often, it is claimed that human evolution is accelerating because technology favors balloon brains on puny bodies. Neither is true. Natural selection's pace is slow; genes are plodding on with building bodies and minds in much the same way as they were for a million or so years, and that's how they'll continue for a long time to come. The adaptations that we bear tell us about long-lost worlds in which our ancestors dwelt. But those same adaptations tell us about our future. For it is not to human nature that we should look for change but to the intriguing new responses, the innovative behavior, that changing environments will elicit from that nature. And this enduring

thread of humanity reminds us that, however novel our environments, their most salient° feature—for us and our descendants, as for our ancestors—is other human beings like ourselves, a meeting of evolved minds.

Words and Meanings

Paragraph

Darwinian	someone who supports the theory of natural selection originated by Charles Darwin (1809–1882), which states that all species arise and develop through genetic variations that increase the individual's ability to survive and reproduce	1
Gray's Anatomy	medical text first published in 1858 and still in use today	
recondite	profound, hidden	
honed	shaped, perfected	
replicating	reproducing, copying	2
Pleistocene	era that began about two million years ago	
predilection	preference	6
pathogens	disease-carrying agents	
Sherlock Holmes	famous fictional detective, the leading character in Sir Arthur Conan Doyle's mystery novels	7
monogamy	practice of having only one mate at a time	
diverge	differ, go in different directions	
consensual	based on the agreement of all participants	9
criminologists	social scientists who study crime and criminals	10
infanticide	murder of a child	11
placenta	organ in the womb connecting mother and fetus	13
inkling	hint or suggestion	14
inadvertent	unplanned, accidental	15
calibrate	measure	
invidious	causing resentment, ill will	
salient	noticeable, prominent	17

Structure and Strategy

1. What strategy does Cronin use in her INTRODUCTION? Does the essay focus primarily on causes or on effects?
2. In paragraph 1, Cronin introduces an ANALOGY, comparing the human mind to a toolbox. Where else in the essay does she use this same analogy? Can you find other instances where the author explains an ABSTRACT idea by comparing it to a CONCRETE example?
3. Paragraph 2 ends with three questions. Where are these questions answered in the essay? What three KEY IDEAS do these questions represent? Rephrase the last sentence of paragraph 2 as a traditional thesis statement.
4. What is the TOPIC SENTENCE of paragraph 3? What strategy does Cronin use to develop it?
5. Find three or four examples of Cronin's use of question-and-answer to develop her points (see, for instance, the first sentence of paragraph 4). Is this informal, conversational style effective, given the seriousness of Cronin's topic?
6. Why are Cronin's ALLUSIONS to the literary figure Sherlock Holmes (paragraphs 7 and 10) appropriate in a causal analysis essay?

Content and Purpose

1. Cronin proposes that human nature is genetically determined. According to paragraphs 1 and 2, how do "our minds and brains" come to share certain characteristics?
2. What fundamental difference between men and women is explored in paragraph 3? How does the theory of natural selection explain this difference (see paragraph 4)?
3. According to the author, what physical characteristic do both men and women find attractive in the opposite sex? How do Darwinians explain the attractiveness of this characteristic?
4. Sex is one way that genes produce copies of themselves. What is another way for genes to promote their survival? How does Darwinian theory alter our traditional notions of the family and of altruism? (See paragraph 10.)
5. Cronin states that criminologists are wrong in their thinking that the family "is the most dangerous place to be." How does she defend the Darwinian point of view against that of the criminologists? Who does Cronin say is most likely to be murdered within a family? Why?

6. According to evolutionary theory, what is the source of sibling rivalry?
7. In your own words, explain why Darwinians think mother and fetus are locked in "irresolvable conflict" (see paragraph 13).
8. According to Cronin, why do we like junk food? What effect is our taste for junk food having on us in a world where we no longer have to hunt to survive?
9. Cronin suggests that the media, like junk food, adversely affect us because they feed us "information that we weren't designed to digest" (paragraph 15). What two negative effects of global communication does Cronin cite to support her point?

Suggestions for Writing

1. Write an essay in which you argue that perception of beauty, sibling conflict, and addiction to fast food are culturally rather than genetically determined.
2. Write an essay that explains a possible evolutionary cause of some aspect of human nature not discussed in Cronin's essay: for example, our religious impulse, inherent curiosity, fear of the dark, consumerism, fondness for jokes, tendency to break promises, xenophobia.
3. Does the theory that humans are creatures of evolution, designed simply to "replicate genes" (in other words, to get our own personal genetic material into the gene pool) appeal to you? Write an essay that details your response and argues either for or against the Darwinian point of view.

The Telephone

ANWAR F. ACCAWI

Anwar F. Accawi was born in the middle of World War II in a small village in the hills of southern Lebanon. He moved to the United States in 1965 when he won a scholarship. Accawi has taught at the English Language Institute at the University of Tennessee since 1979. In 1985, he started writing stories for his children about his childhood home. His book *The Boy from the Tower of the Moon* (1999) is a personal narrative of his boyhood in Lebanon. His essays have appeared in the *Sun*, the *Sewanee Review*, *DoubleTake*, *Now and Then*, *The Best American Essays* (1998), and *Harper's Magazine*.

1   When I was growing up in Magdaluna, a small Lebanese village in the terraced, rocky mountains east of Sidon, time didn't mean much to anybody, except maybe to those who were dying, or those waiting to appear in court because they had tampered with the boundary markers on their land. In those days, there was no real need for a calendar or a watch to keep track of the hours, days, months, and years. We knew what to do and when to do it, just as the Iraqi geese knew when to fly north, driven by the hot wind that blew in from the desert, and the ewes knew when to give birth to wet lambs that stood on long, shaky legs in the chilly March wind and baaed hesitantly, because they were small and cold and did not know where they were or what to do now that they were here. The only timepiece we had need of then was the sun. It rose and set, and the seasons rolled by, and we sowed seed and harvested and ate and played and married our cousins and had babies who got whooping cough and chickenpox—and those children who survived grew up and married *their* cousins and had babies who got whooping cough and chickenpox. We lived and loved and toiled and died without ever needing to know what year it was, or even the time of day.

2   It wasn't that we had no system for keeping track of time and of the important events in our lives. But ours was a natural—or, rather, a divine—calendar, because it was framed by acts of God. Allah himself set down the milestones with earthquakes and droughts and floods and locusts and pestilences°. Simple as our calendar was, it worked just fine for us.

3   Take, for example, the birth date of Teta Im Khalil, the oldest woman in Magdaluna and all the surrounding villages. When I first met her, we had just returned home from Syria at the end of the Big War° and were living with Grandma Mariam. Im Khalil came by to welcome my father home and to take a long, myopic° look at his foreign-born wife, my mother. Im Khalil was so old that the skin of her cheeks looked like my father's grimy tobacco pouch, and when I kissed her (because Grandma insisted that I show her old friend affection), it was like kissing a soft suede glove that had been soaked with sweat and then left in a dark closet for a season. Im Khalil's face got me to wondering how old one had to be to look and taste the way she did. So, as soon as she had hobbled off on her cane, I asked Grandma, "How old is Teta Im Khalil?"

The Boy From The Tower of the Moon, first published by Beacon Press, Boston © Anwar Accawi © Éditions Autrement, Paris, 2010 for the publication in French.

Grandma had to think for a moment; then she said, "I've been   4
told that Teta was born shortly after the big snow that caused the
roof on the mayor's house to cave in."

"And when was that?" I asked.   5

"Oh, about the time we had the big earthquake that cracked the   6
wall in the east room."

Well, that was enough for me. You couldn't be more accurate   7
than that, now, could you? Satisfied with her answer, I went back
to playing with a ball made from an old sock stuffed with other,
much older socks.

And that's the way it was in our little village for as far back   8
as anybody could remember: people were born so many years
before or after an earthquake or a flood; they got married or died
so many years before or after a long drought or a big snow or some
other disaster. One of the most unusual of these dates was when
Antoinette the seamstress and Saeed the barber (and tooth puller)
got married. That was the year of the whirlwind during which
fish and oranges fell from the sky. Incredible as it may sound, the
story of the fish and oranges was true, because men—respectable
men, like Abu George the blacksmith and Abu Asaad the mule
skinner, men who would not lie even to save their own souls—told
and retold that story until it was incorporated° into Magdaluna's
calendar, just like the year of the black moon and the year of the
locusts before it. My father, too, confirmed the story for me. He told
me that he had been a small boy himself when it rained fish and
oranges from heaven. He'd gotten up one morning after a stormy
night and walked out into the yard to find fish as long as his
forearm still flopping here and there among the wet navel oranges.

The year of the fish-bearing twister, however, was not the last   9
remarkable year. Many others followed in which strange and wonderful things happened: milestones added by the hand of Allah
to Magdaluna's calendar. There was, for instance, the year of the
drought, when the heavens were shut for months and the spring
from which the entire village got its drinking water slowed to a
trickle. The spring was about a mile from the village, in a ravine
that opened at one end into a small, flat clearing covered with fine
gray dust and hard, marble-sized goat droppings, because every
afternoon the goatherds brought their flocks there to water them.
In the year of the drought, that little clearing was always packed
full of noisy kids with big brown eyes and sticky hands, and their
mothers—sinewy°, overworked young women with protruding
collarbones and cracked, callused brown heels. The children ran
around playing tag or hide-and-seek while the women talked,
shooed flies, and awaited their turns to fill up their jars with

drinking water to bring home to their napping men and wet babies.
There were days when we had to wait from sunup until late afternoon just to fill a small clay jar with precious, cool water.

10   Sometimes, amid the long wait and the heat and the flies and
the smell of goat dung, tempers flared, and the younger women,
anxious about their babies, argued over whose turn it was to fill up
her jar. And sometimes the arguments escalated into full-blown,
knockdown-dragout fights; the women would grab each other by
the hair and curse and scream and spit and call each other names
that made my ears tingle. We little brown boys who went with
our mothers to fetch water loved these fights, because we got to
see the women's legs and their colored panties as they grappled
and rolled around in the dust. Once in a while, we got lucky and
saw much more, because some of the women wore nothing at all
under their long dresses. God, how I used to look forward to those
fights. I remember the rush, the excitement, the sun dancing on
the dust clouds as a dress ripped and a young white breast was
revealed, then quickly hidden. In my calendar, that year of drought
will always be one of the best years of my childhood, because it
was then, in a dusty clearing by a trickling mountain spring, I got
my first glimpses of the wonders, the mysteries, and the promises
hidden beneath the folds of a woman's dress. Fish and oranges
from heaven . . . you can get over that.

11   But, in another way, the year of the drought was also one of
the worst of my life, because that was the year that Abu Raja, the
retired cook who used to entertain us kids by cracking walnuts on
his forehead, decided it was time Magdaluna got its own telephone.
Every civilized village needed a telephone, he said, and Magdaluna
was not going to get anywhere until it had one. A telephone would
link us with the outside world. At the time, I was too young to
understand the debate, but a few men—like Shukri, the retired
Turkish-army drill sergeant, and Abu Hanna the vineyard keeper—
did all they could to talk Abu Raja out of having a telephone
brought to the village. But they were outshouted and ignored and
finally shunned by the other villagers for resisting progress and
trying to keep a good thing from coming to Magdaluna.

12   One warm day in early fall, many of the villagers were out in
their fields repairing walls or gathering wood for the winter when
the shout went out that the telephone-company truck had arrived
at Abu Raja's *dikkan*, or country store. There were no roads in those
days, only footpaths and dry streambeds, so it took the telephone-
company truck almost a day to work its way up the rocky terrain
from Sidon—about the same time it took to walk. When the truck
came into view, Abu George, who had a huge voice, and, before

the telephone, was Magdaluna's only long-distance communication system, bellowed the news from his front porch. Everybody dropped what they were doing and ran to Abu Raja's house to see what was happening. Some of the more dignified villagers, however, like Abu Habeeb and Abu Nazim, who had been to big cities like Beirut and Damascus and had seen things like telephones and telegraphs, did not run the way the rest did; they walked with their canes hanging from the crooks of their arms, as if on a Sunday afternoon stroll.

It did not take long for the whole village to assemble at Abu 13
Raja's *dikkan*. Some of the rich villagers, like the widow Farha and the gendarme° Abu Nadeem, walked right into the store and stood at the elbows of the two important-looking men from the telephone company, who proceeded with utmost gravity, like priests at Communion, to wire up the telephone. The poorer villagers stood outside and listened carefully to the details relayed to them by the not-so-poor people who stood in the doorway and could see inside.

"The bald man is cutting the blue wire," someone said. 14

"He is sticking the wire into the hole in the bottom of the black 15
box," someone else added.

"The telephone man with the mustache is connecting two 16
pieces of wire. Now he is twisting the ends together," a third voice chimed in.

Because I was small and unaware that I should have stood 17
outside with the other poor folk to give the rich people inside more room (they seemed to need more of it than poor people did), I wriggled my way through the dense forest of legs to get a first-hand look at the action. I felt like the barefoot Moses, sandals in hand, staring at the burning bush on Mount Sinai. Breathless, I watched as the men in blue, their shirt pockets adorned with fancy lettering in a foreign language, put together a black machine that supposedly would make it possible to talk with uncles, aunts, and cousins who lived more than two days' ride away.

It was shortly after sunset when the man with the mustache 18
announced that the telephone was ready to use. He explained that all Abu Raja had to do was lift the receiver, turn the crank on the black box a few times, and wait for an operator to take his call. Abu Raja, who had once lived and worked in Sidon, was impatient with the telephone man for assuming that he was ignorant. He grabbed the receiver and turned the crank forcefully, as if trying to start a Model T Ford. Everybody was impressed that he knew what to do. He even called the operator by her first name: "Centralist." Within moments, Abu Raja was talking with his brother, a concierge° in Beirut. He didn't even have to raise his voice or shout to be heard.

19   If I hadn't seen it with my own two eyes and heard it with my own two ears, I would not have believed it—and my friend Kameel didn't. He was away that day watching his father's goats, and when he came back to the village that evening, his cousin Habeeb and I told him about the telephone and how Abu Raja had used it to speak with his brother in Beirut. After he heard our report, Kameel made the sign of the cross, kissed his thumbnail, and warned us that lying was a bad sin and would surely land us in purgatory. Kameel believed in Jesus and Mary, and wanted to be a priest when he grew up. He always crossed himself when Habeeb, who was irreverent, and I, who was Presbyterian, were around, even when we were not bearing bad news.

20   And the telephone, as it turned out, was bad news. With its coming, the face of the village began to change. One of the first effects was the shifting of the village's center. Before the telephone's arrival, the men of the village used to gather regularly at the house of Im Kaleem, a short, middle-aged widow with jet-black hair and a raspy voice that could be heard all over the village, even when she was only whispering. She was a devout Catholic and also the village *shlikki*—whore. The men met at her house to argue about politics and drink coffee and play cards or backgammon. Im Kaleem was not a true prostitute, however, because she did not charge for her services—not even for the coffee and tea (and, occasionally, the strong liquor called arrack) that she served the men. She did not need the money; her son, who was overseas in Africa, sent her money regularly. (I knew this because my father used to read her son's letters to her and take down her replies, as Im Kaleem could not read and write.) Im Kaleem was no slut either—unlike some women in the village—because she loved all the men she entertained, and they loved her, every one of them. In a way, she was married to all the men in the village. Everybody knew it—the wives knew it; the itinerant° Catholic priest knew it; the Presbyterian minister knew it—but nobody objected. Actually, I suspect the women (my mother included) did not mind their husbands' visits to Im Kaleem. Oh, they wrung their hands and complained to one another about their men's unfaithfulness, but secretly they were relieved, because Im Kaleem took some of the pressure off them and kept the men out of their hair while they attended to their endless chores. Im Kaleem was also a kind of confessor and troubleshooter, talking sense to those men who were having family problems, especially the younger ones.

21   Before the telephone came to Magdaluna, Im Kaleem's house was bustling at just about any time of day, especially at night, when its windows were brightly lit with three large oil lamps, and

the loud voices of the men talking, laughing, and arguing could be heard in the street below—a reassuring, homey sound. Her house was an island of comfort, an oasis for the weary village men, exhausted from having so little to do.

But it wasn't long before many of those men—the younger ones especially—started spending more of their days and evenings at Abu Raja's *dikkan*. There, they would eat and drink and talk and play checkers and backgammon, and then lean their chairs back against the wall—the signal that they were ready to toss back and forth, like a ball, the latest rumors going around the village. And they were always looking up from their games and drinks and talk to glance at the phone in the corner, as if expecting it to ring any minute and bring news that would change their lives and deliver them from their aimless existence. In the meantime, they smoked cheap, hand-rolled cigarettes, dug dirt out from under their finger-nails with big pocketknives, and drank lukewarm sodas that they called Kacula, Seffen-Ub, and Bebsi. Sometimes, especially when it was hot, the days dragged on so slowly that the men turned on Abu Saeed, a confirmed bachelor who practically lived in Abu Raja's *dikkan*, and teased him for going around barefoot and unshaven since the Virgin had appeared to him behind the olive press. **22**

The telephone was also bad news for me personally. It took away my lucrative° business—a source of much-needed income. Before the telephone came to Magdaluna, I used to hang around Im Kaleem's courtyard and play marbles with the other kids, waiting for some man to call down from a window and ask me to run to the store for cigarettes or arrack, or to deliver a message to his wife, such as what he wanted for supper. There was always something in it for me: a ten- or even a twenty-five-piaster piece. On a good day, I ran nine or ten of those errands, which assured a steady supply of marbles that I usually lost to Sami or his cousin Hani, the basket weaver's boy. But as the days went by, fewer and fewer men came to Im Kaleem's, and more and more congregated at Abu Raja's to wait by the telephone. In the evenings, no light fell from her window onto the street below, and the laughter and noise of the men trailed off and finally stopped. Only Shukri, the retired Turkish-army drill sergeant, remained faithful to Im Kaleem after all the other men had deserted her; he was still seen going into or leaving her house from time to time. Early that winter, Im Kaleem's hair suddenly turned gray, and she got sick and old. Her legs started giving her trouble, making it hard for her to walk. By spring she hardly left her house anymore. **23**

At Abu Raja's *dikkan*, the calls did eventually come, as expected, and men and women started leaving the village the way **24** a hailstorm begins: first one, then two, then bunches. The army took them. Jobs in the cities lured them. And ships and airplanes carried them to such faraway places as Australia and Brazil and New Zealand. My friend Kameel, his cousin Habeeb, and their cousins and my cousins all went away to become ditch diggers and mechanics and butcher-shop boys and deli owners who wore dirty aprons sixteen hours a day, all looking for a better life than the one they had left behind. Within a year, only the sick, the old, and the maimed were left in the village. Magdaluna became a skeleton of its former self, desolate and forsaken, like the tombs, a place to get away from.

25   Finally, the telephone took my family away, too. My father got a call from an old army buddy who told him that an oil company in southern Lebanon was hiring interpreters and instructors. My father applied for a job and got it, and we moved to Sidon, where I went to a Presbyterian missionary school and graduated in 1962. Three years later, having won a scholarship, I left Lebanon for the United States. Like the others who left Magdaluna before me, I am still looking for that better life.

Words and Meanings

Paragraph

2	pestilences	disease epidemics
3	Big War	World War II
	myopic	near-sighted
8	incorporated	merged with, became part of
9	sinewy	lean, muscular
13	gendarme	police officer
18	concierge	hotel attendant
20	itinerant	moving from place to place, not resident
23	lucrative	profitable

Structure and Strategy

1. Does this essay focus primarily on cause or on effect? Of what?
2. This essay is divided into two parts: paragraphs 1 through 10 and 11 through 25. Summarize the content of the two halves of the piece.
3. What IRONY is there in paragraph 11, the turning point of the essay?

4. Identify two or three ANECDOTES in the essay that make it clear that the story is being told from the POINT OF VIEW of a child.

5. Identify three descriptive details in paragraph 1 that you think are particularly effective. How do these descriptive elements help support the topic of the paragraph?

6 The ILLUSTRATION developed in paragraphs 3 through 7 contains more dialogue than any other anecdote in the essay. What point is Accawi making here, and why do you think that he uses dialogue to support it?

7. Identify two SIMILES in paragraphs 13 and 17 that are specifically religious in meaning. Are they appropriate in an account of the introduction of technology into a village? Why or why not?

8. What are "Kacula, Seffen-Ub, and Bebsi" (paragraph 22)? Is Accawi's description of the villagers' pronunciation humorous? What is his attitude toward the speakers? How do details such as these influence the TONE of the essay?

Content and Purpose

1. According to Accawi, how did the villagers of Magdaluna mark time before the coming of the telephone? How did they "keep track of the hours, days, months, and years" (paragraph 1)?

2. Identify three memorable people among the villagers that Accawi describes. What descriptive and narrative details does he provide to help you "know" each of these people? How do they come alive to you? How do you think the author feels about each of these characters?

3. Who works harder in Magdaluna, the women or the men? Support your answer with specific references to the essay.

4. The first effect of the telephone on the village community is told through the story of Im Kaleem, "the village *shlikki*" (paragraphs 20 through 22). What is this consequence, and why do you think Accawi chooses Im Kaleem's story to communicate it?

5. The effects of the telephone on two specific people are detailed in paragraph 23. Who are the people, and what happens to them?

6. In paragraph 24, we are told that the "calls did eventually come." What happens then? Where do people go? What happens to Magdaluna itself? Do you think that these effects are all due to the arrival of the telephone in the village?

7. In your own words, describe how Accawi feels about the changes that swept through his world. Refer to specific details from paragraphs 24 and 25.

Suggestions for Writing

1. How do technologies such as the Internet, ATMs, smartphones, or video games change people and their environment? Write an essay describing the effects of a new technology on a person or place you know.
2. Write an essay describing a neighbourhood, town, or village that you know (perhaps one that you or your family came from). What has happened to this place over time? What caused the changes? Your essay should both describe the transformation and communicate your feelings about it.

ADDITIONAL SUGGESTIONS FOR WRITING: CAUSAL ANALYSIS

Choose one of the topics below and write a paper that explores its causes *or* effects. Write a clear thesis statement and plan the development of each KEY IDEA before you begin to write the paper.

1. Alcoholism
2. Cheating in school
3. The popularity of a *YouTube* video that has gone viral
4. Online gambling
5. Polygamy
6. Compulsive shopping
7. The pressure on women to be thin
8. Vegetarianism
9. Peer pressure among adolescents
10. Depression
11. Obesity
12. The trend to postpone childbearing until a couple is in their thirties or even forties
13. A specific phobia that affects someone you know (e.g., planes, snakes, spiders)
14. The attraction of religious cults
15. Marriage breakdown
16. Lying
17. Internet shopping
18. The increasing demand among men for plastic surgery (or spa treatments, cosmetics, etc.)
19. Shyness
20. People's tendency to distrust or dislike people who are different from themselves

UNIT 7

Definition

WHAT IS DEFINITION?

All communication depends on shared understanding. In writing, the writer and the reader must have a common understanding of what the words mean. Sometimes a definition is required to ensure this common understanding. Knowing when and how to define terms clearly is one of the most useful skills a writer can learn. Through definition, a writer creates shared meaning.

There are two basic ways to define terms: the short way and the long way. The short way is sometimes called **formal definition**: a single-sentence definition of a word that may be unclear to the reader. In the model essay "Talking Pidgin," the second paragraph begins with a formal definition: "A pidgin is a simplified language that evolves between groups of people who have no language in common." A fuller, more elaborate definition of pidgin languages follows. The essay as a whole is an example of the long form of definition, called **extended definition**. Extended definition is a kind of expository writing in which the word or idea being defined is the topic of the essay. Extended definition is required when the nature of the thing to be defined is complex, and the writer's goal is to explain in detail *what it is.*

WHY DO WE WRITE DEFINITION?

Definition is a useful way to provide information about a topic. A short, formal definition is often used to introduce an unfamiliar word or technical term. It may also be used to explain an unusual meaning of a word that is normally understood in another way. For instance, a reader might be tempted to think a "pidgin" was a kind of bird if the definition quoted in the paragraph above was omitted. This definition—and the shared understanding between writer and reader that it ensures—is crucial to grasping the definition of hybrid languages presented in the essay.

An extended definition is useful to explain ABSTRACT ideas, as Ian Brown does in his essay on the meaning of irony. Brown acknowledges the challenge of his topic:

> I realize this—irony, I mean—is a dangerously abstract subject. . . . Irony derives from *eironeia*, Greek for dissimulation, and encompasses verbal, literary, situational, dramatic, and cosmic irony and may or may not include sarcasm. . . . It entails a situation in which the surface meaning and the underlying meaning of what is said or done are not the same.

After providing the etymological origins of *irony,* Brown goes on to offer a number of concrete examples that help to ground his definition.

Definition is not restricted to a purely informative or expository function; it can involve argument or persuasion as well. Denise Chong's essay on page 304 develops a definition of "Being Canadian" that people from diverse cultures can relate to. In "Nature or Nurture—What's the Real Test of 'Home'?" on page 297, Ken Wiwa makes some poignant observations about his definition of "home" that will resonate with many people who have left their birthplace behind. June Callwood uses her definition of forgiveness (page 315) as a platform from which she makes a passionate plea for us to understand the costs—and the benefits—of true forgiveness.

HOW DO WE WRITE DEFINITION?

There is no single rhetorical pattern that applies to extended definition. Its development relies instead on one or more of the other patterns explained in this text. In other words, depending on the topic and the AUDIENCE, an extended definition can employ any of a number of organizational patterns, or even a combination of strategies.

It is often helpful to begin your extended definition with a formal definition. To write a formal definition, first put the term you are defining into the general class of things to which it belongs; then identify the qualities that set it apart or distinguish it from the others in that class. Here are two examples of formal definition:

TERM		CLASS	DISTINGUISHING FEATURES
Misogyny	is	the hatred	of women.
Misanthropy	is	the hatred	of people in general.

Constructing a formal definition is a logical way to begin the task of definition. It prevents vague formulations, such as "misogyny is when you don't like women."

Here are two pitfalls to avoid when writing definitions:

1. Do not begin your essay with a word-for-word definition copied from the dictionary. When you're staring at a piece of blank paper, it's hard to resist the temptation to resort to this strategy. But you should resist, because a dictionary definition is boring and often not directly relevant to your own topic.

2. Don't chase your own tail by using in your definition a form of the word you're defining. Stating that "adolescence is the state of being an adolescent" doesn't clarify anything for readers.

A good definition establishes clearly, logically, and precisely the boundaries of meaning. It communicates the meaning in an organizational pattern appropriate to the term and to the reader. To define is an act of creation, and defining terms clearly shows respect for both the ideas you're explaining and the readers you're addressing.

The following model essay—an extended definition of the term "pidgin language"—illustrates definition by example, etymology, and distinctive characteristics.

Talking Pidgin

Introduction (quotation and question to intrigue the reader)

Thesis is a question

Begins with formal definition and adds examples

Pren, man bolong Rom, Wantok, harim nau. Mi kam tasol long plantim Kaesar. Mi noken beiten longen. Can you translate these words? Not likely, unless you are familiar with Tok Pisin, a pidgin language spoken by about a million people in Papua New Guinea. What is a pidgin language?

A pidgin is a simplified language that evolves between groups of people who have no language in common. It is a new "hybrid" language made up of elements derived from its source languages: English and Chinese, for example, or Spanish and Tagalog. Most pidgin languages developed to permit groups to trade with each other. For example, when the Nootka and Chinook peoples living on the Pacific northwest coast of North America came into contact with French and English traders in the nineteenth century, they developed a pidgin language so they could talk and do business with each other. Like all pidgins, this language—Chinook Jargon—combined elements of its source languages: Nootka, Chinook, English, and

French. From the 1830s to the 1920s, from California to Alaska, Chinook Jargon was spoken by people from widely varying language backgrounds who came together to hunt, log, or look for gold. Chinook Jargon expressions are still used on the in the Pacific northwest region today: *mucketymuck* is a slang term for an important person, and *saltchuck* means the sea.

Definition by example

There are hundreds, perhaps thousands, of pidgin languages around the world. Many are based on European languages such as Portuguese, Spanish, French, Dutch, and English, and they reflect the extent of European colonization over the past 500 years. Probably the best-known example is Pidgin English, the language used by British and Chinese traders in ports such as Canton. But pidgins can develop wherever different languages collide. Mogilian is a Choctaw-based pidgin formerly used by Amerindian tribes along the Gulf of Mexico. Pachuco, or "Spanglish," is an English–Spanish hybrid used in Latino communities in the United States. Bazaar Malay is a pidgin derived from Malaysian and Chinese that is widely used in Malaysia and Indonesia.

Definition by etymology

Pidgins are so widespread and so multilingual in origin that linguists (scholars who study the nature of language) are not certain where the word *pidgin* comes from. Some suggest that it derives from the Portuguese word for business, *ocupação;* others think the source is a Chinese-inflected pronunciation of the English word *business*. Some etymologists (linguists who specialize in word origins) theorize that the word comes from the Hebrew *pid yom,* which means *barter*.

Definition by distinctive characteristics

All pidgin languages are characterized by a small vocabulary (a few hundred or thousand words), a simplified grammatical structure, and a narrower range of use than the languages they are based on. Pidgins are unique in that they are the native languages of no one. Speakers use them for a few restricted purposes—usually work and trade—and they use their native tongues for more diverse and complex communications.

Pidgins cease to exist when the contact between the source-language groups diminishes, or when one group adopts the language of the other. In their adaptability and transience, pidgins are excellent examples of the processes of linguistic change. More than any other kind of verbal communication, pidgins demonstrate how resourceful and ingenious humans can be in adapting language to fit their needs.

Conclusion (highlights significance and provides translation of opening quotation)

So what does the opening quotation actually say? It is none other than Shakespeare's famous words from *Julius Caesar:* "Friends, Romans, countrymen, lend me your ears; I come to bury Caesar, not to praise him."

Nature or Nurture—What's the Real Test of "Home"?

KEN WIWA

Journalist, documentarian, and activist Ken Wiwa (b. 1968) was born in Nigeria. His father, the internationally renowned playwright and human rights activist Ken Saro-Wiwa, was executed in 1995 after being imprisoned by the Nigerian military dictatorship. In 1999, Wiwa moved to Canada, where he was writer-in-residence at Massey College at the University of Toronto and a columnist for *The Globe and Mail*. His memoir of his father, *In the Shadow of a Saint*, won the 2001 Hurston-Wright Award for non-fiction writing. In 2005 he returned to Nigeria, where he became Special Advisor to the President on peace, conflict resolution, and reconciliation.

There's no place like home. Whenever I contemplate that phrase, I usually regard it with [ambivalence°], and over the past two weeks I've experienced both sides of its meaning. Watching six years of accumulated belongings from a family life in Canada being loaded into a shipping container would send a shiver of apprehension running through the most footloose nomad. It might be a truism, but it is only when you leave home that you really begin to appreciate it. 1

Without my knowing or suspecting it, Toronto, especially the cul-de-sac where I lived in the west end of the city, now sticks out in the collage of places that spring to mind whenever I think of "home." That street, which was my home base for six increasingly peripatetic° years, is one of those places where everyone 2

Ken Wiwa, "Nature or nurture—what's the real test of 'home'?" *Globe and Mail*, August 12, 2005. Reprinted with permission from the author.

really does know your name. It is odd, considering that I was one of its most transient residents, that I have so many memories of my Toronto street—my neighbours; children playing out on the road and running in between the gardens; the street parties; the cranks, loners and extroverts; the smell of skunks on a summer night; going for a run in High Park and lounging by Lake Ontario in summer—oh and er, shovelling snow in the winter.

3   Friends and neighbours: That's what has imprinted Ridley Gardens as home on my world's interior map. Like the sitcoms that take their names from the things that make us humane and sociable animals, the final episode of our Ridley Gardens life has ended, leaving a gaping hole. In Africa, we say it takes a village to raise a child. That was true in Toronto for my youngest son. He was born at home at Ridley Gardens and nurtured by the street. But as one of my neighbours succinctly put it while watching our sons play soccer one night, moving my family to the U.K. while I shuttle in and out of Africa will make my family life more coherent geographically.

4   For much of the past week, I have been homeless, living between my mother's place and my sister-in-law's house outside London. We're not actually moving to our new place until the end of this month but this halfway house is good preparation for taking what for me is a leap of faith—living outside a big city. I thought I couldn't resist the lure of the big smoke, but darting in and out of London this week, I am surprised at how easily I seem to have let go of my addiction to metropolitan hustle. London is the place I have always regarded as my turf, having spent the longest stretch of my life there. Driving into a half-empty city on a recent Saturday morning was an eerie experience; I imagine it was the underlying caution in the aftermath of the terrorist attacks°. A few days later, I struggled for an hour to get across town on the underground train, trying not to think about who might be carrying a bomb. If nothing else, such thoughts expose you to your prejudices, so you adopt the *sang-froid*° that comes with the territory. Living in a big city like London is a skittish experience these days. You don't have to be mad—but it helps. . . .

5   I escaped to Africa . . . [and tomorrow] I head to the sanctuary of my village. It will be a strange trip for me because the meaning of that home has changed since the last time I was there. When my grandfather passed away in April, he was the last of my grandparents; I have fewer compelling reasons to return to the village. Like anyone raised far away from their roots, the death of grandparents can cut you off. I guess you could call it the law of diminishing returns.

6   The thing about villages in Africa though is that most Africans, like me, have a village, a specific place that is unequivocally° home. And to give up on that place is to abdicate the centre of our

being. As the world turns on its economic wheels, the meaning of home for many of us spins with the dizzying pace of change. I like change, it keeps things fresh. But I also like to feel the ground beneath my feet. And I wonder, in all of this wandering: Is there no place like home any more?

Words and Meanings

Paragraph

ambivalence	experiencing two opposing attitudes or feelings at the same time	1
peripatetic	moving from place to place	2
terrorist attacks	the bombings of London's subway system in July 2005	4
sang-froid	cool, composed attitude	
unequivocally	unarguably; having only one interpretation	6

Structure and Strategy

1. How does the title prepare the reader for the topic Wiwa defines in this essay? Does Wiwa's essay fulfill the expectation that the title sets up in the reader?
2. The essay begins with a CLICHÉ that the author regards with "ambivalence." What two contradictory meanings can you assign to the saying "There's no place like home"?
3. What TV situation comedy does Wiwa allude to in paragraph 2? Can you think of examples of "sitcoms that take their names from the things that make us humane and sociable animals" (paragraph 3)? Have any of these programs influenced your own definition of "home"?
4. Identify and explain the PUN with which the author concludes paragraph 5.

Content and Purpose

1. Explain the meaning of the title. What is the difference between "nature" and "nurture"?
2. Identify the three places Wiwa has called "home" so far. What connection is there between each place and the title of the essay?
3. In which "home" did Wiwa live longest? How does he feel about that place now? Why?
4. In which "home" did Wiwa and his family spend the previous six years? What about their life there will they miss?

5. How does Wiwa feel about his home in Africa? Why has the meaning of that home changed for him?
6. Explain what makes a place a "home," according to Wiwa. Do you agree with his definition? Has he missed any essential characteristics that you would include in your definition of "home"?

Suggestions for Writing

1. In how many "homes" have you lived? Define what "home" means to you.
2. Write an essay about the place where you grew up. Are you as connected to this place as an adult as you were as a child? How does this connection (or lack of connection) have an impact on your life?
3. Read Richard Poplak's "Loaves and Wishes" (page 140) or David Bezmozgis' short story "Tapka" (page 396), both of which deal with the disorienting experience of leaving one's original home. Write an essay that uses Wiwa's essay and either Poplak's or Bezmozgis' piece to explore your own feelings about emigration.

Don't Call Me That Word

LAWRENCE HILL

Lawrence Hill is the author of seven books, including the novels *Any Known Blood* and *Some Great Thing* and the non-fiction book *Black Berry, Sweet Juice: On Being Black and White in Canada*. His latest novel, *The Book of Negroes*, was published around the world. It became a national bestseller in Canada and won various awards including Canada Reads 2009, the Commonwealth Writers' Prize, and the Rogers Writers' Trust Fiction Prize. Much of his writing touches on issues of identity and belonging. Hill, who speaks French and some Spanish, has travelled in Niger, Cameroon, and Mali as a volunteer with Canadian Crossroads International, a non-profit organization that he continues to support as an honorary patron.

1   Growing up in the 1960s in the affluent, almost all-white Don Mills, Ont., I was told by my black father that education and professional achievement were the only viable options for black people in North America. He laid down three rules as if they had been received from the mouth of God: 1) I was to study like the

dickens; 2) anything less than complete success in school or at work was to be regarded as failure; 3) if anybody called me "nigger," I was to beat the hell out of him.

This is the legacy of being black in Canada. You overcompensate for the fluke of your ancestry, and stand on guard against those who would knock you down. Over 400 years of black history here, we have had to overcome numerous challenges: the chains of slave vessels, the wrath of slave owners, the rules of segregation, the killing ways of police bullets, our own murderous infighting, and all the modern vicissitudes° of polite Canadian oppression.

Blacks in Canada, like our metaphorical brothers and sisters all over the world, have a vivid collective memory. We know what our ancestors have been through, and we know what our children still face. Most of us cringe° when we hear the word "nigger." No other word in the English language distills hatred so effectively, and evokes such a long and bloody history.

These days, more people than ever are talking about the word "nigger," as a result of the publication this year of the book *Nigger: The Strange Career of a Troublesome Word*, by Randall Kennedy, a black American law professor at Harvard University. It's a fascinating read, but it raises a troublesome argument that I ultimately reject: Kennedy praises "African American innovators" (by which he means comedians and hip hop stylists) for "taming, civilizing, and transmuting 'the filthiest, dirtiest, nastiest word in the English language.'"

Some misguided white people have bought into this same way of thinking. We have hit the pinnacle of absurdity when white teenagers sling their arms around black friends and ask, "Whassup my nigger?" And some white people seem to want a piece of that word, and feel the need to apply it to their own difficult experiences. The Irish have been referred to as "the niggers of Europe." In the 1970s, Québécois writer Pierre Vallieres titled one of his books *White Niggers of America*. And just the other night, when I visited a drop-in centre catering mostly to black junior high and high school students in Toronto's Kensington Market area, a white teenager decked out in baggy pants and parroting what he imagined to be blackspeak complained that some kids accused him of being a "wigger"—an insulting term for whites who are trying to act black. Whatever that means.

As Randall Kennedy rightly asserts, the word abounds° in contemporary black urban culture. True, when it crops up in hip hop lyrics, it's not intended to carry the hate of the racist. It signals an in-group, brotherly, friendly trash talk. This is well known in American culture but it has penetrated black Canadian culture, too.

Choclair, a leading black Canadian hip hop artist, uses the word "nigga"—a derivation of "nigger"—frequently in his lyrics.

7   Some people might say that the N-word is making a comeback. That the old-style, racist use of the word has faded into history and that it's now kosher° to use the word in ordinary conversation. This argument fails on two counts. First, racists and racism haven't disappeared from the Canadian landscape. The comeback argument also fails because it suggests that reappropriating° the word reflects a new linguistic trend. This is naive. As a way of playing with the English language's most hateful word, black people—mostly young black males—have called themselves "nigger" for generations. The difference now is that these same young blacks have broadcast the word, via music and TV, to the whole world. In the middle-class black cultures I've encountered in Canada and the United States, such a young man usually gets slapped or tongue-lashed by his mother, at just about that point, and he learns that the only time it's safe to use that word is when he's chilling on the street with his buddies. Black people use the word "nigger" precisely because it hurts so much that we need to dance with our own pain, in the same way that blues music dives straight into bad luck and heartbreak. This is very much part of the black North American experience: we don't run from our pain, we roll it into our art.

8   But does that take the sting out of the word? No. And what's the proof of that? We don't use the word around our mothers, our teachers, the people we fall in love with, or our children. "Nigger" is a word that young black men use on each other. But the word still pains most black Canadians. Let me share an image of just how much the word hurts. A friend of mine—a black woman, community activist and graduate student—was dying to read Kennedy's book. She bought it last week, but couldn't bring herself to start devouring it on the subway to work until she had ripped off the cover: she wouldn't allow herself to be seen on the subway with the word "nigger" splashed on the cover of a book, so close to her face.

Words and Meanings

Paragraph

2	vicissitudes	change of circumstances, usually unpleasant
3	cringe	flinch, shrink back, as if in fear of being hit
6	abounds	is commonly found
7	kosher	permissible, legitimate (from the Hebrew word meaning *proper according to Jewish law*)
	reappropriating	reclaiming as one's own

Structure and Strategy

1. What do the examples in paragraph 5 illustrate?
2. How does the CONCLUSION support and summarize the points that Hill makes in his essay?
3. Hill defines the N-word, historically and currently, but his essay is also an example of another rhetorical strategy. What is it?
4. What kind of DICTION does Hill use in this piece? What does his level of language tell you about the author?

Content and Purpose

1. Where and when did Hill grow up? What is his racial heritage? What were his father's three rules? Do the rules involve the "word" that Hill is referring to in his title?
2. According to the essay, how long is the history of black people in Canada? What has been their legacy?
3. Who is Randall Kennedy and what is his view of the N-word? What is Hill's opinion of Kennedy's argument?
4. Does Hill agree that "it's now kosher to use the word in ordinary conversation" (paragraph 7)? What is your opinion on that issue?
5. According to Hill, how have black North Americans dealt with the pain of racism over the centuries?
6. Why is *nigger* "the English language's most hateful word"? What other words are similarly hateful, for the same reason?

Suggestions for Writing

1. Have you ever been called an offensive name because of your race, ethnic origin, gender, or sexual orientation? Define the term by recounting one or more occasions on which it was used and explaining your personal response to the disrespect inherent in that name.
2. Some musicians, comedians, and writers use language usually considered to be offensive as part of their art. Choose a specific artist (or artists) who uses this technique and explain why you think this person's work is (or is not) successful.
3. Most people would agree that directing racial epithets or ethnic slurs at people different from oneself is wrong. But do you think it is all right for them to use what is generally considered to be offensive language when referring to themselves? Write an essay explaining your opinion on this issue.
4. "We don't run from our pain, we roll it into our art" (paragraph 7). In this sentence, Hill refers to the North American black experience; however, the same point could be made

about other races and ethnic groups. Using Hill's sentence as your thesis, write an essay explaining how it applies to a specific ethnic group.

Being Canadian

DENISE CHONG

Vancouver-born Denise Chong (b. 1953) grew up in Prince George, British Columbia. She first worked as an economic adviser to Pierre Elliott Trudeau but left public service in 1984 to begin writing full-time. She edited *The Penguin Book of Canadian Women's Short Stories* (1997) and is the author of a best-selling memoir, *The Concubine's Children* (1994), which chronicles the experiences of her grandparents who came to Canada from China. Her next book, *The Girl in the Picture* (1999), was built around a photograph taken during the Vietnam War of the severely burned Kim Phuc fleeing her napalmed village. Her latest book, *Egg on Mao: The Story of an Ordinary Man Who Defaced an Icon and Unmasked a Dictatorship* (2009), also focuses on human rights. Chong tells the story of Lu Decheng, a worker who defaced a portrait of Chairman Mao during the 1989 protests in China's Tiananmen Square and suffered cruel consequences for his political act.

1   I ask myself what it means to be a Canadian. I was lucky enough to be born in Canada [, so] I look back at the price paid by those who made the choice that brought me such luck.

2   South China at the turn of the century became the spout of the teapot that was China. It poured out middle-class peasants like my grandfather, who couldn't earn a living at home. He left behind a wife and child. My grandfather was 36 when exclusion° came. Lonely and living a penurious existence, he worked at a sawmill on the mud flats of the Fraser River, where the Chinese were third on the pay scale behind "Whites" and "Hindus." With the door to Chinese immigration slammed shut, men like him didn't dare even go home for a visit, for fear Canada might bar their re-entry. With neither savings enough to go home for good, nor the means once in China to put rice in the mouths of his wife and child there, my grandfather wondered when, if ever, he could return to the bosom of a family. He decided to purchase a concubine, a second wife, to join him in Canada.

3   The concubine, at age 17, got into Canada on a lie. She got around the exclusion law in the only way possible: she presented

the authorities with a Canadian birth certificate. It had belonged to a woman born in Ladner, British Columbia, and a middleman sold it to my grandfather at many times the price of the old head tax°. Some years later, the concubine and my grandfather went back to China with their two Vancouver-born daughters. They lived for a time under the same roof as my grandfather's first wife. The concubine became pregnant. Eight months into her pregnancy, she decided to brave the long sea voyage back so that her third child could be born in Canada. [Her] false Canadian birth certificate would get her in. Accompanied by only my grandfather, she left China. Three days after the boat docked, on the second floor of a tenement on a back alley in Vancouver's Chinatown, she gave birth to my mother.

Canada remained inhospitable. Yet my grandparents *chose* to keep Canada in their future. Both gambled a heritage and family ties to take what they thought were better odds in the lottery of life. . . .   4

My own sense, four generations on, of being Canadian is one of belonging. I belong to a family. I belong to a community of values. I didn't get to choose my ancestors, but I can try to leave the world a better place for the generations that follow. The life I lead begins before and lingers after my time.   5

I am now the mother of two young children. I want to pass on a sense of what it means to be a Canadian. But what worries me as a parent, and as a Canadian, is whether we can fashion an enduring concept of citizenship that will be the glue that holds us together as a society. Curiously, Canadian citizenship elicits the most heartfelt response outside Canada. Any Canadian who has lived or travelled abroad quickly discovers that Canadian citizenship is a coveted possession. In the eyes of the rest of the world, it stands for an enlightened and gentle society.   6

Can we find a strong concept of citizenship that could be shared by all Canadians when we stand on our own soil? Some would say it is unrealistic to expect a symbol to rise out of a rather pragmatic° past. We spilled no revolutionary blood, as did France—where the word *citoyen*° was brought into popular usage—or America. Some lament the absence of a founding myth; we don't have the equivalent of a Boston Tea Party. Others long for Canadian versions of heroes to compete with the likes of American images that occupy our living rooms and our playgrounds. The one Canadian symbol with universal recognition is the flag. But where does the maple leaf strike a chord? Outside Canada. On the back packs of Canadian travellers. . . .   7

Some say Canadian citizenship is devalued because it is too easy to come here. But what sets Canadian society apart from others is that ours is an inclusive society. Canada's citizenship act remains more progressive than [the immigration laws of]   8 many countries. Canadians by immigration have equal status with Canadians by birth. In contrast, in western Europe, guest workers, even if they descended from those who originally came, can be sent "home" any time. In Japan, Koreans and Filipinos have no claim to the citizenship of their birth. The plight of the Palestinians in Kuwait after the [first] Gulf War gave the lie to a "free Kuwait."

9   Canadian citizenship recognizes differences. It praises diversity. It is what we as Canadians *choose* to have in common with each other. It is a bridge between those who left something to make a new home here and those born here. What keeps the bridge strong is tolerance, fairness, understanding, and compassion. Citizenship has rights and responsibilities. I believe one responsibility of citizenship is to use that tolerance, fairness, understanding, and compassion to leaf through the Canadian family album together. . . .

10   How we tell our stories is the work of citizenship. The motive of the storyteller should be to put the story first. To speak with authenticity and veracity° is to choose narrative over commentary. It is not to glorify or sentimentalize the past. It is not to sanitize our differences. Nor [is it] to rail against or to seek compensation today for injustices of bygone times. In my opinion, to try to rewrite history leads to a sense of victimization. It marginalizes Canadians. It backs away from equality in our society, for which we have worked hard to find expression.

11   I believe our stories ultimately tell the story of Canada itself. In all our pasts are an immigrant beginning, a settler's accomplishments and setbacks, and the confidence of a common future. We all know the struggle for victory, the dreams and the lost hopes, the pride and the shame. When we tell our stories, we look in the mirror. I believe what we will see is that Canada is not lacking in heroes. Rather, the heroes are to be found within.

12   The work of citizenship is not something just for the week that we celebrate citizenship every year. It is part of every breath we take. It is the work of our lifetimes. . . .

13   If we do some of this work of citizenship, we will stand on firmer ground. Sharing experience will help build strength of character. It will explain our differences, yet make them less divisive. We will yell at each other less, and understand each other more. We will find a sense of identity and a common purpose. We will have something to hand down to the next generation.

14   My grandfather's act of immigration to the new world and the determination of my grandmother, the girl who first came here as a *kay toi neu*°, to chance a journey from China back to Canada so that my mother could be born here, will stand as a gift to all future

generations of my family. Knowing they came hoping for a better life makes it easy to love both them and this country.

In the late 1980s, I [found] myself in China, on a two-year stint living in [Beijing] and working as a writer. In a letter to my mother in Prince George, I confessed that, despite the predictions of friends back in Canada, I was finding it difficult to feel any "Chineseness." My mother wrote back: "You're Canadian, not Chinese. Stop trying to feel anything." She was right. I stopped such contrivances. I was Canadian; it was that which embodied the values of my life.   15

Words and Meanings

		Paragraph
exclusion	the closing off of Chinese immigration to Canada	2
head tax	a fee charged by the Canadian government for each Chinese person entering Canada from 1885 until 1923	3
pragmatic	practical as opposed to idealistic	7
citoyen	citizen (French)	
authenticity and veracity	genuineness and truthfulness	10
kay toi neu	serving girl (Cantonese)	14

Structure and Strategy

1. Identify the METAPHOR at the beginning of paragraph 2. Is it an effective image or a CLICHÉ? Explain.
2. Paragraph 8 is developed mainly by use of examples. What are these examples, and what KEY IDEA do they support?
3. How does Chong support her definition of Canadian citizenship in paragraph 9?
4. What kind of CONCLUSION does the essay use? Is it effective? Why or why not?

Content and Purpose

1. Summarize the experience of the people whose story is told in paragraphs 2, 3, and 4. What is the relationship between them and the author? What is her attitude toward them?
2. What is the question that "worries" Chong as she defines what being Canadian means to her? (See paragraphs 6 through 8.)
3. According to Chong, how do people outside Canada view this country? Do you agree with her? Why or why not?

4. What are some of the obstacles Chong sees to a "concept of citizenship that could be shared by all Canadians" (paragraph 7)?
5. What are the "rights and responsibilities" (paragraph 9) of citizenship expressed in the essay?
6. Paragraph 10 discusses the role of narrative—"How we tell our stories"—as an important element of the "work of citizenship." How does Chong feel about stories that condemn past injustices as a way of demanding compensation? Do you agree with her? Why or why not?
7. According to the essay, how will all Canadians benefit from telling our stories as part of the "work of citizenship" (paragraph 13)?
8. In two or three sentences, summarize Chong's definition of "being Canadian." How does her definition compare with your own understanding of what it means to be Canadian?

Suggestions for Writing

1. Chong maintains, "How we tell our stories is the work of citizenship." Write an essay that tells the story of someone you know who has become a Canadian citizen.
2. Chong argues that seeking compensation for past injustice "leads to a sense of victimization [and] marginalizes Canadians." Do you agree? Why or why not?

Other Meanings, Below the Surface Level—Remember That? Anybody?

IAN BROWN

Ian Brown (b. 1954) is a Canadian journalist and author, winner of nine National Magazine and National Newspaper awards. He is a feature writer for *The Globe and Mail* and a freelance writer for *Maclean's, Financial Post,* and other journals. Brown is the host of CBC Radio's *Talking Books* and anchor of two TVO documentary series, *Human Edge* and *The View from Here.* His book *The Boy in the Moon* (2009), a moving account of his son Walker's rare genetic disorder and its effects on the family, won both British Columbia's. National Award for Canadian Non-Fiction and the Charles Taylor Prize. Brown is also the editor of *What I Meant to Say* (2006), an anthology of essays by prominent Canadian male writers whom Brown invited to write on subjects that they would have liked—but had never been able—to discuss with women.

I saw something genuinely unusual the other day, which was unusual, given how commonplace the unusual is now. I saw a man on the sidewalk holding a Bates List Finder address book. The Bates List Finder was a mechanical address book patented in 1937 and popular in the 1950s and 1960s—an enclosed metal tray, with a snap-down lid, seven and a half inches long and four inches wide. It came in soothing colours like Egg Cream or Avocado, and usually sat next to your (rotary) telephone. 1

A movable arrow down one side clicked through the alphabet until you found the first letter of the name of the person you wanted to call, whereupon you pushed a bar at the bottom of the lid, and it popped open to the page that held all the telephone numbers of all the people you knew whose name began with, say, G—more convenient than an address book, but less industrial than a Rolodex. Sprung open like an eager clam, the device bore a resemblance to a flip phone, except that it was bigger and heavier and wasn't a phone at all. The Bates List Finder address book was very popular with people who longed to be better organized. Those kinds of people still exist. The Bates List Finder address book does not. 2

What made the guy on the sidewalk even more unusual was that he was holding his wide-open Bates List Finder address book to his ear, and "talking" into it—as if it were a cellphone. This was his joke, an old-tech gizmo being used as a new-tech smart phone, to parody the crazy dream of technological progress, not to mention cellphones, the act of walking and talking, and our frantic, human longing for connection. He looked a little crazy, the kind of careening° city dweller whose life resembles performance art even when he doesn't want it to—a man going through the motions of communicating via a technology that couldn't (really) communicate. He was a walking, talking embodiment° of the ironic life, the life we all live now. 3

I realize this—irony, I mean—is a dangerously abstract subject. It attracts obsessives and philosophers, precisely the kind of people one wants to avoid if one is to live a crisp, clear, answer-filled existence. It's a notoriously difficult word to define. Irony derives from *eironeia*, Greek for dissimulation, and encompasses verbal, literary, situational, dramatic and cosmic irony, and may or may not include sarcasm. Whatever, dude. Nice weather we're having—not. Let's go. [*They do not move.*]° 4

5   The least one can say—and perhaps the less one says about irony, the better, which is an ironic thing to say at this point—is that it entails a situation in which the surface meaning and the underlying meaning of what is said or done are not the same. Fancy that. Irony says one thing and means another, and doesn't have a nervous breakdown in the process. To an ironist such as Socrates or Shakespeare, the only thing that is true is that nothing is true without its opposite being true as well. Hence Henry W. Fowler's famously crabby and exasperated definition of irony in his *Modern English Usage*: "A way of shrugging one's shoulders in print."

6   The ironic point of view—the one that sees the world as a series of paradoxes° arising from more or less insoluble problems— has been controversial ever since the German Schlegel brothers° (Friedrich and A.W.) suggested at the outset of the 19th century that a lot of what we think is objectively real and true is, in fact, subjective. Philosopher G.W.F. Hegel° hated the Schlegels, as do people such as Bill O'Reilly and the hardheads at Fox News.

7   Yet another philosophical point of view insists that irony ceased to be a viable philosophical perch° after the attacks on the World Trade Center divided the world into clearly labelled Good and Evil factions. There are even people who make a decent living claiming that we now live in a "post-ironic" age. *Greenberg*, a [2010] movie starring 44-year-old Ben Stiller and directed by 40-year-old Noah Baumbach, is the tale of a failed Generation X musician who can't get over himself long enough to believe in anything. He may be the most charmless character in movie history. He falls for a 26-year-old girl from the new, non-ironic generation, someone willing to believe in—and sleep with—almost anyone who can make her feel authentic. She responds to his nagging nihilism°, he to her promiscuous yes-ness. They are doomed.

8   Still, you have to admit that irony comes in handy these days. Consider Barack Obama, who campaigned against offshore drilling to get elected, but [then] embraced it [only to be faced with the catastrophic British Petroleum oil leak in the Gulf of Mexico]. Here at home, Prime Minister Stephen Harper's Conservative government . . . stonewalled for months about what it knew of the fate of prisoners turned over to Afghan authorities. . . . [Then, over] 12 days, our fearful leaders . . . released 6,700 pages of documents pertaining to the matter. Unfortunately—ironically!—huge swaths of those documents [were] blacked out, "redacted" by censors.

9   Those black strips are physical irony—thousands of pages that hide information by purporting to reveal it. Truthful, and not truthful at all; a bundle of secrets that can't help revealing itself.

10   Which is not a bad description of any of us, the government included.

Words and Meanings

careening	zig-zagging; being thrown from one side to another	3
embodiment	physical presence or form	
Let's go. [*They do not move.*]	quotation from *Waiting for Godot* (1948), Samuel Beckett's famous play about the irony of the human condition	4
paradoxes	A paradox is a seemingly contradictory statement that may nevertheless be true.	6
Friedrich (1772–1829) and A. W. Schlegel (1767–1845)	poets, critics, and leading philosophers of the German Romanticism movement	
G. W. F. Hegel (1770–1831)	major philosopher of German Idealist movement	
viable philosophical perch	a practicable view of the world	7
nihilism	belief that nothing is worth believing in	

Structure and Strategy

1. This piece was published as a column in *The Globe and Mail.* What features of the essay identify it as a newspaper column?
2. The first sentence is a paradox. Identify it. Why is a paradoxical opening an effective INTRODUCTION to an essay on irony?
3. How does the title reflect the author's argument?

Content and Purpose

1. What is a "Bates List Finder" and what does the "guy on the sidewalk" do with it? Why do you think Brown begins his definition with this anecdote? Have you ever seen one of these gadgets, perhaps in the home of an elderly person?
2. How does Brown define irony in paragraphs 4 and 5? What is his own definition?
3. What is the "ironic point of view" (paragraph 6)? How does it deal with reality?
4. According to Brown, are people now in their twenties part of an ironic or post-ironic generation? Do you agree or disagree?

Suggestion for Writing

Write an essay defining the difference between irony and sarcasm. Provide examples from popular culture that illustrate your points.

The Thief, the Thinker, and His Identity

MARK KINGWELL

Mark Kingwell (b. 1963) is a professor of philosophy at the University of Toronto, as well as a public intellectual who has written widely in the popular press. Educated at the University of Toronto, Edinburgh University, and Yale, Kingwell is the author of twelve books, including *The World We Want* (2001) and *Better Living* (1998). In addition to numerous articles in academic journals, Kingwell's essays on culture and politics have appeared in more than 40 mainstream publications, including *Harper's*, *Utne Reader*, *The New York Times Magazine*, *Adbusters*, the *National Post*, and *The Globe and Mail*.

1   The other Mark Kingwell was a cheeky bastard. After a three-day shopping spree at various stereo outlets, home-supply stores and discount jewelry joints, racking almost 20 grand in components, power tools, and diamond chokers, the other Mark Kingwell stopped to get some cash. He wanted a little walking-around money, a bit of dosh°, some peeling paper°, some cake°.

2   The other Mark Kingwell wasn't going to stop just anywhere to get the cash. The other Mark Kingwell was no run-of-the-mill grifter, some cheap punk on a mindless blowout. No, he was a criminal mastermind with a comic-book sense of humour, the Lex Luthor of credit-card fraud. Or maybe he was just an idiot. Anyway, he used the ATM in the deli at the corner of the street where I, the real Mark Kingwell, lived. There it was on the statement, MasterCard cash advance, three hundred dollars, deli. And then the other Mark Kingwell went and had a couple of martinis.

3   Reading the printout of recorded expenses, plotting the other Mark Kingwell's journey through the cash nexus° of modern urban sprawl, was the only time I laughed during the disturbing experience of having my identity stolen. Otherwise it was long, frustrating phone conversations with suspicious security officers, some mid-level "X-Files" paranoia about the wobbly infrastructure of the postindustrial state, and a few afternoons of wild speculation° about who, how, and why.

4   Like other victims of credit card fraud, I alternated between being freaked out and surging with resentment. A couple of weeks ago in *The New York Times Magazine*, a man called Adam Ray

---

recounted his own version of this late-capitalist metaphysical night-mare when a fraud artist in Virginia applied for eight cards in his name. "In less than a month, this guy spent more than $40,000, a large chunk on stuff I'd never buy for myself, like Tommy Hilfiger and Nautica clothes and designer shoes," Mr. Ray said. "He also bought $5,000 worth of Zales diamonds, and while I don't blame the woman who got them, my wife was getting mad because I never bought her such nice things. All the gifts I'd given her suddenly seemed less special."

Mrs. Ray sounds a little, um, demanding, but you see her point.   5
There's something galling° about identity theft, especially if the thief proceeds to splurge by preying on your own good credit. At the same time, if the thief shops at places you don't frequent or care for, you feel oddly offended. I mean, maybe not Tiffany's, but couldn't he at least have gone to Birk's? And doesn't he realize that I myself, the real Mark Kingwell, have issues with how Wal-Mart treats its employees? Pretty soon you're wondering whether identity really is, as marketers insist, the sum of your shopping preferences.

Which just scratches the surface of the philosophical mysteries   6
here. People tend to take their personal identity for granted, but that's simply a mundane refusal to engage the deep questions of existence. Who are you? How do you know? How can you demon-strate it? Are you the same person from one moment to the next? In ancient Greek mythology, the warship of the minotaur-slaying hero Theseus was, over many years, replaced plank by plank. When every single plank had been replaced, was it still the original ship? If the removed planks had been secretly stored and later assem-bled, was *that* the original ship?

Questions best left for the seminar room, you say, but I can tell   7
you that once the consensual fiction° of identity is fractured, and somebody else is in possession of your numbers and passwords, things get weird. It is, for example, remarkably difficult to con-vince a credit agency that you are who you say you are. You keep shouting, "But I'm the real Mark Kingwell!" and "Of course I know my mother's maiden name!" even as you realize that this is exactly what the other Mark Kingwell would say. Before long, you feel like you're in one of those "Star Trek" episodes where you have to prove you're the real Kirk by knowing which way Sulu parts his hair or refusing to shoot McCoy with a phaser.

It doesn't help if you have now and then committed details   8
of your personal life (and drinking habits) to paper. For a while, I wondered if the other Mark Kingwell was indulging in a witty deconstruction of the appearance/reality distinction, or making fun of my "media personality." But then I saw that this was pointy headed crap, and thinking I'd been specially targeted was just

another illusion of identity. I'm merely a statistic in one of North America's fastest growing crime waves. [Former] U.S. attorney-general John Ashcroft [said] he [wanted] to make identity theft a federal offence, which would add two years to any conviction, but as deterrents go, that's chump change. Mr. Ray's impersonator, for example, who bilked more than 50 people out of a half million dollars, got a mere six and a half years on a plea bargain, and he only got caught because he was greedy and stupid.

9   Meanwhile, the vertigo° about personal identity, once experienced, never fully subsides. In "Listening to Bourbon," his sly satire on personality-altering drugs, Louis Menand° offers this compelling assessment of the ancient philosophical puzzle: "The sexual stallion and future world-beater of nineteen, for whom three pizzas and an accompanied hour in the back seat of a car are just the beginning of a decent evening, and the sagging commuter of twenty-five years later, who staggers home hoping only to have the stamina to make it through the first half hour of Charlie Rose°, are nominally 'the same person.' But by virtue of what? Of having the same Social Security number? Identity is the artificial flower on the compost heap of time."

10   That, as Mr. Menand says, is why people need bourbon°. Or in my case, as the still-at-large other Mark Kingwell apparently knows, a martini.

Words and Meanings

Paragraph		
1	dosh, peeling paper, cake	slang terms for cash
3	nexus	connection, link
	speculation	wondering, theorizing
5	galling	bitterly annoying
7	consensual fiction	agreed-upon story
9	vertigo	disorientation, confusion
	Louis Menand	distinguished American writer and literary critic
	Charlie Rose	American TV talk show host (PBS)
10	bourbon	an American whisky

Structure and Strategy

1. Identify the example in paragraphs 4 and 5. What point does it support?

2. What ALLUSIONS does Kingwell use in paragraphs 2, 3, 6, and 7? Are they familiar to you? Does he provide enough context to make them work for you?
3. What is the TOPIC SENTENCE of paragraph 9? What does it mean? How does Kingwell support his point about personal identity?
4. Consider the METAPHOR with which paragraph 9 concludes. Why is it effective?

Content and Purpose

1. Who is the "other Mark Kingwell"? What does he do?
2. Who is the "real Mark Kingwell" and how does he feel about "the other"?
3. What are the "deep questions of existence" that the theft of Kingwell's identity raises for him?

Suggestions for Writing

1. Have you or someone you know ever had your identity stolen? Write an essay about the experience, its consequences, and your own feelings about the experience.
2. Recognizing that this topic is the purest form of speculation, write an essay about the person you will be in 30 years in terms of personal identity. What will you look like? What will you do? How will you live? How similar to or different from the person you are now will you be?

Forgiveness

JUNE CALLWOOD

Author, broadcaster, and activist June Callwood (1924–2007) was born in Chatham, Ontario. She began writing for *The Globe and Mail* in the early 1940s and married noted sportswriter Trent Frayne, keeping her own name because *Globe* policy at that time precluded hiring married women. Callwood eventually wrote many articles and more than twenty books, including ghostwritten autobiographies for famous people such as TV personality Barbara Walters. Yet the abiding passion that animated Callwood's life and career was social justice. She spoke up forcefully for the rights of women, children, gays, the disabled, and the dispossessed. In addition, she championed the cause of freedom of expression,

Reprinted by permission of the estate of June Callwood.

working for the Canadian Civil Liberties Association, PEN Canada, and the Writers' Union of Canada. Callwood founded Casey House in 1988, a hospice providing care to people with AIDS at a time when there was no effective treatment for the fatal disease. She also founded Nellie's, one of the first shelters for abused women. Callwood amassed an impressive array of awards and honorary degrees over the years, including the Order of Canada. A chair of social justice was established in her name at the University of Toronto. Callwood continued to write and promote progressive causes until her death from cancer. Her lifelong commitment to social justice earned her the title Canada's Conscience.

1   A small boy in an industrial city in Ontario was beaten severely many times by his father, to the extent that the boy not infrequently required a doctor to stitch up the wounds. His father, a policeman, sincerely believed that if he beat his son with chains, belts, sticks, and his fists, the boy would not grow up to be gay. That boy, now in his thirties and indelibly a gay man, says he will never forgive his father.

2   "What he did is not forgivable," the man says with composure. "How can it ever be all right to abuse a child? But I have let it go."

3   And a woman, raised on the Prairies in a Finnish home, married a black man and had a son. She showed the infant proudly to her mother, whose reaction was a look of naked disgust. Her mother and that son, now a charming and successful adult, have since developed an affectionate relationship, but the daughter has not forgotten or forgiven the expression on her mother's face. "The best I can do," she says, "is that I have stopped hating her."

4   The ability to forgive is a central tenet° of every major religion in the world—Christian, Judaic, Hindu, Buddhist, and Islamic. Those faiths urge followers to forgive their enemies and, indeed, even to find a way to love those who wrong them. As the twenty-first century dawns, however, the world is making a spectacular mess of such pious admonitions. Instead of goodwill, this is the age of anger, the polar opposite of forgiveness. Merciless ethnic, tribal, and religious conflicts dominate every corner of the planet, and in North America individuals live with high levels of wrath that explode as domestic brutality, road rage, vile epithets, and acts of random slaughter.

5   Many people, like the gay man or the woman in a biracial marriage, find forgiveness an unreasonable dictate. Some assaults on the body or soul are unconscionable°, they feel, and forgiveness is simply out of the question. It satisfies the requirements of their humanity that they gradually ease away from the primitive thoughts of revenge that once obsessed them.

When Simon Wiesenthal, the famed Nazi hunter, was in a   6
German concentration camp, he found himself in a strange situation. He was taken to the bedside of a dying SS officer, a youth
who had killed many Jews, and the young man asked him, a
Jew, for forgiveness. Wiesenthal was silent and left the room, but
was haunted ever after. Thirty years later, he contacted some of
the world's great thinkers and asked, what should I have done?
Theologians such as Bishop Desmond Tutu and the Dalai Lama
gently hinted that he should have been forgiving, for his own sake,
but others, notably philosopher Herbert Marcuse, said that great
evil should never be forgiven. In *The Sunflower*, a collection of fifty-
three responses to Wiesenthal's question, Marcuse wrote sternly
that forgiveness condones° the crime.

The moral vacuum left by the pervasive disuse and misuse   7
of religious tenets has allowed a secular° forgiveness industry to
spring into being. People who yearn desperately to rid themselves
of an obsession for vengeance will seek help in curious places.
Since 1985, the University of Wisconsin–Madison has offered forgiveness studies, and an International Forgiveness Institute was
founded there. Four years ago, the world's first international conference on forgiveness drew hundreds of delegates to Madison.
Stanford University has a forgiveness research project and people
in California, a state on the cutting edge of self-absorption, are
taking part in studies on the art and science of forgiveness. Self-
help shelves in bookstores abound in titles such as *Forgive Your
Parents: Heal Yourself.*

An odious° US daytime television show, *Forgive or Forget*, fea-   8
tures guests who say they owe someone an apology. They describe
their offence, and then, *ta-dah*, the injured party appears on the
appropriately tacky set and either grants or withholds forgiveness.
Will the former foes embrace one another? The titillated° audience
can't wait.

Apologies are iffy because often they are contrived or coerced°.   9
Apologies extracted by judges, mediators, and parents are thin
gruel for the wronged person. One familiar genre of apology,
the one which commences, "I am sorry you are feeling badly," is
particularly counterproductive because there is no admission of
any responsibility; it is the other person's problem for being thin-
skinned. A sincere and remorseful acceptance of blame, however,
can close a wound.

Psychologists are engrossed by the topic and so are theolo-   10
gians, philosophers, psychiatrists, and—surprise—cardiologists.
Unforgiving people, some studies show, are three times more likely
to have heart disease as people who don't carry grudges. These

findings raise the suspicion that the researchers may have the cart before the horse. Heart attacks occur more often in blow-top people who have unfortified egos, the very ones most apt to be relentlessly unforgiving. On the other hand, people who hold tolerant views of human nature and don't seem to nurse grievances unduly tend to have blood pressures in the normal range.

11   Clergy, counsellors, and people who lecture and write books about forgiveness all preach reductionism as a strategy for overcoming hot resentment of someone's nasty behaviour. They say that people who have been harmed should see the hurtful as deeply flawed human beings working out nameless aggressions. Pitiable and inferior, they are examples of failure to thrive. Adults still distressed by abuse, neglect, or rejection in childhood are urged to consider what happened in their parents' childhoods—often, bad parenting comes from being badly parented. The theory is that understanding the reasons for their parents' limitations will enable the offspring to acquire a measure of compassion. Maybe it works. Hillary Clinton apparently forgave her sleazy husband because she knows he had an unhappy childhood.

12   This technique can be applied to almost any injustice and falls within the rapists-were-beaten-as-children, *poor them* school of thought, which for some skeptics veers perilously close to non-accountability. The law and commonsense hold that adults are responsible for what they do. While empathy may help people appreciate why others behave badly, the exercise is somewhat patronizing. The offender is reduced to a contemptible hive of neuroses and ungovernable aberrations°, which accordingly elevates the injured party to a morally superior person.

13   Demonizing the enemy is a common coping mechanism in times of adversity. In military terms, it captures the high ground. Catastrophes such as divorce, job loss, rape, robbery, infidelity, and slander are all assaults on personal dignity and self-respect. A sense of being intact—*safe*—has been violated, and people are dismayed to find themselves for some time emotionally crippled by anger and grief. Betrayal and loss take big chunks out of people's confidence and leave them feeling excruciatingly vulnerable to random harm.

14   The starting place, some therapists say, is to accept that something appalling has happened, and it hurts. Denial, a recourse more favoured by men than by women, won't help. The next step they say, is to develop an off switch. When fury threatens to make the brain reel, people should grasp for distractions. Brooding about revenge only serves to unhinge reason. If people don't rid themselves of wrath, personal growth stops cold. The hard part

comes at the end of the process. The choices are to enter a state of forgiveness, which is a triumph of generosity, or just to put the matter in a box, cover it with a lid, place a brick on the lid, and move on. In healthy people, a perverse° state of mind eventually wears itself out.

In yoga, they say that it takes six years of regularly practising meditation to gain spiritual insight. Forgiveness of a great wrong may take longer. The process can't even begin until the injured person stops crying.   15

Some people are marvellously unbroken by great injustices. Nelson Mandela smiled gently at his adversaries after twenty-seven years of brutal imprisonment. A worldwide figure of wonder, he even invited his white jailer to his inauguration as South Africa's president. In Cambodia, a pastor whose family had been wiped out by the Khmer Rouge baptized and forgave a notorious Khmer Rouge leader known as Duch. A university professor in Virginia had an urge to kill the intruder who beat his mother to death, but stopped himself with the thought, "Whose heart is darker?" And the father of a young girl casually murdered in a street encounter with a teenager she didn't know attended the trial and sat quietly throughout the appalling testimony. He said he would visit the youth in prison. "I do not think I can forgive him," he explained, "but perhaps if I know him I will not hate him."   16

Forgiveness is hard work. A woman, a devout Roman Catholic who forgave the man who tortured and killed her seven-year-old daughter, said, "Anyone who says forgiveness is for wimps hasn't tried it." The reward for giving up scalding thoughts of reprisal° is peace of mind. It is worth the candle°.   17

Words and Meanings

		Paragraph
tenet	principle, strong belief	4
unconscionable	unacceptable	5
condones	excuses	6
secular	having no relation to religion	7
odious	offensive, disgusting	8
titillated	fascinated, delighted by the invasion of another's privacy	
contrived or coerced	made up or forced	9

12	aberrations	deviations from the norm; delusions
14	perverse	obstinate, spiteful
17	reprisal	revenge
	worth the candle	an expression dating from Medieval times to describe an activity that required candlelight to see by; hence, worth the effort

Structure and Strategy

1. Identify the examples provided in the INTRODUCTION (paragraphs 1–3). How do they differ from the examples used in the CONCLUSION (paragraph 17)? Why do you think Callwood chose these differing examples?

2. Callwood identifies a number of ways humans can respond to being wronged, among them denial, excusing or demonizing the wrongdoer, and distraction. Identify the paragraphs that deal with these different responses and the author's objections to them.

3. Analyze the TONE of the essay. What do phrases such as "pious admonitions" (paragraph 4), "cutting edge of self-absorption" (paragraph 7), "odious US daytime television show," and "*ta-dah*" (paragraph 8) indicate about the attitude of the author to the ideas she is expressing?

Content and Purpose

1. What has traditionally been prescribed religious teaching about forgiveness? (See paragraph 4.) According to Callwood, what is happening to this dogma in the twenty-first century? Do the examples used to illustrate her point about this century support this contention?

2. Who was Simon Wiesenthal? Why does Callwood use his experience in the essay? How would you have answered the question he later posed to theologians and philosophers?

3. Why are apologies "iffy," according to Callwood?

4. What may be the physiological consequences of unresolved anger, according to this essay (see paragraph 10)?

5. What is "reductionism"? What is the reductionist strategy for overcoming anger about other people's behaviour that Callwood explains in paragraph 11? Do you think the example Callwood cites in the last sentence of the paragraph is effective?

6. What is the central flaw in this reductionist strategy, according to Callwood (see paragraph 12)?

7. Identify the steps in the process of forgiveness described in paragraph 14. Are there any alternatives for people who have been wronged and cannot forgive?

Suggestions for Writing

1. Write an essay about an injury or injustice that you or someone close to you suffered at the hands of someone else. What happened? What was the response? Were you or the person close to you able to forgive the person who committed the wrong?
2. Have you or someone close to you ever committed an injustice against someone else? Write an essay about the experience. What happened? How did the injured party respond? Was forgiveness possible in the situation?
3. Write an essay that explores the attitude of your religion toward forgiveness.
4. Explain why you think the federal government's response to a group of Canadians (e.g., the Japanese, who were interned during World War II; the Chinese, who were subject to a head tax until 1923, when they were denied the right to immigrate; First Nations peoples, whose children were abused in residential schools) was helpful or not helpful, to the victims, their offspring, and the larger society.
5. Read Lorna Crozier's "What Stays in the Family" (page 65) and apply Callwood's theories about forgiveness to the experiences that Crozier writes about. Do you think she has forgiven her father? Her mother? Should she?

ADDITIONAL SUGGESTIONS FOR WRITING: DEFINITION

Write an extended definition of one of the topics below.

1. Canadian humour
2. Superstition
3. Anxiety
4. Poverty
5. Avatar
6. Terrorism
7. Happiness
8. Social network
9. Racism
10. A good neighbour

UNIT 8

Argument and Persuasion

WHAT ARE ARGUMENT AND PERSUASION?

In Unit 7, we pointed out that some words have specific meanings that are different from their generally accepted meanings. The word ARGUMENT is commonly defined as a disagreement or quarrel, while PERSUASION usually refers to the act of trying to convince someone of something: to share an opinion or, perhaps, to buy a product. In the context of writing, however, the terms "argument and persuasion" refer to specific kinds of writing that have a special PURPOSE—one that is different from the main purpose of expository prose.

The introductions to Units 2 through 7 of this text have explained organizational patterns commonly found in EXPOSITION—writing intended primarily to explain. It is true that a number of the essays in these units contain strong elements of argument or persuasion: consider Margaret Wente's indictment of "bafflegab" in Unit 2, Example, or Gabor Maté's assertion that childhood neglect and abuse—not personal weakness—is the cause of drug abuse in Unit 6, Causal Analysis. Nevertheless, the primary purpose of expository writing is to *inform* the reader—to explain a topic clearly.

Argument and persuasion have a different primary purpose. They attempt to lead the reader to share the writer's beliefs and perhaps even to act on these beliefs. For example, in "Immigration: The Hate Stops Here" (page 366), Michael Ignatieff attempts to convince readers that although Canadians like to think of their country as a haven of tolerance, it may actually be an incubator of ethnic hatred. In a lighter vein, in "Google Never Forgets: A Cautionary Tale," Max

Fawcett wants to persuade us to be mindful that our online profiles can haunt and embarrass us for years. Of course, readers are not likely to be persuaded of anything without clear explanation, so there is always some overlap between exposition and argument. Nonetheless, in this unit we consider argument and persuasion as writing strategies intended mainly to *convince* or *persuade* the reader of an opinion, judgment, or course of action.

WHY DO WE WRITE ARGUMENT AND PERSUASION?

There are two fundamental ways to appeal to readers: through their minds and through their hearts. *Argument* is the term applied to the logical approach, convincing a person by way of the mind. For instance, in "Why I Like to Pay My Taxes," Neil Brooks constructs a thoughtful argument for contributing to the common good. *Persuasion* is the term often applied to the emotional approach, convincing a person by way of the heart. Jane Rule, in "The Harvest, the Kill," makes a strong appeal to the emotions in her persuasive essay about being mindful of the food we eat, whether we harvest it or kill it.

Writers often combine strategies, using logical and emotional appeals together. For example, Jill McCorkle uses the techniques of logical argument as well as a persuasive evocation of her son's childlike need to use "naughty words" in "Cuss Time," an essay in which she argues for freedom of speech and expression. We decide which approach to use—logical, emotional, or a combination of the two—depending on the issue we are discussing.

HOW DO WE WRITE ARGUMENT AND PERSUASION?

While exposition tends to focus on facts, argument and persuasion focus on issues. An **issue** is an opinion or belief that not all people agree on.[1] It is always *controversial,* which literally means "having two sides." To begin to argue an issue, clearly and concisely state your opinion about it. This is your statement of THESIS. Here are three theses from essays in this unit:

I like paying taxes. (Neil Brooks, "Why I Like to Pay My Taxes," page 341)
Halloween is a racist holiday. (Thea Lim, "Take Back Halloween," page 329)

---

[1] Note that an issue must be supportable by external evidence. "I like blue" is not an issue; it is a matter of taste.

Women are the new heavyweights of the workplace. (Margaret Wente, "The New Heavyweights of the Workplace," page 338)

The test of a good thesis for an argument or persuasion paper is whether someone could plausibly argue the opposite POINT OF VIEW: "I hate paying taxes"; "Halloween is a multicultural holiday"; "Men are the heavyweights of the workplace."

Once your opinion about an issue is clearly stated, you need to identify reasons to support it. Why do you believe what you do about the issue? The reasons you identify are the KEY IDEAS you will explore and support in your essay.

Argument/persuasion papers can be structured in a number of ways. How you organize your essay depends on your target AUDIENCE. How much do your readers know about the topic? Are they likely to be biased in favour of or against your opinion? For example, how many people actually *like* to pay taxes? Most—not all—people probably think Halloween is a fun holiday, but they may be intrigued by the idea that it perpetuates racist stereotypes. Men and women may have very different responses to the issue of who is the bread-winner in the family.

Once you've analyzed your audience, you can decide how best to approach them: directly or indirectly. If your readers are likely to be sympathetic to your point of view on an issue, you can state your opinion up front, then outline your reasons for holding that opinion, and then provide the EVIDENCE that supports those reasons. This is the direct approach—basically, the same thesis statement-based organization you've become familiar with in the previous seven units. Our model essay, "Why Good Writing Makes You Sexy," follows this familiar pattern.

On the other hand, if you think your readers are not likely to support your opinion, you would do better to build your case indirectly, setting out definitions, examples, and other evidence before declaring where you stand on the issue. Readers who are confronted early with a statement with which they disagree often do not listen to an explanation of the opposing point of view. People who would normally reject an argument for total freedom of expression are drawn into McCorkle's description of her allowing her little boy a "cuss time" when he can say all the bad words he wants. Another example of a successful indirect approach is "Immigration: The Hate Stops Here," in which Ignatieff is careful to get his audience onside before he states strongly and clearly what Canada expects from immigrants to this country.

One structural pattern is common to both argument and persuasion: the "two sides of the story" approach. This technique is particularly useful when you are arguing a contentious issue that may provoke serious dispute. "Why I Like to Pay My Taxes" is a fully developed example of the "two sides" approach. Neil Brooks carefully considers and dismisses his opponents' anti-tax arguments after he has presented convincing reasons for his pro-tax position. By acknowledging your opponents' position and their arguments, you enhance the credibility of your own position on an issue.

Here are four guidelines for writing effective argument and persuasion:

1. Draft a thesis statement that clearly states your opinion on an issue and, if appropriate, briefly previews your key ideas—your reasons for holding that opinion. (You may or may not include this statement in your final version, but it's a good idea to have it in front of you as you draft your essay.)

2. Think through your key ideas carefully and make sure that you can support them with appropriate and convincing details. Do some research to find supporting EVIDENCE.

3. Assemble accurate, relevant, and sufficient evidence to develop your key ideas.

4. Structure your argument in whatever pattern is most appropriate for your issue and your target audience. Usually, whether you choose to approach your topic directly or indirectly, you save your most compelling reason for the end of the essay so that it will remain in the reader's mind.

Bringing readers over to our side through well-chosen words is a challenge. Argument and persuasion are probably the most formidable writing tasks that we undertake, yet they may also be the most important. Armed with logic, emotions, and words, we can persuade others to agree with us and even to act. Effective persuasion is an art that truly deserves to be called *civilized*.

The model essay that follows takes a light-hearted approach to an old but still timely argument.

Why Good Writing Makes You Sexy

Introduction (challenges the view that writing skill has nothing to do with sex appeal)

This may come as a surprise to you, but being able to write well contributes to your sex appeal. Even more surprising is the fact that not being able to write well decreases your attractiveness to prospective mates. Intrigued? Read on! Writing is an essential skill if you want to achieve three vital objectives: communicate

Thesis
statement

effectively and memorably, obtain and hold satisfying employment, and attract worthy sex partners. Once you understand the influence good communication can have on your life, then you will see how skills such as faultless grammar, sound sentence structure, and an appealing style can transform you from road kill on the highway of life to a turbocharged powerhouse.

Key idea #1:
The reason is
developed by
contrast and
example

Note use of
questions to
engage reader

While spoken communication is, for most of us, easy, natural—almost automatic—it doesn't have the lasting power of written language. Even e-mail, the least permanent form of writing, can be re-read, forwarded, and redirected, attaining a kind of permanence that conversation cannot. Who wants to be the author of a message remembered for its unintended but hilarious grammatical flaws or syntactical blunders, such as a headline reading, "Judge to rule on nude beach"? Writing permits us to organize and present our thoughts effectively. Who hasn't mentally replayed a conversation over and over before finding, when it's too late, just the right comeback to a humiliating putdown? Writing allows the time to ensure that every sentence is precise, memorable, and devastating.

Key idea #2:
The reason is
developed by
contrasting old
and new
business
environments

Note use of
examples to
support key
idea

In business environments, good writing is a predictor of success. People who communicate well do well. This fact is continually emphasized in executive surveys, recruitment panels, and employer polls. At one time, novices heading for a career on the corporate ladder held the attitude that writing was something secretaries did. In today's climate of instant and incessant electronic communication and networked industries, few people can rely on a subordinate to correct their errors or polish their style before their colleagues or clients see their work. Besides, many of those secretaries who could write well are now occupying executive suites themselves. It doesn't matter what career you choose: your effectiveness is going to be judged in part by how well you communicate. Whether you're a health-care worker who must keep comprehensive and accurate notes, an environmental technician who writes reports for both experts and laypeople, or a manager who must defend her need for a budget increase, good writing enhances both the message and the messenger.

Key idea #3:
Developed by
contrasting
the survival
skills required
in prehistoric
times with those
required today
Note use of
descriptive
details

Throughout evolutionary history, men and women have sought mates with the skills and attributes that would enable them to thrive in the environment of the times. Eons ago, female survival depended on choosing a man with a concrete cranium and bulging biceps because he was most likely to repel predators and survive attacks. Prehistoric men selected women for their squat, sturdy bodies and thick fat layer because such females were more likely than their sinewy sisters to survive an Ice Age winter (and even provide warmth). Attraction between the sexes is based on attributes that suggest ability to survive, procreate, and provide. Skills such as spear hurling and fire tending are not in much demand anymore. Today's men and women are on the lookout for mates with updated thriving expertise. Your ability to communicate effectively is one of the skills that places you among the 21st-century elite, those who will rise to the top of the corporate food chain, claiming the most desirable mates as you ascend. Besides, the ability to write melting love letters or clever, affectionate text messages is a far more effective turn-on these days than the ability to supply a slab of mastodon or a well-crafted loincloth. Go ahead—flex those writing muscles, flaunt that perfect style!

Conclusion
emphasizes
significance of
the topic

Why write? Because excellent communication skills are the single most important attribute you can bring to the table, whether you are negotiating for power, profession, prestige, or a partner.

Author answers
the question
"Why write?"
with a deliberate
sentence
fragment
designed to
linger in the
reader's mind

Take Back Halloween

THEA LIM

Thea Lim was born in Toronto in 1981, but she grew up in Singapore. She describes herself as an anti-racist feminist who comes from conservative roots. Her writing has been published by *Utne Reader, The Atlantic Monthly, Bitch Magazine, Jezebel, Canadian Woman Studies/les cahiers de la femme*, and *Second Story Press*, and in multiple textbooks in the fields of composition and sociology. She published her first novel, *The Same Woman*, in 2008. Lim was the first Web editor of the *Shameless Magazine* group blog and she is currently a special correspondent for the blog *Racialicious*.

I'm a Halloween party pooper. I do a dismal job of dressing up. My last costume consisted of a baseball hat with googly eyes and mouse ears. I've only given out candy once. Some years I've even hidden upstairs in the dark, ashamed of my lack of candy, pumpkin and sense of fun. 1

I've always felt like a bit of a jerk for not participating in the festivities. It doesn't come that naturally to me—I spent most of my childhood in a country where Halloween wasn't really celebrated, except as a club night. But since I moved back to North America eight years ago, Halloween has seemed more like an obligation than a party zone, and every year I fail to rise to the challenge. 2

A year ago a new friend pointed out to me . . . [that] Halloween is not just a time to wear fake blood and fishnets, it's also . . . racist! 3

Mainstream North American culture likes to define itself as cultureless, but Halloween is a very cultural practice. Not only is it a little weird (Just look at it from the point of view of an outsider. Send your kids out to strangers' houses and tell them to ask for candy? Decorate your house like a graveyard? Dress up like a sexy version of a public health worker?) it is also based on difference—the point of Halloween is to dress up as "something different." So how do people who are often made to feel visually different—you know, like people of colour—experience Halloween? The average Halloween costume tells us a lot about what we culturally consider to be abnormal. 4

It tells us that dressing up in an overtly sexy way is taboo; in other words, that we're a pretty sex-negative people. It tells us that we are obsessed with strict gender categories [not only] because most little boys and girls have to choose very gender-coded costumes, but also because for many young people Halloween is the one time they can experiment with gender in a socially sanctioned° 5

Reprinted by permission of the author.

way. And if dressing up as "something different" can typically involve wearing geisha make-up, a Native headdress, bling, or a turban, Halloween tells us that our cultural norm is a middle-class, North American, white person.

6   Maybe it's not surprising then, that those of us who are made to feel [that] we are visually different, or those of us who feel culturally marginalized by mainstream North American culture (and we're prolly the same people who are acutely aware that North American cultures are very real, and very definable), feel uncomfortable, guilty, angry or just plain sad at Halloween.

7   Two weeks ago I co-facilitated an anti-racist Halloween workshop for the Toronto Asian Arts Freedom School. And the experience made me feel like less of a funless, googly-hat-wearing, Halloween loser.

8   Our workshop was attended primarily by 1st and 2nd generation Canadian Asian youth, and I was surprised and relieved to hear many people saying some of the things that I'd felt, but never quite been able to articulate. We talked about how as kids we'd felt uncomfortable or silly dressing up at Halloween; that the idea of dressing up as "something different" didn't compute, because every day we felt like "something different." Or that when we tried to imagine ourselves in a traditional costume (like a firefighter or a cheerleader—costumes that are very gendered and raced) it never seemed to fit. It's true that the few times I have dressed up, it's always been as a non-human thing: a tomato, carrot or a bee (that was my agricultural stage).

9   People of colour—especially those who grew up or live racially isolated—have a fear of being conspicuous°. As much as I like attention, I also devote massive energy to trying to blend in. This affects my personality and how I present myself on a fundamental level. The regular attempt to neutralize your race is a basic part of living as a person of colour in a racist culture. I wasn't able to pin down why the holiday where you're supposed to stand out gives me a serious case of the heebiegeebies, until I gave that workshop. It was totally enlightening to hear how much other Freedom Schoolers related; how much Halloween turned our fears of conspicuousness all the way up. You don't dress up because you have a phobia of standing out; you don't wanna stand out; this collective project to stand out freaks you out. But when you don't dress up, you stand out. It's enough to drive anyone under the bed until November 1st.

10   Halloween is not racist in and of itself. Many cultures have some form of Halloween, like the Mexican Day of the Dead, or the Chinese Hungry Ghost Festival. Celebrating Halloween doesn't

have to be a racist act. In fact, I know many people of colour (anti-racist people of colour!) who love Halloween. The main question that we tried to answer in our workshop, was this: even if sometimes we are made to feel as if we don't fit into the mainstream idea of what a North American is, we still are North Americans—and as a North American holiday, Halloween is ours too. So how can we take it back?

Here are four ideas we came up with: 11

1) Go as an aspect of my identity amplified. Sure I'm a mixed   12
race person of colour, and a huge part of my identity stems from that. But I get tired of being boiled down to only that. Sometimes I feel like the parts of my identity that have nothing to do with my racial/cultural identity are less interesting, exotic or sexy to the people around me.

One of our participants had the idea that it might be fun to   13
dress up as something that represented our personal cultures (i.e., the culture of me! the unique combination of everything that has happened to me). For example, if you're a chronically late person, you could wear an enormous, broken wrist-watch. Personally I have an intense (and okay, strange) hatred of wrinkled or bunchy bed covers. I could go dressed up as an immaculate pillow case.

2) Go as a dead version of a racial stereotype. My hair stylist   14
(who is East Asian) works in one of the poshest salons in town (but gives me a large discount so I can justify my coiff). Last year she dressed up in full geisha regalia—except she had a massive bullet wound on her forehead. To me the geisha costume represents a lot of the way East Asian women are sexualised in North America—expected to be submissive and sexually available. There was something ghoulishly satisfying about seeing it paired with such unsettling gore. I liked the idea of taking something that represents the way we've been oppressed, and then putting a gross, unappetizing spin on it.

**3) A costume that somehow indicates that cultural clothes are   15
not a costume.** Some of our participants talked about how, as children, Halloween was the only time they could wear their cultural clothes to school without getting full-out mocked. What effect does it have on us that the only time we can be ourselves is when others are dressing up as the weirdest thing they can think of?

The reason why "ethnic costumes" are so problematic is [that]   16
they posit° a cultural identity as a costume—they compress the complexity and intricacy of an entire culture into dress-up; into something that anyone (or really, usually someone with class and race privilege) has the right to use for the most superficial purposes.

17   One of our participants kicked around the idea of going dressed up in a sari, but with a sign that said "This is not a costume." Or to be less literal: wear your cultural clothes for a week leading up to Halloween, and then wear jeans and a t-shirt on Halloween itself.

18   **4) Throw a "you can *not* wear a costume" party.** I think this was my favourite. Maybe, at least right now, Halloween night just isn't a safe place for sensitive, anti-racist folks. So throw your own anti-racist October 31st party, and for people like me who feel downhearted whenever they try to think of an acceptable Halloween costume, make it a party where you don't have to dress up if you don't want to.

19   Have a safe and anti-racist Halloween. It's seriously more fun than hiding upstairs.

Words and Meanings

Paragraph

5	sanctioned	approved, acceptable
9	conspicuous	standing out, drawing attention
16	posit	assume

Structure and Strategy

Lim's piece appeared as a blog post on *Racialicious,* "a blog about the intersection of race and pop culture." Check it out, and see whether the post fits in among the other posts. Then identify features of Lim's post that are characteristic of blog writing.

Content and Purpose

1. According to Lim, why does she have a hard time with Halloween? What is her racial background?
2. Why does Lim think Halloween looks "a little weird" (paragraph 4) from the point of view of a cultural outsider? Do you agree or disagree? Why?
3. Besides reinforcing racial stereotypes, according to Lim, what else do costumes at Halloween say about North American culture? (See paragraph 5.)
4. What is the fear that Lim argues is common among "people of colour [living] . . . in a racist culture" (paragraph 9)? Do you agree or disagree? Why?
5. Summarize the four strategies that Lim and her workshop partners came up with to make people of colour feel more

comfortable at Halloween. Do you think these ideas would be fun? Why or why not?

Suggestions for Writing

1. Many cultures have a festival or occasion when people dress up in costumes. Write an essay about one of these dress-up festivals with which you are familiar. What is its origin? Purpose? How do you celebrate the festival or mark the occasion?
2. Write a narrative essay about celebrating Halloween (or another costume festival) when you were a child.

Google Never Forgets: A Cautionary Tale

MAX FAWCETT

Max Fawcett is a Vancouver-born and Toronto-raised writer now living in Edmonton. His work has been published in *The Globe and Mail*, the *National Post*, *The Vancouver Sun*, the *Toronto Star*, and *Corporate Knights Magazine*. He is the former editor of *The Chetwynd Echo*, a newspaper in the small northern community of Chewynd, B.C.; a past editor of *Dooneyscafe.com*; and the current managing editor of *Alberta Venture Magazine*.

We all have one, be it a mother, a well-meaning grand-parent or a particularly mischievous college buddy. They're the people who insist on sharing embarrassing stories—which are invariably supported either by a gallery of photographs or a library of shaky home videos—with those you had foolishly hoped would never see them. For example, my mother enjoys producing the front page of the *Vancouver Sun*, circa 1981, on which I am pictured stark naked and sucking on my bottle while sitting on the edge of a public swimming pool on a particularly hot summer day. The upside was the fact that, like my naked baby picture, these embarrassing moments could be managed, the mor-tifying game of show-and-tell limited to small audiences, and its effects mitigated° with healthy doses of self-deprecating° laughter.

1

Originally published in *This Magazine* 1 September 2006. © Max Fawcett. Reprinted with permission of the author.

2   The internet, quite unintentionally, has changed that. Thanks
to what amounts to a universally accessible photographic memory,
the internet essentially creates the digital equivalent of an unau-
thorized biography for everyone who leaves a digital footprint.
This biography is full of things you might like to share and others
you might not, from your comments in an online discussion group
to your Grade 12 graduation pictures or some ill-conceived poetry
you submitted to an online journal a few years ago. Worse still
is the fact that you have almost no control over the biography's
content.

3   Douglas Coupland describes this as our digital "shadow,"
and he believes it has dangerous implications. As he told a *Time*
reporter last spring:

> You've got this thing that follows you no matter where you
> go. It's going to survive your real shadow long after you're
> dead. It's composed of truth, half-truth, lies, vengeance,
> wishful thinking, accuracy, inaccuracy. It grows and grows
> and gets bigger. It's you but it's not you.

It is, in other words, like having the details of a particularly nasty
high-school rumour tattooed on your forehead for the rest of your
life. Worse still to Coupland is the fact that these shadows are no
longer limited merely to the famous and assorted minor celebrities: "Mine's pretty large at the moment but I think in a few years,
everyone's is going to be huge. It won't be just people in the public
light any more," [Coupland] said in the same interview.

4   The ghost writer behind these increasingly common unauthor-
ized biographies is none other than Google, that most trusted and
financially successful search engine. Google, you see, has betrayed
your trust. While it was guiding you to a particularly good restaurant or helping you find a long-lost high-school friend, it was also
collecting the dirt on you and sharing it with anyone who would
listen.

5   The search engine business used to be a competitive one, with
rival engines like Lycos, HotBot and AltaVista battling Google
for market domination. But Google's code won out, in large part
because it was so good at finding a good bed and breakfast in Napa
Valley instead of napalm manufacturers or articles on the dangers of breakfast in bed when you punched "bed and breakfast +
Napa" into the search field. But that superior code is also ruthlessly
efficient at finding every reference, however obscure, tangential
or dated it might be, when an individual's name is searched. As
the *National Post*'s Samantha Grice wrote in March, "the internet's
helpful librarian can become an embarrassing mom who insists on

hanging your dorkiest kid photos above the mantle and incessantly gushing about your less-than-stellar achievements."

I learned this lesson first hand, thanks to an Angelfire/ Geocities website that I created in 1998. I was 18 years old, living in a student residence at UBC and, like many people at the time, relatively unfamiliar with the internet. One of my floor-mates, a computer science student, appealed to my vanity—a winning strategy to this day, unfortunately—by suggesting that I create a webpage. After all, he argued, what was the harm? It was free, and if I either got bored with it or didn't like what I had created I could just delete it and forget about the whole experience. He neglected to mention that I could also forget that it existed. 6

In 2004, I finally remembered. Vanity being one of my chief weaknesses, I was Googling myself—a process in which you enter your own name as a search term on Google and discover your digital reflection—and I discovered, with no small degree of horror, the webpage that I had forgotten. Appropriately titled—appropriate in that it exacted the greatest amount of embarrassment—"Max Fawcett, this is your life," the page was a quintessentially amateurish presentation of my interests at age 18. According to the site, "I'm an honors history student/freelance newspaper writer. On this page you will find my collection of wrestling, *South Park,* and other cool links." Surf through and you could—and according to the ticker positioned at the bottom of the page, 674 people did— find a "shrine" to "the greatest wrestler of all-time, Chris Jericho" as well as "an extensive collection of *South Park* links, images, and episodes." The cherry in this cocktail of shame is the email address provided, greekgod@angelfire.com, a reference both to the summer I had spent in Greece and the fact that, I assume, I was fairly high on myself at the time of the page's construction. 7

The cost of my "bad Google" has been limited to embarrassment, but for others the price of leaving a digital footprint can be much higher. Employers now routinely Google prospective hires, and one ill-considered comment on a weblog five years ago can mean the difference between making the final round of interviews and being passed over in favour of someone without an objectionable Google shadow. A recent Harris Interactive poll found that 23 percent of adult internet users in the United States had searched online for information about their clients, customers, workers and potential employees. 8

Worse still is the fact that these Google-happy bosses often find what they're looking for. Nunavut Tourism employee Penny Cholmondeley—Polar Penny, to her online visitors—stumbled across this unfortunate reality on July 18, 2004, when she was 9 terminated from her job for comments made on her weblog. Intended as a personal journal that would detail her summer in Canada's Arctic for her friends and family, the blog included the occasional unflattering picture of, or critical observation on Iqaluit. Without notice or an opportunity to defend herself, Cholmondeley was fired by Nunavut Tourism after it was tipped off about the existence of the blog by an anonymous source just before the end of her six-month probation period. Polar Penny's experience isn't unique, either. Ironically enough, the next year Google employee Mark Jen was fired after blogging about his first few days at work. Delta Air Lines employee Ellen Simonetti was fired because the airline discovered photos of her in her uniform that she had posted on a website.

10   Perhaps the most infamous° Google shadow in history belongs to Mike Klander, once a powerful organizer for former prime minister Paul Martin and the author of an ill-considered blog posting in which he compared federal NDP candidate Olivia Chow to a certain breed of dog. The post and blog were quickly taken down, but not before Google's robots—the architects of everyone's Google shadow—captured and archived it. Klander resigned, but the blog became a major news story and gravely harmed Klander's boss, then Trinity-Spadina Liberal MP Tony Ianno, who was trying to defeat Chow for a third consecutive time to retain his seat. I'm not sure what Mr. Klander is like as a person, but this seems like an awfully high price to pay for what amounts to a bad joke.

11   The lesson here—ironically, one I'm not heeding, as the publication of this piece will breathe new life into that darkest corner of my Google shadow—is to be careful of what you put on display. The internet, for all of its marvellous technological advances and still greater possibilities, is a more dangerous place than we'd like to admit, and that danger comes not from spam, viruses, worms or even those creepy old men who prowl chat rooms pretending to be 16-year-old girls, but instead from the fact that our every cyberstep, every cyber-thought and every search term is saved, sealed and put on display, without our consent and beyond our control. Consider yourself warned.

Words and Meanings

Paragraph

1	mitigated	moderated, lessened
	self-deprecating	putting oneself down, making fun of oneself
10	infamous	notorious; famous in a bad way

Structure and Strategy

1. What example does Fawcett use to introduce his essay? How does it relate to Google? Why do you think he chose it?
2. What METAPHOR for a person's Google "biography" does Fawcett borrow from Douglas Coupland? Who is Douglas Coupland?
3. Why is the example in paragraph 5 a particularly good one?
4. What is the TONE of the essay? Is it ARGUMENT or PERSUASION?

Content and Purpose

1. What is Fawcett's prime source of embarrassment on the Internet? How did it end up there? How does he describe himself? According to Fawcett, what makes him particularly vulnerable to embarrassing himself in such a fashion?
2. Along with personal embarrassment, Fawcett maintains that people can damage their careers by means of their Google "shadow." What happened to Polar Penny? To Ellen Simonetti? What is ironic about Mark Jen's job loss when his blog entries showed up in a Google search?
3. Do you think what happened to political organizer Mike Klander is "Perhaps the most infamous Google shadow in history"? Can you think of any other people who earned similar infamy on the Internet?
4. Google is not the only possible source of embarrassment online. What is the most common way in which people can create a "digital shadow"?

Suggestions for Writing

1. Check your own "digital shadow" by Googling yourself or assessing an earlier Facebook profile. Write an essay about what you find, whether you knew it was there, and the kind of person that the shadow presents. How close is it to the real you? If you don't happen to like what you find, is it possible to change the "shadow" you?
2. Write a persuasive essay about the issue of privacy in the age of Google and *Facebook*. Is it right for potential employers to check job applicants' profiles online? What other risks can be associated with a person's "digital shadow"?

The New Heavyweights of the Workplace

MARGARET WENTE

Margaret Wente (b. 1950) has enjoyed a successful career in Canadian journalism as both a writer and editor. Born in Chicago, she moved to Toronto in her teens and holds a B.A. from the University of Michigan and an M.A. in English literature from the University of Toronto. Since 1992 she has been a columnist for *The Globe and Mail* and has twice won the National Newspaper Award for her writing. Her first book was the bestseller *An Accidental Canadian* (2004); her latest book is *You Can't Say That in Canada!* (2009).

1   Something interesting has happened with many of the couples I know. The wives have now become the major breadwinners. They have high-powered jobs in design, consulting, medicine, public affairs, HR, law and banking. Many of their husbands are underemployed or semi-retired, not always by choice. One works behind the counter in a retail store. Another keeps the books for a small business. One is a freelance writer whose market has nearly dried up, and another husband has gone back to school for a degree. A couple of others work for their wives' businesses. Several of these men also organize the household chores and do the cooking. Thirty years ago, most of these men handily out-earned their wives. But the situation has reversed.

2   Could this be the future? Very likely. At every age and income level, women are more likely than ever before to be the major or sole breadwinner in the family. The reason is not that more women are working, but that fewer men are. Three-quarters of the people who lost their jobs in the U.S. recession were men, and the hardest-hit sectors were the male worlds of construction, manufacturing and finance. Many of those jobs aren't coming back. In the city of Hamilton—once known as Steeltown—just 2 per cent of the population still works in steel. In Sudbury, the town that nickel built, Inco's unionized labour force has shrunk from 12,000 to around 3,300 souls, who are currently locked in a futile long-term strike° with their foreign owner.

3   Back in 2007, something happened in Canada that got almost no attention. We became the first country in the Western world where women outnumbered men in the work force. At first the gap

---

was small—just one half of 1 per cent—but by 2009, the gap had grown to 3.5 per cent. (Note: Statistics Canada's measure doesn't include the self-employed.) This January, the United States followed us across the threshold.

All evidence suggests the gender shift is permanent. It would 4
be nice to report that the sons of the striking nickel workers have gone off to university to become metallurgical engineers. But they have not. Just 18 per cent of Canadian males between 18 and 21 are currently attending university. Their sisters, though, are doing fine. They outperform their brothers in school and are far more focused on getting the credentials that will land them jobs as dental hygienists, bank clerks, office managers and nurses.

It's now conventional wisdom that a BA is the new minimum 5
requirement for a good job in the postindustrial economy. Today, 58 per cent of all BAs are earned by women. And nearly all the fields that will yield the most employment growth over the next couple of decades are ones already dominated by women. (An exception: janitors.)

A richly reported story in *The Atlantic* magazine ("The End of 6
Men," by Hanna Rosin) argues that these changes in the workplace amount to an unprecedented role reversal, whose cultural consequences will be vast. She notes that even something as fundamental as the sex preferences of parents has changed. Throughout human history, when muscle-power mattered and patriarchy reigned, sons were infinitely more valuable than daughters. But now—from urban America to urban Beijing—people's preferences have tilted toward girls. According to Ms. Rosin, one U.S. outfit that offers sperm selection says requests for girls are running at about 75 per cent.

At the heart of the *Atlantic* piece is one highly provocative 7
question. What if the modern, postindustrial economy is simply more congenial to women than to men?

It's hard not to answer yes. The modern, postindustrial 8
economy rewards people with a high degree of emotional intelligence who can navigate complex social networks. It rewards people who are flexible, adaptable and co-operative, who have good verbal skills, and who can work diligently, sit still and focus long enough to get the credentials they need to land a job. Women tend to be better at these things than men. They're also good at all the gender-neutral stuff, such as sales and analytical skills. Meantime, as muscle jobs vanish, men are showing little or no interest in becoming dental hygienists, kindergarten teachers or anything else that requires a high degree of people skills and nurturing.

It seems that just as women have more aptitude for certain jobs 9
than men, they also have more aptitude for schooling—especially

the long years of schooling you've got to put in to finish university. As Torben Drewes, an economics professor at Trent University, discovered, it's no mystery why more girls get in to university than boys. They're more motivated and they work harder in high school. "Fewer males had aspirations for university education than females and this fact might account for the lower levels of effort among them," he wrote. "However, it is also true that males were not able to produce high school averages (and, therefore, the entry requirement for university) as efficiently as females."

10   Men and women also behave differently once they get there. Here's what guys typically do in first-year university: play video games, work out, watch TV, party. Here's what girls do: study.

11   "If men were operating rationally in an economic sense, they should be flooding into higher education," says Tom Mortenson, a senior scholar at the Pell Institute for the Study of Opportunity in Higher Education in Washington. But people don't always operate rationally. And so we have that most modern of stereotypes—the aimless, slacker man-boy who isn't really qualified for anything and can't quite latch on to the job market.

12   As women bring home more and more of the bacon—and sometimes the whole hog—what will men do? How will relationships between the sexes be renegotiated? How will men figure out new ways to be a man? I have no idea. But for the first time since women relied on men to chase away the lions and bring home a tasty side of mastodon, it's all up for grabs.

Words and Meanings

Paragraph

2   long-term strike   One of the longest in Canadian history, the year-long strike ended in July 2010.

Structure and Strategy

1. The examples in paragraph 1 illustrate a contrast. What is it?
2. What is the TOPIC SENTENCE in paragraph 2? How is its point supported?
3. How does Wente support her point about changes in the work place amounting to "an unprecedented role reversal" (paragraph 6)? Do you agree with Wente's point? Why or why not?
4. What is the contrast in paragraph 10? Is it one that you agree or disagree with? Why?
5. Identify the idiomatic expression and the METAPHOR in the conclusion. How would you answer the question it poses?
6. Why do you think Wente chose the title "The New Heavyweights of the Workplace"?

Content and Purpose

1. What is the "gender shift" Wente refers to in paragraph 4?
2. What percentage of Canadian males between 18 and 21 are currently attending university? The percentage of females? What percentage of B.A. degrees are earned by women? What about B.Sc. degrees? Do you think Wente uses statistics effectively in this essay?
3. According to Wente, what work skills will be highly rewarded in the new "postindustrial economy"? Who does she think tend to have more of these skills, men or women? Do you agree? Why or why not?
4. What STEREOTYPE does Wente refer to in paragraph 11? Can you think of other examples of this stereotype? Does it have any validity?

Suggestions for Writing

1. How have men's and women's roles changed in the past thirty years or so? Write an essay contrasting prevailing gender roles and expectations in your generation as opposed to your parents' generation.
2. Who do you think does better in school, boys or girls? Why? Write an essay explaining the difference, based on your opinion and experience.
3. Write an essay in response to the three questions Wente asks in her concluding paragraph: What will men do in the new economy? How will relationships between the sexes be negotiated? How will men figure out new ways to be a man?

Why I Like to Pay My Taxes

NEIL BROOKS

A professor of law at Osgoode Hall Law School in Toronto, Neil Brooks has taught tax law and policy for more than thirty years. He has published extensively on tax issues and consulted widely for Canada's federal and provincial governments. In addition to serving as a consultant on tax policy and reform to the governments of New Zealand and Australia he has participated in income tax–related projects in countries around the

Neil Brooks, "Why I Like to Pay My Taxes" *Toronto Star*, January 8, 2006. Reprinted with permission of the author.

342 UNIT EIGHT • ARGUMENT AND PERSUASION

globe, among them Lithuania, Vietnam, Japan, China, Mongolia, Ghana,
Zimbabwe, South Africa, Bangladesh, and Sri Lanka. His most recent book
is *The Trouble with Billionaires,* co-authored with Linda McQuaig (2010).

1   I like paying taxes. Taxes allow us to pursue our aspirations
collectively and thus greatly enrich the quality of life for the
average Canadian family. Taxes have brought us high-quality
public schools that remain our democratic treasure, low tuition at
world-class universities, freedom from fear of crippling health bills,
excellent medical services, public parks and libraries, and livable
cities. None of these things comes cheaply.

2   Taxes also assist us in spreading our incomes over our lifetimes
to maximize our well-being by, for example, transferring income
from our high-income years to our retirement years, from times
when we are supporting children to times when we are not, and
from periods when we are well and able to take care of our own
needs to periods when we are ill or suffering from a disability.

3   Just as importantly, the public goods and services that we
purchase with taxes leave working people more secure, healthier,
better educated, more economically secure and therefore better protected against business threats, and thus more able to win their fair
share of the national income that we all collectively produce.

4   Taxes also allow us to discharge our moral obligations to one
another. They enable us to establish democratically controlled
public institutions that attempt to prevent exploitation in market
exchanges and family relations; to ensure mutuality in our inter-
dependence upon each other; to compensate those who are inevitably harmed through no fault of their own by the operation of
a dynamic market economy that we all benefit from; to ensure a
more socially acceptable distribution of income and wealth than
that which results from market forces alone; to strive for gender
and racial equality; and to provide full entitlement and open access
to those services essential to human development. As a result, taxes
buy us a relatively high level of social cohesion and social equality
and therefore the benefits of community existence. What would
any of us have without community?

5   In spite of the fact that they enable us to collectively provide
our most valuable goods and services, no one likes paying taxes.
There is a good deal of public misunderstanding about the role of
taxes in modern democratic states. In large part, this misunderstanding has been fostered by business interests and others who
would like to roll back the economic and social borders of the
public sector so that they can exercise unhindered power in our
society through private markets. Part of their deliberate and clever

strategy has been to use language and concepts in discussing taxes that make it appear self-evident that, while citizens can afford more private goods and services, which businesses produce, they are deluding themselves and living beyond their means if they think they can afford more public goods and services produced by government. Examples of such misleading characterizations of taxes abound. Here are three:

Increased taxes cannot be afforded. This common and compelling-   6
sounding refrain is patently nonsense. Many public goods provided by government and financed by taxes, such as health and education services, are necessities. Therefore, reducing the government supply of these services will not mean that people are no longer paying for them, it will simply mean that they are paying for them in the form of prices demanded by private providers instead of taxes paid to finance their provision through the public sector.

Similarly, when people say that we cannot afford to pay taxes   7
to provide child and elderly care services, presumably they are not saying that we can no longer afford to look after our children or the elderly. What they must mean is that instead of spreading the cost of these services equitably, through the tax system, across the entire population, we should leave them to be borne by women, by and large, who provide these services unpaid in their own homes.

Thus, often when business interests assert that taxes should   8
be reduced it is not because they think we can no longer afford the services that governments provide, but because they want to shift the cost of providing them from themselves and other high-income individuals to low-income families and women working in their homes at tasks that we all benefit from but for which they are not paid.

Taxes are a burden. This common description of taxes is equally   9
misleading. Taxes are the price that we pay for goods and services produced in the public sector from which we all benefit. They are equivalent to amounts we pay as prices for goods and services produced in the private sector. Compounding the deception, at the same time as they speak of public goods as being financed by the "imposition of taxes," business interests often speak of private goods as being financed by "the dollar votes of consumers." Here rational understanding is stood on its head. The vote, which is the symbol of democracy, is assigned to a marketplace transaction, while taxes, which are democratically determined, are treated as being amounts people have no control over but that are imposed on them.

10   **Taxes restrict freedom.** This common objection to taxes subtly reinforces the idea that the public sector simply consumes whatever it purchases with tax money, instead of using the money to deliver goods and services that benefit citizens. Taxes, in fact, increase the amount of freedom in society.

11   In a market economy, to have money is to have freedom. The government transfers over 65 per cent of the taxes it receives to families in need in the form of pensions, child allowances, social assistance, and compensation for work-related injuries or loss of employment. Thus, while it might be said that taxes restrict the freedom of some, they greatly enlarge the freedom of others.

12   Taxes increase our freedoms in other ways, including for example, the freedom to travel by using publicly financed roads and other transportation systems, the freedom to learn and think critically, freedom from concerns over crippling health bills, and the freedom to enjoy public libraries, beaches and parks.

13   To promise, as some politicians are doing, that they are going to cut taxes in order "to allow Canadians to keep more of their hard-earned dollars" is simply a way of saying "forget about recognizing your moral obligations to one another, to heck with pursuing your most noble aspirations collectively and do not worry about securing the blessings of real freedom." These people need a civics lesson. As a famous U.S. jurist noted, taxes are the price we pay for civilization.

14   Ultimately, what is at stake is the question of who will exercise power in our society. Will important sources of power be controlled by a small number of people through private markets? Or will important sources of power remain in the control of the majority of Canadians through democratically elected institutions?

Structure and Strategy

1. Where does Brooks state the THESIS of this essay?
2. This essay is an example of the "two sides of the story" approach explained in the introduction to this unit. Which paragraphs develop the pro-taxes point of view, and which paragraphs deal with the anti-taxes view?
3. How does paragraph 5 contribute to the structure and development of the piece?
4. Who do you think is the intended AUDIENCE for this essay?
5. What CONCLUSION strategy does Brooks use?
6. Is Brooks' essay developed primarily by ARGUMENT or by PERSUASION? Cite examples from the essay to support your opinion.

Content and Purpose

1. What are some examples of "public goods and services" (paragraph 3) that our tax money provides in Canada? Do you agree with the author that without taxes, we would not have "the benefits of community existence" (paragraph 4)?
2. Identify the three points that Brooks uses to explain why he likes paying taxes (paragraphs 2–4). Can you see a pattern in the arrangement of these points?
3. Why does Brooks think that there is a general misunderstanding about what taxes do in a modern democracy?
4. What does Brooks think of individuals and groups who would like to "roll back the economic and social borders of the public sector" (paragraph 5)?
5. What are the three "misleading characterizations of taxes" (paragraph 5), according to Brooks, and how does he counter each of them? Do you agree or disagree with him?
6. What is the relationship between voting and taxes? According to Brooks, which institution gives citizens more choice—democratic elections or the marketplace?
7. What does Brooks think that politicians who promise to cut taxes are really doing?

Suggestions for Writing

1. Which side of the political spectrum—right or left—do you think Brooks reflects in his essay? Do you agree or disagree with his position? Write an essay that argues your point of view.
2. Free public education through high school is one of the public services that are financed by taxes. Should postsecondary education also be tuition-free? Write an essay that argues your position on this issue.
3. Brooks maintains that Canada provides "excellent medical services" (paragraph 1) through its publicly financed health care system. However, there are waiting lists for many medical services, and many Canadians cannot find a family doctor. Write an essay that explores whether Canadians would be better or worse off if they had to pay for some of their medical care themselves.

Cuss° Time

JILL MCCORKLE

Jill McCorkle (b. 1958) teaches creative writing at North Carolina State University. She has written a number of novels and short-story collections, including *Ferris Beach*, *Going Away Shoes*, and *The Cheer Leader*. Her essays and reviews have appeared in *The New York Times Book Review*, *The Washington Post*, and *The American Scholar*, among other publications, and her stories have appeared in *The Atlantic*, *Ploughshares*, *Oxford American*, and *Best American Short Stories*.

1   My dad often told a story from his days as a mail carrier where he confronted a little boy no more than five perched up in a tree in a yard severely marked by poverty and neglect. The kid looked down with dirty face and clothes and said, "Whatcha want, you old son of a bitch?" We laughed at his aggressive assertion, but there was something sad and tender in it, too. There was the recognition of his own reality and the hope that his anger and toughness might in time lead him to a better place.

2   One day when my son was eight, he came into the kitchen while I was cooking and said: "You put bad words in your books, don't you?" No doubt he had overheard my mother, who often tells people who ask about my work: "Well, you'll never find her books in the Christian bookstore." I said that sometimes—when character and situation called for it—I did use strong language, that I couldn't imagine a realistic portrait of human nature, particularly in our contemporary society, without it.

3   "So can I do that?" he asked, and of course I told him absolutely—that when he writes a short story or novel, he will have all the freedom in the world to do so.

4   He pulled a ripped sheet of notebook paper from behind his back. "Would you like to hear the first of my book?"

5   This was when I stopped what I was doing and gave him my full attention, boy in Red Sox shirt and baggy jeans—his uniform of many years. "Now," he said. "Keep in mind that this is a 14-year-old girl who is being made to marry a guy she's never even met and she's mad." I could only assume he had read or heard something in school to inspire this—stories of another culture used to enlighten and remind us of our basic rights and freedoms and how important they are. He paused, giving a very serious look before clearing his throat, shaking the paper, and beginning.

"Goddamnit why would I want to marry that piece of shit boy? I'm 6
damn mad as hell."

He stopped and looked at me, waiting for my response. It was 7
one of those important parental moments, recognized as it is happening, so I took a few seconds. "Well," I said. "You certainly have
captured her anger and frustration." He nodded, a look of great satisfaction on his face, and wandered back to where he was playing
video games. Needless to say I confiscated that piece of paper and
carefully placed it in the box of treasured writings I have saved.
It is right in there with a letter he wrote his sister claiming he had
"Shitey conselars" at a camp he was unhappily attending.

A year or so before this took place, I had given him permission 8
to have what we called "cuss time." It began when I realized that he
was silently mouthing a lot of new vocabulary while riding in the car
or drawing. He saw me see him one day and he was embarrassed, so
I told him I knew that urge to test a word and how important it is to
do so. Thus the origin of cuss time. Every day for five minutes, usually right after school, he could say anything he wanted. He liked to
bounce on the already beaten-up leather sofa while saying the words,
sounds emitted as his feet left the cushion. It was a kind of Trampoline
Tourette's°—*hell, bitch, doo-doo*—and I'll confess I was always happy
that we were never interrupted by UPS or a friend stopping by.
What I found particularly endearing is that in his world, all words
that were considered inappropriate for public voice weighed
exactly the same. *Fart* and *fuck* and *fanny* were equals. *Shit* and *ass*.
When the kitchen timer rang, all cussing ended until the next day.

I found it liberating to watch his liberation. I was a kid who had 9
gotten my mouth washed out with soap regularly, and all that ever
did—other than leave me foaming and gagging—was to make me
furious and determined to say everything even more. It's one of the
most basic laws of human nature, isn't it? The more we are denied
something, the more we want it. The more silence given to this or
that topic, the more power. All you need do is look to the binge-
drinking or eating-disorder cases that surround us, the multitudes
of church sex scandals, to show that the demand for abstinence or
any kind of total denial of thought or expression or action can often
lead to dangerous consequences. When we know we can choose to
do this or that, we don't feel as frantic to do so, to make a sudden
move or decision that might be the worst thing for us.

When our words and actions are filled with possibilities and 10
potential, we are more likely to weigh out the options. I am convinced that the anticipation of cuss time—the *freedom* of cuss time—
kept my son from being overheard by some person in authority
who might have had no choice but to reprimand him and assign
punishment.

11   *Potential* is a powerful word. I remember feeling so sad when my children turned a year old and I knew, from reading about human development, that they had forever lost the potential they were born with to emulate° the languages of other cultures, clicks and hums and throat sounds foreign to me. For that short period of time, a mere 12 months, they could have been dropped anywhere in the world and fully adapted accordingly. But beyond this linguistic loss, we are at risk of losing something far greater each and every time we're confronted with censorship and denial. Perfectly good words are taken from our vocabulary, limiting the expression of a thought or an opinion. I recently read about high schoolers who are not allowed to use the word *vagina*. And what should they say instead? When you read about something like this (just one recent example of many), you really have to stop and wonder. Is this restriction because someone in charge thinks vaginas are bad? I once had a story editor ask me not to use the word *placenta*. I wanted to say: "Now tell me again how you got here?" *Oh, right, an angel of God placed you into the bill of the stork.*

12   Word by single word, our history will be rewritten if we don't guard and protect it, truth lost to some individual's idea about what is right or wrong. These speech monitors—the Word Gestapo (speaking of words some would have us deny and forget)—attempt to define and dictate what is acceptable and what is not.

13   Lenny Bruce, while pushing the First Amendment as far as it can go, famously said, "Take away the right to say *fuck* and you take away the right to say *fuck the government*." And maybe that's *really* what all the rules are about—power and control—someone else's over you. Though I felt the impulse to tell my son cuss time was a secret of sorts, "our own little game," I stifled the urge, knowing what a dangerous and manipulative thing the use of a "secret" can be. Besides, any suggestion of denial of the act would have worked against everything I was trying to give him. Of course, it wasn't any time at all before several little boys started asking to ride the bus home with him. "Can I do cuss time?" they pleaded. I sadly had to tell them the truth: they were not of legal age and so cuss time was something only their own parents could give them.

14   I have often thought what a better, more confident person I would have been if only I had grown up with cuss time instead of soap licking.

15   My first public reading from my work was when I was 25 years old. At the end, as I stood at the podium speaking to people, I noticed an elderly woman slowly making her way down the aisle. I waited for her to reach me only to have her shake a

finger in my face and say, "And you look like such a nice girl!" Unfortunately, I was still conditioned to want her to believe that I was a nice girl, conditioned to care more about what other people thought of me than what I thought of myself. It was only after the fact that I felt angry, that I wanted to go back and ask if she was even paying attention to what I was reading about—a situation of hurt humans expressing their feelings. I wanted to say, you have every right to your opinions and thoughts but that doesn't make you *right*. I wanted to say *fuck you*, and even knowing it would have been completely out of character for me to do so, I like knowing that I *could* have.

By limiting or denying freedom of speech and expression, we 16 take away a lot of potential. We take away thoughts and ideas before they even have the opportunity to hatch. We build a world around negatives—you can't say, think, or do this or that. We teach that if you are safely camouflaged in what is acceptable and walk that narrow road—benign or neutral words, membership in institutions where we are told what to think and believe—then you can get away with a lot of things. You can deny who you are and all that came before you and still be thought of as a *good* person. And what can be positive in that? In fact, what is more positive than a child with an individual mind full of thoughts and sounds and the need to express them who has the freedom to discover under safe and accommodating conditions the best way to communicate something? In other words, you old son of a bitch, I say *Let freedom ring*!

Words and Meanings

cuss	a common pronunciation of the word *curse*, meaning swearing	Title
Tourette's	a neurological disorder characterized by uncontrollable twitching and swearing	8
emulate	reproduce, imitate	11

Structure and Strategy

1. What INTRODUCTORY STRATEGY does McCorkle use to begin her essay? How is it echoed in the CONCLUSION?
2. Identify the contrast the author develops between her experience of saying "bad" words as a child and her son's. How does she feel about what happened to her?

3. Identify the example that McCorkle uses to illustrate the meaning of the word "potential" and the loss of it (see paragraph 11).
4. What METAPHOR does the author use to characterize "speech monitors" (paragraph 12)? Is it appropriate?
5. What is the THESIS of McCorkle's argument?

Content and Purpose

1. What is McCorkle's line of work? How does it relate to the first experience she narrates about her son (paragraphs 2–7)? How old is he at the time? Was it before or after this episode that she granted him "cuss time"?
2. Why did McCorkle originate "cuss time" with her son? What does the little boy do during "cuss time"? How do his friends relate to it? Do you think "cuss time" is a good thing for small children? Why or why not?
3. According to McCorkle, what is "one of the most basic laws of human nature" (paragraph 9)? Do you agree or disagree? Why?
4. How does McCorkle respond to the "elderly woman" (paragraph 15) who criticizes her for language she uses in her writing?
5. According to the author, what are we doing when we take away or limit freedom of speech or expression? Do you agree or disagree? Why?

Suggestions for Writing

1. Bringing up children is not an easy task. Write an essay about the way that you learned about appropriate—and not so appropriate—language and/or actions as a child. How did your parents teach you what they considered to be the right way to talk or behave?
2. Should there be any limits on free speech? What about hate speech or offensive stereotyping or defamation of religion? Should the government have the right to limit those kinds of expression? Write an essay that explains your views and argues your point of view on these issues.

The Potemkin Province

DANIEL FRANCIS

Born (1947) and raised in Vancouver, Daniel Francis is the author of more than 20 books, principally about Canadian history. Titles include *The Imaginary Indian: The Image of the Indian in Canadian Culture* (1992); *National Dreams: Myth, Memory and Canadian History* (1997); and *A Road for Canada: The Illustrated Story of the Trans-Canada Highway* (2006). He was editorial director of the mammoth *Encyclopedia of British Columbia*. His book *L.D.: Mayor Louis Taylor and the Rise of Vancouver* won the City of Vancouver Book Award in 2004. His latest book is *Operation Orca: Springer, Luna and the Struggle to Save West Coast Killer Whales* (2007; with Gil Hewlett).

T he story goes that in 1787 the Russian general Prince Grigori 1
Potemkin erected the façades of village buildings along the banks of the Dnieper River. When his former lover, Empress Catherine the Great, passed by on a tour of her Crimean territories, she was fooled into thinking that the mock villages actually existed and was impressed at the value of her new acquisitions and the accomplishments of her Prince. Ever since, the phrase "Potemkin village" has been used to indicate a situation where a false front disguises or distorts a less pleasant hidden reality.

With the widespread use of the latest tourist slogan, "The 2
Best Place on Earth," British Columbia has elevated itself to the ranks of a "Potemkin Province," a place of false fronts and pretense, marketed to the world as a beauty spot of unlimited abundance in order to obscure a history of pillage° and environmental embarrassments.

Many British Columbians see themselves as living in paradise, 3
the envy of the world. As our homegrown humorist Eric Nicol once observed, "British Columbians like to think of their province as a large body of land entirely surrounded by envy." While many outsiders think of B.C., when they think of it at all, as a rain-sodden outpost of meagre civilization, a province with too much geography and not enough industry, we who are privileged to live here insist that it is, well, the best place on earth.

This smug and grandiose delusion is of relatively recent vin- 4
tage. There was a time, long before the invention of tourism, when visitors to British Columbia saw it as the edge of nowhere, home to cannibals and some of the foulest weather on the planet. "This Coast is as Silent and Solatary [sic] as the House of death," moaned

---

© Daniel Francis. Reprinted by permission of the author.

the captain of one early-nineteenth-century trading vessel, "and I wish that I was as Clear from it I would take Verry good Care that no man Should Ever Catch me in this part of the world again." Early traders called the interior of the province "The Siberia of the Fur Trade," a reference to its isolation and forbidding winters. Later colonists huddled in their scattered settlements, fearful of the local Indians, occasionally dispatching gunboats to enforce their notional° authority. They appreciated the wealth that B.C. offered in the form of plentiful natural resources, but they never would have thought they were living at the centre of the world. That was still London or San Francisco.

5   As the twentieth century began, British Columbians, or at least those involved in the tourist trade, began to feel the need to elevate their rhetoric in order to attract visitors to the mountain parks and coastal hideaways. Once they had conjured up° a place that was more playground than province, they inevitably began to believe their own publicity. Tourist brochures presented a fabricated image of the place, accompanied by breathtaking photographs of the wild coast or the majestic Interior, usually with a totem pole somewhere in the foreground. Early slogans that were used to sum up life here included "The Evergreen Playground," "Always Cool, Never Cold," "The Playground of North America," and, until very recently, "Beautiful British Columbia."

6   Of course these phrases give a partial, cartoonish character to the province. One does not look to the literature of tourist promotion for subtlety or accuracy. Still, to call oneself "The Playground of North America" or even "Beautiful British Columbia" is a far cry from the triumphalist bombast° of "The Best Place on Earth." For the use of the superlative we must thank the Liberal government of Premier Gordon Campbell which began deploying the phrase as the focus of an advertising campaign in 2004.

7   British Columbia is unique in claiming that it is the "best" anything, anywhere. None of the other Canadian provinces feels the need for such a boastful slogan. The state of New Mexico appears to go one giant step further than B.C.; it bills itself as "The Best Place in the Universe." But presumably this is a sly reference to the infamous alien spacecraft that supposedly crashed near the town of Roswell, New Mexico, in 1947, and is done with tongue planted firmly in cheek.

8   The government of British Columbia, on the other hand, displays no sense of humour whatsoever about its claim. The Liberals firmly believe that our province is the best place on earth because they have made it so. (I suppose we should be thankful they did not decide to call us the best people on earth.) To the rest of us, it sounds a bit like

the answer to one of the CBC's sophomoric competitions, doesn't it? Who are the ten most significant Canadians? Where are the three most important places in Canada? What is the Best Place on Earth?

In reality, of course, British Columbia is not a playground. Behind the billboard façade of ski slopes and totem poles, the Potemkin Province is a resource frontier and always has been. The earliest fur traders who arrived in the 1780s found the coastal kelp beds full of sea otter whose thick pelts they obtained from the local First Nations. It is estimated that before the trade laid waste to coastal waters, as many as 300,000 of these cuddly creatures inhabited the North Pacific basin. Within a few decades, otter skins had become a rare commodity and the newcomers had to turn their attention to other resources. 9

Beginning with the sea otter, we have a long history of intolerance and waste when it comes to marine animals. Large whale species such as humpback, minke, and gray were hunted from shore-based whaling operations starting in the 1860s. Humpbacks are a case in point. The last of these great behemoths were massacred on an August day in 1952. "I will never forget that day," recalled fisherman Billy Proctor, the venerable sage° of Echo Bay in the Broughton Archipelago. "I was trolling in the mouth of Knight Inlet, and I seen the old *Nahmint* coming out towing all the old whales alongside. I just about cried. . . . That was the last of the humpbacks in the mainland." The *Nahmint* was a thirty-metre steel catcher boat belonging to the last whaling station on the coast at Coal Harbour in Quatsino Sound on the northwest coast of Vancouver Island. Most of the whales it relied on came from outside waters, but during the 1950s it mopped up the remnant populations in the inner waters inlet by inlet until there were no survivors. The station closed in 1967, but by then there were no whales left anyway. They have only recently begun returning. 10

Seals and sea lions also fell victim to human predators, shot for their skins or because they were thought to be pests that threatened the commercial fishery. Between 1913 and 1969, more than 200,000 harbour seals were killed in B.C. for pelts and bounties. Sea lion rookeries° were blown up with dynamite in the name of predator control. The recent book *Basking Sharks: The Slaughter of B.C.'s Gentle Giants* (New Star Books, 2006) has documented how basking sharks, the second-largest fish in the world, were all but eradicated° from the coast by fisheries officers hunting them down and slicing them in half with a giant knife mounted on the bow of a boat. 11

Orcas, or killer whales, are a special case because they are considered the iconic° animal of the coast, with visitors coming 12 from around the world to get a look at one in the wild. Yet forty years ago they were shot on sight or captured for sale to American aquariums. The hunt was stopped just this side of extinction. Basically, it was open season on any marine animal that seemed to interfere with the salmon fishery or had some commercial value of its own.

13   The experience of the sea otters and the whales has been repeated time and again on the coast. No sooner has a resource—animal, mineral or plant—been identified as valuable to the outside world than it is harvested to the point of extinction. Whether it was the old-growth forests or salmon streams destroyed by logging, the pattern was the same. Nature was commodified° and the commodities were harvested without thought for the future.

14   Nor does this attitude belong to the past. The newspaper brings daily reminders that in the Potemkin Province, development trumps conservation. A few months ago local politicians were on the verge of allowing the construction of a housing development at the mouth of the Adams River, a project which would have threatened one of the most plentiful salmon runs in the world. Local protest stopped the project just in time. Similarly, fish farms are allowed to threaten wild salmon stocks on the coast, while it is only a matter of time before the government gives in to the economic imperative and allows drilling for oil in offshore waters. Add to this the devastation of the pine-beetle plague in the Interior and it is hard not to conclude that the best place on earth is looking the worse for wear.

15   Many British Columbians are nature worshippers, happiest when they are kayaking down a white-water rapid or bounding along a mountain trail. They may approve of the slogan because they believe it. The rest of us are expected to swallow our embarrassment and go along with the illusion. Since the government began using its bloviated° catchphrase, at least one online petition has sprung up asking that it be rescinded. The petition calls it "embarrassingly arrogant," "vague and mostly meaningless," "presumptuous and distasteful," and "shockingly pretentious." They get no argument from me. But in the Potemkin Province, there is little hope that saner, less swollen heads will prevail.

16   Of course, B.C. is a beautiful place. Many places are. But the best place on earth? Not likely. No place is. At the same time, it is our place, a unique place, and it is our responsibility not to wreck it. To date we haven't been doing a very good job. The most irritating thing about the Liberals' slogan is that it tries to put a happy face on failure. We've been given a part of the world to look after

and collectively we should be ashamed of ourselves for the clumsy way we have mishandled it. What we need from our government is a call to action, not an excuse to be complacent°.

Words and Meanings

pillage	to take by force, plunder, rob	2
notional	in name only	4
conjured up	created magically	5
bombast	overblown rhetoric, boasting	6
venerable sage	wise old man	10
rookeries	rocks on which sea lions give birth and nurse their young	11
eradicated	wiped out	
iconic	symbolic	12
commodified	turned into commodities, something to be exploited	13
bloviated	overblown, pompous	15
complacent	smug, self-satisfied	16

Structure and Strategy

1. Identify examples of slogans that the British Columbia tourist industry has used to promote the province over the years.
2. What examples does the author use to illustrate the environmental devastation at the root of British Columbia's resource-based economy?
3. How would you describe the TONE of this essay?
4. Is "The Potemkin Province" an example of ARGUMENT or PERSUASION?

Content and Purpose

1. What is a "Potemkin village"? How did the term originate? Why does it apply to the province of British Columbia?
2. What were the early Europeans who came to British Columbia looking for? How did they regard the place?
3. The author objects to the B.C. slogan "The Best Place on Earth" for two different reasons. What are they? (See paragraphs 3–8 and 9–14.)

4. According to Francis, what has traditionally been the attitude of British Columbians to the natural bounty of their environment?
5. What does Francis think British Columbians and their government need to do? Do you agree or disagree? Why?
6. In paragraph 16, Francis writes, "B.C. is a beautiful place. Many places are. But the best place on earth? Not likely. No place is." What do you think he means?

Suggestions for Writing

1. Read Wade Davis's "The End of the Wild" on page 112. Compare this essay to "The Potemkin Province." What is similar about their subjects and their authors' approach to their subjects? What is different?
2. Research the state of wild salmon stock in British Columbia's mainland rivers. Is the salmon population in a precipitous decline or staging a comeback? What has been the impact of the salmon industry on the British Columbia economy? What are the implications for this resource? (You may want to read Russell Wangersky's "Clinging to The Rock" on page 42, where the depletion of cod stocks forms the background of his look at outport Newfoundland.)
3. British Columbia is not the only province that heavily exploits its natural resources. Choose another province and explain how it has exploited a natural resource.
4. Choose a province that you think does a good job of stewardship; that is, using its natural resources responsibly or sustainably. How and why does this province manage its resources this way?

What's Wrong with Africa

JON EVANS

Jon Evans is a writer, adventure traveller, and software engineer. He has written four crime thrillers, including *Invisible Armies* (2008), the Arthur Ellis Award-winning *Dark Places* (2005), and his most recent work, the graphic novel *The Executor* (2010). Evans spends much of his time backpacking in places like Zimbabwe, the Balkans, and Iraq; he writes articles about politics and technology in the developing world for *The Walrus, Maisonneuve, Wired,*

The Guardian, and *the Globe and Mail.* He blogs for *Wired UK, The Guardian,* and *Tor.com,* a science fiction and fantasy website. His epic quest novel *Beasts of New York* is available free online at beastsofnewyork.com.

"Give me money!" *"Donnes-moi d'argent!"* Go for a walk   1
through rural Kenya, or a town in Rwanda, or downtown
Lusaka, or almost anywhere south of the Sahara and north
of Botswana, and at some point children will rush up to you and
make that appeal. Not beggars, you understand, just kids hanging
out and playing—until they see someone rich.

It's easy, and wrong, to think of such children as Africa writ   2
small, to imagine the whole continent as desperate for handouts,
afflicted with the famous "culture of dependency." The prevailing
attitude is that white people screwed up the place, so white people
must pony up to fix it. That attitude exists among Westerners and
Africans alike, and aid agencies do nothing but strengthen the sentiment. But it's really just a symptom.

Africa's fundamental problem is the omnipresent notion that   3
good things do not come from striving, but only from providence°;
that the key to success and happiness is "seize opportunity when
it knocks," not "fight to make what you want happen." Ever hear
of attribution theory? It claims that happy people view personal
triumphs as the result of their inherent qualities, and setbacks
as flukes caused by external forces, while depressed people see
the reverse. Well, if there's such a thing as cultural attribution,
then Africa is afflicted by a strange and pathological version of it;
many of its inhabitants see *everything,* good or bad, as the result of
external chance.

Why? Because it's true. Across sub-Saharan Africa, fortune is   4
so fickle that effort is rarely rewarded. So many factors can and do
torpedo ambition: corruption, disease, drought, natural disaster,
tribal politics, power cuts, bad tourist PR, incompetent leaders, etc.
The same fatalism° that helps African citizens cope with the endless
slings and arrows hurled in their direction also leads inevitably,
and correctly, to a "striving doesn't work" mentality.

Is there hope? Of course there's hope—but it doesn't come   5
from the West. I'm with Paul Theroux, Graham Hancock, Dambisa
Moyo, Hernando de Soto and pretty much everybody I've ever
met in Africa who is not part of the aid industry: most development aid is actively harmful. Selling goods for less than production cost is dumping, a business practice condemned as predatory
because it undercuts nascent° producers who can't compete with
below-market prices. Aid is just dumping with the price set to zero.
Medical aid and disaster relief are necessary. There might even be

a few other aid projects actually worth the effort poured into them. But in general, I say kill it all.

6   The horror stories are legion. Donated clothes decimate local textile industries. Shells of buildings, silted dams, and unfinished "pilot projects" dot the African landscape. Food-aid convoys in Sudan tithed most of their cargo to the warring forces in exchange for safe passage, perpetuating the very conflict they were trying to alleviate. Young white people flock to expensive hotels in brand-new four-wheel-drives for useless "conferences" that amount to paid exotic vacations. Peace Corps yahoos° are trained and flown out at great cost to teach Western hairdressing or dig wells that people will never use.

7   And that's without going into the soft side effects of that horrifying "culture of dependency." In Zimbabwe, for example, before Mugabe went mad, a rural community deliberately allowed water to pool and destroy a dam, because then the Norwegians who built it would come back to fix it and spend more money. But aid's worst consequence is the continuation, and amplification, of the attitude that change must always come from outside. My friend Gavin Chait calls it "the recolonization of Africa through aid."

8   Still, it's Africa's governments, not its NGOs, that are primarily at fault for the continent's pervasive fatalism. The whole point of government is to create an environment where striving for success is a realistic option. Most African governments fail spectacularly: tribal, incompetent, inefficient, unbelievably bureaucratic, jawdrop-pingly corrupt, they are machines built to rob people rather than help them.

9   The influence of a meritocratic° middle class might restrain the kleptocrats°, and exemplify how striving leads to success—but only if they were also members of a majority ethnic group. (Asian or Lebanese minorities often run sub-Saharan Africa's most successful businesses.) So how do you get an African middle class? Education is important, but it isn't enough. An average kid with time, tools and a full belly will always outperform a genius kid who comes in hungry from fieldwork. No, to become middle-class, first you do what every smart African who can afford to does: you get the hell out of the place.

10   But not forever. Despite what the media tells you, Africa is not war-torn Darfur or Somalia. Most African nations are phenom-enally beautiful, oozing with untapped potential, places to go back to. In the meantime, the African diaspora°, connected via phone cards and the internet, send money back to their relatives, or divide their time between the First World and their homeland.

The second migration, just as important, is rural to urban. I   11
used to wonder why the gargantuan° shantytowns that surround
African cities—anarchic°, filthy, often violent—even existed. I'd far
rather live in a rural village. But those who move from the country
to the shantytowns are willing to risk that misery in exchange for
a shot at a new life and success. Most will fail. But they connect
the cities to the villages. Like the overseas diaspora, they too send
remittances°; they support friends and relatives who also come
and try their luck in the big city; and they're how ideas, money and
education flow from town to mud hut.

Of course, they have a little help from an amazing revolu-   12
tion that has swept across the so-called Dark Continent. Hop in
a *matatu*, walk down a road, stop in a remote village for a Coke,
and what do you see? Cell phones by the thousand: worn on lan-
yards° by individuals, or rented by the minute at roadside stalls.
"They walk for half a day just to reach a road, and then they pull
out a mobile," marvels a friend who lives in Africa. According
to the World Bank, one in five Africans has a cell phone; that's
roughly one per family. For the first time in the continent's history, people can talk (and text) to their faraway family and
friends.

The better the communication links, the tighter the bonds,   13
the more overseas Africans can and will send remittances, invest
capital, provide know-how and new tools, chip away at the colossal
inefficiencies that consume so much of Africa's vast potential and
pull their extended families up into a new middle class. The same
process can echo out from the shantytowns to the rural villages,
hoisting the next generation into position to make the same leap.
That's the great hope.

But wait: here's an even greater one. Most of the developing   14
world leapfrogged over copper-wire landlines straight to cell
phones. What if, similarly, they are about to jump from abaci°
straight to smartphones, hardly touching computers in between?
And what if that changes, well, everything?

This isn't just pie-in-the-sky Pollyannaism°. Yes, cell phones in   15
Africa are the economic equivalents of cars here, and today's smartphones are Ferraris. But in 2004, a new Motorola RAZR cost $650.
Today? $75. That's what today's Androids, BlackBerries and iPhones
will cost in 2014, by which time they'll have permeated even mud
huts and ramshackle shantytowns. And they'll all be bought with
cold hard cash—Africa's peerless mobile-phone industry is mostly
private, viciously competitive and quite profitable.

It's hard to overstate what a huge difference those smart-   16
phones are likely to make. Today, only 3 percent of Africans have

any internet access at all. Their smartphone revolution will be like our three information revolutions—computer, internet, mobile—happening *all at once.*

17   In 1978, China was poorer than all but a few corners of Africa are today. Then Deng Xiaoping introduced structural reforms, and thirty years on, the Middle Kingdom is a superpower. Putting the internet at the fingertips of hundreds of millions of Africans for the very first time will mark a transformation no less significant than Deng's reforms. It's easy to imagine this information revolution triggering growth comparable to that of China and India since the 1970s; growth that in only a few years could create far more wealth than all the lost decades and squandered billions of aid.

18   Will that happen? God knows. AIDS alone may end that hope entirely. (Its prevalence, despite massive public education, is another artifact of Africa's fatalism.) Corruption, tribalism or sheer brutal dictatorship might destroy it, as in Zimbabwe. But there is hope, and it's real and tangible. We might help provide the technology, but the ultimate solutions lie within Africa. We can do our part, by buying African, spending tourist dollars, and helping with disaster relief. But real hope, real change, doesn't come from outside, and never will.

Words and Meanings

Paragraph

3	providence	good fortune, good luck (often associated with divine intervention)
4	fatalism	attitude that "what will be will be," that one cannot change destiny
5	nascent	emerging, just coming into existence
6	yahoos	jerks
9	meritocratic	based on merit (rather than on ethnicity, family ties, or political alliance)
	kleptocrats	corrupt government officials; thieving bureaucrats
10	diaspora	people who have left their homeland, often for political reasons, to live abroad
11	gargantuan	enormous
	anarchic	lawless
	remittances	payments of money sent to those still living in the homeland

lanyards	cord worn round the neck for carrying a light object	12
abaci	plural of *abacus*, which is an ancient counting device consisting of beads strung on wires	14
Pollyannaism	foolish or blind optimism (after the heroine of *Pollyanna*, the 1913 novel by Eleanor Porter)	15

Structure and Strategy

1. Identify the comparison the author develops in paragraphs 1 and 2. Is it presented as the cause of problems in Africa?
2. What is the TOPIC SENTENCE of paragraph 3? Where else in the essay does the author continue to develop this topic?
3. What is the TONE of this essay? What is Evans' attitude toward Africa?
4. Can one legitimately generalize about an entire continent, as Evans' title suggests his essay does? Why or why not? Where in the essay does the author narrow his focus?

Content and Purpose

1. How does Evans define what he calls African "fatalism" in paragraphs 3 and 4?
2. Why does Evans propose ending aid to Africa, apart from "medical aid and disaster relief" (paragraph 5)? How does he support his argument?
3. Identify the two migrations that Evans argues are required if African nations are to prosper.
4. What does Evans see as the role of technology in Africa's future?
5. What countries are cited as examples of the kind of development that Africa could achieve?
6. Ultimately, is Evans optimistic or pessimistic about Africa's future? Where does he think meaningful change comes from?

Suggestions for Writing

1. Do some research on a person who has encouraged the world to give aid to Africa. (U2's Bono and Canada's Stephen Lewis come to mind.) Assess their work, and write an essay about the overall effectiveness of their efforts, either countering or supporting Evans' argument in "What's Wrong with Africa."
2. Write an essay about the issue of people from a poor country going to work in a wealthy country and sending money back to

their families. How does this kind of migration affect the family? Given that these migrants are often educated and ambitious, how does their exodus affect the society that is left behind?

The Harvest, the Kill

JANE RULE

Jane Rule (1931–2007) grew up in Plainfield, New Jersey. She moved to British Columbia in 1956 and began to write lesbian-themed fiction. Her books include *Desert of the Heart* (1964), later made into the movie *Desert Hearts* (1985); *This Is Not for You* (1970); *The Young in One Another's Arms* (1977); and *A Hot-Eyed Moderate* (1985). Rule received the Order of Canada in 2007 in a ceremony held, at her request, on Galiano Island, where she had lived for more than thirty years.

1   I live among vegetarians of various persuasions and moral meat eaters; therefore when I have guests for dinner I pay rather more attention to the nature of food than I would, left to my own imagination.

2   The vegetarians who don't eat meat because they believe it to be polluted with cancer-causing hormones or because they identify their sensitive digestive tracts with herbivore° ancestors are just cautious folk similar to those who cross the street only at the corner with perhaps a hint of the superstition found in those who don't walk under ladders. They are simply taking special care of their lives without further moral deliberation°.

3   Those who don't eat meat because they don't approve of killing aren't as easy for me to understand. Yesterday, as I pried live scallops from their beautiful, fragile shells and saw them still pulsing in the bowl, ready to cook for friends for whom food from the sea is acceptable, it felt to me no less absolute an act of killing than chopping off the head of a chicken. But I also know in the vegetable garden that I rip carrots untimely° from their row. The fact that they don't twitch or run around without their heads doesn't make them less alive. Like me, they have grown from seed and have their own natural life span which I have interrupted. It is hard for me to be hierarchical° about the aliveness of living things.

There are two vegetarian arguments that bear some guilty   4
weight for me. The first is the number of acres it takes to feed
beef cattle as compared to the number of acres it takes to feed
vegetation. If there ever were a large plan to change our basic
agriculture in order to feed everyone more equably°, I would support it and give up eating beef, but until then my not eating beef
is of no more help than my eating my childhood dinner was to the
starving Armenians. The second is mistreatment of animals raised
for slaughter. To eat what has not been a free-ranging animal is to
condone° the abuse of animals. Again, given the opportunity to support laws for more humane treatment of the creatures we eventually
eat, I would do so, but I probably wouldn't go so far as to approve
of chickens so happy in life that they were tough for my table.

The moral meat eaters are those who believe that we shouldn't   5
eat what we haven't killed ourselves, either gone to the trouble of
stalking it down or raising it, so that we have proper respect for the
creatures sacrificed for our benefit.

I am more at home with that view because my childhood sum-   6
mers were rural. By the time I was seven or eight, I had done my
share of fishing and hunting, and I'd been taught also to clean my
catch or kill. I never shot anything larger than a pigeon or rabbit.
That I was allowed to use a gun at all was the result of a remarkably indulgent° father. He never took me deer hunting, not because
I was a girl but because he couldn't bear to shoot them himself. But
we ate venison° brought to us by other men in the family.

I don't remember much being made of the sacredness of the   7
life we took, but there was a real emphasis on fair play, much of it
codified° in law, like shooting game birds only on the wing, like not
hunting deer with flashlights at night, like not shooting does°. But
my kinfolk frowned on bait fishing as well. They were sportsmen
who retained the wilderness ethic of not killing more than they
could use. Strictly speaking, we did not need the food. (We could
get meat in a town ten miles down the road.) But we did eat it.

Over the years, I became citified. I still could and did put live   8
lobsters and crab in boiling water, but meat came from the meat
market. Now that I live in the country again, I am much more
aware of the slaughter that goes on around me, for I not only eat
venison from the local hunt but have known the lamb and kid on
the hoof (even in my rhododendrons°, which is good for neither
them nor the rhododendrons) which I eat. The killers of the animals
are my moral, meat-eating neighbors. I have never killed a large
animal, and I hope I never have to, though I'm not particularly ten-
derhearted about creatures not human. I find it hard to confront the
struggle, smell, and mess of slaughter. I simply haven't the stomach
for it. But, if I had to do it or go without meat, I would learn how.

9   It's puzzling to me that cannibalism is a fascinating abomination to vegetarian and meat eater alike, a habit claimed by only the most vicious and primitive tribes. We are scandalized by stories of the Donner Party or rumors of cannibalism at the site of a small plane crash in the wilderness, a boat lost at sea. Yet why would it be so horrifying for survivors to feed on the flesh of those who have died? Have worms and buzzards more right to the carcass?

10   We apparently do not think of ourselves as part of the food chain, except by cruel and exceptional accident. Our flesh, like the cow in India, is sacred and taboo°, thought of as violated° even when it is consigned° to a mass grave. We bury it to hide a truth that still must be obvious to us, that as we eat so are we eaten. Why the lowly maggot is given the privilege (or sometimes the fish or the vulture) denied other living creatures is a complex puzzle of hygiene, myth and morality in each culture.

11   Our denial that we are part of nature, our sense of superiority to it, is our basic trouble. Though we are not, as the producers of margarine would make us believe, what we eat, we are related to what we harvest and kill. If being a vegetarian or a moral meat eater is a habit to remind us of that responsibility, neither is to be disrespected. When habit becomes a taboo, it blinds us to the real meaning. We are also related to each other, but our general refusal to eat our own flesh has not stopped us from slaughtering each other in large and totally wasted numbers.

12   I am flesh, a flesh eater, whether the food is carrot or cow. Harvesting and killing are the same activity, the interrupting of one life cycle for the sake of another. We don't stop at eating either. We kill to keep warm. We kill for shelter.

13   Back there in my rural childhood, I had not only a fishing rod and rifle, I had a hatchet, too. I cleared brush, cut down small trees, chopped wood. I was present at the felling of a two-thousand-year-old redwood tree, whose impact shook the earth I stood on. It was a death more simply shocking to me than any other I've ever witnessed. The house I lived in then was made of redwood. The house I live in now is cedar.

14   My ashes may nourish the roots of a living tree, pitifully small compensation for the nearly immeasurable acres I have laid waste for my needs and pleasures, even for my work. For such omnivorous° creatures as we are, a few frugal° habits are not enough. We have to feed and midwife° more than we slaughter, replant more than we harvest, if not with our hands, then with our own talents to see that it is done in our name, that we own to it.

The scallop shells will be finely cleaned by raccoons, then made   15
by a neighbor into wind chimes, which may trouble my sleep and
probably should until it is time for my own bones to sing.

Words and Meanings

herbivore	creature that eats only plants	2
deliberation	thought, consideration	
untimely	before they are fully grown	3
hierarchical	organized in order of rank or importance	
equably	evenly, fairly	4
condone	forgive, excuse	
indulgent	the opposite of strict	6
venison	deer meat	
codified	written down as rules or laws	7
does	female deer	
rhododendrons	large, flowering bushes common in B.C. gardens	8
taboo	forbidden	10
violated	abused, dishonoured	
consigned	delivered, handed over to	
omnivorous	creatures that eat both animals and plants	14
frugal	saving, conserving	
midwife	assist in the birth of animals	

Structure and Strategy

1. In paragraph 1, Rule divides her neighbours into two categories: vegetarians and moral meat eaters. What is the function of paragraphs 2 through 4 and 5 through 7? What relation do they have to the opening paragraph?
2. In which paragraph does Rule explicitly state the opinion that forms the basis for her ARGUMENT? Why do you think she introduces this statement so late in the essay?
3. Explain what makes the concluding sentence of this essay effective and memorable. What powerful images come together to reinforce Rule's point about the interdependency of all forms of life?

Content and Purpose

1. What two classes of vegetarians does Rule identify?
2. What are the "two vegetarian arguments" presented in paragraph 4? Do they appeal to the intellect or to the emotions? Do you find either of these arguments persuasive? Why is Rule not a vegetarian herself?
3. What is a "moral meat eater"? Does Rule herself fit into this category?
4. What childhood experiences contributed to Rule's adult views about the morality of "harvesting and killing"?
5. According to Rule, why is there such a strong taboo on cannibalism? (See paragraphs 9 through 11.)
6. According to Rule, what do humans deny about themselves that leads to an absence of responsibility for the natural world? How does she relate this denial to burial rituals?
7. Paragraphs 12 through 14 illustrate how we exploit nature, consuming far more than we return. What, according to Rule, do we need to acknowledge before we can correct this imbalance?

Suggestions for Writing

1. Write an essay persuading the reader to adopt (or give up) a vegetarian lifestyle. Appeal to your reader's intellect and emotions in your attempt to convince the reader to give up (or eat) meat.
2. Do you agree or disagree with the contention that wearing fur or leather clothing is a violation of animal rights? Write an essay in which you convince your reader of the reasonableness of your opinion.

Immigration: The Hate Stops Here

MICHAEL IGNATIEFF

Michael Ignatieff (b. 1947) is leader of the Liberal Party of Canada. Before entering politics in 2005, he served as director of the Carr Center for Human Rights at Harvard University and taught at leading universities around the globe. Born and raised in Toronto, the son of a Russian émigré diplomat and a Canadian mother, Ignatieff is considered an expert on democracy, human rights, and international affairs. He is a versatile writer, having written plays, movies, and award-winning works of fiction and non-

"Immigration: The Hate Stops Here" by Michael Ignatieff, *Globe and Mail*, October 25, 2001. Reprinted by permission of the author.

fiction. Among his recent works are *The Lesser Evil: Political Ethics in an Age of Terror* (2004) and *True Patriot Love* (2009).

anadians tell the story of immigration to our country in 1
terms of two myths: that we are a welcoming people, and
that we are welcoming because those we welcome are only
too happy to leave their hatreds behind. When the two myths are
put together, they allow us to imagine Canada as a haven, a place
where people abandon their own hatreds and escape the hatreds
that drove them from their homes. This double myth is both self-
congratulatory and self-deprecating. A safe haven is not necessarily
a very exciting place—but better to be dull than dangerous. Most
newcomers have lived our dullness as deliverance.

But now we must ask two other questions. Were we ever as 2
welcoming as the myth made us out to be? And now, in a world
transfigured by terror, are we sure that newcomers are leaving their
hatreds behind?

A multicultural Canada is a great idea in principle, but in 3
reality it is more like a tacit contract of mutual indifference.
Communities share political and geographical space, but not necessarily religious, social or moral space. We have little Hong Kongs,
little Kabuls, little Jaffnas, just as we once had little Berdichevs,
little Pescaras, little Lisbons. But what must we know about each
other in order to be citizens together?

In 1999, a moderate Tamil intellectual I greatly admired was 4
blown to pieces by a car bomb in Colombo by an extremist Tamil
group. His offence: seeking a peaceful solution to the Sri Lankan
catastrophe through negotiations with the Sinhalese government.
After I went to Colombo to denounce the act of terror that had
claimed his life, I began receiving Tamil magazines arguing that
anyone from the Tamil community who sought non-violent solutions to political problems was a stooge or a fool.

The French call this strategy *la politique du pire*°: endorsing 5
strategies to make things worse so that they cannot possibly get
better. I came away from these Tamil magazines feeling that I could
say nothing to the persons who had written them. The punch line
of my story is that the postmarks were Canadian; they had been
printed and published on my native soil.

The point of the story is not to turn on the Tamil community; 6
most members despise the sort of rhetoric that I, too, despise. The
point is that we need to rethink larger Canadian myths about the
passage to Canada as a passage from hatred to civility. Is it true
now? Was it ever true?

In the 1840s, the Irish brought their hatreds with them on 7
the emigrant ships. Emigrants from the Balkans did not forget or

forgive the oppression that caused them to flee. After the Second World War, emigrants from territories under Soviet tyranny came to this country with all their hatreds still alive. It is an innocent, liberal assumption to suppose that hatred is always bad. It's a necessity to hate oppression. I think, for example, of the Baltic Canadians who, whenever the Soviet Bolshoi Ballet toured Canada, held up signs outside the theatre protesting Soviet tyranny. These people now seem more morally aware than those, and they included me, who thought it was time to acquiesce in the facts of life, i.e., the permanent Soviet occupation of Eastern Europe.

8   It is not always right for exile and emigration to be accompanied by political forgetting. Remembering a conquered or oppressed home is one of the duties of emigrants. The problem is that exile can freeze conviction at the moment of departure. Once in exile, groups fail to evolve; they return, once their countries are free, speaking and behaving as if it were still 1945. A case in point: Croatian exiles, who escaped to Canada in the 1940s to flee Josip Broz Tito's° imposition of Communist rule over Yugoslavia, remained more nationalistic than they would have in Tito's postwar Croatia. In exile, few could bear to learn that the country they had lost was also guilty of atrocities against Jews, Serbs, Roma and other minorities. Facing up to the reality of Ante Pavelic's° wartime regime was hard enough in Zagreb; it was harder in Toronto. Indeed, it was often said in Zagreb that the chief support for the most intransigent and aggressive Croatian nationalism after independence was to be found, not in Zagreb, but in Toronto.

9   Dual allegiances are complex: A newly-minted Canadian citizen who would not dream of assassinating a fellow citizen from some oppressor group does not hesitate to fund assassinations in the old country. Sometimes emigration is accompanied by the guilt of departure. This guilt makes diaspora groups° more violent and more extreme than those that live in the country where the oppression is taking place. Diaspora nationalism is a dangerous phenomenon because it is easier to hate from a distance: You don't have to live with the consequences—or the reprisals.

10   Canadians, new and old, need to think about what role their diasporas play in fanning and financing the hatreds of the outside world. The disturbing possibility is that Canada is not an asylum from hatred but an incubator of hatred. Are we so sure that acts of terror in Kashmir do not originate in apparently innocent funding of charitable and philanthropic appeals in Canadian cities? Are we certain that the financing of a car bomb in Jerusalem did not begin in a Canadian community? Do we know that when people die in Colombo, or Jaffna, there's no Canadian connection?

I don't have answers to these questions and it would be inflam- 11
matory to make allegations without evidence. My point is only
to ask us to rethink our myths of immigration, particularly that
innocent one that portrays us as a refuge from hatred. It is clear that
this was never entirely true: Many immigrant groups that make
their lives here have not been extinguishing, but rather fanning, the
hatreds they brought with them.

It would be a good idea to get the rules for a multicultural 12
Canada clear to all. Canada means many things—and in the debate
about what it means, new voices are as valuable as older ones—but
one meaning is indisputable. We are a political community that has
outlawed the practice and advocacy of violence as an instrument of
political expression. We have outlawed it within, and we need to
outlaw it without. Just as we have laws against racial incitement or
the promulgation of ethnic hatred in order to protect our new citizens
from bigotry, abuse and violence, so we must have laws for the prose-
cution of anyone in Canada who aids, abets, encourages or incites acts
of terror. There may be political causes that justify armed resistance,
but there are none that justify terrorizing and murdering civilians.

The distinction between freedom fighters and terrorists is not 13
the relativist° quagmire°. There are laws of war governing armed
resistance to oppression, as there are laws of war governing the
conduct of hostilities between states. Those who break these laws
are barbarians, whatever cause they serve. Those who target civilians to cause death and create fear are terrorists, no matter how just
their armed struggle may be. States that use terror against civilians
are as culpable as armed insurgents.

Coming to Canada is not the passage from hatred to civility 14
that we have supposed. And frankly, some hatred—of oppression, cruelty, and racial discrimination—is wanted on the voyage.
But Canada must keep to one simple rule of the road: We are not a
political community that aids, abets, harbours or cultivates terror.

So it is appropriate to say to newcomers: You do not have to 15
embrace all our supposed civilities. You can and should keep the
memory of the injustice you have left firmly in your heart. But the
law is the law. You will have to leave your murderous fantasies of
revenge behind.

Words and Meanings

		Paragraph
la politique du pire	literally, "the worst kind of politics"	5
Josip Broz Tito	Communist dictator of Yugoslavia, 1945 to 1980	8

8	Ante Pavelic	the Croatian "Butcher of the Balkans," responsible for the deaths of some one million Serbs, Jews, and Roma during and after World War II
9	diaspora groups	ethnic or religious communities who have left—or been exiled from—their homeland and have established settlements elsewhere
13	relativist	relativism is a theory that considers values (e.g., truth, morality) as "relative" rather than absolute; i.e., there is no black or white—right or wrong—only shades of grey.
	quagmire	swampy ground where one cannot find sure footing; a metaphor for the relativists' view of values being conditional rather than absolute. In a quagmire, one is neither in water nor on solid ground

Structure and Strategy

1. With what introductory strategy does Ignatieff begin this essay? Read the first paragraph aloud. Identify some of the stylistic features that capture attention and make it memorable.
2. What are the functions of paragraphs 2 and 6? How do they move the ARGUMENT forward?
3. What is the TOPIC SENTENCE of paragraph 7? What kind of development is used to support it?
4. What AUDIENCE did Ignatieff have in mind for this essay? How do you know?
5. How would you describe Ignatieff's TONE?
6. With what concluding strategy does Ignatieff end his essay? Is his CONCLUSION effective? Why?
7. Is this essay primarily an argument or a persuasive piece?

Content and Purpose

1. What are the two "myths" that Canadians believe about immigration to this country? Why does Ignatieff think that they are more myth than reality?
2. It's often said that immigrants to the United States enter a "melting pot," whereas immigrants to Canada become part of a "mosaic." How would you explain the difference? In which paragraphs does Ignatieff allude to this supposed Canadian model?
3. What is the IRONY that underlies the personal ANECDOTE Ignatieff recounts about the tragic death of a moderate Tamil intellectual?

4. Do you think that Ignatieff believes that, once they arrive here, immigrants from strife-torn nations should somehow forget the politics that may have driven them to Canada?
5. What is "diaspora nationalism" (paragraph 9), and what does Ignatieff think of it?
6. Ignatieff's proposals for dealing with ethnic hatred in a multicultural Canada are presented in paragraph 12. Summarize them in your own words.
7. What does Ignatieff see as the difference between freedom fighters and terrorists? Do you agree or disagree?

Suggestions for Writing

1. Do you agree or disagree with Ignatieff's argument that the "rules for a multicultural Canada" must be made clear to all (paragraph 9)? Write an essay explaining your opinion.
2. Read Denise Chong's "Being Canadian" (page 304). Compare Chong's view of what immigrants should maintain—or leave behind—from their original culture with Ignatieff's view.
3. Honour killings are a cultural transplant that horrify most Canadians. Write an essay about the origins of honour killings and ways to eliminate them.

ADDITIONAL SUGGESTIONS FOR WRITING: ARGUMENT AND PERSUASION

Choose one of the topics below and write an essay based on it. Think through your position carefully, formulate your opinion, and identify logical reasons for holding that opinion. Construct a clear thesis statement before you begin to write the paper.

1. Violence against an established government is (or is not) justified in certain circumstances.
2. Racial profiling is (or is not) necessary for the police to protect society against criminals.
3. Locally grown food is (or is not) a way to improve our diet and the planet.
4. Print newspapers and magazines are (or are not) doomed as the online world expands.
5. The government of Canada should (or should not) decriminalize the use of marijuana.
6. Males and females should (or should not) play on the same sports teams.
7. Parents should (or should not) be legally responsible for property damage (e.g., vandalism, theft) caused by their underage children.

8. Children should (or should not) be responsible for the care of their elderly parents.
9. Critically ill patients should (or should not) be permitted to end their lives if and when they choose.
10. A teacher should (or should not) aim most of the course work at the weakest students in the class.
11. Online pornography is (or is not) harmful.
12. The Canadian Armed Forces should (or should not) be assigned to combat in addition to peacekeeping missions.
13. Racism in Canada is (is not) increasing.
14. Grades in college/university courses should (or should not) reflect a student's effort as well as achievement.
15. Argue for or against the following statement: "One thing is certain: offering employment—the steady kind, with benefits, holiday pay, a measure of security, and maybe even union representation—has fallen out of economic fashion" (Naomi Klein).

UNIT 9

Fiction

INTRODUCTION

Once upon a time. . . .

The short stories in Unit 9 are our gift to you. We have not included fiction in the previous editions of *Canadian Content* because first-level Canadian college and university writing courses tend to focus on non-fiction writing. Most introductory courses emphasize exposition and argument: writing that relies on verifiable facts to explain something in a clear and persuasive way.

Fiction—a story based in the writer's imagination—belongs to another world, but a fascinating and engaging one that complements the fact-based world of exposition and argumentation. The phrase *"Once upon a time"* has a hypnotic power over children, who naturally love stories. Adults can be similarly captured by a good work of fiction. We look to fiction to entertain and amuse us, to be sure. But wonderful stories also offer us the unique opportunity to get into the minds, hearts, and experiences of other people—opportunities we would otherwise never have shared. Fiction's ability to create empathy—to enable us to see the world through someone else's eyes—is a powerful capacity that enlarges our experience and enhances our common humanity.

The stories collected here are fine ones. They deal with elemental concerns: love, marriage, friendship, home, family, loss. All are Canadian, mostly by younger writers who reflect the remarkable diversity of our country. They live and write here but their origins are as varied as their stories.

We have arranged the stories from west to east, according to the geographical regions they represent. Ivan E. Coyote's "She Comes Home a Moth" is set in Whitehorse; Madeleine Thien's "Simple Recipes" takes place in Vancouver; and Alissa York's "The Back of the Bear's Mouth" is set in the Yukon bush. Moving east,

Amber Hayward's "Shelterbelt" is a story from the Prairies; David Bezmozgis's "Tapka" is set in immigrant-rich Toronto; and Roger Burford-Mason's "Treading Water" takes place in Northern Ontario. Tilya Gallay Helfield's "Stars" is a story from and about Montreal; Jennifer Stone's "Prerequisites for Sleep" comes from the Maritimes; and the collection concludes with a rattling ghost story from Cape Breton, Alistair MacLeod's "As the Birds Bring Forth the Sun."

Read and enjoy!

She Comes Home a Moth

IVAN E. COYOTE

Ivan E. Coyote is a writer and performer. She is the author of five books: four story collections, *Close to Spider Man, One Man's Trash, Loose End,* and *The Slow Fix,* as well as a novel, *Bow Grip.* She is a long-time columnist for *Xtra!* in Toronto and *Xtra! West* in Vancouver. Coyote is also an audience favourite at music, poetry, spoken word, and writers' festivals from Anchorage to Amsterdam. Originally from the Yukon, Ivan lives in Vancouver.

Everyone on our street had kids. It was that kind of street: Hemlock Street, a dusty little L-shaped road with a fence at one end. I wouldn't call the place where our street stopped a dead end, though, because that's where it all started: the old dump road, the power line, the veins in a leaf-like network of trails that led to our places. The places we built forts, tobogganed in green garbage bags, and learned how to ride after our dads took the blocks off our pedals.

My mom tells the story of how she met your mom, awake in the night, pacing in front of the living room window, a small, crying bundle in her arms. That bundle was me. There was only one other light on the block, in the house right across the street. Inside the light stood a woman, holding a baby. She shrugged, a you-too, huh? kind of movement with her shoulders, and waved at my mother.

They didn't get a chance to meet for a couple more days—your mom worked in the evenings and mine in the day—but they would be together late at night, in their windows, with the road and the dark between them, in separate circles of light.

One Friday night your mom knocked on our door. "Could you take her?" She meant you. "Pierre and I, we need to go away for a couple of hours. Can you watch my baby? Her name is Valerie."

So I only remember a time when there was you. You can remember details, whole conversations and dates; I cannot. I remember colours, our hands stained with cranberries. You had long brown hair. We both had a pair of red pants.

We were always together. Your dad called us cheese and crackers. We never kissed.

I liked how you hardly said anything when there were adults around, but how when we were alone your soft voice spilled out plans: now how 'bout we play this? We usually fundamentally disagreed on what we were or should be playing, but never considered other partners.

I remember when your grandmother came to visit from France; her voice was bigger than she was, and your father was the interpreter. She shook her head and laughed at my mother. "How come everyday you send this one out looking like a butterfly, and she comes home a moth?"

You always kept your knees clean.

My mom let us use her bike one day. We were going to the store, and her bike had a basket in front. It was way too big for me, but I pedalled with much concentration, my tongue pressed between my lips. You sat on the seat, legs dangling, your summer-brown thumbs in my belt loops.

We had to go down the big hill next to the meadow where boys smoked cigarettes sometimes, and your grip on my waist tightened. "You're driving too *faaaast*. Slow *dooown*." Your voice was bumpy from the gravel and potholes on the road.

Unfamiliar with the physics of a three-speed, I slammed on what turned out to be the front brakes, and that's when the tragedy happened. The road rash would heal, the hole in the knee of my cords could be mended, but your hair? Now we were in trouble. One of your braids had gotten caught in the spokes of the front wheel as we went over the handlebars, and been chopped off. We immediately aborted the mission and went straight back to your place.

We called out as soon as we came through the front door, our faces grim and tear-streaked. Your father came flying naked out of the shower, and did the preliminary medical inspections with no clothes on at all. Only when he realized there were no broken bones or stitches needed did he disappear back into the bathroom, returning with bandaids and iodine, a damp towel around his waist.

He shook his head sadly at your lopsided braid: "Just wait till your Maman gets home." Hair was a female domain; it was she that we would have to answer to for this, and we knew it. "How did you let this happen?" He was looking at me when he asked.

I slunk home, and told the story to my mother. The only thing more horrifying to me than what had happened to your hair was the sight of my very first naked man, hairy and dark and smelling of aftershave.

My mom had a logical explanation for this.

"Well, you know how the Salezes are different from us? Like how Grace lets you guys colour on the walls in Val's room, but I would kill you both if you did that here? Well, that's why Pierre had no clothes on. They're French."

This made perfect sense to me at the time.

I don't remember the day you left, I just remember you being gone. I think it was the first time I ever missed someone. Everyone else I loved never went anywhere. And France was such a far away place, farther even than Vancouver, too far away to phone, too far away to hope you would ever come back.

Twenty years later I saw your name on an ad. You had a video camera and were looking for gigs. It couldn't be you, but I called anyway.

"Is your name Valerie Salez?"

"Did you used to live in the Yukon?"

"Was your father French? Did your mother talk a lot?"

We were only blocks away. I went to your place that same night. We said the same thing to each other at exactly the same time right before you hugged me.

"You haven't changed a bit."

Simple Recipes

MADELEINE THIEN

Madeleine Thien was born in Vancouver in 1974, the only Canadian-born child of Malaysian–Chinese immigrant parents. She studied at Simon Fraser University and the University of British Columbia. Her short story collection *Simple Recipes* (2001) won numerous awards. Her second book, *The Chinese Violin* (2002), is a children's story about a young girl who emigrated from China with her father. Thien published her first novel, *Certainty*, in 2006.

There is a simple recipe for making rice. My father taught it to me when I was a child. Back then, I used to sit up on the kitchen counter watching him, how he sifted the grains in his hands, sure and quick, removing pieces of dirt or sand, tiny imperfections. He swirled his hands through the water and it turned cloudy. When he scrubbed the grains clean, the sound was as big as a field of insects. Over and over, my father rinsed the rice, drained the water, then filled the pot again.

The instructions are simple. Once the washing is done, you measure the water this way—by resting the tip of your index finger on the surface of the rice. The water should reach the bend of your first knuckle. My father did not need instructions or measuring cups. He closed his eyes and felt for the waterline.

Sometimes I still dream my father, his bare feet flat against the floor, standing in the middle of the kitchen. He wears old buttoned shirts and faded sweatpants drawn at the waist. Surrounded by the gloss of the kitchen counters, the sharp angles of the stove, the fridge, the shiny sink, he looks out of place. This memory of him is so strong, sometimes it stuns me, the detail with which I can see it.

Every night before dinner, my father would perform this ritual—rinsing and draining, then setting the pot in the cooker. When I was older, he passed this task on to me but I never did it with the same care. I went through the motions, splashing the water around, jabbing my finger down to measure the water level. Some nights the rice was a mushy gruel. I worried that I could not do so simple a task right. "Sorry," I would say to the table, my voice soft and embarrassed. In answer, my father would keep eating, pushing the rice into his mouth as if he never expected anything different, as if he noticed no difference between what he did so well and I so poorly. He would eat every last mouthful, his chopsticks walking quickly across the plate. Then he would rise, whistling, and clear the table, every motion so clean and sure, I would be convinced by him that all was well in the world.

My father is standing in the middle of the kitchen. In his right hand he holds a plastic bag filled with water. Caught inside the bag is a live fish.

The fish is barely breathing, though its mouth opens and closes. I reach up and touch it through the plastic bag, trailing my fingers along the gills, the soft, muscled body, pushing my finger overtop the eyeball. The fish looks straight at me, flopping sluggishly from side to side.

My father fills the kitchen sink. In one swift motion he overturns the bag and the fish comes sailing out with the water. It curls and jumps. We watch it closely, me on my tiptoes, chin propped up on the counter. The fish is the length of my arm from wrist to elbow. It floats in place, brushing up against the sides of the sink.

I keep watch over the fish while my father begins the preparations for dinner. The fish folds its body, trying to turn or swim, the water nudging overtop. Though I ripple tiny circles around it with my fingers, the fish stays still, bobbing side-to-side in the cold water.

For many hours at a time, it was just the two of us. While my mother worked and my older brother played outside, my father and I sat on the couch, flipping channels. He loved cooking shows. We watched *Wok with Yan*, my father passing judgement on Yan's methods. I was enthralled when Yan transformed orange peels into swans. My father sniffed. "I can do that," he said. "You don't have to be a genius to do that." He placed a sprig of green onion in water and showed me how it bloomed like a flower. "I know many tricks like this," he said. "Much more than Yan."

Still, my father made careful notes when Yan demonstrated Peking Duck. He chuckled heartily at Yan's punning. "Take a wok on the wild side!" Yan said, pointing his spatula at the camera.

"Ha ha!" my father laughed, his shoulders shaking. "*Wok* on the wild side!"

In the mornings, my father took me to school. At three o'clock, when we came home again, I would rattle off everything I learned that day. "The brachiosaurus," I informed him, "eats only soft vegetables."

My father nodded. "That is like me. Let me see your forehead." We stopped and faced each other in the road. "You have a high forehead," he said, leaning down to take a closer look. "All smart people do."

I walked proudly, stretching my legs to match his steps. I was overjoyed when my feet kept time with his, right, then left, then right, and we walked like a single unit. My father was the man of tricks, who sat for an hour mining a watermelon with a circular spoon, who carved the rind into a castle.

My father was born in Malaysia and he and my mother immigrated to Canada several years before I was born, first settling in Montreal, then finally in Vancouver. While I was born into the persistence of the Vancouver rain, my father was born in the wash of a monsoon country. When I was young, my parents tried to teach me their language but it never came easily to me. My father ran his thumb gently over my mouth, his face kind, as if trying to see what it was that made me different.

My brother was born in Malaysia but when he immigrated with my parents to Canada the language left him. Or he forgot it, or he refused it, which is also common, and this made my father angry. "How can a child forget a language?" he would ask my mother. "It is because the child is lazy. Because the child chooses not to remember." When he was twelve years old, my brother stayed away in the afternoons. He drummed the soccer ball up and down the back alley, returning home only at dinner time. During the day, my mother worked as a sales clerk at the Woodward's store downtown, in the building with the red revolving W on top.

In our house, the ceilings were yellowed with grease. Even the air was heavy with it. I remember that I loved the weight of it, the air that was dense with the smell of countless meals cooked in a tiny kitchen, all those good smells jostling for space.

The fish in the sink is dying slowly. It has a glossy sheen to it, as if its skin is made of shining minerals. I want to prod it with both hands, its body tense against the pressure of my fingers. If I hold it tightly, I imagine I will be able to feel its fluttering heart. Instead, I lock eyes with the fish. *You're feeling verrrry sleepy*, I tell it. *You're getting verrrry tired.*

Beside me, my father chops green onions quickly. He uses a cleaver that he says is older than I am by many years. The blade of the knife rolls forward and backward, loops of green onion gathering in a pyramid beside my father's wrist. When he is done, he rolls his sleeve back from his right hand, reaches in through the water and pulls the plug.

The fish in the sink floats and we watch it in silence. The water level falls beneath its gills, beneath its belly. It drains and leaves the sink dry. The fish is lying on its side, mouth open and its body heaving. It leaps sideways and hits the sink. Then up again. It curls and snaps, lunging for its own tail. The fish sails into the air, dropping hard. It twitches violently.

My father reaches in with his bare hands. He lifts the fish out by the tail and lays it gently on the counter. While holding it steady with one hand, he hits the head with the flat of the cleaver. The fish falls still, and he begins to clean it.

In my apartment, I keep the walls scrubbed clean. I open the windows and turn the fan on whenever I prepare a meal. My father bought me a rice cooker when I first moved into my own apartment, but I use it so rarely it stays in the back of the cupboard, the cord wrapped neatly around its belly. I have no longing for the meals themselves, but I miss the way we sat down together, our bodies leaning hungrily forward while my father, the magician, unveiled plate after plate. We laughed and ate, white steam fogging my mother's glasses until she had to take them off and lay them on the table. Eyes closed, she would eat, crunchy vegetables gripped in her chopsticks, the most vivid green.

My brother comes into the kitchen and his body is covered with dirt. He leaves a thin trail of it behind as he walks. The soccer ball, muddy from outside, is encircled in one arm. Brushing past my father, his face is tense.

Beside me, my mother sprinkles garlic onto the fish. She lets me slide one hand underneath the fish's head, cradling it, then bending it backwards so that she can fill the fish's insides with ginger. Very carefully, I turn the fish over. It is firm and slippery, and beaded with tiny, sharp scales.

At the stove, my father picks up an old teapot. It is full of oil and he pours the oil into the wok. It falls in a thin ribbon. After a moment, when the oil begins crackling, he lifts the fish up and drops it down into the wok. He adds water and the smoke billows up. The sound of the fish frying is like tires on gravel, a sound so loud it drowns out all other noises. Then my father steps out from the smoke. "Spoon out the rice," he says as he lifts me down from the counter.

My brother comes back into the room, his hands muddy and his knees the colour of dusty brick. His soccer shorts flutter against the backs of his legs. Sitting down, he makes an angry face. My father ignores him.

Inside the cooker, the rice is flat like a pie. I push the spoon in, turning the rice over, and the steam shoots up in a hot mist and condenses on my skin. While my father moves his arms delicately over the stove, I begin dishing the rice out: first for my father, then my mother, then my brother, then myself. Behind me the fish is cooking quickly. In a crockery pot, my father steams cauliflower, stirring it round and round.

My brother kicks at a table leg.

"What's the matter?" my father asks.

He is quiet for a moment, then he says, "Why do we have to eat fish?"

"You don't like it?"

My brother crosses his arms across his chest. I see the dirt lining his arms, dark and hardened. I imagine chipping it off his body with a small spoon.

"I don't like the eyeball there. It looks sick."

My mother tuts. Her nametag is still clipped to her blouse. It says *Woodward's*, and then, *Sales Clerk*. "Enough," she says, hanging her purse on the back of the chair. "Go wash your hands and get ready for supper."

My brother glares, just for a moment. Then he begins picking at the dirt on his arms. I bring plates of rice to the table. The dirt flies off his skin, speckling the tablecloth. "Stop it," I say crossly.

"*Stop it,*" he says, mimicking me.

"Hey!" My father hit his spoon against the counter. It *pings*, high-pitched. He points at my brother. "No fighting in this house."

My brother looks at the floor, mumbles something, and then shuffles away from the table. As he moves farther away, he begins to stamp his feet.

Shaking her head, my mother takes her jacket off. It slides from her shoulders. She says something to my father in the language I can't understand. He merely shrugs his shoulders. And then he replies, and I think his words are familiar, as if they are words I should know, as if maybe I did know them once but then I forgot them. The language that they speak is full of soft vowels, words running together so that I can't make out the gaps where they pause for breath.

My mother told me once about guilt. Her own guilt she held in the palm of her hands, like an offering. But your guilt is different, she said. You do not need to hold on to it. Imagine this, she said, her hands running along my forehead, then up into my hair. Imagine, she said. Picture it, and what do you see?

A bruise on the skin, wide and black.

A bruise, she said. Concentrate on it. Right now, it's a bruise. But if you concentrate, you can shrink it, compress it to the size of a pinpoint. And then, if you want to, if you see it, you can blow it off your body like a speck of dirt.

She moved her hands along my forehead.

I tried to picture what she said. I pictured blowing it away like so much nothing, just these little pieces that didn't mean anything, this complicity that I could magically walk away from. She made me believe in the strength of my own thoughts, as if I could make appear what had never existed. Or turn it around. Flip it over so many times you just lose sight of it, you lose the tail end and the whole thing disappears into smoke.

My father pushes at the fish with the edge of his spoon. Underneath, the meat is white and the juice runs down along the side. He lifts a piece and lowers it carefully onto my plate.

Once more, his spoon breaks skin. Gingerly, my father lifts another piece and moves it towards my brother.

"I don't want it," my brother says.

My father's hand wavers. "Try it," he says, smiling. "Take a wok on the wild side."

"No."

My father sighs and places the piece on my mother's plate. We eat in silence, scraping our spoons across the dishes. My parents use chopsticks, lifting their bowls and motioning the food into their mouths. The smell of food fills the room.

Savouring each mouthful, my father eats slowly, head tuned to the flavours in his mouth. My mother takes her glasses off, the lenses fogged, and lays them on the table. She eats with her head bowed down, as if in prayer.

Lifting a stem of cauliflower to his lips, my brother sighs deeply, he chews, and then his face changes. I have a sudden picture of him drowning, his hair waving like grass. He coughs, spitting the mouthful back onto his plate. Another cough. He reaches for his throat, choking.

My father slams his chopsticks down on the table. In a single movement, he reaches across, grabbing my brother by the shoulder. "I have tried," he is saying. "I don't know what kind of son you are. To be so ungrateful." His other hand sweeps by me and bruises into my brother's face.

My mother flinches. My brother's face is red and his mouth is open. His eyes are wet.

Still coughing, he grabs a fork, tines aimed at my father, and then in an unthinking moment, he heaves it at him. It strikes my father in the chest and drops.

"I hate you! You're just an asshole, you're just a fucking asshole chink!" My brother holds his plate in his hands. He smashes it down and his food scatters across the table. He is coughing and spitting. "I wish you weren't my father! I wish you were dead."

My father's hand falls again. This time pounding downwards. I close my eyes. All I can hear is someone screaming. There is a loud voice. I stand awkwardly, my hands covering my eyes.

"Go to your room," my father says, his voice shaking.

And I think he is talking to me so I remove my hands.

But he is looking at my brother. And my brother is looking at him, his small chest heaving.

A few minutes later, my mother begins clearing the table, face weary as she scrapes the dishes one by one over the garbage.

I move away from my chair, past my mother, onto the carpet and up the stairs.

Outside my brother's bedroom, I crouch against the wall. When I step forward and look, I see my father holding the bamboo pole between his hands. The pole is smooth. The long grains, fine as hair, are pulled together, at intervals, jointed. My brother is lying on the floor, as if thrown down and dragged there. My father raises the pole into the air.

I want to cry out. I want to move into the room between them, but I can't.

It is like a tree falling, beginning to move, a slow arc through the air.

The bamboo drops silently. It rips the skin on my brother's back. I cannot hear any sound. A line of blood edges quickly across his body.

The pole rises and again comes down. I am afraid of bones breaking.

My father lifts his arms once more.

On the floor, my brother cries into the carpet, pawing at the ground. His knees folded into his chest, the crown of his head burrowing down. His back is hunched over and I can see his spine, little bumps on his skin.

The bamboo smashes into bone and the scene in my mind bursts into a million white pieces.

My mother picks me up off the floor, pulling me across the hall, into my bedroom, into bed. Everything is wet, the sheets, my hands, her body, my face, and she soothes me with words I cannot understand because all I can hear is screaming. She rubs her cool hands against my forehead. "Stop," she says. "Please stop," but I feel loose, deranged, as if everything in the known world is ending right here.

In the morning, I wake up to the sound of oil in the pan and the smell of French toast. I can hear my mother bustling around, putting dishes in the cupboards.

No one says anything when my brother doesn't come down for breakfast. My father piles French toast and syrup onto a plate and my mother pours a glass of milk. She takes everything upstairs to my brother's bedroom.

As always, I follow my father around the kitchen. I track his footprints, follow behind him and hide in the shadow of his body. Every so often, he reaches down and ruffles my hair with his hands. We cast a spell, I think. The way we move in circles, how he cooks without thinking because this is the task that comes to him effortlessly. He smiles down at me, but when he does this, it somehow breaks the spell. My father stands in place, hands dropping to his sides as if he has forgotten what he was doing mid-motion. On the walls, the paint is peeling and the floor, unswept in days, leaves little pieces of dirt stuck to our feet.

My persistence, I think, my unadulterated love, confuse him. With each passing day, he knows I will find it harder to ignore what I can't comprehend, that I will be unable to separate one part of him from another. The unconditional quality of my love for him will not last forever, just as my brother's did not. My father stands in the middle of the kitchen, unsure. Eventually, my mother comes downstairs again and puts her arms around him and holds him, whispering something to him, words that to me are meaningless and incomprehensible. But she offers them to him, sound after sound, in a language that was stolen from some other place, until he drops his head and remembers where he is.

Later on, I lean against the door frame upstairs and listen to the sound of a metal fork scraping against a dish. My mother is already there, her voice rising and falling. She is moving the fork across the plate, offering my brother pieces of French toast.

I move towards the bed, the carpet scratchy, until I can touch the wooden bed-frame with my hands. My mother is seated there, and I go to her, reaching my fingers out to the buttons on her cuff and twisting them over to catch the light.

"Are you eating?" I ask my brother.

He starts to cry. I look at him, his face half hidden in the blankets.

"Try and eat," my mother says softly.

He only cries harder but there isn't any sound. The pattern of sunlight on his blanket moves with his body. His hair is pasted down with sweat and his head moves forward and backward like an old man's.

At some point I know my father is standing at the entrance of the room but I cannot turn to look at him. I want to stay where I am, facing the wall. I'm afraid that if I turn around and go to him, I will be complicit, accepting a portion of guilt, no matter how small that piece. I do not know how to prevent this from happening again, though now I know, in the end, it will break us apart. This violence will turn all my love to shame and grief. So I stand there, not looking at him or my brother. Even my father, the magician, who can make something beautiful out of nothing, he just stands and watches.

A face changes over time, it becomes clearer. In my father's face, I have seen everything pass. Anger that has stripped it of anything recognizable, so that it is only a face of bones and skin. And then, at other times, so much pain that it is unbearable, his face so full of grief it might dissolve. How to reconcile all that I know of him and still love him? For a long time, I thought it was not possible. When

I was a child, I did not love my father because he was complicated, because he was human, because he needed me to. A child does not know yet how to love a person that way.

How simple it should be. Warm water running over, the feel of the grains between my hands, the sound of it like stones running along the pavement. My father would rinse the rice over and over, sifting it between his fingertips, searching for the impurities, pulling them out. A speck, barely visible, resting on the tip of his finger.

If there were some recourse, I would take it. A cupful of grains in my open hand, a smoothing out, finding the impurities, then removing them piece by piece. And then, to be satisfied with what remains.

Somewhere in my memory, a fish in the sink is dying slowly. My father and I watch as the water runs down.

The Back of the Bear's Mouth

ALISSA YORK

Alissa York was born in Athabasca, Alberta, to parents who moved there from Australia. Her novels include *Mercy* (2003), *Effigy* (2007), and *Fauna* (2010). Her short fiction has appeared in various literary journals and anthologies, and in the short story collection *Any Given Power* (1999). She has lived all over Canada, and now makes her home in Toronto.

God knows how long Carson was watching me before I caught on—it was dark where he was sitting, like he'd brought some of the night in with him. I matched his look for a second, and a second was all it took. He stood up out of his corner and made for the bar.

I saw this show on the North one time. About the only part I remember was these bighorn sheep all meeting up at the salt-lick. They were so peaceful, side by side with their heads bent low, and no rutting or fighting, no matter if they were old or up-and-coming, no matter if they were male or female, injured or strong. That's the way it was with me and Carson. Neither one of us said much. We just sat there side by side, and it felt like the natural thing.

First published in *Any Given Power*, Alissa York (Winnipeg: Arbeiter Ring Publishing, 1999). Reprinted by permission of the author.

When the time came, Carson just stood and made for the doorway, the same slow bee-line stride he'd taken to the bar. Beside me, the bartender cleared our glasses and talked low into his beard. "Think twice little girl, the Northern bushman's a different breed."

But then Carson looked back at me over his shoulder, and just like a rockslide, I felt myself slip off the barstool and follow.

The truck took its time warming up, so we sat together in the dark, both of us staring at the windshield like we were waiting for some movie to start.

"Robin," he said finally, "I figure you got no place to go."

I turned my head his way a little. I was just eighteen and he must've been forty, but none of that mattered a damn.

"No Carson, I don't."

"Well." He handed me a cigarette and put one to his own lips, leaving it hanging there, not lighted. I brought the lighter out of my coat pocket and held the flame up in front of his face, the flicker of it making him seem younger somehow, a little scared.

After a minute I sat back and lit my own.

I must've fallen asleep on the drive. It was no wonder with the hours I'd been keeping—hitching clear across the country in just under three weeks. God knows how I landed in Whitehorse, except I remember hearing some old guy in a truckstop talking about it, calling it the stop before the end of the line.

I opened my eyes just as Carson was laying me out on the bed. The place was dark and cold as a meat locker. It stunk of tobacco and bacon, oiled metal and mould and mouse shit, but somewhere underneath all that was Carson's smell—a gentle, low-lying musk. I know it sounds crazy, but I'll bet that smell was half the reason I went with him in the first place.

I pulled the blanket around me and sat up, watching the shadow that was him pile wood into the stove. He lit the fire, then settled back into the armchair, watching me where I sat. I'd always hated people staring at me. I guess that's why I left school in the end—the teachers and everyone staring at your clothes, your hair, staring into your skull. But Carson was different. His eyes just rested on me, not hunting or digging, just looking because I was there, and more interesting than the rug or the table leg.

Who knows how long we sat like that. I remember him pulling a couple more blankets down from a cupboard, laying one around my shoulders and leaving the other at the foot of the bed.

In the morning sun was all through the place. The bed was an old wrought iron double, with only my side slept in. Coals burnt low in the stove. A grizzly head hung over the bed, mounted with its mouth wide open and the teeth drawn back like a trap.

Carson was nowhere, so I stepped outside and lit a smoke. It was warm, the sun already burning holes in the snow. We were in the bush alright, the clearing was just big enough for the cabin, the outhouse, and the truck. The dirt road that led in to the place closed up dark in the distance, like looking down somebody's throat. A skinny tomcat squeezed out the door of the outhouse and sat washing what was left of one of its ears. The trees grew thick and dark, and the sounds of jays and ravens came falling.

I found Carson round back of the cabin, bent over the carcass of a deer. There was another one in the dust nearby, a buck with small, velvety antlers. Carson looked up at the sound of my footsteps, his eyes all quick and violent.

"Morning," I said.

"Morning."

"You get those this morning?"

"— No."

Something told me to shut up. I walked back round to the door and went inside. The place looked like it hadn't ever been cleaned, so I threw a log in the stove, put the kettle on top, and set about finding some rags and soap.

He never touched me for the whole first week. A couple of times he walked up close behind me and stood there, smelling my hair or something, and I waited for his hand on me, but it didn't come.

The days passed easily. I got the place clean, beat the rugs and blankets, swept out the mouse shit, oiled the table, and washed the two windows with hot water and vinegar. I even stood up on the bed and brushed the dust out of the grizzly's fur. There were gold hairs all through the brown, lit up and dancing where the sunlight lay on its neck.

Carson never thanked me for cleaning up, and I never thanked him for letting me stay. On my eighth night there he turned in the bed and I felt him pressing long and hard into the back of my thigh. He held me tight, but it didn't hurt. He fit into me like something I'd been missing, like something finally come home.

Carson was sometimes gone for part of the night, or all of it. He either went out empty and brought a carcass back, or went out with a carcass or two and came back empty. Usually it was caribou or deer, but one time there was a lynx. He let me touch the fur. It felt just the same as a regular cat—a few hairs came away in my hand.

Time went by like this, me cooking and cleaning and watching, sometimes reading the *Reader's Digest* or some other magazine from a box in the cupboard, sometimes just sitting and smoking on the doorstep, watching the forest fill up with spring. Carson got more comfortable when I'd been there for awhile, started teaching me how to shoot the rifle—first at empty bean tins, then at crows and rabbits that came into the clearing. When I finally hit a rabbit, Carson let out a whoop and ran to get it. Then he took the gun from my hands and held the rabbit up in front of my face. Its hindlegs were blown clear off. I felt my fingers go shaky when I reached for its ears, felt tears come up the back of my throat when I took it from him, the soft, dead weight of it in my hand.

One night I got Carson to let me go along. That sounds like I had to talk him into it, but really all I said was, "Can I come?"

"You can't talk if you do."

"You heard me talk much?"

"— Alright."

It was like driving through black paint—the headlights cut a path in front of the truck, and the dark closed up behind us. I had to wonder how Carson found his way around, how he ever managed to get back home. When we got a ways off the main road, he slowed right down and started zigzagging, the headlights swishing over the road and into the bush, then back over the road to the other side.

I was just nodding off when Carson cut the engine, grabbed the gun and jumped out into the dark. I caught a yellow flash of eyes in the bush, then came the shots, the gun blazing once, twice, and the moose staggered into the lights, forelegs buckling, head slamming into the dirt.

Carson pulled a winch out from under the seat and rigged it up to some bolts in the bed of the truck. We got the moose trussed up, but it took us forever to get it in the back.

"This is a big one," I said, not sure if it was true. I'd only ever seen one from far away, standing stock-still in a muskeg, the way they do.

"Not one," he said, "two. Springtime, Robin."

The next night Carson headed off on his own and I was just as glad. I was still trying to lose the picture of that moose's head hitting the ground.

It seems like it would be creepy being out there in the middle of God-knows-where, Yukon Territory, but I got used to it pretty fast. Even when I was alone it felt safer than any city I'd been through— all those junkies and college kids and cars.

One night though, I woke up slow and foggy, feeling like I couldn't breathe. It took a while for me to realize that tomcat was sitting on me, right on my chest, and when my eyes got used to the dark I could make out the shape of a mouse in its jaws.

I'm no chicken, but that dead mouse in my face scared the shit out of me. I threw the cat clear across the room, and the mouse flew out of its mouth and landed somewhere near the foot of the bed. The tom yowled for a minute, then found the mouse and settled down. I swear I didn't close my eyes until dawn. I just lay there, listening to that cat gnawing and tearing at the mouse, snapping the bones in its teeth.

I'd been out there for a couple of months as close as I could guess, and I had no ideas about leaving. It wasn't that Carson was such great company—half the time he wasn't there, and the other half he was busy skinning something, or cleaning his guns, or doing God knows what round back of the cabin. At night was mostly when we met up. He'd climb into the bed after me, and hold me hard and gentle, always the same way, from the back with me lying on my side. I didn't mind—it felt good, and I figured he was shy about doing it face to face. It made sense, a man who lives out in the bush on his own for so long.

By that time I was sure I was pregnant. I hadn't bled since I'd been there, my tits were sore, and my belly had a warm, hard rise in it. One night when Carson was lying behind me, I took his hand and put it there. I turned my face around to him, and even though it was dark as the Devil, I could tell he was smiling. I don't know that I've felt that good before or since.

I only asked Carson about the hunting once.

"Carson, all these animals —"

The way he looked at me made me think of that first day, when he looked up from that deer like he was a dog and I was some other dog trying to nose in on the kill. His eyes were really pale blue, sometimes almost clear. They didn't usually bug me, but times like that I always thought of that riddle—the man gets stabbed with an icicle, and it melts, and then where's the murder weapon?

It was maybe a week or two later when I woke up to the sound of Carson coming home in the truck. That alone told me there was something wrong—usually he coasted up to the cabin and came in without waking me up. I was lighting the lamp when he threw open the door.

"Can you drive?"

"What's wrong?"

"Can you drive!"

"Yes!"

"Get dressed."

"What's wrong Carson?"

"Goddammit Robin!"

I crawled out from under the covers and grabbed for my clothes. He jumped up on the bed and stood where my head had been, reaching one hand deep into the grizzly's mouth. I thought he'd lost it for sure, but a second later he jumped back down and stuck a fistful of money in my face, twenties and fifties, a fat wad of them.

"There's more up there," he said, "if I don't come back you come and get it, just reach past the teeth and push the panel. And watch you don't cut your hand."

He shoved the truck keys into the pocket of my red mack.

"Carson," I said, and my voice came out funny. I was thinking about what he said, about him maybe not coming back.

"Get going. Lay low in Whitehorse. I'll find you."

"But where will you go?"

"Out in the bush. Get going."

He touched my hair for a second, then held the door open and pushed me outside.

I got a room at the Fourth Avenue Residence. I didn't check in until morning, after spending the whole night driving around in the dark, scared shitless. When dawn came and I finally saw the road sign I'd been hoping for, I felt about two steps from crazy.

Whitehorse was waking up when I pulled into town. I bought a bottle of peroxide at the Pharmasave, and a big bag of Doritos, then I found the Fourth Ave. And parked around back.

First thing I did in my room was eat the whole bag of Doritos, fast, like I hadn't had anything for days. Then I took the scissors from the kitchen drawer and cut off all my hair. It fell onto the linoleum and curled around my feet, shiny black as a nest of crows. I left the peroxide on until it burned, and when I rinsed it out and looked at myself in the mirror I had to laugh. And then I had to cry.

I slept the whole day and through the night, and the next morning I went down to the front desk and bought a pack of smokes, two Mars Bars and a paper. I folded the paper under my arm and I didn't look at the front page until I was back in my room. I ate the Mars Bars while I read, and my hunger made me remember the baby. Our baby—mine and Carson's.

PITLAMPER GOES TOO FAR
Conservation Officer Harvey Jacobs was shot and badly wounded late last night when he surprised a lone man pitlamping on a back-road off the Dempster Highway. The man who fired at Jacobs is believed to be one Ray Carson, who has a cabin in the area. RCMP have issued a warrant for Carson's arrest and ask that anyone with information pertaining to his whereabouts come forward. Jacobs took a single .38 bullet in his right side. He is currently in intensive care . . . .

I lay on my back on the bed, until it felt like the baby was screaming for something to eat. I thought about going out, but I ended up calling for pizza.

I was in the corner store when I heard. The old bitch behind the counter leaned across to me and said, "Did you hear? They got that nut case, Carson."

I looked down at the lottery tickets, all neat and shiny under a slab of plexiglas.

"They had to take the dogs in after him. Got him cornered up in the rocks of a waterfall, but he turned a gun on them. Well, they had to shoot him, the stupid bugger—"

She kept on talking, but that was the last I heard. I closed the door on her voice, walked up the road a ways, and sat down in the weeds. I thought about staying there forever, thought about the grass growing up around my shoulders, turning gold and seedy, then black and broken under the snow.

Then I thought about the baby and figured I better get up.

Shelterbelt

AMBER HAYWARD

Amber Hayward is an author and poet who lives in Hinton, Alberta, on the eastern edge of Jasper National Park. She and her husband own the Black Cat Guest Ranch, where they host murder mystery weekends scripted by Hayward. Her most recent book is *Stolen Children*, the final book in her trilogy *Children of the Panther*; the first two volumes are *The Healer* and *Darkness of the God*.

If you stare at the sun hard enough, it dries the tears in your eyes right up. And afterwards, if you look around at the rest of the sky or the barn or something, there's all these black and purple dots that look really neat. Some kids like video games but this can be just as good, especially when you're already in trouble for refusing to share the computer with your little brother.

Sisters aren't great but brothers are a hundred times worse. A sister might act like a part-time mom, telling you what to do and nagging sometimes, but she can also be really nice, maybe bake cookies if she knows you're feeling down. She could use the computer if she needed it for homework, but she wouldn't be on it for hours playing games and then lie about it, say that someone else used it all day.

If you had a mom like some kids do, one who doesn't have to work weekends, she'd be around all day Saturday and she'd know who was telling the truth, there wouldn't be this big fight and she wouldn't have to say, "Just get out of my sight, the both of you. I don't want to see or hear from you for at least an hour."

If you didn't have to share a room with your brother, maybe you could go there and read or something, but when you share a room, most times you can't be in there at the same time or there'll be fighting for sure. So if he gets the room first and you live in a pretty small house, the only way to stay out of your mom's sight is to go outside.

Around seven o'clock on a September Saturday night can be really pretty. The sky goes this orange colour and the sun gets big and red, like in a science fiction movie; the clouds reach across the sky in rows, like rows of wheat in the sky.

If you run to the end of the shelterbelt and back three times, you're usually too tired to be mad or sad when you're done. If you run to the end of the shelterbelt and just keep going, across the quarter section that was the first one your dad had to sell, your legs get tired at first and it's hard to breathe, but before long you

---

Reprinted by permission of the author.

start feeling strong, like you could run forever, catch up to that big old setting sun and live in a land where all the houses are huge and airy like the fields, with walls the same gold colour as the sky, where the people are tall and beautiful, and wise and kind.

But you have to be careful when you start running like that, keep an eye on your watch so you aren't late for the dinner your mom will have ready by eight and be sure to get your chores in the chicken house done before ten when your dad gets home for the dinner he eats with your mom. If you kept running like that, and you added to all the worries your folks already have, you'd be really really sorry. You might even have to lie at the clinic about where you got that bruise on your cheek. And you'd have to listen to your brother that night saying you deserve it because you are such a fuck-up, and you won't even want to tell your mom that he said a swear, because it'd just make more trouble.

Why can't you remember the exact moment your brother became your enemy the way you know your dad changed from the very day he took the job in town? If you think back, you're like a grampa or something, only remembering good things—walking to the irrigation ditch together, barefoot in the soft hot dust of the road beside the shelterbelt, building the tree house in the big old cottonwood next to the little house where Grandmother Frame lived until she died. And beating up Jeremy Wolitski because he called your brother a baby on the first day of Grade One.

You know you should have other friends. That's what your mom and your sister keep telling you. But at school town kids stick with town kids and farm kids stick with farm kids. And most of the farm kids in your grade have moved away. The only boy left is Jeremy Wolitski, the bully, and he's best friends with your little brother instead of you.

If a person could have chickens for friends, you'd have lots of friends. When you were little, you were always crawling up the ramp of the chicken house and in the door where the chickens went to get to their nesting boxes. You could see them on their shelves behind the big doors your mom used to collect the eggs. You could even feel underneath the hens, all warm and soft with the hot round eggs on the straw, and they never pecked you. But they did peck your brother when he followed you in there, so you had to stop. He followed you everywhere when he was small.

The chickens still like you better than they do anyone else but this doesn't make you feel as good as it once did. Your dad never says what he used to about you being a natural farmer. And you don't like the new chicken house. You think the chickens probably hate you for it. They have to stay in their wire cages all the time and the eggs roll away the minute they lay them. They don't get to go outside and fool around in the yard, maybe even get out of the fence and hide their eggs at the bottom of a stack of old tires.

If you stop halfway down the shelterbelt, you might find the spot where Becky from the next farm used a string tied between two trees, an old chair and some broken china to make a play house. You and Becky were the mom and dad and you'd only let your brother play if he agreed to be the baby. The string and the chair are gone but there's still an old cardboard sign nailed to one tree. The letters are too faded to read now but it used to say, "Annie Reed keep out!" Annie's dad is a rich guy from town who bought the Peters' farm and he built Annie a great play house just like a real house, but she was no fun to play with and she made fun of Becky's play house.

If Becky hadn't moved away two years ago, she might still be your friend, even if she is a girl. Or maybe she'd be hanging out with Annie and her stuck-up town kid friends. Even though you begged her not to, your mom invited Annie to your birthday party last year. Annie got all the kids going about what a cheap party it was—no big fat goodie bags for all the kids, no bowling or movie, just hot dogs and dumb games like Monopoly. You took everyone to the hay barn and let them pick out kittens to take home, but Annie said she was allergic to kittens and to hay.

There was a fight that night when your dad had to drive around after he got home from work, picking up kittens from kids whose parents wouldn't let them keep them. And your mom asked you why you did it and you said because it was such a cheap party and you'd rather have no party at all. And your mom cried and said she'd worked really hard and if that's how you felt, that's the last party you'd ever have.

And when your dad got home, he was yelling about how if you think they're made of time and money, well, you just have another think coming. You could tell he wanted to hit you, the way you want to break your brother's stuff sometimes but you're afraid you won't be able to stop if you start. So you kept quiet and far away from your dad and he just yelled at you a little more then he went out and killed the kittens.

It used to be when your dad got mad, he'd go out in the fields, no matter how late at night, walk around and do whatever work needed doing, pick rocks or dig up a stump in the meadow down by the creek, hoe a bit, pull thistles out of the ditches so they didn't spread. Now the only land he still owns is that bottom land and he never goes there and he doesn't care much about the fields he leases back for growing hay and oats. But when he put his fist through the kitchen wall the same time he slapped you and cut your face with his ring, your mom said he had to take it outside, so now he chops wood when he's mad.

The winter before last there were big winds and seven trees in the shelterbelt blew over, splitting along the white heartwood. But it took the new owner until September to decide that he didn't want that firewood for himself so your dad could have it after all. The neatest thing was that the trees got leaves anyhow, all bent over and broken like they were. You liked to go out there, sit on the trunks like a bench, bounce up and down a little but not too much. They were clinging to life and you didn't want to make it harder, break their last connection to their roots, even though your mom said she once saw poplar fence rails that were cut off at both ends but still had new leaves.

You thought it was too bad when your dad took the chain saw to the trees, even though that huge pile of logs waiting to be split is like a promise of protection. He's split a lot of wood while you've sat inside, maybe in your room with your mom talking to you and your brother making faces from behind her back, or maybe in your sister's room while she tries to talk some sense into you.

And it doesn't do any good to remember the times when you were younger and you got in trouble for something like leaving the gate to the chicken yard open or tracking mud into the kitchen and he'd slap you quick on the bum, not too hard, and then whisper to your mom that he did far worse when he was a kid. Because that doesn't happen any more.

One time you were sitting on the stairs that led to the attic bedrooms, listening to big fat upside-down flies on the window sill rotate themselves to death and you heard your dad come in from splitting wood and your mom asked him, "Didn't you skip classes too when you were a kid," and he said it was different now, kids need their education and anyway why didn't anyone consider how he felt, to hear about it from his boss who's married to the school principal, everyone at work heard about it before he did.

And you wonder if things will be better or worse when you move to town. Because that's the next thing, you heard them talking about it one night when you were listening through the heat vent in the upstairs hall. How could it be better for your dad? He won't have the wood pile. And your family won't have the money from the chickens and the eggs and the hay. But you can't ask about it. You aren't supposed to know about it.

And you wonder why your dad won't let you split wood, even though you promise you'll be careful and not cut off your little toe the way he did when he was ten. Because you couldn't cut wood, you used to go over to Becky's abandoned house and throw rocks through the windows when you were mad. The bright clash of breaking glass made you feel good, until you got caught. That night a lot of wood got split.

Now all you can do is run, try to outrun thoughts about what moving into town will be like, about saying goodbye to the chickens and the shelterbelt and the play house and the hay shed cats. And you wonder, when your father killed the kittens that night, cutting off their heads with his axe, was it just like splitting wood?

Tapka

DAVID BEZMOZGIS

Born in Riga, Latvia, in 1973, David Bezmozgis immigrated to Toronto with his parents in 1980. He is an award-winning writer and filmmaker, and his stories have appeared in numerous publications including *The New Yorker, Harper's, Zoetrope, All-Story,* and *The Walrus.* His first book, *Natasha and Other Stories* (2004), was published in the United States and Canada and then translated into more than a dozen languages. His work has been broadcast on NPR, BBC, and the CBC, and his stories have been anthologized in *The Best American Short Stories 2005* and *2006.* As a filmmaker, Bezmozgis was a screenwriting fellow at the Sundance Labs, where he developed his first feature, *Victoria Day,* which premiered in competition at the Sundance Film Festival in 2009. His website is www.bezmozgis.com.

Goldfinch was flapping clotheslines, a tenement delirious with striving. 6030 Bathurst: insomniac, scheming Odessa. Cedarcroft: reeking borscht in the hallways. My parents, Soviet refugees but Baltic aristocrats, took an apartment at 715 Finch, fronting a ravine and across from an elementary school—one respectable block away from the Russian swarm. We lived on the fifth floor, my cousin, aunt, and uncle directly below us on the fourth. Except for the Nahumovskys, a couple in their fifties, there were no other Russians in the building. For this privilege, my parents paid twenty extra dollars a month in rent.

In March of 1980, near the end of the school year but only three weeks after our arrival in Toronto, I was enrolled in Charles H. Best Elementary. Each morning, with our house key hanging from a brown shoelace around my neck, I kissed my parents goodbye and, along with my cousin Jana, tramped across the ravine—I to the first grade, she to the second. At three o'clock, bearing the germs of a new vocabulary, we tramped back home. Together, we then waited until six for our parents to return from George Brown City College, where they were taking an obligatory six-month course in English—a course that provided them with the rudiments of communication along with a modest government stipend.

In the evenings, we assembled and compiled our linguistic bounty.

Hello, havaryew?
Red, yellow, green, blue.
May I please go to the washroom?
Seventeen, eighteen, nineteen, twenny.

Joining us most nights were the Nahumovskys. They attended the same English classes and travelled with my parents on the same bus. Rita Nahumovsky was a beautician who wore layers of makeup, and Misha Nahumovsky was a tool-and-die maker. They came from Minsk and didn't know a soul in Canada. With abounding enthusiasm, they incorporated themselves into our family. My parents were glad to have them. Our life was tough, we had it hard—but the Nahumovskys had it harder. They were alone, they were older, they were stupefied by the demands of language. Being essentially helpless themselves, my parents found it gratifying to help the more helpless Nahumovskys.

After dinner, with everyone gathered on cheap stools around our table, my mother repeated the day's lessons for the benefit of the Nahumovskys and, to a slightly lesser degree, for the benefit of my father. My mother had always been an exceptional and dedicated student, and she extended this dedication to George Brown City College. My father and the Nahumovskys came to rely on her detailed notes and her understanding of the curriculum. For as long as they could, they listened attentively and groped desperately toward comprehension. When this became too frustrating, my father put on the kettle, Rita painted my mother's nails, and Misha told Soviet *anekdoti*.

In a first-grade classroom a teacher calls on her students and inquires after their nationalities. "Sasha," she says. Sasha says, "Russian." "Very good," says the teacher. "Arnan," she says. Arnan says, "Armenian." "Very good," says the teacher. "Lyubka," she says. Lyubka says, "Ukrainian." "Very good," says the teacher. And then she asks Dima. Dima says, "Jewish." "What a shame," says the teacher. "So young and already a Jew."

The Nahumovskys had no children, only a white Lhasa Apso named Tapka. The dog had lived with them for years before they emigrated and then travelled with them from Minsk to Vienna, from Vienna to Rome, and from Rome to Toronto. During our first month in the building, Tapka was in quarantine, and I saw her only in photographs. Rita had dedicated an entire album to the dog, and, to dampen the pangs of separation, she consulted the album daily. There were shots of Tapka in the Nahumovskys' old Minsk apartment, seated on the cushions of faux-Louis XIV furniture; there was Tapka on the steps of a famous Viennese palace; Tapka at the Vatican, in front of the Colosseum, at the Sistine Chapel, and under the Leaning Tower of Pisa. My mother—despite having grown up with goats and chickens in her yard—didn't like animals and found it impossible to feign interest in Rita's dog. Shown a picture of Tapka, my mother wrinkled her nose and said, "Phoo." My father also couldn't be bothered. With no English, no money, no job, and only a murky conception of what the future held, he wasn't equipped to admire Tapka on the Italian Riviera. Only I cared. Through the photographs, I became attached to Tapka and projected upon her the ideal traits of the dog I did not have. Like Rita, I counted the days until Tapka's liberation.

The day Tapka was to be released from quarantine, Rita prepared an elaborate dinner. My family was invited to celebrate the dog's arrival. While Rita cooked, Misha was banished from their apartment. For distraction, he seated himself at our table with a deck of cards. As my mother reviewed sentence construction, Misha played hand after hand of *durak* with me.

"The woman loves this dog more than me. A taxi to the customs facility is going to cost us ten, maybe fifteen dollars. But what can I do? The dog is truly a sweet little dog."

When it came time to collect the dog, my mother went with Misha and Rita to act as their interpreter. With my nose to the window, I watched the taxi take them away. Every few minutes, I reapplied my nose to the window. Three hours later, the taxi pulled into our parking lot, and Rita emerged from the back seat cradling animated fur. She set the fur down on the pavement where it assumed the shape of a dog. The length of its coat concealed its legs, and, as it hovered around Rita's ankles, it appeared to have either a thousand tiny legs or none at all. My head ringing "Tapka, Tapka, Tapka," I raced into the hallway to meet the elevator.

That evening, Misha toasted the dog: "This last month, for the first time in years, I have enjoyed my wife's undivided attention. But I believe no man, not even one as perfect as me, can survive so much attention from his wife. So I say, with all my heart, thank

God our Tapka is back home with us. Another day and I fear I may have requested a divorce."

Before he drank, Misha dipped his pinkie finger into his vodka glass and offered it to the dog. Obediently, Tapka gave Misha's finger a thorough licking. Impressed, my uncle declared her a good Russian dog. He also gave her a lick of his vodka. I gave her a piece of my chicken. Jana rolled her a pellet of bread. Misha taught us how to dangle food just out of Tapka's reach and thereby induce her to perform a charming little dance. Rita also produced Clonchik, a red-and-yellow rag clown. She tossed Clonchik under the table, onto the couch, down the hallway, and into the kitchen; over and over, Rita called, "Tapka, get Clonchik," and, without fail, Tapka got Clonchik. Everyone delighted in Tapka's antics except my mother, who sat stiffly in her chair, her feet slightly off the floor, as though preparing herself for a mild electric shock.

After the dinner, when we returned home, my mother announced that she would no longer set foot in the Nahumovskys' apartment. She liked Rita, she liked Misha, but she couldn't sympathize with their attachment to the dog. She understood that the attachment was a consequence of their lack of sophistication and also their childlessness. They were simple people. Rita had never attended university. She could derive contentment from talking to a dog, brushing its coat, putting ribbons in its hair, and repeatedly throwing a rag clown across the apartment. And Misha, although very lively and a genius with his hands, was also not an intellectual. They were good people, but a dog ruled their lives.

Rita and Misha were sensitive to my mother's attitude toward Tapka. As a result, and to the detriment of her progress with English, Rita stopped visiting our apartment. Nightly, Misha would arrive alone while Rita attended to the dog. Tapka never set foot in our home. This meant that, in order to see her, I spent more and more time at the Nahumovskys'. Each evening, after I had finished my homework, I went to play with Tapka. My heart soared every time Rita opened the door and Tapka raced to greet me. The dog knew no hierarchy of affection. Her excitement was infectious. In Tapka's presence, I resonated with doglike glee.

Because of my devotion to the dog, and their lack of an alternative, Misha and Rita added their house key to the shoelace hanging around my neck. During our lunch break and again after school, Jana and I were charged with caring for Tapka. Our task was simple: put Tapka on her leash, walk her to the ravine, release her to chase Clonchik, and then bring her home.

Every day, sitting in my classroom, understanding little, effectively friendless, I counted down the minutes to lunchtime. When the bell rang, I met Jana on the playground and we sprinted across the grass toward our building. In the hall, our approaching foot-steps elicited panting and scratching. When I inserted the key into the lock, I felt emanations of love through the door. And once the door was open Tapka hurled herself at us, her entire body consumed with the ecstasy of wagging. Jana and I took turns embracing her, petting her, covertly vying for her favor. Free of Rita's scrutiny, we also satisfied certain anatomical curiosities. We examined Tapka's ears, her paws, her teeth, the roots of her fur, and her doggy genitals. We poked and prodded her, we threw her up in the air, rolled her over and over, and swung her by her front legs. I felt such overwhelming love for Tapka that sometimes, when hugging her, I had to restrain myself from squeezing too hard and crushing her little bones.

It was April when we began to care for Tapka. Snow melted in the ravine; sometimes it rained. April became May. Grass absorbed the thaw, turned green; dandelions and wildflowers sprouted yellow and blue; birds and insects flew, crawled, and made their charac-teristic noises. Faithfully and reliably, Jana and I attended to Tapka. We walked her across the parking lot and down into the ravine. We threw Clonchik and said, "Tapka, get Clonchik." Tapka always got Clonchik. Everyone was proud of us. My mother and my aunt wiped tears from their eyes while talking about how responsible we were. Rita and Misha rewarded us with praise and chocolates. Jana was seven and I was six; much had been asked of us, but we had risen to the challenge.

Inspired by everyone's confidence, we grew confident. Whereas at first we made sure to walk thirty paces into the ravine before releasing Tapka, we gradually reduced that requirement to ten paces, then five paces, until finally we released her at the grassy border between the parking lot and the ravine. We did this not because of laziness or intentional recklessness but because we wanted proof of Tapka's love. That she came when we called was evidence of her love, that she didn't piss in the elevator was evi-dence of her love, that she offered up her belly for scratching was evidence of her love, that she licked our faces was evidence of her love. All of this was evidence, but it wasn't proof. Proof could come in only one form. We had intuited an elemental truth: love needs no leash.

That first spring, even though most of what was said around me remained a mystery, a thin rivulet of meaning trickled into my cer-ebral catch basin and collected into a little pool of knowledge. By the end of May, I could sing the ABC song. Television taught me to say "What's up, Doc?" and "super-duper." The playground introduced me to "shithead," "mental case," and "gaylord." I seized upon every opportunity to apply my new knowledge.

One afternoon, after spending nearly an hour in the ravine throwing Clonchik in a thousand different directions, Jana and I lolled in sunlit pollen. I called her shithead, mental case, and gaylord, and she responded by calling me gaylord, shithead, and mental case.

"Shithead."

"Gaylord."

"Mental case."

"Tapka, get Clonchik."

"Shithead."

"Gaylord."

"Come, Tapka-lapka."

"Mental case."

We went on like this, over and over, until Jana threw the clown and said, "Shithead, get Clonchik." Initially, I couldn't tell if she had said this on purpose or if it had merely been a blip in her rhythm. But when I looked at Jana her smile was triumphant.

"Mental case, get Clonchik."

For the first time, as I watched Tapka bounding happily after Clonchik, the profanity sounded profane.

"Don't say that to the dog."

"Why not?"

"It's not right."

"But she doesn't understand."

"You shouldn't say it."

"Don't be a baby. Come, shithead, come my dear one."

Her tail wagging with accomplishment, Tapka dropped Clonchik at my feet.

"You see, she likes it."

I held Clonchik as Tapka pawed frantically at my shins.

"Call her shithead. Throw the clown."

"I'm not calling her shithead."

"What are you afraid of, shithead?"

I aimed the clown at Jana's head and missed.

"Shithead, get Clonchik."

As the clown left my hand, Tapka, a white shining blur, oblivious to insult, was already cutting through the grass. I wanted to believe that I had intended the "shithead" exclusively for Jana, but I knew it wasn't true.

"I told you, gaylord, she doesn't care."

I couldn't help thinking, Poor Tapka. I felt moral residue and looked around for some sign of recrimination. The day, however, persisted in unimpeachable brilliance: sparrows winged overhead; bumblebees levitated above flowers; beside a lilac shrub, Tapka clamped down on Clonchik. I was amazed at the absence of consequences.

Jana said, "I'm going home."

As she started for home, I saw that she was still holding Tapka's leash. It swung insouciantly from her hand. I called after her just as, once again, Tapka deposited Clonchik at my feet.

"I need the leash."

"Why?"

"Don't be stupid. I need the leash."

"No, you don't. She comes when we call her. Even shithead. She won't run away."

Jana turned her back on me and proceeded toward our building. I called her again, but she refused to turn around. Her receding back was a blatant provocation. Guided more by anger than by logic, I decided that if Tapka was closer to Jana then the onus of responsibility would be on her. I picked up the doll and threw it as far as I could into the parking lot.

"Tapka, get Clonchik."

Clonchik tumbled through the air. I had put everything in my six-year-old arm behind the throw, which still meant that the doll wasn't going very far. Its trajectory promised a drop no more than twenty feet from the edge of the ravine. Running, her head arched to the sky, Tapka tracked the flying clown. As the doll reached its apex, it crossed paths with a sparrow. The bird veered off toward Finch Avenue, and the clown plummeted to the asphalt. When the doll hit the ground, Tapka raced past it after the bird.

A thousand times we had thrown Clonchik and a thousand times Tapka had retrieved him. But who knows what passes for a thought in the mind of a dog? One moment a Clonchik is a Clonchik, and the next moment a sparrow is a Clonchik.

I shouted at Jana to catch Tapka and then watched in abject horror as the dog, her attention fixed on the sparrow, skirted past Jana and directly into traffic. From my vantage point on the slope of the ravine, I couldn't see what happened. I saw only that Jana broke into a sprint and I heard the caterwauling of tires, followed by Tapka's shrill fractured yip.

By the time I reached the street, a line of cars already stretched a block beyond Goldfinch. At the front of the line were a brown station wagon and a pale-blue sedan blistered with rust. As I neared, I noted the chrome letters on the back of the sedan: D-U-S-T-E-R. In front of the sedan, Jana kneeled in a tight semicircle with a pimply young man and an older woman with very large sunglasses. Tapka lay on her side at the center of their circle. She panted in quick shallow bursts. She stared impassively at me, at Jana. Except for a hind leg twitching at the sky at an impossible angle, she seemed completely unharmed. She looked much as she did when she rested on the rug at the Nahumovskys' apartment after a vigorous romp in the ravine.

Seeing her this way, barely mangled, I felt a sense of relief. I started to convince myself that things weren't as bad as I had feared, and I tentatively edged forward to pet her. The woman in the sunglasses said something in a restrictive tone that I neither understood nor heeded. I placed my hand on Tapka's head, and she responded by opening her mouth and allowing a trickle of blood to escape onto the asphalt. This was the first time I had ever seen dog blood, and I was struck by the depth of its color. I hadn't expected it to be red, although I also hadn't expected it to be not-red. Set against the gray asphalt and her white coat, Tapka's blood was the red I envisioned when I closed my eyes and thought: red.

I sat with Tapka until several dozen car horns demanded that we clear the way. The woman with the large sunglasses ran to her station wagon, returned with a blanket, and scooped Tapka off the street. The pimply young man stammered a few sentences, of which I understood nothing except the word "sorry." Then we were in the back seat of the station wagon with Tapka in Jana's lap. The woman kept talking until she finally realized that we couldn't understand her at all. As we started to drive off, Jana remembered something. I motioned for the woman to stop the car and scrambled out. Above the atonal chorus of car horns, I heard: "Mark, get Clonchik."

I ran and got Clonchik.

For two hours, Jana and I sat in the reception area of a small veterinary clinic in an unfamiliar part of town. In another room, with a menagerie of afflicted creatures, Tapka lay in traction, connected to a blinking machine by a series of tubes. Jana and I had been allowed to see her once but were rushed out when we both burst into tears. Tapka's doctor, a woman wearing a white coat and furry slippers resembling bear paws, tried to calm us down. Again, we could neither explain ourselves nor understand what she was saying. We managed only to establish that Tapka was not our dog. The doctor gave us coloring books, stickers, and access to the phone. Every fifteen minutes, we called home. Between phone calls, we absently flipped pages and sniffled for Tapka and for ourselves. We had no idea what would happen to Tapka; all we knew was that she wasn't dead. As for ourselves, we already felt punished and knew only that more punishment was to come.

"Why did you throw Clonchik?"

"Why didn't you give me the leash?"

"You could have held on to her collar."

"You shouldn't have called her shithead."

At six-thirty, my mother picked up the phone. I could hear the agitation in her voice. The ten minutes she had spent at home not knowing where I was had taken their toll. For ten minutes, she had been the mother of a dead child. I explained to her about the dog and felt a twinge of resentment when she said, "So it's only the dog?" Behind her I heard other voices. It sounded as though everyone were speaking at once, pursuing personal agendas, translating the phone conversation from Russian to Russian until one anguished voice separated itself: "My God, what happened?" Rita.

After getting the address from the veterinarian, my mother hung up and ordered another expensive taxi. Within a half hour, my parents, my aunt, and Misha and Rita pulled up at the clinic. Jana and I waited for them on the sidewalk. As soon as the taxi doors opened, we began to sob uncontrollably, partly out of relief but mainly in the hope of engendering sympathy. I ran to my mother and caught sight of Rita's face. Her face made me regret that I also hadn't been hit by a car.

As we clung to our mothers, Rita descended upon us.

"Children, what, oh, what have you done?"

She pinched compulsively at the loose skin of her neck, raising a cluster of pink marks.

While Misha methodically counted individual bills for the taxi-driver, we swore on our lives that Tapka had simply got away from us. That we had minded her as always but, inexplicably, she had seen a bird and bolted from the ravine and into the road. We had done everything in our power to catch her, but she had surprised us, eluded us, been too fast.

Rita considered our story.

"You are liars. Liars!"

She uttered the words with such hatred that we again burst into sobs.

My father spoke in our defense.

"Rita Borisovna, how can you say this? They are children."

"They are liars. I know my Tapka. Tapka never chased birds. Tapka never ran from the ravine."

"Maybe today she did?"

"Liars."

Having delivered her verdict, she had nothing more to say. She waited anxiously for Misha to finish paying the driver.

"Misha, enough already. Count it a hundred times, it will still be the same."

Inside the clinic, there was no longer anyone at the reception desk. During our time there, Jana and I had watched a procession of dyspeptic cats and lethargic parakeets disappear into the back rooms for examination and diagnosis. One after another they had come and gone until, by the time of our parents' arrival, the waiting area was entirely empty and the clinic officially closed. The only people remaining were a night nurse and the doctor in the bear-paw slippers, who had stayed expressly for our sake.

Looking desperately around the room, Rita screamed, "Doctor! Doctor!" But when the doctor appeared she was incapable of making herself understood. Haltingly, with my mother's help, it was communicated to the doctor that Rita wanted to see her dog. Pointing vigorously at herself, Rita asserted, "Tapka. Mine dog."

The doctor led Rita and Misha into the veterinary version of an intensive-care ward. Tapka lay on her little bed, Clonchik resting directly beside her. At the sight of Rita and Misha, Tapka weakly wagged her tail. Little more than an hour had elapsed since I had seen her last, but somehow over the course of that time Tapka had shrunk considerably. She had always been a small dog, but now she looked desiccated. She was the embodiment of defeat. Rita started to cry, grotesquely smearing her mascara. With trembling hands, and with sublime tenderness, she stroked Tapka's head.

"My God, my God, what has happened to you, my Tapkochka?"

Through my mother, and with the aid of pen and paper, the doctor provided the answer. Tapka required two operations. One for her leg. Another to stop internal bleeding. An organ had been damaged. For now, a machine was helping her, but without the machine she would die. On the paper, the doctor drew a picture of a scalpel, of a dog, of a leg, of an organ. She made an arrow pointing at the organ and drew a teardrop and colored it in to represent blood. She also wrote down a number preceded by a dollar sign. The number was fifteen hundred.

At the sight of the number, Rita let out a low animal moan and steadied herself against Tapka's little bed. My parents exchanged a glance. I looked at the floor. Misha said, "My dear God." The Nahumovskys and my parents each took in less than five hundred dollars a month. We had arrived in Canada with almost nothing, a few hundred dollars, which had all but disappeared on furniture.

There were no savings. Fifteen hundred dollars. The doctor could just as well have written a million.

In the middle of the intensive-care ward, Rita slid down to the floor and wailed. Her head thrown back, she appealed to the fluorescent lights: "*Nu*, Tapkochka, what is going to become of us?"

I looked up from my feet and saw horror and bewilderment on the doctor's face. She tried to put a hand on Rita's shoulder, but Rita violently shrugged it off.

My father attempted to intercede.

"Rita Borisovna, I understand that it is painful, but it is not the end of the world."

"And what do you know about it?"

"I know that it must be hard, but soon you will see. . . . Even tomorrow we could go and help you find a new one."

My father looked to my mother for approval, to insure that he had not promised too much. He needn't have worried.

"A new one? What do you mean, a new one? I don't want a new one. Why don't you get yourself a new son? A new little liar? How about that? New. Everything we have now is new. New everything."

On the linoleum floor, Rita keened, rocking back and forth. She hiccupped, as though hyperventilating. Pausing for a moment, she looked up at my mother and told her to translate for the doctor. To tell her that she would not let Tapka die.

"I will sit here on this floor forever. And if the police come to drag me out I will bite them."

"Ritochka, this is crazy."

"Why is it crazy? My Tapka's life is worth more than a thousand dollars. Because we don't have the money, she should die here? It's not her fault."

Seeking rationality, my mother turned to Misha—Misha who had said nothing all this time except "My dear God."

"Misha, do you want me to tell the doctor what Rita said?"

Misha shrugged philosophically.

"Tell her or don't tell her, you see my wife has made up her mind. The doctor will figure it out soon enough."

"And you think this is reasonable?"

"Sure. Why not? I'll sit on the floor, too. The police can take us both to jail. Besides Tapka, what else do we have?"

Misha sat on the floor beside his wife.

I watched as my mother struggled to explain to the doctor what was happening. With a mixture of words and gesticulations, she got the point across. The doctor, after considering her options, sat down on the floor beside Rita and Misha. Once again, she tried to put her hand on Rita's shoulder. This time, Rita, who was still rocking back and forth, allowed it. Misha rocked in time to his wife's rhythm. So did the doctor. The three of them sat in a line, swaying together, like campers at a campfire. Nobody said anything. We looked at each other. I watched Rita, Misha, and the doctor swaying and swaying. I became mesmerized by the swaying. I wanted to know what would happen to Tapka; the swaying answered me.

The swaying said: Listen, shithead, Tapka will live. The doctor will perform the operation. Either money will be found or money will not be necessary.

I said to the swaying: This is very good. I love Tapka. I meant her no harm. I want to be forgiven.

The swaying replied: There is reality and then there is truth. The reality is that Tapka will live. But, let's be honest, the truth is you killed Tapka. Look at Rita; look at Misha. You see, who are you kidding? You killed Tapka and you will never be forgiven.

Treading Water

ROGER BURFORD-MASON

Roger Burford–Mason (1943–1998) worked as a teacher, writer, and broadcaster in England before moving to Canada in 1988. His first collection of short stories, *Telling the Bees,* published in Canada in 1990, drew on observations of life in the country of his birth, while his second collection, *Beaver Picture and Other Stories,* explored life in his beloved adopted country. His short story "The Rat-Catcher's Kiss," first published in *Exile* magazine, was short-listed for the prestigious Journey Prize, the annual award for short fiction by the best of Canada's new writers. Other stories have appeared in literary magazines in Canada and the United Kingdom He authored three biographies: one was on Roy Vernon Sowers, a legendary figure in the antiquarian book world; another, *Travels in the Shining Island,* was on James Evans, missionary and inventor of the Cree syllabary alphabet. His third biography was his last work, *A Grand Eye for Glory,* about Group of Seven founder Franz Johnston. It was published just before he died.

L ater, I found out it had been the hottest weekend since they began keeping records. It was as if the whole world had been stunned by the heat; even the cicadas were silent. The lake road was shimmering as I drove, illusions of water, mirages.

I thought of Mal Proctor sweating in his blubber, and I smiled.

I wasn't hot. The air conditioning in my truck is powerful, though it sucks up gas like you wouldn't believe. But as they say, you've got to give something to get something.

I hit the logging road and took the left trail which comes out onto a concession road above the lake. When I reached it, I parked and switched off the engine and the air with it. It was cool enough inside the cab, and I was parked under trees so I wasn't getting the direct sun.

The Basie tape I'd been listening to ended. I turned it over and let the seat back a little. I was late myself, and it was past three o'clock. Mal had said he'd check in around three. Typical. Not that I had anything particular to do, but I'd just as soon have been puttering around at the cottage where if I got too hot I could dive into the water to cool off.

Mal, you bastard, you'll get yours one day.

"Christ, Don, do you ever sleep sound!"

I opened my eyes. Mal's pink face hung at the window, peering in, shiny with a thin film of sweat. He had that worried look—partly squinting, partly disdainful—like he's thinking, "Shit, so what's this I got to deal with now?"

I touched the button and the window slid down smoothly. The dense heat of the afternoon was like a blow in the face.

"Electric windows, eh?" he said, screwing his plump face up. "Geez, Don, that's a real drain on your battery. Do you know what electric windows suck outta your battery?"

Go suck yourself, Mal.

"You're late," I said. "You stop for a full course dinner or something?"

He scowled at his watch, an irritated, involuntary glance.

"Goddam highways," he said.

I knew Mal. I knew I was supposed to infer that he was late because of some holdup on the road and not because he couldn't get himself together enough to leave at the right time which was usually what happened. "Why the fuck do you live in such a goddam remote place anyway?"

So people like you aren't always dropping in, Mal.

"Did you ever see it hot like this?" He was stooped over, getting back into his Chevy. He looked back at me with a complaining face. "It was some hot on the highway," he said. "We're talking hot."

"So? You got air."

"It's screwed or something," he said through his open window. "C'mon, let's go."

His air wasn't screwed. Edith told me a long time ago that he had disconnected it to save gas. I slid the window up and switched the air on again. I could see him drumming his fat fingers on his steering wheel as I turned the truck around and headed off back down the logging road to the lake.

We parked under the trees, and I got out and went over to him. He was writing in a small black notebook.

"Two hundred and thirteen kilometres," he said, looking up. "It's two hundred and thirteen kilometres, Don."

It was a complaint against geography, against geological history, against human settlement, against the arrangement of all the hills and streams, the small villages and road junctions that had been strung out along his route, out of spite, specifically to make his trip more difficult and time consuming.

"I put twenty bucks of gas in before I left," he worried. "Y'think that'll get me back too?"

I shrugged. I didn't know or care whether it would get him home or not. For all I cared, he could be stranded late at night by the roadside in some godforsaken little village where everyone is deaf and goes to bed at eight every evening.

"How much did you use getting here? You can figure it out."

He wrote some more in his black book.

"Just about make it if I don't use any while I'm here."

I snorted. What gas was he going to use shacked up at my cottage in the middle of the lake for the weekend?

"Did you bring a bag?"

"Christ, Don, give me a break, will you?"

He locked his door and checked all the others. "I didn't bring much."

Of course you didn't, you tightwad.

"But you did get some beers?"

He opened the trunk.

"Couldn't find a beer store open," he said, dragging a gaping sports bag out of the trunk with stuff just jammed into it.

Not that you had the whole week to get yourself organized and buy beer at least?

"The one at the end of your street was closed, eh?"

He straightened up and shrugged. "I told Edith to get me a two-four." He threw the bag into the boat. "But I guess she forgot."

"Hey, so you don't get to drink any beer this weekend," I said without a trace of humour. "Cause I've only got enough for me."

He gave me another worried look to see if I was joking. "Get outta here, Don," he said with an uncertain laugh. "You got beer. You wouldn't be stuck up here without any, I know you!"

About that at least he was right.

"Yeah, Mal," I said slowly, loading each word, "but what you got to worry about is am I going to give you any."

He swallowed and blinked furiously.

"I know you, Don," he repeated lamely. "Anyway, I brought you the Saturday papers from the city."

He settled himself in the middle of the boat. He was surprisingly nimble and assured in it considering he was so overweight and such a klutz every other way. "C'mon, I need some cool water and a cold beer."

I cast off the lines and jumped into the stern.

My cottage is on an island in the lake. I've only got a little old 9 h.p. two-stroke, so it's about twenty minutes from dock to dock. Call it three kilometres and you wouldn't be far out.

The water was like float-glass, deep, deep green and to my fingers trailing over the back, like warm silk. Even with Mal's bulk amidships, we seemed to be barely denting the surface, though in our wake a deep troughing *V* arrowed out towards the shoreline.

"Still here, huh?" Mal shouted as we rounded an outcrop of rock and began our approach to my dock. "It's a wonder that little shack doesn't just slide into the lake and disappear."

I cut the engine and immediately the only sound was the swish of the water under the gunwales as I steered us in.

"It'll outlast us both," I said. I leaned out of the boat and tied the stern line to the ring. "Take that forward line and run it through the ring."

But just getting up to attempt it, he nearly turned us over.

"It's O.K., Mal," I said, jumping out onto the dock. "Leave it alone, I'll fix her."

I tied the bow line securely and held out my hand towards Mal. He put his hand out to take mine.

"Not your hand, Mal," I said with an edge of scorn. "The bag. Hand me up the bag."

He grunted and held up the bag. I took it and turned abruptly to the cottage, leaving him to scramble out the best way he could.

It was cool in the cottage. I put Mal's bag down in the middle of the floor.

"Put that in your room, Mal," I said as he came in, but he pushed straight past me to get a beer from the refrigerator.

He came back into the living room, unscrewing his beer. "It's O.K.," I said when I saw he'd taken only one. "I'll get my own."

"What? Oh, yeah. Sorry, Don, didn't think."

Do you ever, fat man?

He sat down heavily into my big old comfortable armchair.

"I needed this."

I got a beer and uncapped it.

"Take your bag into your room, Mal. Don't leave it there where one of us is going to fall over it."

"Later," he said, nudging it with his foot to where it wouldn't be in the way.

"Now, Mal," I said.

He had taken up a magazine and was skimming through it. It was one of my *Practical Photographers* so there wasn't much in it that he'd understand.

"Jesus H.!" he said, holding a double page spread open towards me. "Look at her tits!"

I picked up his bag and took it to the door.

"Don, what the fuck?"

I threw it out the door and let the screen door shut with a bang.

"I said I'd fix it later," he said aggrieved. "What's the big deal? What d'you wanna go and do that for?"

"I like this place tidy, Mal," I said. "Bags in rooms, food in the cupboards, beer in the fridge, and the canoe paddles in their rack. T-I-D-Y, get it?"

He grunted and took another pull at his beer.

"I hope you didn't break anything in that bag," he grumbled. "Pitching it out like that."

"Was there something in it to break, Mal?" I said. "I mean, we know there wasn't any beer in it, don't we? What did you do, pack ketchup? Did you bring your own mayonnaise?"

He looked quizzically at me.

"What the fuck's with you, Don?" he said, the complaining note gone out of his voice. "You asked me to come up here, remember? I don't think it was me called you outta the blue to ask if I could come for the weekend. Did I do that?"

We were silent. I stood at the window watching the sun slanting across the still water. There's a smaller island than mine just opposite the cottage. It's about half a mile from my place at its nearest point. The whole of the side I was looking at was in deep shade. It would be so cool over there this time of the afternoon.

"I'm going to swim," I said.

I went straight out to the dock, peeling off my T-shirt as I went. I stepped out of my shorts and dove in.

I swam underwater for as long as I could hold my breath and then surfaced on my back, treading water. Mal was standing on the dock.

"What if some of these people that live around here come by?" he called.

"They'll see my cock," I shouted back, blowing water like a walrus. "Why don't you get outta that stuff and swim too? Then they could see two cocks!"

If yours isn't buried in all that blubber.

Mal shook his head and said something I didn't catch as I sucked a deep breath and dived. When I surfaced, I swam with steady strokes out towards the island.

A quarter of a mile out, I turned on my back. Mal was a small, plump figure on the dock.

"This is great," I said. "What more could you want on a hot day?"

I didn't raise my voice. I knew that on an afternoon like that, with no other sounds and the water still like a mirror, he'd be able to hear me even if I swam clear over to the island.

"Time was, I used to be a good swimmer," he said.

His voice carried strangely, sounding richer and deeper than usual. I swam backstroke towards the dock.

"When I was a kid I could really swim," he said, "before I let myself go—."

I laughed in disbelief. "You can swim?"

"Sure I can swim," he answered hotly. "You fucking jocks think you're the only guys can do things!"

I swam to the dock and pulled myself up onto the hot planks.

"Show me," I said. "I never heard Edith say you could swim."

"What the fuck would she know whether I can swim or not," he said sourly.

Not yet. It's not time yet.

"So show me."

"I will," he snapped. "You think I'm just a fat loser, huh? Just like her. Well, watch this."

He wrenched off his shirt, his shoes and his socks, and pulled off his baggy grey pants. For a moment he stood in his boxer shorts, poised to dive, and then he took a header.

He didn't dive badly, considering—well, not a belly flop, anyway. He broke the surface about forty feet from the dock.

"O.K.?" he challenged.

"Swim," I said. "I want to see you swim."

He duck-dived and swam away from the dock with short, steady strokes.

"That's not bad, Mal," I shouted. "I think you've got something there."

He swam out another hundred feet or so and then trod water.

"So what d'you think now?" There was a note of satisfaction in his voice. "Is that swimming or is that swimming?"

"That's swimming," I conceded. "You look as if you might have been pretty good at it once. A bit of practice and I bet you'd be a strong swimmer again."

But I noticed that coming in he wasn't pulling so strongly, and by the time he was hanging onto the dock, he was panting.

"You'd soon get it back," I said. "I guess it's like riding a bike or having sex: once you've done it, you never forget how."

He ducked under the water and came up, shaking the water off his head like a dog.

"I used to be good," he said again.

He bobbed a couple of times in the water for lift and then pulled himself up onto the dock.

"I bet I was one of the best swimmers in my year at school."

He lay on his back in the sunshine.

"That's neat water," he said. "It felt good."

I didn't say anything, and in a few moments he was snoring. I left him where he was and went to get another beer.

I did some chores around the cottage that took me a while, and when I went to find Mal, he was sitting in the big room with my photographic magazines looking for more girls with big tits. Two empty beer bottles lay on their sides on the rug, and he was swigging from a third.

"Help yourself to a beer or two," I said.

Edith is about the most generous person I know, and Mal is about the most shamelessly cheap. You went anywhere with him, it'd be in your car with your gas, and if you were eating with him in a restaurant, he always had to go to the men's room when the waiter came with the bill.

But it's hard to embarrass Mal about his cheapness. You can be oblique or you can be direct, it doesn't seem to faze him at all. I guess he's heard it all before and lived to sponge another day.

He put the bottle down in his lap and gave the irritating, choked-off laugh he can't help when he's caught out in some act of stinginess.

"I'll bring 'em next time, Don," he said, his eyes sliding away to the magazine. "My treat, eh?"

"Go in the kitchen and set the table, Mal," I said. "I'm making the supper so you can be the housemaid."

He laughed again and sucked some more beer out of his bottle. I turned back from the door.

"Do it now Mal," I said coldly. "Don't think I wouldn't throw your supper out there too."

I went into the kitchen to begin cooking, and in a moment Mal lumbered in.

"Lead the way, chief," he said. That's how Mal shows you he's going to do what you say, but he expects you to take the responsibility for it.

"Just look, Mal, you'll find everything."

He crashed about the kitchen, throwing open cupboards and rattling drawers, and in a few moments he'd set the table in a rudimentary fashion.

"We having wine or beer?"

I turned from the pork chops I was grilling.

"You didn't bring any wine, Mal," I said. "And I'm rationing the beers from here on. You already had more in an afternoon than I've had since I fetched them from the beer store Wednesday."

Mal laughed his choked laugh and opened the fridge, but I'd taken the rest of the beers out of the fridge and buried them in the earth-box under the back steps.

"This is childish, Don," he said.

Welshing on your obligations is childish, Mal.

"Put water out on the table," I said. "It'll be better for us anyway."

It wasn't the most fun of a meal I've ever had. Mal was pissed off that I'd taken the beer out of the fridge and wouldn't tell him where it was, and I was regretting letting Edith talk me into inviting him to the cottage for the weekend.

You owe me, Edith.

"So, Mark Spitz," I said as we were finishing, "you going to come for a swim with me after supper?"

He wiped his mouth on the back of his hand.

"You still think I can't handle it, eh?" he said. "You know what? Maybe I'll get into it again, get it back, like you said."

"Sure," I encouraged him. "You can swim at your condo, can't you? Or maybe join the Y?"

"Not the same as swimming in a deep fucking lake though, is it?"

I agreed it wasn't.

"You gonna swim far tonight?"

I told him that I usually took a long one in the evening. Daytimes I go in for comfort, to be cool; in the evenings I swim for the exercise.

"So, how far?"

"Maybe out to the island," I said. "Maybe right around it."

He looked doubtfully at me.

"No way can you swim around that island," he said flatly.

"Why's that, Mal?" I said with a calculated sneer. "Because you couldn't? I do it at least once a week."

"No way," he repeated. "It'd take you all night."

"An hour," I said.

"No way."

"An hour, that's all."

I got up and began to stack the dirty dishes. "And you're washing up, Mal," I said, carrying the dirty stuff to the draining board. "I'll dry."

"Only an hour?" he said. "Around the whole island?"

I nodded. "Once a week at least."

We finished up the dishes and went down to the dock. I began peeling off my clothes.

"How far do you reckon I could swim?" he said. "Right now, I mean, without any more practice?"

I shook my head. "Not far," I said. "You were puffing this afternoon and you only did a couple hundred yards."

"I was just getting my wind," he said. "I can handle it."

"How far do you think?" I said.

He thought about it.

"I bet I could make it to the island," he said. "If I took my time."

He looked as if he really believed it, too.

"Go for it," I said. "I'll swim beside you if you like."

He was almost grateful.

And he made it. O.K., so the last couple of hundred yards he was fading, but he made it to the rocks.

He lay back gasping for air, sucking it down greedily into his lungs.

"Now how are you going to get back?" I said when he'd got his breath back.

But doing it had really buoyed him up.

"I'm gonna swim back!"

I shadowed him back across the lake until he was near enough to the cottage not to be in any danger. Then I turned and swam back out to the eastern point of the island, down its length and back to the cottage. It took me about three quarters of an hour.

When I got back to the cottage and dried myself, Mal was still hyped about his swim.

"I wasn't in such bad shape that time," he said. "When I got back to this side, I mean. Jesus H., Don, a few more days and I'd have her licked!"

A few more days? God forbid.

"You can work on it at the Y," I said, going into the kitchen to put the kettle on to make tea. It was still a lovely, warm evening, but having been in the water for an hour, I was chilled.

Mal stood at the window and watched evening darken over the lake. All along the far shore, lights began to pinprick the gloaming as people settled down with their drinks, their evening meals, their satellite television and rented videos. Somewhere, way across the lake, someone was playing music with a steady thumping bass line that seemed to set the evening air throbbing.

"Don."

He'd come to stand in the kitchen doorway.

"I know you don't like me."

I didn't answer, and he went on as if he wasn't looking for an answer anyway.

"And I know you think I'm a heap of crap who can't do anything. Just like your precious fucking sister does."

"Maybe she'd think differently," I said quietly, "if you gave her a reason to."

He ignored me.

"And I don't give a fuck about her either, if you really want to know. But this is what I'm telling you now, and you'd better believe it. I'm gonna make it around the island before I leave tomorrow night."

I gave a short, mirthless laugh. "You're dreaming, Mal," I said. "It takes time."

"Fuck you!"

Oh, Edith, the things I do for you.

I had agreed to invite him to spend the weekend at the cottage, to give her a chance to clear her stuff out of their apartment. She was determined to leave him, and I didn't give her any arguments.

But I still didn't understand why he'd agreed to come. Usually cottages, boats, the outdoor life—he avoided them all like the plague.

"And he hits me," she had said at last when I'd got her to stop crying. "The last couple of times we argued, he hit me."

I hit him because he hit my little sister, sir. He can't do that.

I was thinking about it as I drifted off to sleep, and I was thinking about it when I woke up. It was ten to six.

As I stood at the kitchen sink filling the kettle to make coffee, I saw something dark bobbing in the water. Mal's head, over by the east end of the island.

I got my binoculars. It was Mal, all right, ploughing along with short, surprisingly strong strokes, clumsy but effective, and getting closer to the rocks at the east end of the island with every stroke.

I watched him as he crawled out of the water onto the fine sand beach beneath the rocks. He sat hunched over his knees, and I guessed he'd be panting heavily, but after a few moments he waded into the water again and began to swim back towards the cottage. It was just after seven when he came in looking for coffee.

"I could smell it half a mile out in the lake," he said. "Didn't you make some toast, too?"

At ten o'clock he set out again, only this time he rounded the rocks and I didn't see him for a little while. When I did see him again, maybe three quarters of an hour later, he was coming back on his tracks. He hadn't attempted to go right around.

I made a snack lunch and brought it down to the dock with a couple of beers. He ate without speaking, and when he'd finished, he went to his room and lay on the bed.

At three o'clock he swam again, strong, surging strokes away from the dock and then back again, and though a few bursts made him pant, he recovered very quickly and did some more.

"O.K.," he said. "Let's do it."

I was splitting logs for the fireplace when he found me. I pretended I didn't know what he meant.

"You know fucking well what," he said. "I'm going to show you once and for all. You're gonna eat shit, man."

I told him he was being stupid. That no one could do what he was aiming to do without building up a lot more strength and stamina.

"It's about three miles altogether," I warned him.

"Piss on it," he said. "I can do it. I know I can. And I want to see your smartass face when I do! Get in the fucking boat and follow me."

I went into the cottage and grabbed a paddle.

He swam strongly and steadily in the strokes of a good swimmer, not a weekend bather—not panting, not even breathing heavily. Just stroke after stroke, monotonous, steady, strong, moving inexorably forward.

We rounded the rocks at the east end of the island in twenty-five minutes and set out along the far side where the sun was still bright, though it was falling towards the horizon perceptibly as we went on.

"You were surprised I came," he said suddenly.

"I guess," I said.

"Edith asked you to invite me."

I didn't answer him.

"So she could pack and leave," he said, without breaking his steady stroke.

"How did you know?"

"I knew," he said.

"And you still came?"

"Why would I spoil her little game?"

"It's no game, Mal," I said. "She's leaving you."

"And she got big brother to set it up?"

"She got big brother to help her leave a man who was treating her like a piece of shit."

"You know why she's leaving me?"

"Yes, I know why. Because you're mean, and you like to put her down all the time, and you despise her and everything she likes and has ambitions for, and because you use your mind to screw her up."

"She said that?" He was treading water.

"No, I figured it out from how I feel about you."

He blew water.

"And I know she's tired of wondering whether she'll come home from work and find you ready to take a swing at her."

"That's a good one," he said.

"And while we're talking about it, Mal," I said angrily, "why do you hit her?"

He didn't speak for several seconds.

"Because she's always needling me, and because she's so fucking stupid," he said "And because she deserves it."

He was swimming again, speaking between breaths. I could hear he was labouring now.

"Mal," I said. "She should have left you years ago."

"Don't think she didn't try," he said, panting.

We were just rounding the western point of the island, but he was really beginning to suffer. His steady strokes had broken into short, choppy grabs at the water. He was hardly swimming at all. He moved the way his life did, no movement forward, just treading water.

"I don't think I can make it, Don," he said. "I'm about beat."

He moved in towards the canoe to hold the painter that was trailing in the water off the stern, but I dipped the paddle and manoeuvred out of his reach.

"Don't be stupid, Don," he said, an edge of alarm in his voice. He was treading water in circles, trying to grab the painter.

I sculled the canoe several yards away from him and watched him flounder.

"You might have guessed I wouldn't let you go on smacking Edith around," I said. "I've always looked out for her since we were kids."

I banged the paddle blade flat on the water. It sounded like a shot and sent a sheet of water into his face. "Who'd care if I let you drown?"

"Don't fuck around, Don," he said, splashing towards me. "I need to hold onto the rope."

I paddled further off, drawing him away from the rocks as he tried to grab the painter.

"What you need is a lesson, Mal," I said.

"Don!" There was real panic in his voice. He floundered frantically towards the canoe, but I eased away from him.

"Don," he pleaded, gulping for air. "Please. I can't. . . ."

He splashed frantically.

I sat in the canoe just out of his reach and watched him wonder if he was going to drown. His eyes were big with fear and he kept calling to me, "Don! Don!"

When he looked as if he really might go under, I pointed with the paddle.

"To your left, Mal," I said. "There's an outcrop of rock there. You can put your feet down."

He splashed around until his feet grounded on the rock.

"Are you crazy, Don? What the fuck do you think you're doing?"

He sounded strangely calm, almost resigned.

"Giving you a taste of the shit you've given Edith over the years, you miserable bastard," I said.

He sat back on the rocks in water up to his armpits.

"What are you going to do?"

I back-paddled and then sat at rest.

"I'm going to go back to the cottage and have a few beers," I said.

"What about me?"

"You'll manage," I said, sliding the paddle into the water.

"To your island?" He sounded frightened.

I circled him. "I don't care," I said.

"I don't know if I can make it," he said quietly.

"Then you've got two choices," I said. "You can sit on the rock until morning and hope someone comes by in a boat—but I imagine you know that up here it can get real cold at night. Or you can wait 'til you've got your strength back and try and swim back."

I pointed the canoe at the cottage and dug a few deep strokes.

"And Mal," I called back to him. "Edith has had enough of you, so if I hear you have so much as thought about doing anything about her leaving, I'll come over to your place and break your legs."

When I got back to the cottage, I got out the binoculars. Mal hadn't moved.

After I had changed, I made myself a sandwich and drank a beer. I packed Mal's bag and threw it on the dock and went back inside with the canoe paddle to put it in the rack. I looked at him with the binoculars and he still hadn't moved. I closed all the windows securely and locked the door.

I threw a short length of two-by-four into the canoe. It would take time, but he'd get back to his car eventually.

I cast off the lines and got into the boat. As I was starting the engine, I saw his head bobbing in the water.

It was midnight when I returned from the village and parked the truck under the trees by the dock on the lake road. Mal's Chevy was gone and there was no sign of the canoe. I guessed that he'd just set it adrift. It would turn up.

I got into the boat and rode the dark, friendly water, back to the cottage.

Stars

TILYA GALLAY HELFIELD

Born and raised in Ottawa, Tilya Gallay Helfield lived for many years in Montreal before moving to Toronto. Her writing has appeared in *The Fiddlehead, Viewpoints,* and *carte blanche.* Helfield is also a visual artist (printmaking, painting, and fibre art) whose work can be found in public and private collections in Canada, the United States and Europe.

After the wartime regulations were published in the newspapers during World War II, my mother told my father in no uncertain terms that she had quite enough to do sewing blackout curtains for the rest of the windows in the house, so he could just paint our cellar windows black. I remember scraping holes in the paint so I could peek inside. At night, the wartime blackout was so pervasive I imagined that God had painted the sky black like our cellar windows, and then chipped away a bit of the paint here and there so He could spy on me through the twinkling hole-stars.

We had other stars closer to home—stars mounted on cardboard hanging in the windows facing our street: bronze stars, for soldiers in the service; silver, for those missing in action; gold for those who had died in the service of our country.

We became accustomed to news of death and disaster during those wartime years. The Allied casualty lists were published on the front page of the daily papers and there were shocked whispers in the Jewish community about relatives lost in the death camps. Everyone we knew had at least one close relative in uniform overseas, but our block was particularly hard hit. Down the street from us, a bronze star hung in the Stokeley family's window for their oldest boy Frank, who was in the RCAF overseas. Another, next door in Mrs. Woollcott's window, for her husband, who was a commander in the navy. A third hung in the window directly across the street from our house for Major Coates, who had been fighting in North Africa since the beginning of the war.

My father claimed that he'd prefer to fight a war overseas any day than have to stay home with Mrs. Coates, who tried to use her grass-widowhood to get Dad to help her with chores around the house. Dad was exempted from war duty because he was almost forty, had three children, poor eyesight, and was doing important war work for the National Research Council, but I was embarrassed that he was one of the few men left on our block between the ages of twenty and forty who was not in uniform.

Next door to the Coates' house, the MacMillans displayed two bronze stars for their sons serving in Italy. The gold star in the Murphys' window was for their only son, who had died at Dunkirk. The silver star in Jamie West's window was for his father, a Brigadier, who was missing in action. The Fines hung a gold star in their window the day the telegraph boy rode up on his bicycle to inform them their son had died at Dieppe. But we continued going to work, attending school and participating in social events. My friend Myrna brought her brother Frank's letters, blackened by the censor's pen, to read aloud to our class. Mrs. Murphy put on her nurse's uniform and took the bus to work at the Ottawa Civic Hospital every morning. A bit long in the tooth for it, according to my mother, but it was wartime and beggars can't be choosers. Only Mrs. Woollcott acknowledged her fear and loneliness by lying on her living room chesterfield all day sipping Canadian Club from a Royal Doulton cup.

The closest relative we had in the war was my father's cousin Bernie from Glace Bay. He and my father had been named for a mutual grandfather, but my father was short and stout, with greying frizzy hair, thick horn-rimmed glasses, and clothes that reeked of tobacco. Bernie, fifteen years younger, was tall and slim, with dark wavy hair and eyes the colour of his Air Force blues. The moment he walked in the door, put his cap on my head and winked at me, I fell madly in love with him.

During the three weeks he was with us, he played tennis with my sister Joan and me and then bought us hot dogs and Orange Crushes to distract us while he tried to return Mum's graceful backhand. After supper, we all sat on the front veranda watching the sunset leech the colours from the sky until only Bernie's eyes and teeth and his glowing pipe gleamed in the indigo night.

When Bernie was sent overseas, I took his letters to school to read to my class and went with my mother to the post office twice a month to mail parcels to him. About six months after he shipped out, his letters stopped. A telegram finally arrived saying that he was missing in action, presumed dead. I remember going to school the next day and telling my friend Myrna how devastated we all were, and how she tossed her hair and said she didn't know why, it wasn't as if he was a brother, just a cousin. We heard months later that he had bailed out of his bomber during an air raid and was a prisoner of war somewhere in Germany.

He came home after the war terribly thin, with dark shadows under his dull eyes. He didn't say a word at dinner and when we sat out on the front veranda afterwards, he lit one cigarette from another with shaking hands. He married an Ottawa girl and went back to Nova Scotia to live. Years later, when he died, prematurely grey and stooped with disease and disappointment, I mourned the handsome young captain with the wavy hair and Air Force blue eyes who had died during that wartime summer so long ago.

Colonel MacMillan was an old man whose great white moustache, straw hat and carved cane made him look like the cover cartoon on an *Esquire* magazine. He and his wife, who were both very deaf, sat on their shaded front veranda in matching rocking chairs and listened to the radio with the volume turned up very loud. Every day at noon, twelve bongs rang out from Big Ben and a British voice announced, "Here is the BBC News."

Simultaneously, diagonally across the street, Radio-Canada began its news broadcast from the Duprés' front room, so that if you stood on an imaginary diagonal drawn between the Duprés' house and the MacMillans', you could listen to the news every noon hour in stereophonic French and English. It used to drive my mother crazy, and she would go around the house at lunchtime slamming all the windows shut against the noise.

The Dupré family, who lived two doors down from us, were the only French-Canadians on our block and the only Roman Catholics. They didn't socialize with any of the neighbours, but they were polite, said "*Bonjour*," and commented on the weather when we met.

Mme. Dupré was a short, plump woman with a large bosom and white hair that she wore rolled up over her ears and gathered into a bun at the nape of her neck. She spent her days cooking and cleaning for her large family, and we often got odd glimpses of her slapping bedding over the bedroom windowsills or beating scatter rugs against her veranda railing. Every morning she stomped outside, wearing a flowered apron over her housedress, and turned the garden hose on the fetid mess the milkman's horse made when it urinated in the street during its morning rounds.

M. Dupré, who was short and stocky, usually wore a dark blue suit, white shirt and conservative tie, his black hair slick as patent leather. After supper, however, he came out in his shirtsleeves and watered the small patch of grass in front of his house until it glittered like glass.

On Saturday afternoons, he pushed his lawn mower across the lawn while his blue shirtsleeves ballooned over their metal clips, and the back of his neck, sans collar and tie, reddened in the afternoon sun. He drove his big black Buick out of his driveway only to take the family to mass on Sunday mornings or for a drive in the Gatineau on Sunday afternoons.

M. Dupré was too old to be in uniform, his son Pierre too young. Pierre, his youngest child, was in my class at school although he was two years older. He had failed the year before because of truancy, bad marks, and misbehaviour in class. Perfectly bilingual, he easily passed his French orals, but failed his written French because of his bad spelling and grammar. He hung around with a gang of tough French guys who went to St. Pat's and wore black leather jackets and pomaded ducktails. They came to pick him up at all hours of the day and night in a '36 Buick with a defective muffler and broken tail lights, cursing at the tops of their voices with equal facility in English and French. Whenever they saw me sitting on my front veranda they slowed down and yelled, "Redhead, pissed in bed, five cents a cabbage head!" and roared off, gears grinding and tires squealing, laughing and yelling something in French about "*les maudits juifs*." I once asked my mother what a "piston bed" was and she went to speak to Mme. Dupré and after that there was a certain coolness between them. I didn't have to ask what *"maudits juifs"* meant.

The Duprés also had two daughters. The younger one, wearing impossibly high heels and a smart little chapeau, took the streetcar every day to her job as a sales clerk in a hat shop on Rideau Street. The older one had just moved from the Beauce with her son and her husband, a pale skinny man with a big Adam's apple and a weak chin, to live with her parents while she looked for a house in Ottawa, and her husband applied for a job in the Civil Service. She was having a difficult second pregnancy and spent most of her time in bed, so Mme. Dupré had to look after her grandson, Ti-Guy.

Our remaining neighbours were fairly equally divided between Protestants and Jews. We had little in common with the Protestants and they rarely spoke to us beyond passing the time of day, but the Jewish families often socialized together. Most of the parents were the same age, and their children played together and went to the same Hebrew school. These two solitudes, imposed by differing languages and religions, were broken only once that I can remember—during that one summer when Ti-Guy came to live on our street.

Ti-Guy was about four years old. He was an unhappy child with a pale blotchy face, dirty blond hair, watery blue eyes, and runny nose. His name was Guy, (pronounced "Gee" with a hard G), the same as his father's, so they called him "Petit Guy" or "Ti-Guy" in joual. Mme. Dupré was constantly changing his clothes, wiping his dripping nose, washing his dirty hands and face and calling for him from various upstairs windows, *"Ti-Guy, Ti-Guy, viens icitte."*

Ti-Guy lived under a constant black cloud. Once he ran directly into the path of a bakery truck. Mike Melamed, who lived over his father's drugstore on Rideau, was playing football in front of the Duprés' house. He had just made a long spiralling pass to his brother Mark, who let the football fall to the ground and dived instead for Ti-Guy, scooping him up in his arms and hurling himself onto our lawn as the truck screeched to a shuddering halt. Ti-Guy's grandmother ran out of her house shrieking and sobbing with relief and carried him home to clean him up. The neighbourhood women returned to the chairs on their verandas, shaking their heads with relief.

After that, his grandmother tied him with a harness and rope to the tree in the front yard to keep him from running into the road, but he always worked himself loose and took off again. He scraped his knees on our gravel driveway, cut his hands on the thorns of the Murphys' rose bushes, and fell out of our apple tree. He teased the Woollcotts' sheepdog until the poor beast lost its patience and nipped him on the ankle. He stole apples from the MacMillans' front yard and chased their cats under their veranda, only to reappear with angry red claw marks down his face.

One day, my brother Ray decided that Ti-Guy would make a perfect victim in an ant-eating torture scenario he'd devised. He and his friends, Stephen Woollcott and Donnie Stokeley, tied Ti-Guy up and were in the process of burying him neck-deep in the hole they were digging in the driveway at the side of our house, when one of the boards shoring up the sides of the hole came loose and dirt began to slip down like sand in an hourglass, burying Ti-Guy. We heard the boys' screams while we were still at the breakfast table and my mother, Joan and I raced down the summer-kitchen steps to the edge of the hole. The crown of Ti-Guy's small blond head was barely visible above the sifting dirt. My mother kicked off her mules, gathered up her cretonne dressing gown and leaped into the hole. She grabbed Ti-Guy by the hair and pulled his face clear so he could breathe, while we all scrabbled frantically in the shifting dirt. When Mum finally pulled him out, she dusted him off and turned on Ray.

"How could you do such a stupid thing?" she shrieked.

"It wasn't my fault. We were just playing 'Prisoner,'" Ray sobbed. "How was I to know the dirt would fall in?"

Mum told Joan and me, "Take Ti-Guy home to his grandmother at once. Offer her my sincere apologies and assure her that Ray will be severely punished." She sent Stephen and Donnie home and turned back to Ray. "You go to your room. We'll see what your father has to say when he gets home." This deferral of punishment was a favourite ploy of hers, since it gave Ray an entire dread-filled day in which to anticipate my father's return. Joan and I each took one of Ti-Guy's grimy hands and led him to his grandmother's house, two doors away.

Mme. Dupré was watering the morning glories along her veranda railing when she caught sight of us. *"Doux Jésus!"* she cried, dropping the hose so that it spattered her shoes and stockings. *"Que c'est qu'y a faitte encore!"*

I began to explain, but my French just wasn't up to it. Mme. Dupré administered several good swats to Ti-Guy's rear end and hauled him into the house, and we could hear his howls through their open windows all the way back to our house.

But Ti-Guy couldn't be discouraged. The next day, Joan picked some berries from Mrs. Kantor's honeysuckle hedge next door while the old lady was preoccupied with her afternoon soap opera.

Joan set them out on three little dolls' dishes on her tea table on our veranda and went into the house to get her dolls dressed for a tea party. When she came back out, Ti-Guy was sitting on one of the small chairs, whimpering and rubbing his stomach. The tiny plate in front of him was empty. Suddenly he jumped up, vomited into my mother's hydrangea bushes and ran home crying.

The next day he appeared none the worse for wear, to my enormous relief, because I had lain sleepless all night, terrified that he had been poisoned.

The next afternoon, Ti-Guy climbed up on the railing of our veranda and fell about six feet into the driveway below. He got up, rubbing the back of his neck, and ran home crying to his grandmother, who put down the bowl of peas she was shelling and took him into the house. When he came out again, his hands and face were washed and he was wearing a clean shirt, but he didn't play. He just sat on his front steps, whimpering and rubbing his neck. His parents took him to the hospital after supper—his father carried him, wrapped in a blue blanket, to the car and put him in his mother's lap in the front seat while Mme. Dupré stood at the curb beside her husband, twisting her apron in her hands.

We were sitting out front after supper the next evening, watching my father water the front lawn, when the entire Dupré family drove up to their house and got out of the car. Mme. Dupré and her daughters were crying. M. Dupré and his son-in-law walked slowly up the front walk with their hands clasped behind their backs. Even Pierre looked strangely subdued. Ti-Guy was nowhere in sight.

Mrs. Murphy came running from her house across the street. "It was the meningitis," she told my mother. "He never had a chance, poor little thing." She and my mother, who until then had merely nodded politely in passing, now clung to each other wordlessly. All the women in the neighbourhood came out of their houses and gathered at the foot of our front steps, as if drawn by a magnetic force. Even Mrs. Woollcott felt her way unsteadily down her front steps, clutching her robe around her with shaking hands, tears streaming down her face.

I knew that soldiers were dying in battle overseas, that bombs were destroying the great cities of Europe. But now it seemed that death had leaped the vast ocean like a stream and settled into the street where we lived.

My mother stood on our front lawn clasping her hands to her chest as though they covered an open wound. At last she went into the house. I followed her into the kitchen, where she had begun to pull out bowls and spatulas and measuring utensils from cupboards and drawers. She measured out flour and sugar and some of our precious butter, mixed the batter with short vicious strokes, slapped out the dough on the wooden board with the rolling pin and slashed it with wicked jabs of the cookie cutter. While the cookies were baking, she scoured the counters and sloshed steaming soapy water over the linoleum floor, dabbing angrily at her tear-filled eyes with the wad of Kleenex she always kept rolled up in her sleeve.

When the cookies were ready, she told me to bring them over to the Dupré house. I made my way up their walk with leaden feet and stood at the door, desperately trying to remember the few appropriate French expressions I knew. I had never been inside their house, and I didn't know how Catholics behaved when there was a death in the family. The warm plate slid between my damp hands and the smell of oatmeal was making me queasy. When M. Dupré opened the door, I stammered in English, "My, my mother sent these. Our deepest sympathies for your loss."

He led me inside, down a narrow hall to the kitchen, where the family sat at a table covered with a blue checked cloth, drinking tea. The house was just like ours, except for the cross hanging on the wall. I'd always thought they were different from my family, but they acted just like Jews did when someone had died.

I put the plate of cookies on the table and repeated, "My mother sent these. Our deepest sympathy for your loss."

They looked at me with red-rimmed eyes. No one spoke. I didn't know what else to say. To my horrified embarrassment, I burst into tears and ran out of the house.

I ran home, climbed the stairs to my room, went in and shut the door. I opened my closet door, pulled out a canvas board and my paint box and pencils, and sat down at my desk and began to sketch. When I was satisfied with my drawing, I squeezed out tubes of cadmium yellow medium and gold ochre, mixing and blending the colours on my palette until I had just the right shade of gold. Then I began to paint.

The next afternoon, I watched the Duprés get into their car and drive away to the funeral home for the wake. I checked to make sure that my painting was dry, then slipped over to their house and hung up my painted gold star in their front window for everyone to see.

Prerequisites for Sleep

JENNIFER STONE

Jennifer Stone lives in Mineville, Nova Scotia, with her husband and son. Her fiction has appeared in *Other Voices, FreeFall, The Fiddlehead,* the *Wascana Review, carte blanche,* and *The Antigonish Review.*

It rained through the night and early morning, tearing the petals from the lilies in the garden. They lay on the ground like pieces of satin tinged with rust. The sky looked bruised, as if it had more crying to do. Anita stood in the kitchen looking out at the day through the screen of the back door. The thin lines of mesh made everything appear slightly out of focus.

"Some people believe that it is good luck to have rain on your wedding day," Judith said cheerfully.

Anita poured coffee into her favourite mug, a black one with a large white A on the side and a chip in the rim, then sat down at the table next to her aunt. Lately, she thought of her aunt as Saint Judith, Saint Jude for short. What else could she be after taking on the responsibility of raising Anita when her mother and father died? Judith had given up the career of an overseas correspondent to become a weekly columnist and an instant parent. In fourteen years, she had never heard the woman complain. Any regrets, if she had them, were not voiced.

"Kevin's mother has rented enough tents to create an upscale refugee camp," Anita said, scooping two heaping teaspoons of sugar into her coffee.

"It is nice of the Sinclairs to host the wedding." Judith ventured. "Kevin's a dear, but you know we would have never been able to put on a spread for that family. Oh, they are always pleasant to everyone and not snobby by any means, but they are used to certain things. Do me a favour, don't get so used to certain things that you won't eat my macaroni and cheese casserole."

"Well Kevin is her only child," Anita said. "Some women like taking care of such details. I'm not one of them. The things I decided to take care of are more than enough wedding details for me. And I don't think you have to worry about the casserole. It's still my favourite." The spoon, hitting the mug as she stirred, underlined her words with porcelain-steel music.

"I know what you mean about wedding details," said Judith. "They aren't my forte, that's for sure."

Reprinted with permission from Jennifer Stone. First published in carte blanche — carte-blanche.org.

"Do you ever wish that you had married?" Anita said. She searched her aunt's face as she posed the question. Up until she was sixteen, Anita would look for her mother in Judith's face; but the more she had looked the more she noticed the differences between the two sisters. What she saw these days was that the years had been good to Judith. Her mother, no longer accumulating time, existed only in the photo albums and old videos stored in the hall closet.

"Oh, I think if the right person had come along, I would have married," said Judith, "but who's to say that the right person still can't show up. Fifty-two is not that old you know." Her voice shifted and she leaned back in the kitchen chair to look directly at her niece. "Don't go thinking that you're the reason I didn't get married. I had plenty of offers, just none that I could live with."

Anita brushed her teeth and jumped into the shower, surveying her body as she adjusted the water temperature. She had put on a few pounds since they announced the engagement, but not a noticeable amount. At her final fitting last week, the dress was perfect. How lucky she had been to find one she liked that was on sale.

It was at a little boutique that Kevin's mother had recommended, located in Barberry Market, an area of old stone houses that had been turned into upscale businesses. The signs hanging from each were understated and catered to a clientele that didn't need to be screamed at. She drove down with Judith one afternoon, thinking they would just look. They found a parking spot on the other side of a street split by a median with a couple of benches and some annual beds. It was the end of April and the empty gardens filled the air with an organic smell of damp soil.

They looked at several dresses, but she kept coming back to the same one. "Go ahead, try it on," the woman said, unzipping the clear plastic so the gown could be viewed better.

Her reflection: auburn hair, freckled skin, white dress, shouted at her without words. Was she ready for this? She didn't know whether to laugh or cry.

"It suits you," Judith said.

"This particular gown is part of a special promotion," the salesclerk said. "Reduced because of the arrival of new stock."

Today that special promotion was hanging on the back of her bedroom door.

They met the rest of the girls at the beauty salon at eleven, Ingrid and Wendy, Anita's friends and Kevin's cousin Michelle, since he didn't have a sister.

Ingrid greeted them with over-exaggerated hugs and kisses that made Anita feel like a plush toy that had been returned after an unplanned absence. "You do realize," Ingrid teased, "that by this time tomorrow you will no longer be a single entity but part of a pair."

"Like shoes," laughed Wendy.

"Or salt and pepper shakers," said Michelle.

"I don't know if I should be jealous or relieved," said Ingrid.

By the time they left the salon, the sky was clear, the sidewalks, nothing but strips of glare. Anita wondered whether or not this had any bearing on her luck, now that both the sun and the rain had made an appearance on her wedding day.

"Just in time for photos," Judith said. Leave it to Judith to say the right thing.

Judith excelled at saying the right thing. After the funeral, she and Anita had returned to the house, which was empty for the first time in days. Someone had tidied up, depriving them of the much-needed busy work. Anita flopped down on the sofa, no longer feeling like the preteen who, just the previous week, had gone to a sleepover with her friends. She had returned the following morning to find a police car waiting in the driveway. Anita resented that loss almost as much as she resented her absent mother and father and the stoned kid who ran the red light. Judith came in and sat down next to her. "I always wanted to learn how to play one of those things," she said, pointing to the Nintendo system on the shelf below the TV. "How 'bout we order a pizza and you can teach me?"

That night they slowly allowed themselves to laugh, and yell at the characters that jumped across the television screen, and then to slip into a realm where silliness prevailed. Afterwards they slept, waking late the following day with a new understanding of the roles they had inherited in each other's lives, knowing that anything either one of them did from now on would impact the other.

Judith gave her away. That was something that Anita insisted on and Kevin agreed. It was only right. They walked down the aisle arm in arm amidst harp music and the rustle of satin and silk, neither one shaking or teary eyed, no mention of what Anita's mother or father may have felt; no need to, they had stopped dwelling on the past years before.

"Kevin's uncle Gerald would be glad to walk you down the aisle," his mother had suggested along with several other options, all male as dictated by tradition. His mother was not one for

altering institutions. But she was also not one for fighting small battles so in the end she concurred.

Mrs. Sinclair liked Anita and thought of her as hard-working
and smart, not some spoiled bimbo who couldn't see past her next
visit to the spa. Although she had always been comfortable, the
older woman had learned the same lessons that Anita had at an
early age; that nothing was to be taken for granted and that important things can disappear, the way her brother had disappeared
into the river; and afterwards, the way her mother had disappeared
into the bottle. Of all the girls that Kevin had been involved with,
Anita had the most substance. The least she could do for the girl
is give her a beautiful wedding. And a beautiful wedding dress
for that matter, no one needs to know of the arrangement made
between her and the owner of the boutique.

I think I'm switching to autopilot," Kevin whispered in her ear part
way through the receiving line.

Anita smiled. She could think of nothing better than sitting
down and putting her feet up. "Tell me again why we didn't consider eloping," she retorted while waiting for his grandfather to
close the gap in the stream of people. Kevin laughed and bent to
kiss her enthusiastically on the mouth. The room burst into a round
of applause.

"Okay break it up," said Kevin's grandfather leaning forward
to peck Anita on the cheek.

Next in line was Richard. His face, like a statue with stone eyes
and a rigid jaw, moved towards her. "Will you be going by Mrs.
Sinclair now, or do you intend to keep your own name?" His question surprised her.

At dinner, Judith had made a speech that was both happy and sad.
She talked about their life together and about new beginnings, the
one they undertook fourteen years earlier and the one that Anita
and Kevin were now embarking on. "I believe that Anita can
manage anything that comes her way, including you, Kevin," she
quipped. A statement that was followed by laughter, along with
whoops and whistles from Kevin's friends.

The rest of the day went off without a hitch. Everyone would
remember it as a lovely event. Mrs. Sinclair had taken their wishes
and transformed them into a choreographed work of art. Anita
tried to imagine how Kevin's mother would use those skills on the
many committees and boards that she was a member of.

She was curled up in the king-size bed next to Kevin. He had
slipped quickly into sleep after they had made love. To her, it

doesn't arrive as easy so she slid out from under the covers and grabbed the complimentary terry robe. The hotel room was on the top floor, overlooking the harbour. A fog rolled above the water looking pinkish yellow from city lights that never allow darkness to settle or stars to shine. Standing in the window, Anita continued to revisit the day in her thoughts. For her this is a nightly habit, rehashing the events of her life in twenty-four-hour segments, one of her prerequisites for sleep.

Richard had come to the wedding. Richard who managed university the way she did, on part-time jobs and student loans, barely making ends meet as he worked his way towards being a heart specialist. She knew he would be excellent, he had already filled a hole in hers.

"It's up to you," he had said to her, "but I think you should go. Why stay home all alone when you can go out and enjoy yourself?"

So she decided to go, taking transit to the closest intersection then walking the rest of the way. The music could be heard all the way down the street, mostly bass, turned up and throbbing like a heart. It started to rain and she was without an umbrella so she ran. A little later, when she was standing in a crowd chatting and sipping a rum and coke, she felt two hands rest on her shoulders and heard a voice from behind. "Even soggy, you're a sight for sore eyes."

That night with Kevin was a fluke. Who would have thought they would run into each other at a party that Richard couldn't attend because he had to work. She and Kevin had been together several years earlier, the summer she was eighteen. No commitments, there were universities to attend and careers to secure. Sex was something that had happened between them. It happened again, aided by memories and alcohol.

There was the baby to think about. She had been on antibiotics at the time, for an ear infection. A warning came with her birth control pills. She had read it only once in her teens when she first started taking the oral contraceptives. She considered an abortion, discussed the option with her doctor. He told her she needed to make a decision quickly, but she let the deadline pass. It wasn't that she was religious or that she thought it was wrong. Some days it seemed perfectly right; other days, not right for her.

The child could belong to either of them; both have similar features. Kevin was so excited when she told him. "We'll get married," he said. "I hope it's a girl."

Anita had weighed her options and made her decision. It was a decision she would consider every time she handed over her baby to the nanny that Kevin's mother offered to procure, and when she returned to university to continue her education debt free. Later she would consider it again when her daughter walked down the aisle as flower girl at Judith's wedding and upon seeing a photo announcing that Richard had become Head of Cardiology. She would consider it every night for the rest of her life. This was something she knew for a fact while standing in the window watching the shoreline become obscure.

As Birds Bring Forth the Sun

ALISTAIR MACLEOD

Alistair MacLeod (b. 1936) grew up in Cape Breton, Nova Scotia. He still spends his summers there, writing in a clifftop cabin looking west toward Prince Edward Island. He financed his education by working as a logger, a miner, and a fisherman, and he writes vividly and sympathetically about such work. He studied at Nova Scotia Teachers College, St. Francis Xavier University, the University of New Brunswick, and Notre Dame, where he took his Ph.D. He was a professor of English at the University of Windsor for many years. Macleod published two internationally acclaimed collections of short stories: *The Lost Salt Gift of Blood* (1976) and *As Birds Bring Forth the Sun* (1986). MacLeod's novel, the powerful *No Great Mischief*, was published in 1999.

Once there was a family with a Highland name who lived beside the sea. And the man had a dog of which he was very fond. She was large and grey, a sort of staghound from another time. And if she jumped up to lick his face, which she loved to do, her paws would jolt against his shoulders with such force that she would come close to knocking him down and he would be forced to take two or three backward steps before he could regain his balance. And he himself was not a small man, being slightly over six feet and perhaps one hundred and eighty pounds.

She had been left, when a pup, at the family's gate in a small handmade box and no one knew where she had come from or that she would eventually grow to such a size. Once, while still a small pup, she had been run over by the steel wheel of a horse-drawn cart which was hauling kelp from the shore to be used as fertilizer.

It was in October and the rain had been falling for some weeks and the ground was soft. When the wheel of the cart passed over her, it sunk her body into the wet earth as well as crushing some of her ribs; and apparently the silhouette of her small crushed body was visible in the earth after the man lifted her to his chest while she yelped and screamed. He ran his fingers along her broken bones, ignoring the blood and urine which fell upon his shirt, trying to soothe her bulging eyes and her scrabbling front paws and her desperately licking tongue.

The more practical members of his family, who had seen run-over dogs before, suggested that her neck be broken by his strong hands or that he grasp her by the hind legs and swing her head against a rock, thus putting an end to her misery. But he would not do it.

Instead, he fashioned a small box and lined it with woollen remnants from a sheep's fleece and one of his old and frayed shirts. He placed her within the box and placed the box behind the stove and then he warmed some milk in a saucepan and sweetened it with sugar. And he held open her small and trembling jaws with his left hand while spooning in the sweetened milk with his right, ignoring the needle-like sharpness of her small teeth. She lay in the box most of the remaining fall and into the early winter, watching everything with her large brown eyes.

Although some members of the family complained about her presence and the odour from the box and the waste of time she involved, they gradually adjusted to her; and as the weeks passed by, it became evident that her ribs were knitting together in some form or other and that she was recovering with the resilience of the young. It also became evident that she would grow to a tremendous size, as she outgrew one box and then another and the grey hair began to feather from her huge front paws. In the spring she was outside almost all of the time and followed the man everywhere; and when she came inside during the following months, she had grown so large that she would no longer fit into her accustomed place behind the stove and was forced to lie beside it. She was never given a name but was referred to in Gaelic as *cù mòr glas*, the big grey dog.

By the time she came into her first heat, she had grown to a tremendous height, and although her signs and her odour attracted many panting and highly aroused suitors, none was big enough to mount to her, and the frenzy of their disappointment and the longing of her unfulfilment were more than the man could stand. He went, as the story goes, to a place where he knew there was a big dog. A dog not as big as she was, but still a big dog, and he brought him home with him. And at the proper time he took the *cù mòr glas* and the big dog down to the sea where he knew there was a hollow in the rock which appeared only at low tide. He took some sacking to provide footing for the male dog and he placed the *cù mòr glas* in the hollow of the rock and knelt beside her and steadied her with his left arm under her throat and helped position the male dog above her and guided his blood-engorged penis. He was a man used to working with the breeding of animals, with the guiding of rams and bulls and stallions and often with the funky smell of animal semen heavy on his large and gentle hands.

The winter that followed was a cold one and ice formed on the sea and frequent squalls and blizzards obliterated the offshore islands and caused the people to stay near their fires much of the time, mending clothes and nets and harness and waiting for the change in season. The *cù mòr glas* grew heavier and even larger until there was hardly room for her around the stove or under the table. And then one morning, when it seemed that spring was about to break, she was gone.

The man and even his family, who had become more involved than they cared to admit, waited for her but she did not come. And as the frenzy of spring wore on, they busied themselves with readying their land and their fishing gear and all of the things that so desperately required attention. And then they were into summer and fall and winter and another spring which saw the birth of the man and his wife's twelfth child. And then it was summer again.

That summer the man and two of his teenaged sons were pulling their herring nets about two miles offshore when the wind began to blow off the land and the water began to roughen. They became afraid that they could not make it safely back to shore, so they pulled in behind one of the offshore islands, knowing that they would be sheltered there and planning to outwait the storm. As the prow of their boat approached the gravelly shore, they heard a sound above them, and looking up they saw the *cù mòr glas* silhouetted on the brow of the hill which was the small island's highest point.

"*M'eudal cù mòr glas,*" shouted the man in his happiness—*m'eudal* meaning something like dear or darling; and as he shouted, he jumped over the side of his boat into the waist-deep water, struggling for footing on the rolling gravel as he waded eagerly and awkwardly toward her and the shore. At the same time, the *cù mòr glas* came hurtling down toward him in a shower of small rocks dislodged by her feet; and just as he was emerging from the water, she met him as she used to, rearing up on her hind legs and placing her huge front paws on his shoulders while extending her eager tongue.

The weight and speed of her momentum met him as he tried to hold his balance on the sloping angle with the water rolling gravel beneath his feet, and he staggered backwards and lost his footing and fell beneath her force. And in that instant again, as the story goes, there appeared over the brow of the hill six more huge grey dogs hurtling down towards the gravelled strand. They had never seen him before; and seeing him stretched prone beneath their mother, they misunderstood, like so many armies, the intention of their leader.

They fell upon him in a fury, slashing his face and tearing aside his lower jaw and ripping out his throat, crazed with blood-lust or duty or perhaps starvation. The *cù mòr glas* turned on them in her own savagery, slashing and snarling and, it seemed, crazed by their mistake; driving them bloodied and yelping before her, back over the brow of the hill where they vanished from sight but could still be heard screaming in the distance. It all took perhaps little more than a minute.

The man`s two sons, who were still in the boat and had witnessed it all, ran sobbing through the salt water to where their mauled and mangled father lay; but there was little they could do other than hold his warm and bloodied hands for a few brief moments. Although his eyes "lived" for a small fraction of time, he could not speak to them because his face and throat had been torn away, and of course there was nothing they could do except to hold and be held tightly until that too slipped away and his eyes glazed over and they could no longer feel his hands holding theirs. The storm increased and they could not get home and so they were forced to spend the night huddled beside their father's body. They were afraid to try to carry the body to the rocking boat because he was so heavy and they were afraid that they might lose even what little of him remained and they were afraid also, huddled on the rocks, that the dogs might return. But they did not return at all and there was no sound from them, no sound at all, only the moaning of the wind and the washing of the water on the rocks.

In the morning they debated whether they should try to take his body with them or whether they should leave it and return in the company of older and wiser men. But they were afraid to leave it unattended and felt that the time needed to cover it with protective rocks would be better spent in trying to get across to their home shore. For a while they debated as to whether one should go in the boat and the other remain on the island, but each was afraid to be alone and so in the end they managed to drag and carry and almost float him toward the bobbing boat. They laid him face-down and covered him with what clothes there were and set off across the still-rolling sea. Those who waited on the shore missed the large presence of the man within the boat and some of them waded into the water and others rowed out in skiffs, attempting to hear the tearful messages called out across the rolling waves.

The *cù mòr glas* and her six young dogs were never seen again, or perhaps I should say they were never seen again in the same way. After some weeks, a group of men circled the island tentatively in their boats but they saw no sign. They went again and then again but found nothing. A year later, and grown much braver, they beached their boats and walked the island carefully, looking into the small sea caves and the hollows at the base of the wind-ripped trees, thinking perhaps that if they did not find the dogs, they might at least find their whitened bones; but again they discovered nothing.

The *cù mòr glas*, though, was supposed to be sighted here and there for a number of years. Seen on a hill in one region or silhouetted on a ridge in another or loping across the valleys or glens in the early morning or the shadowy evening. Always in the area of the half perceived. For a while she became rather like the Loch Ness monster or the Sasquatch on a smaller scale. Seen but not recorded. Seen when there were no cameras. Seen but never taken.

The mystery of where she went became entangled with the mystery of whence she came. There was increased speculation about the handmade box in which she had been found and much theorising as to the individuals who might have left it. People went to look for the box but could not find it. It was felt she might have been part or a *buidseachd* or evil spell cast on the man by some mysterious enemy. But no one could go much farther than that. All of this caring for her was recounted over and over again and nobody missed any of the ironies.

What seemed literally known was that she had crossed the winter ice to have her pups and had been unable to get back. No one could remember ever seeing her swim; and in the early months at least, she could not have taken her young pups with her.

The large and gentle man with the smell of animal semen often heavy on his hands was my great-great-great-grandfather, and it may be argued that he died because he was too good at breeding animals or that he cared too much about their fulfilment and well-being. He was no longer there for his own child of the spring who, in turn, became my great-great-grandfather, and he was perhaps too much there in the memory of his older sons who saw him fall beneath the ambiguous force of the *cù mòr glas*, the youngest boy in the boat was haunted and tormented by the awfulness of what he had seen. He would wake at night screaming that he had seen the *cù mòr glas a'bhàis*, the big grey dog of death, and his screams filled the house and the ears and minds of the listeners, bringing home again and again the consequences of their loss. One morning, after a night in which he saw the *cù mòr glas a'bhàis* so vividly that his sheets were drenched with sweat, he walked to the high cliff which faced the island and there he cut his own throat with a fish knife and fell into the sea.

The other brother lived to be forty, but, again so the story goes, he found himself in a Glasgow pub one night, perhaps looking for answers, deep and sodden with the whisky which had become his anaesthetic. In the half darkness he saw a large, grey-haired man sitting by himself against the wall and mumbled something to him. Some say he saw the *cù mòr glas a'bhàis* or uttered the name. And perhaps the man heard the phrase through ears equally affected by drink and felt he was being called a dog or a son of a bitch or something of that nature. They rose to meet one another and struggled outside into the cobblestoned passageway behind the pub where, most improbably, there were supposed to be six other large, grey-haired men who beat him to death on the cobblestones, smashing his bloodied head into the stone again and again before vanishing and leaving him to die with his face turned to the sky. The *cù mòr glas a'bhàis* had come again, said his family, as they tried to piece the tale together.

This is how the *cù mòr glas a'bhàis* came into our lives, and it is obvious that all of this happened a long, long time ago. Yet with succeeding generations it seemed the spectre had somehow come to stay and that it had become *ours*—not in the manner of an unwanted skeleton in the closet from a family`s ancient past but more in the manner of something close to a genetic possibility. In the deaths of each generation, the grey dog was seen by some—by women who were to die in childbirth; by soldiers who went forth to the many wars but did not return; by those who went forth to feuds or dangerous love affairs; by those who answered mysterious midnight messages; by those who swerved on the highway to avoid the real or imagined grey dog and ended in masses of crumpled steel. And by one professional athlete who, in addition to his ritualized athletic superstitions, carried another fear or belief as well. Many of the man's descendants moved like careful haemophiliacs, fearing that they carried unwanted possibilities deep within them. And others, while they laughed, were like members of families in which there is a recurrence over the generations of repeated cancer or the diabetes that comes to those beyond middle age. The feeling of those who may say little to others but who may say often and quietly to themselves, "It has not happened to me," while adding always the cautionary "yet."

I am thinking all of this now as the October rain falls on the city of Toronto and the pleasant, white-clad nurses pad confidently in and out of my father's room. He lies quietly amidst the whiteness, his head and shoulders elevated so that he is in that hospital position of being neither quite prone nor yet sitting. His hair is white upon his pillow and he breathes softly and sometimes unevenly, although it is difficult ever to be sure.

My five grey-haired brothers and I take turns beside his bedside, holding his heavy hands in ours and feeling their response, hoping ambiguously that he will speak to us, although we know that it may tire him. And trying to read his life and ours into his eyes when they are open. He has been with us for a long time, well into our middle age. Unlike those boys in that boat of so long ago, we did not see him taken from us in our youth. And unlike their youngest brother who, in turn, became our great-great-grandfather, we did not grow into a world in which there was no father's touch. We have been lucky to have this large and gentle man so deep into our lives.

No one in this hospital has mentioned the *cù mòr glas a'bhàis*. Yet as my mother said ten years ago, before slipping into her own death as quietly as a grownup child who leaves or enters her parents' house in the early hours, "It is hard to *not* know what you do know."

Even those who are most sceptical, like my oldest brother who has driven here from Montreal, betray themselves by their nervous actions. "I avoided the Greyhound bus stations in both Montreal and Toronto," he smiled upon his arrival, and then added, "Just in case."

He did not realize how ill our father was and has smiled little since then. I watch him turning the diamond ring upon his finger, knowing that he hopes he will not hear the Gaelic phrase he knows too well. Not having the luxury, as he once said, of some who live in Montreal and are able to pretend they do not understand the "other" language. You cannot *not* know what you do know.

Sitting here, taking turns holding the hands of the man who gave us life, we are afraid for him and for ourselves. We are afraid of what he may see and we are afraid to hear the phrase born of the vision. We are aware that it may become confused with what the doctors call "the will to live" and we are aware that some beliefs are what others would dismiss as "garbage." We are aware that there are men who believe the earth is flat and that the birds bring forth the sun.

Bound here in our own particular mortality, we do not wish to see or see others see that which signifies life's demise. We do not want to hear the voice of our father, as did those other sons, calling down his own particular death upon him.

We would shut our eyes and plug our ears, even as we know such actions to be of no avail. Open still and fearful to the grey hair rising on our necks if and when we hear the scrabble of the paws and the scratching at the door.

Appendix

SAMPLE ESSAY PRESENTED IN MLA STYLE

1.25 cm *2.5 cm*

2.5 cm

Marlowe 1

Jessica Marlowe

COMM 120

Professor N. Waldman

30 Sept. 2011

Author's name, course name and number, instructor's name, date

What Makes You Happy?

Essay title, centred

What makes you happy: A great new outfit? A baby's

smile? A hefty bonus cheque? Human happiness is a

complicated question, one that is attracting increased

attention from psychologists, sociologists, and policy

Essay double-spaced throughout

makers. There is even a new academic discipline,

Happiness Studies, that focuses on what "happiness"

means and how people try--and often fail--to achieve

it. "Happiness" in this context does not mean joy, or

merriment, or cheerfulness, or any other synonym you

may find in your thesaurus. It means a high level of

satisfaction with one's life. For most people, good health,

Thesis statement

meaningful work, and positive personal relationships are

basic requirements for happiness. Those are the givens.

The variables most often cited are material wealth,

personal residence, and family ties.

What we own is, of course, a function of how much

disposable income we have. We often assume that the

Marlowe 2

more money we have, the happier we will be because we can buy more "stuff": a high-end auto, designer clothes, state-of-the-art electronics, fabulous footwear, dazzling jewellery, a yacht--the list is endless. But beyond a certain level of comfort, research suggests that owning more "stuff" does not translate into more happiness. In "But Will It Make You Happy?" Stephanie Rosenbloom (B1) recounts the experience of a young couple with well-paying jobs, a spacious apartment, two cars, and piles of household goods who felt, despite it all, dissatisfied with their lives. They gave away most of their possessions and downsized to a small studio apartment, while he went back to school and she started a business from home. Their income dropped dramatically, but so did their spending. Now debt-free, they travel, do volunteer work, and say that they are happier than they have ever been.

Summary

Another example is software engineer Kelly Sutton, who pared down his life to a laptop, iPad, Kindle, two hard drives, a few items of clothing, and towels and bed linens, and documented the purge on his blog, TheCultofLess. com. Sutton sums up his experience this way:

Long quota-tion with words omitted (ellipses) and words changed (in square brackets)

> While I don't consider myself to be some sort of ascetic or societal recluse, I've found that more stuff equates to more stress. Each thing I own[ed]

Marlowe 3

came with [an] expectation of responsibility. . . .

I glance[d] into my desk drawers and [saw] my

neglect. (Qtd. in Bielski L4)

> Full paren-
> thetical source
> citation; see
> item 2 in
> Works Cited

These examples bear witness to the old adage that

money can't buy happiness, and the latest academic

research confirms that traditional wisdom. A recent study

finds that having money actually "impairs people's ability

to savor everyday positive emotions and experiences"

(Quoidbach 759).

> Short quota-
> tion within
> text; full
> parenthetical
> source citation;
> see item 7 in
> Works Cited

On the other hand, money can buy something that

does contribute to happiness: positive experience. The

experience could be a memorable vacation; a backyard

pool for the whole family to enjoy; a biking excursion

with friends; season's tickets to the theatre or a sports

event; a weekend camping expedition; or even a relaxing

day at the spa. While a new car provides a pop of pleasure

when we first drive it home, we quickly get used to it, and

the thrill is gone. Or, worse, our neighbour comes home

with a better one, and we succumb to envy for his shinier,

more expensive vehicle.

The craving for material possessions is insatiable;

acquiring the new clothes or smart phone we long for

leads, sadly, to higher expectations but not increased

satisfaction. But the pleasure of a satisfying experience

Marlowe 4

can be savoured over time. British philosophy professor

Short quotation; abbreviated source citation (author's name given in the text); see item 3 in Works Cited

A.C. Grayling maintains, "A man who has a thousand pounds and spends it on a wonderful trip to the Galapagos Islands is a rich man indeed: the experiences, the things learnt, the differences wrought in him by both, are true wealth (2008)."

Related to conspicuous consumption is another happiness variable, our homes. Where we live influences our happiness, both on the macro (the country) and micro (the home) levels. The Scandinavian countries consistently score highest in happiness surveys. For example, in the 2010 *Gallup World Poll* survey, Denmark, Finland, and Norway topped the list of 155 countries surveyed. Denmark ranked first, with 82% of respondents reporting themselves as "thriving." Sweden tied with the Netherlands for fourth place. Canada placed eighth. Francesca Levy describes the survey methodology Gallup used in this poll:

Long quotation; abbreviated source citation (author's name and title of source given in the text); see item 4 in Works Cited

First, they asked subjects to reflect on their overall satisfaction with their lives, and ranked their answers using a "life evaluation" score between 1 and 10. Then they asked questions about how each subject had felt the previous day. Those answers allowed researchers to score their "daily experiences"--things like

Marlowe 5

whether they felt well rested, respected, free of pain and intellectually engaged. Subjects that reported high scores were considered "thriving." The percentage of thriving individuals in each country determined our rankings. (N. pag.)

As one would expect, a certain level of affluence is reflected in these findings, but it is surprising to those of us living in the Frozen North to find that a warm climate is not a factor that contributes significantly to happiness. The five least happy countries (Sierra Leone, Cambodia, Comoros, Burundi, Togo) are all impoverished-and-hot countries. The United States, by most measures the richest country in the world, falls below Canada at number 14 with 57 percent of respondents reporting themselves as thriving. These rankings suggest that the happiness of a country depends on the degree to which its economic and social welfare--the social safety net--is assured.

Our immediate surroundings--the space we live in-- influence our happiness, too. People work hard to achieve a comfortable home with enough space for their family. Yet there is increasing evidence that bigger, fancier homes do not necessarily translate into happier occupants. For one thing, in Canada's major cities, affordable large

Marlowe 6

homes with big lots exist only in the suburbs, a fact that means a long, stressful daily commute for the family's breadwinners. Apart from the huge carbon footprint of the jumbo house and the two gas-guzzling cars, the personal costs to the family can be very high. Charles Montgomery emphasizes this point in "Me Want More Square Footage":

Modified long quotation from article in an anthology; abbreviated source citation; see item 6 in Works Cited

> [P]eople who live in low-density sprawl are more likely to die violently than their inner-city cousins--thanks mostly to car accidents. . . . [S]uburban kids are far more likely to get hooked on drugs and booze. Why? Not enough chill-out time with their parents, for one thing. And where are suburban parents in those crucial after-school hours? Drumming their dashboards on marathon commutes home from distant offices. (59–60)

Thinking about where we live, of course, leads us to the third factor in the happiness equation: the people with whom we live. While an adult may choose to live alone or with a group of like-minded friends, most of us live in families. Russian writer Leo Tolstoy famously began his

Short quotation; abbreviated source citation; see last item in Works Cited

classic novel *Anna Karenina* with the words: "All happy families are alike; each unhappy family is unhappy in its own way" (1). Whether or not Tolstoy is right, there is no question that a person's family--both the birth family and the family one chooses or creates--significantly

Marlowe 7

influences his or her happiness. Coming from a

troubled family is a strong predictor of unhappiness.

Those who have been born into a dysfunctional family

must work long and hard to overcome the emotional

damage of their background; if they do not, they are

likely to repeat the damaging behaviour in the family they

form on their own as adults (Maté 254–257).

Paraphrase; full source citation; see item 5 in Works Cited

On the other hand, healthy marriages and families

correlate to higher levels of happiness and well-being in

life. Studies tell us that married people tend to be happier

than single people. Adding children to the mix, however,

complicates the association between family and happiness.

Once an infant joins the family, caregiving takes over one's

life. The work is endless with small children. Older parents

especially, who have become accustomed to independence,

may find that a baby's incessant demands lower their

day-to-day satisfaction with life. This dissatisfaction

usually diminishes as the child grows and becomes more

independent, although the adolescent years often present

a whole new set of challenges. A 2009 study cited in the

Journal of Happiness Studies reviews the positives and the

negatives of having children and concludes that children

greatly increase people's satisfaction with life if they have

the time, the financial resources, and the right partner to

share them with. (Angeles).

Summary of journal article; abbreviated source citation; see first item in Works Cited

Marlowe 8

Possessions, property, and parenthood: all are mixed

blessings. Perhaps the key to happiness must remain a

mystery. Some people maintain a happy equilibrium even

in challenging circumstances; other people struggle to be

happy with a life that most would envy. Mark Holder, a

professor at UBC Okanagan, provides a helpful overview

of advice from happiness researchers to put us on track

(qtd. in Shore): nurture social relationships, seek well-

being rather than wealth, choose good friends, don't

compare yourself to celebrities, cultivate gratitude, be

active, complete tasks, help others, develop a hobby,

appreciate the good moments, and don't bear grudges.

Forgive people. Perhaps these deceptively simple

maxims--not fame, fortune, or fabulous wealth--hold the

key to lasting happiness.

Paraphrase of Holder's comments in a book by Shore; see second-last item in Works Cited

Marlowe 9

Works Cited

Angeles, Luis. "Children and Life Satisfaction." *Journal of Happiness Studies* (2009) <doi:10.1007/s10902-009-9168-z>.

Bielski, Zosia. "Keeping Down with the Joneses." *Globe and Mail* 28 August 2010: L4.

Grayling, A.C. "Happiness Is the Measure of True Wealth." *Telegraph* 10 April 2008 <http://www.telegraph.co.uk/comment/3557112/Happiness-is-the-measure-of-true-wealth.html>.

Levy, Francesca. "The World's Happiest Countries." *Forbes* 14 Jul 2010 <www.forbes.com/2010/07/14/world-happiest-countries-lifestyle-realestate-gallup.html>.

Maté, Gabor. "Embraced by the Needle." *Canadian Content.* 7th ed. Eds. Nell Waldman and Sarah Norton. Toronto: Nelson, 2011. 254–257.

Montgomery, Charles. "Me Want More Square Footage." *Canadian Content.* 7th ed. Eds. Nell Waldman and Sarah Norton. Toronto: Nelson, 2011. 57–62.

Quoidback, Jordi, Elizabeth W. Dunn, K.V. Petrides, and Moïra Mikolajczak. "Money Giveth, Money Taketh Away: The Dual Effect of Wealth on Happiness." *Psychological Science* (2010): 759–763 <doi:10.1177/0956797610371963>.

Marlowe 10

Rosenbloom, Stephanie. "But Will It Make You Happy?"

New York Times 8 August 2010: B1, B4.

Shore, Randy. "A Scientific Approach to Happiness."

Vancouver Sun 4 Aug 2010 <http://communities.

canada.com/vancouversun/blogs/greenman/

archive/2010/08/04/a-scientific-approach-to-

happiness.aspx>.

Tolstoy, Leo. Anna Karenina. Trans. Richard Pevear and

Larissa Volokhonsky. New York: Penguin Books,

2000. (Original work published in 1878.)

GLOSSARY

ABSTRACT and **CONCRETE** are terms used to describe two kinds of nouns. **Abstract nouns** name ideas, terms, feelings, qualities, measurements—concepts we understand through our minds. For example, *idea, term, feeling, quality,* and *measurement* are all abstract words. **Concrete nouns**, on the other hand, name things we perceive through our senses: we can see, hear, touch, taste, or smell what they stand for. *Author, rhythm, penguin, apple,* and *smoke* are all concrete nouns.

An **ALLUSION** is a reference to something—a person, a concept, a quotation, or a character—from literature, history, mythology, politics, or any other field familiar to your readers. For instance, if you were to describe one of your friends as "another Tiger" (referring to the professional golfer Tiger Woods), the reader might picture a high-performance athlete with a superb golf swing or a man who shamed himself through marital infidelity.

There are two guidelines for the effective use of allusions. First, allude to events, books, people, or quotations that are known to your readers. If your readers have never followed golf, they will have no mental image of Tiger Woods, so they will be no better informed; worse, they may feel frustrated because they are "missing something." Detailed knowledge of your intended audience and their cultural frames of reference will help you choose appropriate allusions.

Second, be sure your allusions are clear and unambiguous. A reference to "King" could mean Mackenzie King, B. B. King, Stephen King, or Martin Luther King, Jr. Who knows? Imagine the confusion if the reader has the wrong King in mind.

AMBIGUITY: An ambiguous statement is one that has two or more meanings. An ambiguous action is one that can be interpreted in more than one way. When used deliberately and carefully, ambiguity can add richness of meaning to your writing; however, most of the time ambiguity is not planned and leads to confusion. For instance, the statement "He never has enough money" could mean that he is always broke, or that he is never satisfied no matter how much money he has. As a general rule, it is wise to avoid ambiguity in your writing.

An **ANALOGY** is a comparison. Writers explain complicated or unfamiliar concepts by comparing them to simple or familiar ones. For instance, one could draw an analogy between life's experiences and a race: the stages of life—infancy, childhood, adolescence, maturity, old age—become the laps of the race, and the problems or crises of life become the hurdles of an obstacle course. If we "trip and fall," we've encountered a crisis; if we "get up and continue the race," we refuse to let the crisis defeat us. See Richard Lederer's "Writing Is. . . ." (page 209) for an extended analogy between the act of writing and throwing a Frisbee. Analogies are often used for stylistic or dramatic effect, as well as to explain or illustrate a point.

ANALYSIS means looking at the parts of something individually and considering how they contribute to the whole. In essay writing, the common kinds of analysis are **process analysis** and **causal analysis**. See the introductions to Unit 3, Process Analysis (page 133), and Unit 6, Causal Analysis (page 251), for more detailed explanations.

An **ANECDOTE** is a short account of an event or incident, often humorous, that is used to catch the reader's interest and illustrate a point. Writers frequently use this technique to introduce an essay. See paragraph 1 of "Just Walk On By" by Brent Staples (page 263) and paragraphs 1 to 3 of June Callwood's "Forgiveness" (page 316) for examples of effective anecdotes.

ARGUMENT/PERSUASION: See RHETORICAL MODES.

The **AUDIENCE** is the writer's intended reader or readers. Knowing their level of understanding, their interests, and their expectations of what they are reading is critically important to the writer. TONE, level of vocabulary, the amount of detail included, even the organizational structure, will all be influenced by the needs of the audience.

When you speak to children, you instinctively use simple, direct language and short sentences. You adapt your speaking style to suit your listeners. Similarly, good writers adapt their prose to suit their readers. Before you begin to write, think about your readers' knowledge of your topic, their educational background, and their probable age level. These factors will influence their interests and, consequently, their initial attitude to your paper. Will they approach it with interest? Or will they pick it up with a yawn? (If the latter is the case, you will have to work harder.) Never talk down to your readers, but don't talk over their heads, either, or they will stop reading.

To get an idea of how a writer adjusts information, structure, style, and tone to appeal to his or her target audience, contrast Judy Brady's "Why I Want a Wife," written for feminist readers of the 1970s, with Margaret Wente's "The New Heavyweights of the Workplace," written for general readers in 2010.

The **BODY** of any piece of writing is the part that comes between the INTRODUCTION and the CONCLUSION. In a PARAGRAPH, the body consists of sentences supporting and developing the TOPIC SENTENCE, which identifies the paragraph's KEY IDEA. In an essay, the BODY consists of paragraphs that explain, discuss, or prove the essay's THESIS.

CHRONOLOGICAL ORDER means time order. Items or ideas that are introduced chronologically are discussed in order of *time sequence*. Historical accounts are usually presented chronologically. In a chronological arrangement of KEY IDEAS, TRANSITIONS such as *first, second, third, next, then, after that,* and *finally* help to keep your reader on track. See the introduction to Unit 3, Process Analysis (page 133), for further details.

A **CLICHÉ** is a phrase or expression that has been used so often that it no longer conveys much meaning. Any phrase that you can automatically complete after reading the first two or three words is a cliché. Consider, for example, the expressions *better late than* _____, *easier said than* _____, and *as pretty as a* _____. The endings are so predictable that readers can (and do) skip over them.

CLIMACTIC ORDER is the arrangement of points in order of importance. Writers usually arrange their KEY IDEAS so that the most important or strongest idea comes last. Thus, the paper builds up to a climax.

COHERENCE is the continuous logical connection between the KEY IDEAS of a piece of writing. In a coherent paper, one paragraph leads logically to the next. Ideas are clearly sequenced within a paragraph and between paragraphs. The topic is consistent throughout, and the writer has supplied carefully chosen and logical TRANSITIONS such as *also, however, nevertheless, on the other hand, first, second,* and *thus.* If a paper is coherent, it is probably unified as well. (See UNITY.)

COLLOQUIALISM: Colloquial language is the language we speak. Expressions such as *guys, okay, a lot,* and *kids* are acceptable in informal speech but are not appropriate in essays, research papers, or reports. Contractions (such as *they're, isn't, it's,* and *let's*) and abbreviations (such as *TV, ads,* and *photos*) that are often used in speech are appropriate in writing only if the writer is consciously trying to achieve a casual, informal effect, as we have attempted in our unit introductions.

CONCLUSION: The conclusion of any piece of writing is what will stay with your reader; therefore, it should be both logical and memorable. A good conclusion contributes to the overall UNITY of the piece, so a conclusion is no place to throw in a new point you just thought of, or a few leftover details. Your conclusion should reinforce your THESIS, but it should not simply restate it or repeat it word for word (boring). Here are five strategies you can choose from to create an effective conclusion:

> *Refer back to your introduction.* "Refer" does not mean "repeat." It means alluding to the content of your introduction and, if the connection is not obvious, clarifying the link for your readers. Good examples of this strategy include "Dispatches from the Poverty Line" (page 104) and "What I Have Lived For" (page 199).

Ask a rhetorical question—one that is intended to emphasize a point, not to elicit an answer. See the concluding paragraph of "Listen Up" (page 177).

Issue a challenge. See the conclusion of "She Said, He Said" (page 207).

Highlight the value or significance of your topic. See the last paragraph of "Why Good Writing Makes You Sexy" (page 328)

Conclude with a relevant, thought-provoking quotation. See the final paragraph of "Talking Pidgin" (page 297).

There are several other techniques you can use to conclude effectively: provide a suggestion for change, offer a solution, make a prediction, or end with an ANECDOTE that illustrates your THESIS. Whatever strategy you choose, you should leave your reader with a sense that you have completed your discussion of your thesis, not that your paper has "just stopped."

CONCRETE: See ABSTRACT/CONCRETE.

CONNOTATION and **DENOTATION:** The **denotation** of a word is its literal or dictionary meaning. **Connotation** refers to the emotional overtones the word has in the reader's mind. Some words have only a few connotations, while others have many. For instance, "house" is a word whose denotative meaning is familiar to all; it has few connotations. "Home," on the other hand, is also denotatively familiar, but this word has rich connotative meanings that differ from reader to reader. (See, for example, the essay by Ken Wiwa on page 297.)

To take another example, the word "prison" is denotatively a "place of confinement for lawbreakers convicted of serious crimes." But the connotations of the word are much deeper and broader: when we hear or read the word "prison," we associate emotions like anger, fear, despair, or loneliness with it. A careful writer will not use this word lightly: it would be inappropriate, and therefore bad style, to refer to your workplace as a "prison" simply because you don't like the location of your office or the length of the lunch break.

CONTEXT is the verbal background of a word or phrase—the words that come before and after it and determine its meaning. For example, the word "period," which has many different meanings, refers to a particular kind of sentence structure in Eva Hoffman's "Lost in Translation" (page 123).

When a word or phrase is taken *out of context,* it is often difficult to determine what it originally meant. Therefore, when you are quoting from another writer, be sure to include enough of the context so that the meaning is clear to your reader.

DEDUCTION is the logical process of applying a general statement to a specific instance and reasoning through to a conclusion about that instance. See also INDUCTION.

DESCRIPTION: See RHETORICAL MODES.

DICTION refers to the choice and arrangement of words in a written work. Effective diction is that which is suited to the topic, the AUDIENCE, and the PURPOSE of the piece. Good writers do not carelessly mix formal with colloquial language, Standard English with dialect or slang, or informal vocabulary with technical JARGON or archaisms (outmoded, antique phrases). Writing for a general audience about the closing of a neighbourhood grocery store, a careful writer would not say, "The local retail establishment for the purveyance of essential foods and beverages has shut its portals for the last time." This statement is pretentious nonsense (see GOBBLEDYGOOK). A careful writer would say, "The corner store has been closed." This statement conveys the same meaning, but it states the message concisely and appropriately.

EMPHASIS: A writer can highlight important points in several ways: through *placement* (the essay's first and last sections are the most prominent positions); *repetition;* or *phrasing.* Careful phrasing can call attention to a particular point. Parallel structure, a very short sentence or paragraph, even a deliberate sentence fragment are all emphatic devices. A writer can also add emphasis by developing an idea at greater length; by directly calling attention to its significance; or by inserting expressions such as "significantly" or "most important." TONE, particularly IRONY or even sarcasm, can be used to add emphasis. Finally, diction can be used as an emphatic device. See Sarah Walker's "How to Perform a Tracheotomy" (page 137), Nick Mamatas' "The Term Paper Artist" (page 193), and Robert Patterson and Charles Weijer's "D'oh! An Analysis of the Medical Care Provided to the Family of Homer J. Simpson" (page 214) for examples of distinctive diction.

EVIDENCE in a piece of writing functions the same way it does in a court of law: it proves the point. Evidence can consist of facts, statistical data, examples, expert opinions, surveys, illustrations, quotations or PARAPHRASES. Charts, graphs, and maps are also forms of evidence and are well suited to particular kinds of reports.

A point cannot be effectively explained, let alone proved, without evidence. For instance, it is not enough to say that outsourcing (the practice of sending jobs offshore) is displacing many Canadian workers. You need to find specific examples of companies, jobs, and statistics to prove the connection. What makes a paper credible and convincing is the evidence presented and the COHERENCE with which it is presented. See Wade Davis's "The End of the Wild" (page 112) for an example of effective use of several kinds of evidence.

EXPOSITION: See RHETORICAL MODES.

FIGURES OF SPEECH are words or phrases that mean something more than the literal content of individual words or phrases. Writers choose to use figurative language when they want the reader to associate one thing with another. Some of the more common figures of speech include SIMILES, METAPHORS, IRONY, PERSONIFICATIONS, and PUNS.

GENERAL and **SPECIFIC: General words** refer to classes or groups of things. "Bird" is a general word; so is "bread." **Specific words** refer to individual members of a class or group; e.g., "penguin" or "Government Brown" (see Richard Poplak's "Loaves and Wishes" for an explanation of Government Brown bread). Good writing is a careful blend of general and specific language. (See also ABSTRACT/CONCRETE.)

GOBBLEDYGOOK is a type of JARGON characterized by wordy, pretentious language. Writing that has chains of vague, abstract words and long, complicated sentences—sound without meaning—is gobbledygook. See the example included under DICTION.

ILLUSTRATION: See the introduction to Unit 2.

INDUCTION is the logical process of looking at a number of specific instances and reasoning through to a general conclusion about them. See also DEDUCTION.

INTRODUCTION: The introduction to any piece of writing is crucial to its success. A good introduction catches the reader's attention, identifies the THESIS of the piece, and establishes the TONE. It "hooks" the reader, making him or her curious to see what you have to say. Here are five different attention-getters you can use:

> *Begin with a story related to your topic.* The story could be an ANECDOTE (a factual, often humorous account of an incident) or a scenario (an account of an imagined situation). See the opening paragraph of Noreen Shanahan's "My Life as a Cleaner" (page 92) for an example of an opening anecdote.

> *Begin with a striking fact or startling statistic.* See the first paragraph of "Listen Up" (page 177).

> *Set up a comparison or contrast to hook your reader.* See the introduction to Jeffrey Moussaieff Masson's "Dear Dad" (page 146) for a comparison and the introduction to Jessica Marlowe's "What Makes You Happy?" (page 20) for a contrast.

> *Begin by stating a common opinion that you intend to challenge.* See "Why Good Writing Makes You Sexy" (page 326).

> *Begin with a question or series of questions.* See the introduction to "The Trouble with Readers" (page 252).

Other strategies you might want to experiment with include beginning with a relevant quotation, offering a definition (yours, not the dictionary's), or even telling a joke. You know how important first impressions are when you meet someone. Treat your introductory paragraph with the same care you take when you want to make a good first impression on a person. If you bait the hook attractively, your reader will want to read on.

IRONY is a way of saying one thing while meaning something else, often the opposite of what the words themselves signify. To call a hopelessly ugly painting a masterpiece is an example of verbal irony.

For an extended example of verbal irony, see Sarah Walker's "How to Perform a Tracheotomy" (page 137). Situations can also be ironic: in David Bodanis's "Toothpaste" (page 185), we learn that a health-and-beauty product is concocted from disgusting ingredients; in Anwar F. Accawi's "The Telephone" (page 283), the instrument that was supposed to enhance the life of a village in fact destroys it. See Ian Brown's essay on page 308 for an extended discussion and examples of different kinds of irony.

Irony is an effective technique because it forces readers to think about the relationship between seemingly incompatible things or ideas. Robert Patterson and Charles Weijer's "D'oh! An Analysis of the Medical Care Provided to the Family of Homer J. Simpson" is an example of extended irony. The article seems to recommend Dr. Riviera over Dr. Hibbert as a model for Canadian family doctors in the twenty-first century, but a careful reading of the evidence the authors call upon will lead the reader to a different conclusion.

JARGON is the specialized language used within a particular trade, discipline, or profession. Among members of that trade or profession, jargon is an efficient, timesaving means of communication. Outside the context of the trade or profession, however, jargon is inappropriate because it inhibits rather than promotes the listener's or reader's understanding. Another meaning of jargon—the meaning usually intended when the word is used in this text—is pretentious language or GOBBLEDYGOOK, which means using words in a misguided attempt to impress readers rather than to convey meaning.

KEY IDEAS are the main points into which the development of a THESIS is divided. (See also PARAGRAPH.)

A **METAPHOR** is a figurative rather than a literal comparison. An effective metaphor is one that draws a fresh, imaginative connection between two dissimilar things. Dennis Dermody, for example, writes that a movie theatre is "a jungle ... filled with a lot of really stupid animals" ("Sit Down and Shut Up or Don't Sit by Me," page 182). An apt, unusual metaphor makes the writer's idea memorable.

NARRATION: See RHETORICAL MODES.

ORDER refers to the arrangement of information (KEY IDEAS) in a paper. While you are still in the planning stage, choose the order most appropriate to your THESIS. There are four arrangements to choose from:

Chronological order means in order of time, from first to last.

Climactic order means arranging your points so that the strongest one comes last (the climax). Present your second-strongest point first, then tuck in your not-so-strong point(s) where it will attract least attention, and conclude with your clincher.

Causal or *logical order* refers to the arrangement of key ideas that are logically/causally linked. One point must be explained before the next can be understood. In process and causal analysis, where there is a direct and logical connection between one point and the next, this arrangement of key ideas is the obvious one to choose.

Random order is a shopping-list kind of arrangement: the points can be presented in any order without loss of effectiveness. Random order is appropriate only when your key points are all equal in significance and not logically or causally linked. You will rarely find a topic that can be developed in random order.

A **PARAGRAPH** is a unit of prose made up of a group of sentences dealing with one point or KEY IDEA. In an essay, you argue or explain your THESIS in a number of key ideas. Each key idea is developed in one or more paragraphs.

Most paragraphs have a TOPIC SENTENCE—a sentence that states the point of the paragraph and is often (but not always) the first or second sentence. The sentences that follow develop the point using one or more supporting strategies: examples, specific details, definition, quotation or paraphrase, comparison and/or contrast. All sentences in the paragraph should be clearly related to its key idea.

Each paragraph should be COHERENT and UNIFIED and should lead the reader smoothly to the next (see TRANSITION). The essays of Bertrand Russell (page 199) and Wade Davis (page 112) deserve careful analysis: their paragraphs are models of form.

PARALLELISM describes a series of words, phrases, clauses, or sentences that are all expressed in the same grammatical construction. In a parallel sentence, for example, the items in a series would be written as single words, phrases, or clauses. Julius Caesar's famous pronouncement, "I came, I saw, I conquered," is a classic example of parallelism.

Parallelism creates symmetry that is pleasing to the reader. Lack of parallelism, on the other hand, can be jarring: "His favourite sports are skiing, skating, and he particularly loves to sail." Such potholes in your prose should be fixed up before you hand in a paper. For example, "What Sam says, she means; and she delivers what she promises, too" would be much more effective if rewritten in parallel form: "What Sam says, she means; what she promises, she delivers."

Because the human mind responds favourably to the repetition of rhythm, parallelism is an effective device for adding EMPHASIS. "What I Have Lived For" (page 199) contains numerous examples of parallelism in DICTION, SYNTAX, and PARAGRAPH structure.

To **PARAPHRASE** is to put another writer's ideas into your own words. You must acknowledge the original writer as the source of the idea. If you don't, you are guilty of plagiarism.

Paraphrasing is essential when you are writing a research paper. Once you have gathered the information you need from various sources and created an original thesis to work with, you write the paper, drawing on your sources for supporting evidence but expressing the sources' ideas in your own words.

A paraphrase should reflect both the meaning and the general TONE of the original. It may be the same length or shorter than the original (but it is not a PRÉCIS). For more information on paraphrasing, including instructions and examples, see our website: www.cancon7e.nelson.com.

PERSONIFICATION is a figure of speech in which the writer gives human qualities to an inanimate object or an abstract idea. For instance, if you write, "The car screeched to a halt," you are comparing the sound of the car's brakes to a human voice. (You are also guilty of using a cliché.) Strive for original and insightful personifications; otherwise, you will be trapped by CLICHÉS.

PERSUASION: See RHETORICAL MODES and the introduction to Unit 8, Argument and Persuasion.

POINT OF VIEW, in EXPOSITION, means the narrative angle of the essay: Who's telling the story? (In PERSUASION and ARGUMENT, point of view can also mean the writer's opinion in the essay.)

If the writer identifies himself as "I," the essay is written from the first-person point of view. In this case, we expect to encounter the writer's own opinions and first-hand experiences. Wangersky's "Clinging to The Rock" is the only essay in Unit 1 that is not written in the first person. One of the reasons this piece leaves a distinct impression with the reader is the writer's choice of a third-person point of view.

If the writer is not grammatically "present," the essay is written from the third-person point of view. Many of the essays in Units 3 through 8 are written in the third person. The writer uses "one," "he," "she," and "they," and the result is more formal than an essay written in the first person.

A careful writer maintains point of view consistently throughout an essay; if a shift occurs, it should be for a good reason, with a particular effect in mind. Careless shifts in point of view confuse the reader.

A **PRÉCIS** is a condensed SUMMARY of an article or essay. It is one-quarter to one-third the length of the original. The examples and ILLUSTRATIONS are omitted, and the prose is tightened up as much as possible. All the KEY IDEAS are included; most of the development is not.

A **PUN** is a word or phrase that brings to the reader's mind two meanings at one time. Max Eastman, in his book *Enjoyment of Laughter*, classifies puns into three sorts: atrocious, witty, and poetic. The person who wrote, "How does Dolly Parton stack up against Mae West?" was guilty of an atrocious pun. Russell Wangersky's title "Clinging to The Rock" contains a witty pun, as does Paul Quarrington's "Home Ice." Poetic puns go beyond the merely humorous double meaning and offer the reader a concise, original comparison of two entities, qualities, or ideas. Richard Poplak's title, "Loaves and Wishes," is a poetic play on the Biblical "loaves and fishes."

PURPOSE means the writer's intent: to inform, to persuade, or to amuse, or a combination of these. See RHETORICAL MODES.

RHETORICAL MODES: The word "rhetoric" means the art of using language effectively. There are four classic modes, or kinds, of writing: exposition, narration, description, and argument/persuasion. The writer's choice of mode is determined by his or her PURPOSE.

EXPOSITION is writing intended to inform or explain. Expository writing can be personal or impersonal, serious or light-hearted. The various methods of exposition (such as definition, comparison, process analysis, and the rest) are sometimes called *rhetorical patterns*.

NARRATION tells a story. Examples of narrative writing are often found in ANECDOTES or ILLUSTRATIONS within expository prose. Michael Ignatieff's "Deficits" (page 71) and Lorna Crozier's "What Stays in the Family" (page 65) are good examples of the use of narration to develop a THESIS.

DESCRIPTION is writing that appeals to our senses: it makes us see, hear, taste, smell, or feel whatever is being described. Descriptive writing is often used to help develop KEY IDEAS in a piece of EXPOSITION or ARGUMENT. In addition to the essays in Unit 1, see the essays by David Bodanis (page 185), Germaine Greer (page 219), and Anwar F. Accawi (page 283) for examples of effective description.

ARGUMENT, sometimes called PERSUASION, is writing that sets out not only to explain something but also to convince the reader of the validity of the writer's opinion on an issue. Sometimes its purpose goes even further, and the writer attempts to motivate the reader to act in some way—in these instances, the writer is aiming for PERSUASION. Like exposition, argument conveys information to the reader, but not solely for the purpose of making a topic clear. Argument seeks to reinforce or to change a reader's opinion about an issue.

SATIRE is a form of humour, sometimes light-hearted, sometimes biting, in which the writer deliberately attacks and ridicules something: a person, a political decision, an event, an institution, a philosophy, or a system. The satirist uses exaggeration, ridicule, and IRONY to achieve his or her effect. There is often a social purpose in satire: the writer points to the difference between the ideal—a world based on common sense and moral standards—and the real, which may be silly, vicious, alienating, or immoral, depending on the object of the satirist's attack. Many of the authors of the selections in this book employ satire in the development of one or more of their KEY IDEAS: for example, "How to Perform a Tracheotomy" (page 137) is an example of an extended satire.

A **SIMILE** is a stated or explicit comparison between two things. Most similes are introduced by *like* or *as*. Russell Wangersky creates a striking simile in "Clinging to The Rock": "a handful of fishing sheds, their sides weathered to a uniform silver-grey, stand like forgotten teeth on a half-buried lower jaw" (page 42).

SPECIFIC: See GENERAL/SPECIFIC.

A **STEREOTYPE** is a fixed idea that a person holds about another person or group of people, an idea based on prejudice rather than reality.

Stereotypes are based on generalizations: broad conclusions about whole classes of people. For example: women are poor drivers; truck drivers are illiterate; teenagers are boors. Stereotypical notions about races and nationalities are particularly objectionable: think of the well-known "Newfie" jokes, for example.

A careful writer avoids stereotypes, unless he or she is using them for satiric purposes. Unthinking acceptance of others' assumptions is a sure sign of a lazy mind. See Pat Capponi's "Dispatches from the Poverty Line" (page 104) for an interesting exploration of stereotypes.

STYLE is the distinctive way a person writes. When two writers approach the same topic, even if they share many of the same ideas, the resulting works will be different. The difference is a product of the writers' personal styles. DICTION, sentence structure, paragraph length, TONE, and level of formality all contribute to style.

Good writers adapt their style to their AUDIENCE and PURPOSE. Academic writers and business writers do not write the same way because they are not writing for the same readers or for the same reasons. Similarly, good writers adapt their style to suit their topic. This stylistic adjustment is almost instinctive: you would not write an informal and humorous account of a teenage suicide, nor would you use a highly formal style in a promotional piece on new toys for the holiday season.

A **SUMMARY** is a brief statement, in sentence or paragraph form, of the KEY IDEAS of an article or essay. Compare PRÉCIS and PARAPHRASE. For instructions and examples, see www.cancon7e.nelson.com.

SYNTAX is the arrangement of words in a sentence. Good syntax means not only grammatical correctness, but also effective word order and variety of sentence patterns. Good writers use short sentences and long ones, simple sentences and complex ones, and natural-order sentences and inverted-order ones. The choice depends on the meaning and EMPHASIS the writer wants to communicate. See "Sentences: Kinds and Parts," www.cancon7e.nelson.com.

A **THESIS** is the particular approach to or point about a topic that the writer wants to communicate to the reader in an essay. It is often expressed in a *thesis statement*. (See "How to Write to Be Understood," page 6 of the Introduction.) Sometimes professional writers do not include an identifiable thesis statement in their essay or article. For less experienced writers, however, a clearly stated thesis—one that expresses the central idea that everything in the essay is designed to support and explain—is the best guide that can be provided for a reader. Equally important, it helps the writer to stay focused.

TONE reflects the writer's attitude to the topic and to his or her intended AUDIENCE. For instance, a writer who is looking back with longing to the past will use a nostalgic tone. An angry writer might use an indignant, outraged tone, or an understated, ironic tone—depending on the topic and purpose of the piece.

Through DICTION, POINT OF VIEW, sentence structure, PARAGRAPH development, and STYLE, a writer modulates his or her message to suit the knowledge, attitude, and expectations of the target audience. Examples of superb control of tone are Michael Ignatieff's sympathetic "Deficits" (page 71), Paul Quarrington's humorously informative "Home Ice" (page 152), the Dalai Lama's "Many Faiths, One Truth" (page 178), and Jane Rule's thoughtful, meditative "The Harvest, the Kill" (page 362).

A **TOPIC SENTENCE** is a sentence that identifies the main point or KEY IDEA developed in a paragraph. The topic sentence is usually found at or near the beginning of the paragraph.

TRANSITIONS are linking words or phrases. They help connect a writer's sentences and paragraphs so that the whole piece flows smoothly and logically. Here are some of the most common transitions used to show relationships between ideas:

To show a time relation: first, second, third, next, before, during, after, now, then, finally, last

To add an idea or example: in addition, also, another, furthermore, similarly, for example, for instance

To show contrast: although, but, however, instead, nevertheless, on the other hand, in contrast, on the contrary

To show a cause–effect relationship: as a result, consequently, because, since, therefore, thus

See also COHERENCE.

UNITY: A piece of writing has unity if all of its parts work together to contribute to the ultimate effect. A unified piece (paragraph, essay, article, report) develops one topic in one tone. Unity is an important quality of any piece of prose: each sentence of a paragraph must relate to and develop the KEY IDEA expressed in the TOPIC SENTENCE; each paragraph must relate to and develop the THESIS of the paper.

author index